PRACTICAL AIDS

for

CATHOLIC TEACHERS

PRACTICAL AIDS
for
CATHOLIC TEACHERS

A Handbook of Material and Teaching
Devices for Use in the Lower Grades
of Parochial Schools

By

SISTER MARY AURELIA, O.S.F., M.A.
Sisters of St. Francis, Millvale, Pa.

And

REV. FELIX M. KIRSCH, O.M.CAP., LITT.D
Capuchin College, Catholic University, Washington, D. C.

WITH NUMEROUS ILLUSTRATIONS

ST. AUGUSTINE ACADEMY PRESS
HOMER GLEN, ILLINOIS

Imprimi Potest.
    Thomas Petrie, O.M.Cap.
      Provincial.

Nihil Obstat.
    Arthur J. Scanlan, S.T.D.
      Censor Librorum.

Imprimatur.
    ✠ Patrick Cardinal Hayes
     Archbishop of New York.

New York, Aug. 18, 1928.

ACKNOWLEDGMENTS

The authors wish to express their thanks to the following authors and publishers for selections which they permitted to be taken from their works: His Eminence, William Cardinal O'Connell for hymn from "The Holy Cross Hymnal"; Rev. John Francis Quinn, S.J., for the poem "A Christmas Gift"; The Salvatorian Fathers for selections from "Tell Us Another" by Rev. Winfrid Herbst, S.D.S.; The Sisters of Loretto for selections from the "Loretto Series of Language Busy Work"; The Carmelite Convent of Boston for selections from "Petals of a Little Flower" translated by Susan L. Emery; The Devin-Adair Company for "The Mother's Quest" from "Songs for Sinners" by Rev. Hugh Francis Blunt; The Century Co. for the poem "Night and Day" by Mary Mapes Dodge from "St. Nicholas Songs"; Houghton Mifflin Company for extracts from poems by Alice and Phoebe Cary; P. J. Kenedy and Sons for "Christmas Chant" and "A Child's Wish" by Father Abram Ryan; Little, Brown & Company for poems by Louisa M. Alcott, Christina Rossetti, and Harriet McEwen Kimball; The National Catholic Welfare Conference, Washington, D. C., for selections from "Health through the School Day," by Mary E. Spencer; Charles Scribner's Sons for verses by R. L. Stevenson, Eugene Field, and Mary Mapes Dodge.

This book was originally published in 1928 by Benziger Brothers.
This facsimile edition reprinted in 2018 by St. Augustine Academy Press.

ISBN: 978-1-64051-042-5

PREFACE

The present book is an attempt to pool the experiences of many teachers. Let any one visit our Catholic schools and he will discover veritable geniuses in the difficult art of making men and women of the little boys and girls, and of leading them unto Christ. The writer has often looked on and asked himself, "Would it not be helpful to other teachers to learn of this method or of that device?" The present book is an answer to this question. Questionnaires were sent to leaders in the profession, and it is largely from their generous responses that *Practical Aids for Catholic Teachers* has been compiled. Of course, the book is not intended to suggest a rule-of-thumb procedure. All that the book purports to do is to stimulate the initiative of our Catholic teachers by telling them of some of the methods employed so successfully by their sisters in the profession. The teacher, to succeed in her work, must always be individualistic. Yet, the observing of the work of others will not kill originality, but will in reality stimulate initiative. And it is the opportunity for such observation and consequent stimulation that the present book intends to offer.

For instance, the morning talks are not intended to serve as material to be memorized. Indeed, their very form would forbid the work of memorizing. No attempt has been made in the talks to write them down to the level of the first- or the second-grade. All that is offered is the material that may suggest to the teacher thoughts that she might wish to tell in her own way to her particular group. The morning talks are expected to prove, not a crutch to the weak, but an alpenstock to the strong.

So, too, with all the other material presented. The book represents the results, as it were, of observing many classrooms, and it is hoped that our teachers will be helped especially in their teaching of religion. The writer trusts that the book will bring to many of our teachers the stimulation received in this regard by one Sister—Sister Mary Callista, a Sister of Mercy—who saw some of the methods advocated here carried out successfully in the Thomas Edward Shields Memorial School in Washington, D. C., and then reported as follows on what she had observed:

> The aim of the teacher of religion should be the development of a Christlike character by giving the child an opportunity *"to do the truth in charity"* in order that he may in all things grow up in Him Who is the head, even unto Christ (Eph. IV, 15). Learning is an *active* process. We have natural desires, which are basic not only to learning but to every act of virtue, but it is necessary to transform the natural urge into a supernatural desire. Development is an internal process and the result of personal experience. The experiences of the child are various, and various, too, are the means which modern psychology and education offer to link up these experiences. Which of these means seems to afford the greatest opportunity for activity, for the satisfaction of natural instincts, for making his own the experience which the child is attempting to live through? Surely the industrial arts. The work at the Thomas Edward Shields Memorial School demonstrates how successfully these may be employed in teaching religion.
>
> The industrial arts as employed in the school include construction work, paper cutting, clay modeling, drawing, painting, carpentering, sewing, and all the activities involved in the use of the sand table as well as in costuming and staging in preparation for dramatization. In these activities, technique is mastered quickly; for, as Bonser and other writers remind us, very little attention is given to the development of skill, for the hand work is always rated as subordinate to the brain work.
>
> What are some of the possibilities of the sand table? None of us who have had the joy of living near the ocean fail to experience a thrill at the thought of building in moist sand, and everybody once upon a time reveled in mud pies. There is no doubt about the children's attitude toward the sand table. But how use it in a

project in religion? The second-graders, for instance, in November, were studying the life of our Blessed Mother before the birth of Our Lord. This was their remote preparation for Christmas. After the story had been told and retold in an interesting way, and the children had "discussed" it, and dramatized it, they succeeded in reproducing the scene on the sand table. They were particularly enthusiastic about Mary's home which they had constructed of a brown corrugated carton, divided into two rooms. Nothing was wanting that little fingers could model or cut out of paper. There was the loving sacrifice of a sample of Palm Olive soap which completely covered the tiny clay-modeled dresser, and a cherub-faced infant doll was acting the part of St. Joseph to the entire satisfaction of his ardent admirers, who delightedly pointed out his bench and clay-modeled tools. Other classes worked out the story of Christmas, telling the story as they worked. Each child was anxious to make a hill of Judea, or a tree or a house for Bethlehem, and all took delight in adding something to the Cave. The whole childhood of Our Lord has been worked out successfully in this way. When they begin their Bible history stories, the children delight in reproducing the garden of Eden, the stories of the Ark, of Moses, of Joseph, etc. In Lent, the Stations might be represented. Just as the children delight in dramatizing the Mission stories of the Far East, or Africa, or Alaska, so they delight in reproducing the scenes after seeing them in the Mission magazines. It is surprising how cleverly they reproduce an African hut, an Eskimo igloo, a Chinese pagoda, or an Indian wigwam.

What are some of the possibilities in paper cutting? In sand table projects, the children will utilize trees, and villages like Bethlehem, or figures cut from magazines or catalogues, and pasted on cardboard. The little ones take joy likewise in picturing their stories on posters. The laws of perspective and proportion must be observed, and the physical setting should be as true to nature as possible. In this way the child is prepared for the study of the fine arts, and will acquire at least some appreciation of the Church's contributions in this direction. What was the inspiration of the great religious painters? The same religious truths which we are teaching to-day. Our little ones feel some of this creative joy in making posters of the incidents in the life of Our Lord and His saints. It is preferable in those scenes which have much detail, to use pictures cut from catalogues or magazines and have the children cut freehand the background after they have designed the setting. Silhouette is often very effective, especially in representing such scenes as the flight into Egypt, the visit of the Wise Men, and incidents in the public life of Our Lord. Posters may be used also to stimulate interest in the missions. In the upper grades the titles may be printed, or letters may be cut out and pasted on the posters. This activity may well lead up to a consideration of the illuminated manuscripts produced under the inspiration of the Church.

Making booklets is another activity that brings interesting results. The fourth-graders who searched through magazines for suitable pictures to present the works of the various days to complete their "Creation Books" certainly learned that story. The "Miracle Books" were not less interesting or instructive. Fourth-graders decided to symbolize the various miracles of Our Lord's public life. Among the symbols were ears and eyes, and in one instance a stiff little man with a very large ear trumpet.

The booklets may be made for various feasts, and numberless are the designs which might be suggested for covers for Thanksgiving, Christmas, Easter, St. Valentine's Day, etc. A by-product of this activity is the lesson of thoughtfulness and gratitude; for the children rarely make these booklets for themselves, but usually as surprises for mother or father.

Sewing is by no means a lost art, and simple costumes improvised by the children may impress on them the lessons we are striving to make their own. All children love to play a part, especially when they do their own costuming. It is beyond doubt that the little lady of seven who draped herself in a blue mantle and a white veil, and knelt piously to receive the Angel's greeting, and then piped in her baby voice: "I'm not good enough to be God's Mother," had caught the spirit of the best beloved Handmaid. Fascinating and cultural are the studies of altar laces and linens, of vestments, and of tapestries.

PREFACE

vii

> Are the lessons in religion really learned when so much time is given to these industrial arts? The test demanded by Christ is met *not by those that say, but by those that do.* What do you find these normal, happy little people doing during a free activity period? When the pre-Christmas project of our blessed Mother's home was being studied, several children made work-baskets for Our Lady, and some moulded donkeys for her to ride to St. Elizabeth. While they were working out their ideas that were struggling for expression, they were also working in the impression. One has but to see them at the Children's Mass, coming back from Holy Communion, to realize that they are growing up in Him, or to see them in the classroom, showing a readiness and quick resourcefulness in assisting one another, to realize that they are learning *to do the truth in charity.* (The Catholic Educational Review, March, 1928, pp. 174, ff.)

It is teaching of this kind that the present book aims to present chiefly by apt illustrations, and hence it is hoped that *Practical Aids for Catholic Teachers* will be welcomed by our Sisters as a helpmate in the noble and arduous task to which they have consecrated their lives.

There remains the pleasant duty of expressing grateful appreciation to the teachers who by furnishing material or by giving advice have made possible the present book. A special debt of gratitude is due to the Rev. Peter J. Bernarding, M.A., himself a teacher of fine experience, who offered a number of helpful suggestions and who spent many hours in preparing the manuscript for the press.

FELIX M. KIRSCH, O.M. CAP.

Washington, D. C.
April 18, 1928.

CONTENTS

PART ONE

MORNING EXERCISES: TALKS, STORIES, MEMORY GEMS

PREFACE v

Introduction

THE MORNING EXERCISES............. 3
   How to Conduct the Morning Exercises.. 3
   The Use of Pictures.................... 4
   A Suggestion for Friday Morning....... 4
   Memory Gems, Mottoes, Quotations...... 4
   How to Use Memory Gems in the Primary Grades 4

Section I

GENTLE VIRTUES

1. CHEERFULNESS 5
   The Cheerfulness of St. Francis..... 5
   Boys and Girls Can Imitate St. Francis 5
   Practice 6
2. CHEERFULNESS AND SUNSHINE. 6
   How Children Can Bring Sunshine to Others 6
   Practice 6
3. CHEERFUL THOUGHTS........... 6
   Are You Always Cheerful?.......... 7
   Practice 7
4. CHEERFULNESS IS CONTAGIOUS 7
   Habit of Cheerfulness............. 7
   Practice 7
5. CHEERFUL WORDS.................. 8
   Cheerful Words Bring Sunshine to Others 8
   Cheerful Words in the Home....... 8
   Practice 8
6. KIND WORDS....................... 9
   Kind Words Make for Peace........ 9
   Practice 9

7. THE CHARM OF KINDNESS....... 9
   Be Kind to the Poor, the Sick and the Aged 9
   Practice 10
8. PEACE AND HAPPINESS......... 10
   Example of Catholic Children...... 10
   Practice 10
   The Example of Jesus, Mary and Joseph and the Saints 11
9. CHEERFULNESS IN OUR ACTIONS 11
   St. Francis and the Wolf........... 11
   Kind Actions Speak Louder than Words 12
   Practice 12
10. SMILING FACES BRIGHTEN THE WORLD 13
   The Smile of Your Guardian Angel.. 13
   Practice 13
11. THE SUNSHINE OF THE HEART.. 13
   Keep the Sun Shining in Our Class Room 13
   Practice 14
12. HAPPINESS IN GOODNESS........ 14
   A Game without a Fight........... 14
   Practice 14
13. FRUITS OF CHEERFULNESS..... 15
   Cheerfulness Is Like Music........ 15
   Practice 16
14. JESUS' LOVE FOR CHILDREN.... 16
   Jesus in the Tabernacle............ 16
   Practice 16
15. PRACTICE MAKES PERFECT..... 16
   Begin to Practice at Home......... 17
   Practice 17
16. SPREADING SUNSHINE........... 17
   A Sunshine Club.................. 17
   Practice 17

17. POLITENESS 18	34. THANKFULNESS 33
Thinking of Others............. 18	God's Many Gifts............... 33
Practice 19	Practice 33
18. POLITENESS IN THE HOME...... 19	35. APPRECIATING OUR PARENTS... 33
The Golden Rule................ 19	A Daily Prayer of Thanksgiving.... 34
Practice 20	Practice 34
19. GOOD MANNERS IN SCHOOL...... 20	36. THE GIFT OF FOOD, CLOTHES AND SHELTER 34
Politeness to Teachers............ 20	God's Creatures Serve Us......... 34
20. GOOD HELPERS IN THE SCHOOL. 20	Practice 34
How to Treat Visitors............ 21	37. THE GIFT OF HEALTH........... 34
21. PATIENCE WITH OTHERS........ 22	Practice 35
The Gift of Sympathy............ 22	38. THE STORY OF THANKSGIVING DAY 35
22. KINDLINESS 22	The Hour of Need............... 35
The Happiest Place on Earth...... 23	Practice 36
Practice 23	39. THE GOODNESS OF GOD......... 36
23. KINDLINESS AND POLITENESS ARE TWIN SISTERS............. 23	Practice 36
Little Ladies and Gentlemen....... 24	40. THE GIFT OF FAITH............. 36
Practice 24	Praying for the Heathen.......... 37
24. THE GOLDEN KEYS............. 24	Helping the Missionaries.......... 37
Practice 26	Practice 38
25. USING THE GOLDEN KEYS....... 26	
Making Amends.................. 27	

Section II

STERNER VIRTUES

26. A KIND ACT, *A Story*............ 27	1. OBEDIENCE 38
27. KINDNESS TO ANIMALS.......... 27	Necessity of Obedience........... 38
The Little Flower's Pet........... 28	Example of the Holy Child........ 39
Practice 28	Obedience to God 39
28. THE HERMIT AND THE LION, *A Story* 28	Practice 39
Practice 29	2. THE COMMANDMENTS OF GOD... 39
29. TIT FOR TAT, *A Story*............ 29	God Is Present Everywhere........ 40
30. KINDNESS TO BIRDS............. 29	Practice 40
God's Little Creatures............ 30	3. "OF COURSE, GOD IS EVERYWHERE!" *A Story* 40
Practice 30	4. OBEDIENCE TO PARENTS........ 41
31. OUR LITTLE SISTERS THE BIRDS 30	How Children Should Obey........ 41
What Children Can Do for Their Little Sisters, the Birds 31	The Example of Christ............ 41
How a Little Robin Learned a Lesson 31	Practice 41
Practice 32	5. "CAN'T I DO SOMETHING FOR YOU, PAPA?" *A Story*............ 42
32. OUR PETS 32	6. OBEDIENCE TO THE TEACHER.. 42
Too Much Petting................ 32	Why Children Must Obey the Teacher 42
33. THE GRATEFUL ELEPHANT, *A Story* 33	

No Order without Obedience........	43
Practice	43
7. OBEDIENCE WINS GOD'S FAVOR.	**43**
Practice	44
8. RIGHTS AND DUTIES OF CITIZENS	**44**
Self-Control	45
Practice	45
9. WORK	**45**
We All Must Work...............	46
Practice	47
10. WORKING UNDER COMPULSION..	**47**
Learn to Like Your Work..........	47
Practice	47
11. PREPARING FOR OUR LIFEWORK	**47**
Your Lesson of To-day Prepares for Your Work To-morrow	48
Practice	48
12. THE BLESSING OF WORK........	**48**
Do the Right Kind of Work..........	49
Practice	49
13. ORDERLINESS	**49**
A Place for Everything and Everything in Its Place...............	49
Practice	50
14. HELPFULNESS	**50**
How to Be Helpful to Others........	51
Practice	51
15. SCHOOL ATTENDANCE...........	**51**
Order Is Heaven's First Law........	52
Practice	52
16. HELPFULNESS AT HOME........	**52**
Ways of Helping...................	52
Practice	53
17. THE SPIRIT OF HELPFULNESS...	**53**
Helping Your Town................	53
Practice	54
18. TRUTHFULNESS	**54**
Why We Should Be Truthful........	54
Practice	54
19. MAKING EXCUSES	**55**

Unconscious Lying	55
Practice	56
20. LYING AND UNHAPPINESS........	**56**
Pretending to Be	56
Practice	56
21. VARIETIES OF UNTRUTHFULNESS	**56**
Speaking Untruthfully about Others.	57
Practice	57
22. HONESTY	**58**
Dishonesty Is Quite Frequent.......	58
Practice	58
23. HONESTY IN SCHOOL WORK.....	**58**
Honesty in Play....................	59
Rules of Honesty...................	59
Practice	59
24. STEALING	**59**
The Habit of Borrowing	60
Practice	60
25. LOST AND FOUND..	**60**
Keeping Your Promises.............	61
Practice	61
26. AN HONEST BOY, *A Story*........	**62**
27. COURAGE	**62**
The Meaning of Courage...........	62
Practice	63
28. COURAGE IN FACING HARD DUTY	**63**
Courage in Playing a Manly Game...	63
Practice	64
29. DARING TO DO RIGHT............	**64**
Manly Sports	65
Practice	65
30. COURAGE OF THE SAINTS	**65**
A Family of Heroes................	65
Practice	66
31. CLEANLINESS	**66**
Keeping out of Puddles.............	66
Practice	66
32. KEEPING YOUR SKIN CLEAN.....	**67**
Frequent Baths....................	67
Practice	67

CONTENTS

33. KEEPING YOUR TEETH CLEAN.. 67
    Why Teeth Decay................. 67
    Practice 68

Section III

SELF-CONTROL

1. SELF-CONTROL 69
    Runaway Ponies 69
    Practice 69
2. NECESSITY OF SELF-CONTROL.. 70
    Control of the Senses............. 70
    Practice 70
3. SELF-CONTROL IN CHILDREN.... 70
    Self-Control Is Our Protection...... 71
4. CONTROLLING OUR THOUGHTS.. 71
    The Uselessness of Idle Thoughts.... 72
    Practice 72
5. CONTROLLING OUR WORDS 72
    The Tongue Is Like a Fire.......... 73
    Practice 73
6. HOW TO CONTROL THE TONGUE. 73
    A Helpful Rule.................. 73
    Practice 73
7. THE CONTROL OF OUR TEMPER.. 73
    Ready to Fight.................. 74
    Practice 75
8. UGLINESS OF BAD TEMPER..... 75
    Blaming Others.................. 75
    Practice 76
9. CONSCIENCE 76
    The Reward of a Good Conscience... 77
    Practice 77
10. DAILY EXAMINATION OF CONSCIENCE 77
    The Help of Confession............ 77
    Practice 78
11. REGULATING YOUR CONSCIENCE 78
    Four Things Necessary............ 78
    Practice 78
12. A CHILD'S CHRISTIAN DAY...... 79
    Help of the Guardian Angel........ 79
    Practice 80
13. SPENDING YOUR DAY WELL..... 80
    Daily Mass and Communion........ 80
    Prayers Before and After Meals.... 80
    Practice 81
14. CONDUCT AT TABLE............ 81
    Sharing Your Good Things......... 81
    Practice 82
15. HOW TO END THE DAY.......... 82

Section IV

THE LIFE OF CHRIST

1. THE FEAST OF CHRISTMAS...... 83
    Practice 84
2. WHY JESUS CAME DOWN UPON EARTH 84
    Practice 85
3. UNSELFISHNESS OF JESUS IN THE CRIB 85
    Practice 86
4. THE SELFISHNESS OF SOME CHILDREN 86
    Practice 87
5. THE FRIEND WHO IS WITH US ALWAYS, *A Story*................ 87
6. PREPARATIONS MADE THROUGHOUT THE WORLD FOR CHRISTMAS 88
    Practice 89
7. A CHILD'S PREPARATION FOR CHRISTMAS 89
    Practice 90
8. PIOUS EXERCISES IN PREPARATION FOR CHRISTMAS........... 90
    A Bed for the Holy Infant.......... 91
9. JESUS' LOVE FOR PURE HEARTS 92
    Practice 92
10. JESUS' LOVE FOR KIND HEARTS. 92
    Practice 93
11. THE CHRIST CHILD, *A Story*...... 93

12. MARY AND JOSEPH ON THEIR WAY TO BETHLEHEM............ 95	28. THE LAST SUPPER............ 114
Practice 96	Practice 116
13. THERE WAS NO ROOM FOR THEM IN THE INN.................... 96	29. JESUS IN THE HANDS OF HIS ENEMIES 116
Practice 96	Practice 117
14. THE SHEPHERDS HASTEN TO THE CRIB 97	30. THE SIGN OF THE CROSS....... 118
	31. THE LESSON OF THE PASSION.. 118
Practice 98	Jesus Is Taken to Pilate........... 118
15. LONGING FOR JESUS............ 98	Practice 119
Practice 98	32. JESUS IS SCOURGED AND CROWNED WITH THORNS....... 119
16. THE CHRISTMAS CLOAK, *A Story*. 98	
17. DRAMATIZING THE STORY OF CHRISTMAS 99	Bear Your Sufferings Patiently..... 120
	Practice 120
18. THE WISE MEN GO TO VISIT THE CRIB 99	33. PILATE CONDEMNS JESUS TO DEATH 120
Practice 101	Cowards Are Not Respected........ 120
19. THE WISE MEN IN BETHLEHEM. 101	Practice 121
The Wise Men Teach You a Lesson.. 102	34. JESUS ON THE WAY TO CALVARY 121
20. THE FLIGHT INTO EGYPT....... 103	The Death of Jesus............... 121
The Holy Innocents............... 103	Showing Our Love for Jesus Crucified 122
Practice 104	
21. THE HOLY FAMILY IN EGYPT.... 104	Practice 123
Practice 105	35. THE LESSONS OF THE CROSS... 123
22. THE BOY JESUS AT HOME....... 106	Our Sins Crucify Jesus Anew....... 123
The Example of Jesus............. 106	Practice 123
Practice 107	36. THE WAY OF THE CROSS........ 126
23. THE CHILDHOOD DAYS OF JESUS 107	
Jesus Prepared Himself for His Life Work 107	**Section V**
	THE BLESSED SACRAMENT
Practice 108	
24. JESUS AT NAZARETH............ 108	1. THE SANCTUARY LAMP......... 126
Practice 110	Practice 127
25. JESUS GOES TO THE TEMPLE WITH HIS PARENTS............ 110	2. THE WISDOM OF A LITTLE GIRL, *A Story* 127
The Journey from Nazareth to Jerusalem 111	3. THE VERY GREATEST ACT OF LOVE 127
The Child Jesus Is Lost........... 111	4. THE SACRED HEART OF JESUS.. 128
Practice 112	What the Heart of Jesus Teaches Us. 129
26. THE SUFFERINGS AND DEATH OF OUR LORD................. 113	Practice 129
	5. HONORING THE BLESSED SACRAMENT 130
Judas Sells Our Lord............. 113	
Practice 113	Practice 131
27. THE SIN OF JUDAS............ 114	6. "WE DON'T TALK IN CHURCH!" *A Story* 131
Practice 114	

7. THE SAINTS AND THE BLESSED SACRAMENT 131
    Saint Imelda 131
    Saint Paschal Baylon............. 132
    The Little Flower of Jesus........ 132
    Practice 133

8. "I AM NOT POOR!" *A Story*........ 133

Section VI

THE BLESSED VIRGIN AND THE SAINTS

1. DEVOTION TO THE BLESSED VIRGIN 134
    Why the Blessed Virgin Is Honored So Highly 134
    St. Theresa's Love for the Blessed Virgin 134
    Practice 135

2. MARY'S SPECIAL LOVE FOR CHILDREN 135
    Practice 135

3. CHILDHOOD OF THE BLESSED VIRGIN 135
    Practice 136

4. THE LIFE OF THE BLESSED VIRGIN IN THE TEMPLE............. 137
    Practice 137

5. THE BLESSED VIRGIN OUR MODEL 138
    Practice 139

6. MARY'S PURITY................. 139
    Practice 139

7. HUMILITY OF THE BLESSED VIRGIN 139
    The Gifts of God Should Not Make Us Proud................. 140
    Practice 140

8. KINDNESS OF THE BLESSED VIRGIN 140
    Practice 141

DEVOTION TO THE SAINTS....... 142
    What Is a Saint?................. 142
    We Do Not Adore the Saints........ 142
    What the Saints Do for Us......... 142
    Practice 142

10. HONOR DUE TO SAINTS......... 143
    How We Honor the Saints........ 143
    Practice 143

11. CELEBRATING THE FEASTS OF SAINTS 143
    Practice 144

12. A BOY SAINT..................... 144
    Practice 145

13. PROTECTED BY AN ANGEL, *A Story* 146

Section VII

THE CHILD APOSTOLATE

1. LITTLE APOSTLES 146
    Good Example Teaches Others...... 146
    Practice 147

2. UNSELFISHNESS OF LITTLE APOSTLES 147
    Sharing with Others the Gifts Received from God................. 147
    Practice 148

3. GRATITUDE OF LITTLE APOSTLES 148
    Many Graces and Blessings......... 148
    Practice 149

4. HOW TO BE LITTLE APOSTLES... 149
    The Boy Apostle................. 149
    Practice 150

5. LITTLE MISSIONARIES........... 150
    Practice 151

6. BOYS AS MISSIONARIES.......... 151
    Practice 152

7. KIND CHILDREN ARE LITTLE MISSIONARIES 152
    Good Example Leads Others to Do Good 152
    Practice 152

8. THE APOSTOLATE OF PRAYER... 152
    Practice 153

CONTENTS

PART TWO
CLASSROOM PROJECTS

Section I

SCHOOL CALENDARS—FEASTS—SPECIAL DAYS

1. SCHOOL CALENDARS 157
    How to Make the Calendars........ 157
2. SUBJECTS FOR POSTER CALENDARS 157
3. A SUNSHINE CALENDAR......... 160
    The Chart of Holy Joy............ 160
4. MODEL FOR CALENDARS........ 160
5. DAYS OF SPECIAL INTEREST IN THE LOWER GRADES............ 160
    Labor Day 188
    Columbus Day 189
    Halloween 189
    Thanksgiving Day 189
    Christmas 190
    Holy Week 190
    Mother's Day 190
6. FEASTS OF THE CHURCH........ 191
    September 191
    October 194
    November 205
    December 207
    January 208
    February 211
    March 213
    April 217
    May 218
    June 219
7. CHARTS, POSTERS AND BLACKBOARD DRAWINGS.............. 224
    The Blessed Virgin's Rose Garden... 224
    The Rosary 224
    Little Friends of the Holy Souls..... 224
    Friends of Jesus 225
    Sheep Around the Crib........... 225
    The Crown of Thorns............ 226
    Flowers for May................ 226
8. NAME DAYS AND BIRTHDAYS... 227

Section II

SAND TABLE PROJECTS

1. SAND TABLE WORK.............. 227
    Equipment 228
    Sand 229
    Trees 229
    Grass 229
    Water 229
    Roads, Streets, Hills and Mountains.. 229
    Snow 229
    Houses, Bridges, Fences........... 229
    Clay for Modeling................ 229
    People, Animals.................. 229
    How to Work Out a Project on the Sand Table.................... 229
2. SAND TABLE PROJECTS IN RELIGION 230
    Adam and Eve in Paradise........ 230
    Adam and Eve Driven out of Paradise 230
    Cain and Abel................... 230
    Cain Kills Abel.................. 230
    Noe and the Ark................. 230
    Noe and His Family Leaving the Ark 230
    The Story of Moses.............. 230
    The Story of Joseph.............. 230
    The Birth of Christ............... 231
    The Flight into Egypt............. 232
    The Holy Family at Nazareth....... 232
    The Stations of the Cross.......... 232
    Calvary 232
    A Grotto of Lourdes.............. 232
    Through the Year with the Sand Table 232
3. MISSIONARY PROJECTS ON THE SAND TABLE.................... 232
    China 233
    American Indians................ 233
    Eskimo 233
    Africa 233

Section III

DRAMATIZATION

1. DRAMATIZATION IN THE CLASSROOM 234
   - Lack of Definite Method 234
   - Dramatization Not a Form of Recreation 235
   - Dramatization Should Benefit All Pupils 235
   - A Finished Production Is Not the Aim 235
   - The Kind of Stories to Be Used for Dramatization 235
   - Method of Procedure 236
   - Summary and Illustration 237
2. STORIES DRAMATIZED 238
   - Cain and Abel 238
   - The Building of the Ark 239
   - Noe's Offering—The Rainbow 239
   - The Story of Joseph 239
   - The Story of Moses 241
   - The Adoration of the Shepherds ... 242
   - The Adoration of the Magi 242
   - Jesus Blessing Little Children ... 243
   - St. Francis and the Wolf 243
   - St. Francis Preaching to the Birds ... 244
   - Blessed Herman Joseph and the Infant Jesus 244
   - Blessed Herman Joseph—Pantomime 245
   - The Boy and the Wolf 245
   - Legend of Corpus Christi—Material for Dramatization 246
3. GYMNASTIC STORIES 247
   - The Little Flower of Jesus and Her Nurse Go to Church 247

Section IV

MUSIC

1. MUSIC IN THE CLASSROOM 248
2. CREATING MUSIC 249
3. MUSICAL CONVERSATION 250
4. THE SINGING OF SONGS IN THE CLASSROOM 251
5. MUSIC IN ITS RELATION TO PLAYS AND GAMES 252
6. DEVICES TO AID THE SINGING TEACHER 253
   - The Singing Voices of the Children .. 253
   - How to Help Monotones 254
   - Mottoes and Slogans for the Music Class 255
7. FOLK SONGS 255
8. SONGS FOR THE LITTLE ONES ... 256

Section V

CLASSROOM AIDS AND DEVICES

1. SCHOOLROOM DECORATIONS 258
   - Pictures in the Schoolroom 259
2. PRACTICAL AIDS AND DEVICES . 259
   - A Bee-Hive 259
   - An Airship Race 259
   - A Race Across the Country 259
   - The Flight of the Birds 260
   - Across the Sea or Across the Lake .. 260
   - Birds on Wires 260
   - Birds on Trees 260
   - Banners and Pennants 261
   - Badges—Armbands 261
   - Home-Made Stencils 261
   - A Scrap Album 261
   - Friday Afternoon Programs 262
   - Bulletin Board 262
   - Exhibiting Work 262
   - Suggestions for Busy Work 263
   - Correct Copying 263
   - Charts to Teach the Use and Meaning of Religious Articles 264
   - To Teach the Story of the Passion of Christ 264
3. SCHOOL MANAGEMENT 264
   - Passing to and from Seats 264
   - To Secure Regular Attendance 265
   - To Cure Tardiness 266
   - To Secure Punctuality 266
   - To Teach the Making of a Good Intention 266

To Teach Thoughtfulness........... 266
Teaching Pupils to Be Tidy........ 266
Lessons in Peace.................. 267

Section VI

DRAWING AND CONSTRUCTION WORK

1. CORRELATING THE COURSE IN ART WORK WITH THE COURSE IN RELIGION..................... 268
2. LITTLE THINGS FOR LITTLE HANDS TO DO................... 269
3. SUPPLEMENTARY WORK IN DRAWING AND CONSTRUCTION.. 271
   Teaching Direction................ 271
   Single Curves..................... 271
   Color Perception.................. 271
   Tearing Trees..................... 273
   Making and Decorating Envelopes... 273
4. PAPER CUTTING.................. 273
   Border Designs 275
   Tree Stencils 275
   How to Make a Boat................ 276
   How to Make a Rosary.............. 276
   How to Make a Small Banner........ 276
   Trees 276
5. LETTER CUTTING................. 279
6. CONSTRUCTION WORK FOR THE SAND TABLE..................... 279
   A House........................... 279
   Log House 279
   Church 280
   Cornstalk Houses and Furniture.... 280
   Cigar Box Furniture............... 281
   Houses of Bethlehem............... 281
   An Altar.......................... 281
   Candlesticks 282
7. TELLING STORIES WITH PICTURE CUT-OUTS 282
8. THE USE OF POSTERS IN TEACHING RELIGION................... 283

9. POSTER PROJECTS................ 284
   Guardian Angel Poster............. 284
   St. Francis and the Wolf.......... 284
   St. Francis and the Birds......... 284
   The Landing of Columbus.......... 284
   Thanksgiving Day Poster........... 285
   The Birth of Jesus................ 286
   The Three Kings................... 286
   The Flight into Egypt............. 286
   The Boy Jesus at Nazareth......... 289
   The Holy Family................... 289
   St. Joseph and the Child Jesus.... 289
   The Annunciation.................. 289
   A Candlemas Procession............ 289
   The Way of the Cross.............. 289
   Calvary 290
   The Resurrection.................. 290
   An Altar of the Blessed Virgin.... 290
   Various Subjects.................. 290
   Missionary Posters................ 292
   Alphabet Posters Illustrating the Lives of the Saints 292
10. MAKING BOOKLETS................ 293
    Creation Booklet 293
    Picture Booklet 294
    Bird Booklet 294
    Flower Booklet 294
    Fruit Booklet..................... 294
    Saint Booklet..................... 294
    Thankful Booklet 294
    Christmas Booklet................. 294
    St. Patrick Booklet............... 294
    St. Joseph Booklet................ 294
    A Penance Booklet................. 295
    Easter Booklet 295
    Mass Booklet 295
    Mother Booklet 295
    Mission Booklet 295
    Vocation Booklet.................. 295

BIBLIOGRAPHY 296

PART ONE
MORNING EXERCISES
MORNING TALKS—STORIES—MEMORY GEMS

INTRODUCTION TO PART ONE

THE MORNING EXERCISES

The first ten or fifteen minutes in school are probably the most important part of the day. Teachers who have learned to appreciate the opportunities of this time, plan for it more carefully than for any other part of the day's work. They realize that the morning exercises are the keynote to the work of the day. The primary end of these exercises is to secure the interest and attention of the pupils and to put them into a healthy and happy frame of mind that will last throughout the day.

The morning exercises may be simply devotional, that is, they may consist of selections from the Sacred Scriptures, the Life of Christ or the Lives of the Saints; or they may be purely ethical or moral, including talks on character, the virtues, habits, or concrete presentations of truth, beauty and goodness, which will be an inspiration to right living. Incidentally these exercises will furnish the teacher abundant opportunities for the use of poetical quotations, pictures, stories, and songs.

The morning exercises here given consist of morning talks, stories, memory gems, and poems. A definite, specific act should be decided upon for practice during the day. A card with a suitable motto or slogan written or printed upon it, hung in the front of the room, will serve to remind the children of the resolution made in the morning. This card should be removed as soon as it has served its purpose.

How to Conduct the Morning Exercises

After the opening prayer the teacher may conduct the Morning Exercises in one of the following ways:

1. Give the talk on whatever subject appeals to you for the day.
2. Teach a quotation, memory gem, or poem related to the topic discussed in the morning talk.
3. Tell a story illustrating the subject discussed.
4. Let the children sing a suitable song or hymn.
5. When a feast occurs, give a talk on this feast.
6. When the children can read and write let them help to suggest a suitable practice for the day. Then let a child write it on the blackboard where it may remain all day. The practices given at the end of each day's morning talks are only suggestive and their use, of course, is optional. Others, more practical and more suitable may suggest themselves to the teacher and her pupils.

A second plan is the following:

1. Let the children sing a suitable song or hymn after the opening prayer.
2. Then give the morning talk.
3. Repeat a quotation or other selection previously learned, or teach a new one.
4. Occasionally tell a story related to the subject of the morning talk.

Other methods, more appropriate, perhaps, will suggest themselves to the teacher. It is not necessary to follow exactly any of the plans outlined here. Good results will be obtained, however, only by faithfully adhering to some definite plan. The teacher, of course, must vary her manner of presenting the material according to the needs of her class.

With children in the first grade, very little can be done the first month or two, and the quotations, memory gems, or poems are merely to be read or recited by the teacher to the class. As soon as the children are able to memorize short selections, the teacher may introduce a few choice ones, taking care to use only those that carry the greatest appeal to her pupils. Experienced teachers know that pupils are not alike in their response to appeals made by quotations and poems.

The Use of Pictures

The use of pictures in connection with the morning talks should be confined to a general study of them. It is not intended that the teacher conduct a regular picture study lesson at this time. Such a study should be deferred to the language period. In regard to the use of the pictures recommended, the teacher might wish to secure small copies for the children and have them make booklets into which they may paste the pictures used during a certain period. Making booklets is a fascinating occupation for the little ones, and the impression made by the lesson taught in connection with the picture will make the preservation of the pictures in booklets more desirable. When the children are able to form sentences, they may be required to write one or two under the pictures in their booklets.

A Suggestion for Friday Morning

On Friday morning it will be well to sum up the week's practices and to praise the efforts made by the little ones. Recall briefly the more important points. Emphasize particularly the presence of God everywhere.

It is not intended that the teacher should use the exact words given in these talks; they are merely suggestions. The teacher should use her own judgment in the matter. In some schools, there are several grades in one room; in others, the children of the first grade may be older than is here supposed, so that it will be necessary for the teacher to adapt her language to the capacity of her particular class.

Memory Gems, Mottoes, Quotations

The study and memorizing of poetry stores the mind of the child with beautiful thoughts and expressions that will influence his future life. Not all poems studied, however, should be memorized; likewise not all of the poem need be committed to memory. Only those parts which seem worth remembering should be selected for memorizing. Such selections are aptly called memory gems.

The learning of memory gems in school is a valuable practice. It is a well-known fact that what is thoroughly committed to memory in childhood is not only memorized more easily, but is retained more tenaciously. We realize the truth of this when we find that stanzas of poetry learned in our childhood days are as fresh in our memories as if they had been learned yesterday.

Memory gems, therefore, should be carefully selected. Use them only as they have a bearing on the lesson being taught. When you are giving the class a talk on kindness, obedience, cheerfulness, select a memory gem that bears on the subject you are discussing.

How to Use Memory Gems in the Primary Grades

Poems and quotations may be used in many ways.

1. The teacher may read or recite to the class a poem or a quotation in connection with the morning talk.
2. The children may be asked to commit to memory poems and quotations for special occasions.
3. The teacher may write the selection on the blackboard for the children to copy and memorize.
4. Occasionally review all the poems and quotations learned. This may be done on Friday afternoon, or on any other suitable occasion. Sometimes when the lessons drag and the children are dull and listless let them recite their favorite memory gems. Ask the children to tell you why they like a certain selection.

Do not require too many poems or quotations to be memorized. Learning and thoroughly understanding and appreciating a few choice selections will be better than storing the memory with useless and meaningless rhymes and jingles. When the children are able to appreciate the beautiful thought contained in a line of poetry, they have acquired the ability to make these thoughts and ideals part of their lives.

PART ONE

SECTION I

GENTLE VIRTUES

1. CHEERFULNESS

The Cheerfulness of St. Francis

Many years ago, there was born in Assisi, a beautiful town of Italy, a little boy who grew up to be a very holy man. He was St. Francis, who was always kind, gentle, loving and cheerful. His parents were very rich, but Francis gave everything he had to the poor, because he wanted to be like Jesus Who was poor when He lived in this world.

When Francis was a boy, his father and mother taught him to speak French. They also taught him to sing pretty songs. In those days wandering singers went from place to place, singing beautiful songs and playing on sweet-toned instruments. Francis liked to listen to these singers and often sang and played when going with his friends through the streets of his home town. Francis had a beautiful voice. People liked to hear him sing.

Francis was always cheerful and happy. He was loved by everybody. He had many friends and was usually the merriest among his companions. He was always first in the gay processions in which the young people of those days took part. Francis was very kind to the poor and the sick. He was ever ready to help others. His face shone with the happiness that was in his heart. He was cheerful and pleasant to all and he carried sunshine with him wherever he went.

When Francis was about twenty-four years old a war broke out between Assisi and a nearby city. Francis became a soldier and went to fight for his native city. He liked the uniform, just as many young men do to-day. He liked the music and the marching. But Francis was soon taken prisoner and for a whole year he was shut up in prison. This was a hard blow to the lively Francis. Yet even in the dungeon he did not lose his gayety and cheerfulness. The soldiers were very lonesome in their dark prison, but Francis cheered them by his gay songs and bright, happy manner. Many times he felt homesick, longing for his dear mother, his kind father and his gay friends and companions. But his sunny nature made him forget his own troubles and devote himself to cheer and comfort his fellow prisoners. Once when the soldiers asked Francis how he could always be so happy and cheerful when he was a prisoner and far from home and his loved ones, he answered: "I must be happy. Some day I shall be loved all over the world." Of course, his companions could not understand Francis, but his bright and joyful manner helped them to bear their sufferings more patiently.

Boys and Girls Can Imitate St. Francis

Did you ever stop to think that you too could make others happy by being pleasant and cheerful? Like St. Francis, you can do much to make your home happy and joyous. Everybody loved St. Francis because he was kind, gentle and loving. If you are kind to others, if you treat them gently and lovingly, you also will make every one about you happy and cheerful. St. Francis was bright and happy even while he was in a dark prison. He carried the sunshine in his heart and tried to make others feel cheerful and happy also. Do you ever try to make others happy? What can you do to help others to be cheerful? We shall try during this month to be like St. Francis and spread happiness and cheerfulness all around us.

Practice:

1. I will think often of the cheerfulness of Saint Francis.
2. I will make somebody cheerful to-day.

A single sunbeam is enough to drive away many shadows.
—*St. Francis of Assisi.*

> Love is the sunshine
> That warms into life
> For only in darkness
> Grow hatred and strife.

> The clouds are dark,
> 'Tis true,
> But right behind
> Shines the blue.
> *Louisa M. Alcott.*

2. CHEERFULNESS AND SUNSHINE

My dear children, what do you think it was that made every one like St. Francis so well? It was his happy, sunny disposition. He was cheerful and pleasant to all, especially to the sick and the poor. His face showed the happiness that filled his loving heart. Do you think you could be like St. Francis in your home? By being cheerful and pleasant to every one you could bring sunshine into the lives of those with whom you live. Cheerfulness is like the sunshine. Just as the sun warms and brightens the earth, so a cheerful boy or girl can make the home bright and warm by a smiling face and pleasing manners. Without the sun the world would be cold and dark; without pleasant and cheerful children, the world would be sad and dreary.

How Children Can Bring Sunshine to Others

How lovely it would be if all the boys and girls in this class would always have smiling, sunny faces! I wonder if all could be cheerful and sweet-tempered to-day? To be cheerful and sweet-tempered is not always easy. Sometimes it is very hard to smile and to appear happy and cheerful. But if you try to make yourselves think only pleasant and beautiful thoughts, you will not find it so very hard after all. First, then, you will have to put away from you all gloomy and discontented thoughts. If you allow your thoughts to dwell only on good and beautiful things you will be able to show the happiness that you feel in your faces. Smiling faces bring sunshine everywhere. If you try earnestly to think about things that are pure, good and wholesome, you will not find it hard to smile. People enjoy being with those who are cheerful, smiling and happy. Bright eyes, rosy lips, red cheeks, and a cheerful face show that a child is happy and healthy. But the only real happiness that is worth while consists in right doing and right thinking. You must fill your minds with happy, cheerful thoughts if you wish to spread sunshine about you.

Practice:

1. When I see some person sad or troubled, I will try to cheer him.
2. I will try to keep a smiling face to-day.

> In the world is darkness,
> So we must shine—
> You in your small corner,
> And I in mine.
> *Emily H. Miller.*

3. CHEERFUL THOUGHTS

Did you ever notice how pretty everything looks after a storm, when the sun shines again? Before the storm, it was dark; the birds flew away to their nests; little children ran home to their mothers; every one tried to get to shelter and safety. The rain came and after a few minutes the darkness disappeared and the sun shone as brightly as before. Then the birds came out of their nests and sang merrily again; the little boys and girls ran out of their homes and played happily once more. Every one was delighted that the sun shone again. People walked along more briskly and the whole country seemed to be brighter and fresher. Everybody likes the sunshine; it makes a person feel bright and cheerful. You like the sunshine also, because it makes you feel light and happy. If the sun did not shine this world would be very dreary indeed. So it is with children. If little boys and girls do not try to be happy and cheerful, they make everybody around them sad and gloomy. Everybody loves children because they are nearly always smiling and cheerful.

Are You Always Cheerful?

Still, I am sorry to say, there are also boys and girls that are cross and peevish. When these children come into the house, they throw their things about the room, tease the baby, torment the cat, and quarrel with their brothers and sisters. Then mother must correct them. Such boys and girls think everybody dislikes them, and they may be right about it, too. If such children keep on acting in that way, they will grow up to be very ill-tempered men and women. No one will want to be near them. But I know that the boys and girls in this class do not want to grow up in this way. Therefore you must try every day to become more pleasant and agreeable. You must try in every way to grow better and better, and soon you will become so used to being kind and pleasant to every one, that you will always be so. If you wish to grow up to be pleasant, cheerful men and women, you must begin to practice now. You cannot wait till you have grown up. So try again to-day to think beautiful thoughts, and to keep your faces smiling and happy.

Practice:

1. I will be careful to-day not to hurt any one's feelings.
2. As soon as I notice that I am not thinking of cheerful things, I will try to think of the kind St. Francis.

> Laugh a bit and sing a song,
> Where they are, there's nothing wrong;
> Joy will dance the whole world through,
> But it must begin with you.

4. CHEERFULNESS IS CONTAGIOUS

I am sure you feel happy every evening when, before going to bed, you think of how many people you helped to cheer during the day. At the same time you helped yourself most of all. Every time you had a kind and cheerful thought, your face showed it; and if you keep on in this way for a long time, your face will begin to show the lovely thoughts that are in your mind. Your father and mother, brothers and sisters were also happy when they saw how pleasant you were trying to be. Can you tell me what makes you feel so bright and cheery? It is because you are trying to please your teacher by listening well to what she tells you. This makes you feel glad and joyful. Since all in this room are helping to make sunshine for others, all are happy and joyous. When I look at your smiling faces this morning, I cannot help thinking how greatly pleased God is with the children in this room to-day.

Habit of Cheerfulness

But you must keep on every day, every hour and every minute trying to think happy and beautiful thoughts. Each day it will become easier. Soon we shall learn to be pleasant all the time. We shall try to drive away all unpleasant and unlovely thoughts.

Practice:

1. I will try to be cheerful all day.
2. I will try to make some one happy to-day by cheering him up.

> Smiles win many friends.
>
> Smiles are like sunshine.
>
> Life is like a mirror; if you smile,
> Smiles come back to greet you.

REVIEW

I see by your happy faces this morning that you have tried very hard this week to think only good and beautiful thoughts. Did you find it very difficult to be cheerful this week? Can you tell me how you tried to be cheerful? That is right, Mary, tell us how you made mother happy this week. (Let the children tell you about some of their experiences in this respect. Draw them out on the subject.) If a visitor came into our classroom to-day, I am sure he would be pleased to see so many smiling faces. He would know at once that you are trying very hard to be good and happy. You must not stop thinking fine and beautiful thoughts, because you want to grow to be noble men and women some day. Try to bring sunshine to every one. Think often of the great St. Francis and strive as he did to bring joy and happiness to others.

> Work a little, sing a little,
>   Whistle and be gay;
> Read a little, play a little,
>   Busy all the day.
>
> Talk a little, laugh a little,
>   Don't forget to pray;
> Be a bit of merry sunshine,
>   All the blessed day.

5. CHEERFUL WORDS

One day when St. Francis was walking along the road with some other friars, he saw many birds in the trees nearby. He turned to his companions and said: "Wait for me here on the road, and I will go to preach to my sisters, the birds." Francis went towards the birds. They sang and chirped merrily as if they wanted to show Francis how glad they were that he came. Then Francis spoke to them. The birds flew down from the trees and sat quietly on the ground near Francis. They listened very closely till Francis had finished his sermon. This is what Francis spoke to them:

"My little brothers and sisters, listen to me! God loves you dearly; He is very good to you. He gives you the beautiful fields and the lovely trees. He gives you wings to fly and water from the brooks to drink. He gives you feathers to keep you warm. So you have much for which to be thankful. Sing His praises, my little brothers and sisters, and thank Him for all His goodness to you."

When St. Francis had finished speaking, he made the sign of the cross over them and they flew away singing their sweetest songs. Thus the words that Francis spoke cheered the little birds and they went happily to their trees, singing and praising the Lord.

We see that the kind and cheerful words of the Saint gave happiness even to the little birds. Like St. Francis, we also can make life brighter and happier for others by speaking words of kindness and good cheer.

Cheerful Words Bring Sunshine to Others

How bright and happy every one looks this morning! See the pretty picture on this calendar.[1] Are we going to have another "Sunshine Week?" How many want to help to make this another week filled with the sunshine of cheerful thoughts and kind and loving words? I see all of you wish to help. We shall learn more ways to be cheerful and happy. You have been trying to keep yourselves cheerful by thinking of bright, happy and pleasant things. You know this will make your faces lovely and that Jesus will be pleased with His own little boys and girls. We shall now learn to speak kind and cheerful words and so bring sunshine to every one about us.

Cheerful Words in the Home

Do you like any one to speak roughly to you? When some one speaks kindly and pleasantly to you, you like that person, do you not? Do you want others to love you? Then you must also learn to speak only kind and cheerful words. Start to-day to speak kindly to all, especially to those at home. Sometimes when you come home from school you find your little brother or sister has taken your toys and broken them. When you see that, you become angry and say some unkind things. That makes your little brother or sister cry; mother will scold you for this, and instead of being glad that you are at home, she will be happy when you must go to school again. Surely you do not want to grow up in such a way that you are always quarreling with others. This would make you bad-tempered and you would find out that no one cares to have you near.

Suppose, that instead of scolding or striking your little brother or sister, you were to say quietly and kindly that you were sorry your toys were broken, and that you hope that it may never happen again. Do you not think your little brother or sister would be sorry? Be kind to father and mother to-day, and be very careful to say only kind and cheerful words. Ask your Guardian Angel to help you.

Practice:

1. When I play with my little brother or sister, I will not say cross or angry words.
2. When mother asks me to do anything, I

---

[1] See design for "Sunshine Calendar" page 187.

will tell her cheerfully that I will do it at once.

>As sunshine and rain,
>Pleasure and pain,
>   Each day on some must fall,
>So the wise thing to do
>If we only knew,
>   Is to make the best of all.

6. KIND WORDS

Did you try yesterday to say kind and pleasant words to baby at home? to father and mother? to brothers and sisters? Do you think they liked it? Or did you forget yourself and say hateful and disagreeable things at home? Kind thoughts and pleasant words will help every one to get on better in this life. If people are kind to one another, they get on so much better everywhere. Did you ever go with mother to visit your uncle or aunt? Did you enjoy being with them? You did? And why? Because every one tried to be very kind and cheerful. You had a pleasant time with your little cousins, because they played games and tried hard to make things agreeable for you. Or, perhaps, you did not enjoy yourself there. And why not? Because your little cousins quarreled with you, or perhaps you said unkind things yourself. If boys and girls want to be really happy, they must learn to get along with other children. This means that they must learn to play without quarreling and wrangling when they lose. They must not cheat, nor say that others cheat.

Kind Words Make for Peace

I said before that every one likes a bright, cheerful, pleasant boy or girl. Your playmates will like you better if you do not say unkind or hateful things. Boys and girls must try to be pleasant and cheerful with their companions. If all would say only pleasant words, no one would quarrel. Boys and girls should play every day, but they should be careful not to wrangle and quarrel about their games. They should give in when others are in the right, and if their playmates are quarrelsome, they should leave them and play with other children. If the little boys and girls in this room would try to be kind and cheerful towards their playmates, how delightful it would be! Do you think Jesus quarreled with His playmates? I am sure He did not. He played many games with His boy friends, but they did not quarrel nor say unkind things to one another. See whether you cannot be like Jesus in your games to-day.

Practice:
1. I will not quarrel with my playmates to-day.
2. If my playmates begin to quarrel, I will try to say something kind to make them stop.

>Be always sunny, cheerful, and bright,
>Whatever happens, day or night.

7. THE CHARM OF KINDNESS

Now that we have tried to use only kind and gentle words, we shall soon find out how easily we can make people like us. There are boys and girls whom everybody likes; and there are others whom no one likes. One of the reasons for this is, that some boys and girls are always pleasant and agreeable, while others are usually ill-tempered and disagreeable. No one likes children who look sullen and ill-natured. Such boys and girls will find it hard to get along with others. People like bright and cheerful children, for they know that cheerful boys and girls have good hearts. Only the good can always be cheerful and happy.

On your way home from school, in your home, or in the homes of your playmates you will often meet strangers. Now these people will be able to tell at once whether you are a well-trained, pleasant boy or girl, or whether you are ill-natured and disagreeable. How will they be able to tell this? They will only have to look at you; if your face is happy and full of sunshine, they will know that you are trying to be good. When they speak to you and you answer them pleasantly and cheerfully, they will be delighted to know you.

Be Kind to the Poor, the Sick and the Aged

You ought to be very careful to speak kindly to all strangers and particularly ought you to be pleasant and cheerful to the poor, to the sick and to old people. Grandfather and grandmother will be pleased with you if you treat them kindly and speak to them pleasantly. Old people and those that are sick like kind, gentle words. Remember that some day you, also, may be old; some day sickness will come to you and you will then be glad that you were always kind and gentle to the sick and to the aged. God will bless you for every kind word spoken to cheer others. To-day, try to speak pleasantly to strangers when they speak to you, and to old people, if there are any near you. Also be especially kind to any sick person you know.

Practice:
1. I will try to say some kind and cheerful words to my grandfather or grandmother, or to any other old person I know.
2. If anyone I know is ill, I will visit him and try to cheer him.

> A cheerful spirit gets on quick;
> A grumbler in the mud will stick.

8. PEACE AND HAPPINESS

Have you had a chance yesterday to say something kind and cheerful to any one? To whom? Do you think they liked it? Was it very hard to do? Did you feel happy afterwards? What made you feel happy? Now you see how easy it is to make others happy. You can do it every day and many times a day, and each time you do something to make others happy, you will be making a better boy or girl of yourself. Sometimes we hear people complain about little boys and girls playing on the street or walking along the way. Some children make so much noise, that they are a constant disturbance to others. Perhaps you are going along talking loudly and making much noise, thereby disturbing a poor sick person. It does not look well for Catholic boys and girls to quarrel with one another on their way home from school. Do you think that little Jesus would like such conduct? Or your blessed Mother? Or your Guardian Angel? Besides, if you act in this way, people will say, "Just look at those Catholic children! Isn't it scandalous the way they behave?" And they will blame your parents and teachers for your bad behavior.

Example of Catholic Children

You do not want people to say such things about the boys and girls in this room, do you? Then you must try to be gentle and quiet on the street. When you play, you must not be so noisy as to disturb others. If you know there is a sick person in a certain house near the street in which you usually play, you will either play very quietly or you will go elsewhere. If you speak loudly or shout at one another, that is not doing what a mannerly child should do. Others are always watching you and will form their opinion, either good or bad, from the way in which you behave on the street. Then too, other boys and girls, seeing how quietly and mannerly you act at play will follow your example. Try to-day to speak quietly on the street and to cause no one annoyance by your play.

Practice:
1. I will play quietly on the street or in the yard to-day.
2. I will not speak roughly to my companions.

> Kind words are like sunbeams
> That sparkle as they fall;
> And loving smiles are sunbeams,
> A light and joy to all.

To the Teacher:—Show the picture of St. Francis preaching to the birds. Recall to the children the story of St. Francis and his sermon to the birds. How attentively they listened to the kind and gentle words of the Saint! Dramatize the story.

REVIEW

My dear children, this week you have tried to be careful about your words. You resolved to speak only kind and cheerful words to every one around you. I am sure you felt very happy on account of this. Now if you try to speak in this way always, you will do much to make yourselves good men and women when you grow up. But it will not be easy always, for sometimes you will have to deal with people who are not kind, but rough in their ways and in their words. But if you are very careful yourself and try to be cheerful, others will try to be kind and cheerful.

ST. FRANCIS PREACHING TO THE BIRDS

The Example of Jesus, Mary and Joseph and the Saints

Let us try every day in our lives to be very kind and cheerful, especially in our words. We can do much good by our words. If we always think of Jesus, how kindly He was, even when helping Mary and Joseph at their work, we shall also be gentle always. Can you imagine what little Jesus was thinking about all day long? I am sure it was about heaven and the angels and His dear Mother. He did not have many pretty toys, but He was satisfied, because He knew they were all His Mother could give Him. He did not quarrel with His playmates, although I know some of them must have been pretty rough; but when Jesus played with them they tried to be quiet and peaceful just as Jesus was.

Mary and Joseph also were quiet and gentle in their everyday life. We cannot imagine either of these holy persons speaking unkindly or harshly to any one. Then, do not forget the example of the gentle St. Francis. Every one loved him because he always spoke kindly to all. People followed him everywhere because they loved to look at his cheerful face and hear his gentle voice telling them to love the good God Who made us all. Even the birds came to him and listened attentively to his gentle words. Try very hard, therefore, to have happy, pleasant and cheerful thoughts at all times and everywhere, at home, in school and on the street. Always and everywhere remember that as Catholic boys and girls you should show every one that you are trying to follow Jesus by speaking gently and kindly to all.

> Just being happy
> Is a fine thing to do;
> Looking on the bright side,
> Rather than the blue.

9. CHEERFULNESS IN OUR ACTIONS

St. Francis and the Wolf

In the days of St. Francis, when he lived in the city of Gubbio, a fierce wolf often appeared in the city. This wolf was so terrible that he devoured not only animals, but even men. Every one feared him. The people dared not go out of the city, for they feared they might meet this terrible wolf.

Now Francis was very sorry for the people and he said: "I will go out to meet the wolf." The people said: "Do not go, for the fierce beast will surely kill you." But Francis made the sign of the cross and set out to find the wolf. Many people followed him at a safe distance. When the wolf saw Francis, he ran towards him with his jaws wide open. Francis walked up to the wolf and made the sign of the cross over him. The wolf stopped suddenly. He looked at Francis, but did not try to hurt him.

Then Francis spoke to the wolf: "Come here, Brother Wolf. I command you in the name of Jesus Christ that you do not harm me or any other person." Strange to tell, the wolf closed his terrible jaws and came meekly as a lamb and laid himself down at the feet of St. Francis. Francis then spoke:

"Brother Wolf, you do much harm in these parts, and you have done great evil, killing and devouring God's creatures without His leave. Not only have you killed and devoured beasts, but you have dared to kill men. For this you ought to be hanged as a murderer. The people are afraid of you and hate you. But I want to make peace between you and them, so that you will do them no more harm, and so that they will forgive you."

The wolf listened attentively to St. Francis. He sat up and wagged his tail. He held up a paw for Francis to take. In this way he was trying to show that he promised to be good. Then Francis said: "Brother Wolf, if the people of this town promise to feed you, will you promise to be good and not to kill any one? I know that you killed for food because you were hungry. You did not know that it was wrong. Do you promise?"

The wolf bowed his head, plainly showing that he wished to promise. Then Francis said: "Brother Wolf, I want you to give me some token of your promise." Then St. Francis stretched out his hand and the wolf put a paw into his hand. This was a sign that he would keep the promise he made to St. Francis. Then St. Francis commanded the wolf to follow him into the city. And the wolf obediently followed after him like a lamb. The people wondered greatly when they saw the wolf following St. Francis like a pet dog. The news spread throughout the town and soon a larger number of men, women and children gathered in the market-place to see St. Francis and the wolf. The people were still afraid, but St. Francis told them of the promise he made to the wolf that the people would feed him daily, and of the promise the wolf made never again to harm the people. The wolf once more put a paw into the hand of St. Francis and the people greatly rejoiced and praised and thanked God.

The wolf kept his promise. For two years he went through the streets of the city and the people gave him food. He never harmed any one again. When the people saw the wolf going about so meekly and gently, they were reminded of the great holiness of St. Francis and of all the good he had done for them.

My dear children, you can learn from this story how God rewards good actions when they are done to help others. St. Francis was so gentle in his words and in his actions that even the fierce wolf obeyed him. Had St. Francis been gruff and harsh, the wolf would not have been tamed so easily. You can learn another lesson from this kind and gentle saint, namely, that by your actions as well as by your words you can help to make others happy.

Kind Actions Speak Louder Than Words

How many have tried to think happy and cheerful thoughts and say kind and cheerful words? I see that most of you have tried. That is right. I think Jesus will be pleased with all of His children in this room. But we must try to do a little more now. Even without speaking to others we can show that we are happy. You know little boys and girls sometimes are naughty and disagreeable, particularly at home. They are sometimes so unruly that mother is very sad about it and wishes she did not have such naughty boys or girls. Now let me see what you can do to make mother happy. Suppose you try to be pleasant and cheerful when you do something for mother or for somebody else. Suppose, when mother tells you to watch the baby, or wash the dishes, or go to the store, you say cheerfully, "All right, mother," and smile to show that you are glad that you can do something for mother. You can play quietly and happily with little brother or sister, or you can sing while you wash the dishes, and the boys can whistle while they go to the store or work about the yard. This will help to make everyone at home feel happy and cheerful.

Practice:
1. I will be very kind to all at home to-day.
2. I will do my work quietly and cheerfully to-day.

As welcome as sunshine in every place
Is the beautiful smile of a good-natured face.

10. SMILING FACES BRIGHTEN THE WORLD

St. Francis did not wait to be asked to help the people of Gubbio, but went cheerfully as soon as he heard about the great harm the wolf was doing. No doubt, when the wolf saw the smiling and happy face of the Saint, he knew that St. Francis had not come to hurt him. Here again you can follow the example of St. Francis. When you are to do a thing, especially if what you are about to do is hard or unpleasant, it will help you very much if you try to be as cheerful about it as possible. Doing a thing cheerfully and willingly will help you to do it more quickly and it will also give you less trouble. If others see how cheerfully you do your work, it will make them cheerful too. Many times mother is very tired after a day of hard work, but when she sees her little boy or girl willingly and cheerfully trying to help her, it will make her feel happy and she will not feel so weary.

The Smile of Your Guardian Angel

How pleased your Guardian Angel must be when he sees his little boy or girl trying to be kind and cheerful, in order to make every one happy. There are some children, however, who begin to cry every time they must do something they do not like to do. Suppose every one should cry each time something disagreeable were to be done; this world would be a very sad place, would it not? You do not like to be called a "cry baby," do you? Well, then you must learn to do all your work so gladly that by and by you will get used to doing everything quickly and cheerfully. When you ask your playmate for a ball, you do not like him to throw it at you or speak roughly to you. But if he smiles and says, "Certainly, here it is," you feel happy and you are pleased to have such a kind friend. Are you always pleasant with your classmates? Do you always speak kindly and cheerfully to the little boys or girls you know? Suppose you try to-day to be kind and pleasant to the boys and girls you meet. Be especially careful to treat every one as you would wish to be treated by them.

Practice:

1. I will try to practice the following:

    Be to others kind and true
    As you would have them be to you.

2. I will be careful to be pleasant and cheerful even if I do not feel like it.

I will try in everything I say or do to make the world more bright.

11. THE SUNSHINE OF THE HEART

Are you trying to carry sunshine with you everywhere? Do you like sunny days? Do you know how you can always have sunny days? How can you do that, Willie? Very good, Willie. I see that you have been trying to make sunshine for every one. How pleasing it would be, if all the children in this class would carry the sunshine with them every day! You know that you can do so, if you wish. If you have sunshine in your hearts, that is, if you continually think only good and beautiful thoughts and thereby try to please God, you will have sunshine in your faces also. And if you show by your faces that you have the sunshine in your hearts, you will not fail to put sunshine into the lives of others.

I told you before that the only happiness worth while is that which follows right doing and right thinking. Doing your duty, that is obeying those whom God has placed over you, is one of the means to make sunshine in your heart. Then also by making others happy and helping to bring cheer and sunshine to those with whom we live, we help to make our own hearts happier and our faces brighter. We must put aside all sullen and gloomy thoughts and think of bright and cheery things. It does not take much to make children happy. So it will not be very hard to bring sunshine into your hearts and lives, because it will be easy to be happy when you do all that is asked of you.

Keep the Sun Shining in Our Class Room

Some children forget that in school also they can help to make things pleasant and cheerful. The sun can be shining inside the school room even if it is not shining outside. You know that if you try hard to listen to me, your lessons will not seem so hard and you can easily learn them. You know also that if you obey me, if you do not talk and laugh and disturb other children, you please me very much and help to make me happy. There are many boys and girls in this room. It is not easy for me to teach so many; but I love little boys and girls, and I like to speak to you about God and little Jesus and His dear Mother and your Guardian Angels. I want you to do all you can to please Jesus. It pleases me also when I know that you obey father and mother and when you are kind to baby brother or sister and to all the others at home. When I see a little boy or girl naughty and lazy, it makes me feel sad for I know that such a child is not trying to please Jesus. Try very earnestly to keep the sun shining in our room to-day.

Practice:

1. I will be very attentive to my teacher to-day.
2. I will watch over myself so that I may not cause any disturbance to-day.

A light heart lives long.

12. HAPPINESS IN GOODNESS

Another day has come for us; God gives us a new day that we may work for Him and earn for ourselves many graces and blessings. To be sure, God does not expect small children to work as hard as father and mother. You are not strong enough for that. You will have to go to school a long time first to learn how to use your brain; you must also build up strong bodies, so that you may grow up to be healthy men and women. If you are not strong and healthy you will not be able to do much work and you cannot have much pleasure either. But one thing you can easily do, that is, be cheerful and pleasant at your work and your play and so make all about you happy also. You have learned many ways for doing this, but you must keep doing it every day. If you stop and think, "Oh well, I'll just be naughty this once. Afterwards I can be good again!" or "I'll strike my little brother this time; I'll not do it again," that will make it all the harder not to do it the next time you feel like doing it.

A Game Without a Fight

You can play games and have plenty of fun at the same time without fighting or quarreling, can you not? If you remember what I told you about making others happy, it will be easy to learn to play without getting noisy and quarrelsome. Sometimes on your way home from school you meet a boy or girl you do not like. Now, would it not please Jesus if you talked very kindly and pleasantly, instead of making faces or calling names?

Perhaps one of your little playmates is ill and cannot run about and play. If mother permits it, you could visit your little friend to cheer him by talking to him about things that will interest and please him. In this way you can bring the bright sunshine to your sick playmate and he will feel happy even though he cannot leave his bed. Of course, if he is so very sick that no one is allowed to see him, then the best thing you can do is to go to Jesus and ask Him to make your playmate well.

Little children can also be kind and cheerful to old people. Sometimes children are thoughtless and cause pain and sorrow to these dear old folks by laughing at them. Perhaps your grandfather and grandmother cannot walk well, and you could help to make them happy and feel the sunshine of your loving heart if you were careful to do little acts of kindness for them. For example, you could fetch the things they need and so save them many steps. Think now what people you can make happy to-day. Make up your mind what you are going to do to help them.

Practice:

1. I will try to do at least one kind act for grandfather or grandmother, or some other old or sick person I know.
2. I will visit my little playmate and bring him some pictures or story books.

A good laugh is sunshine in the house.
Thackeray.

REVIEW

Recall briefly all you have said about cheerfulness. Cheerful boys and girls are like the sunshine. The sunshine cheers and brightens the world. Without the warm rays of the sun the earth would be cold and dreary. Nothing could grow. So it is with cheerfulness. Without it people would be sad and gloomy. No one would find pleasure in any thing. There cannot be much happiness and content where there is little or no cheerfulness.

To be cheerful always and everywhere is not easy. But we can learn to be cheerful. By thinking good and beautiful thoughts, by speaking pleasant and cheerful words, and by doing kind acts, we can soon become pleasant and cheerful. Then when our hearts are filled with this holy joyousness, our faces and manners will show it and others will be made happy also.

How every one loves the good St. Francis! Even to-day, more than seven hundred years after his death, people everywhere speak of the kind and gentle saint. Saint Francis was always pleasant and cheerful to every one. Even the animals loved this cheerful saint. The little birds loved him and listened to his kind words. They did not fear St. Francis. They knew he was gentle and kind and would not hurt them. Then, there was the fierce wolf. No one dared to go near him. He killed and devoured even people. But when the gentle St. Francis spoke to him, he became as meek as a lamb. So it was with other saints. All of them were gentle and peaceful. It is this that helped to make them great saints. They tried to follow our Lord. Jesus was gentle and kind. He was cheerful and pleasant. His face beamed with a joyous sunshine, more beautiful even than the sunshine we see around us. People followed Jesus everywhere because He was always so kind and loving to all. Above all, He was kind to the poor, to the sick and to those in trouble.

Can we not try to be a little like Jesus? The saints followed His example. We have seen what one of these saints did to become like Jesus. We can easily act like St. Francis by being kind, gentle, and pleasant with all, and then we shall one day became a true follower of the Divine Savior Who said, "Learn of Me, for I am meek and humble of heart."

> Try to be cheerful,
> Never be fearful,
>   Or think that the sky will fall.
> Let the sky tumble,
> Fear not the rumble,
>   It never can hurt you at all.

13. FRUITS OF CHEERFULNESS

You know you can have cheerful and pleasant thoughts; you can speak kind and gentle words, and you can do many pleasing acts. Now you must remember that little boys and girls grow every day and what they do now as little children will help to make them the kind of men and women they are some day going to be. You have learned that cheerfulness is like the sunshine. But this kind of sunshine does not depend on the weather; it depends only on ourselves. It is the sunshine we make for ourselves and others by our good deeds. Do you know any cheerful people? Who is the most cheerful boy or girl you know? Who is the most cheerful man you know? The most cheerful woman? Do you like them? Do other people like them?

Cheerfulness Is Like Music

How many of you like music? I see quite a number. A smile is also like music, and a cheerful face is like a sweet song. A smiling face makes many people forget their troubles. Some people are not happy. Perhaps they are very poor, or sick, or they have no friends. Some of these people are sad all the time. But once in a while a kind person will try to cheer them and make them smile.

You are young, you have not the troubles and unhappiness of most grown people. But many grown people would not now be so unhappy, if they had learned, when they were as young as you, how to smile and be cheerful. Perhaps they were boys and girls who did not know about the great joy to be found in trying to have sunshine always. They grew up and their faces did not shine with happiness as they should have. Instead, their sullen, gloomy looks made people stay away from them, and, of course, they did not get along well with others. Try to-day to remember that your thought must be good and beautiful if you wish to be happy and cheerful.

Practice:
1. When ugly or unpleasant thoughts come to my mind, I will at once think of something pleasant and cheerful.
2. I will often look at the picture of Jesus to-day and think of His great love for us.

> Trip lightly over trouble,
> Trip lightly over wrong;
> We only make it double
> By dwelling on it long.

14. JESUS' LOVE FOR CHILDREN

To-day I wish again to speak about the joy and pleasure a lovely, smiling face gives to all who look upon it. That is why most people love children. (Show the picture of Jesus blessing little children.) Look at this picture. What makes these children so pretty? Is it the clothes they wear? Is that what you think, Mary? "No, their smiling faces." You are quite right, Mary, it is the happy, smiling faces of the little ones. See the little boy kneeling down. How eagerly the other children are waiting for Jesus to put His hand on their heads! Do you think there are any children there who are ill-natured and disagreeable? Do you see any children there whose faces show that they were pouting or grumbling?

Jesus in the Tabernacle

I am sure you wish you had been with these children at the time Jesus blessed them. Jesus in the tabernacle in church also wants to bless the children in this room. If He sees your smiling, cheerful faces, He will be much pleased. He knows it is not always easy to be cheerful and pleasant. That is why He will bless especially those children who try to be like Him. Jesus was gentle and kind. When He was little like you, He was always cheerful and pleasant, and when He walked along the street, people turned to look at Him again, and wondered Who this gentle and charming Boy was.

Practice:
To-day you can make a special effort to be cheerful and pleasant by resolving:
1. To keep from frowning, or pouting, or looking sullen.
2. To look pleasant and cheerful, no matter what happens.

Be good, do good, and you will be happy.

15. PRACTICE MAKES PERFECT

Have you ever helped to make any one forget his troubles by being happy and cheerful your-

JESUS BLESSING THE LITTLE CHILDREN

self? Never let a day pass without trying to make some one feel happier and more cheerful. You know that when a boy wants to be a baseball player, he must play often, for the more he practices, the better player he will be. If your sister practices on the piano every day, she will soon be a good pianist. In the same way, if you try to be pleasant and cheerful every day, you will soon be able to do it without much trouble.

Resolve that to-day you will try to speak only kind and pleasant words to those at home and at school. When you go home to-day, go about the house and see to how many persons you can speak kindly. Just try it and see how quickly you can make others feel happy when you yourself are cheerful. Start as soon as you reach home.

Begin to Practice at Home

When you reach home, you will probably find mother tired and weary because baby was cross and she had so much work to do. That will be a good chance to practice cheerfulness. Say something pleasant to cheer her. Offer to help her and see how quickly you can make her smile. Perhaps you can play with the baby for a while and so give mother a chance to finish her work. You can do the same for your brothers and sisters. They may be tired and therefore not feel like being cheerful and pleasant. Perhaps father comes home from work so very tired that he does not feel like being cheerful. You can talk to him and tell him all about what you learned in school to-day and what you did all day long. Father will be pleased to hear about all these things and will soon forget that he is tired. In order to help you to keep your resolution to-day, decide now what you are going to do.

Practice:

1. I will help mother with her work, when I come home from school to-day.
2. I will try to make my father cheerful by telling him what I learned in school to-day.

The world is so full of a number of things,
I'm sure we should all be as happy as kings.
Robert Louis Stevenson.

16. SPREADING SUNSHINE

We have to-day another chance to see how many persons we can make happy by being pleasant and cheerful ourselves. You have by this time found how everybody likes boys and girls who wear sunny faces and who smile and try to make others sunny and happy also. Let us count the stars this morning on our "Sunshine Calendar." Who has more stars? I see the boys are trying to beat the girls.[1] You have to keep smiling, girls, or the boys will beat you. Is it growing easier to be sunny and cheerful? Do you sometimes think about St. Francis and the birds?

A Sunshine Club

Now here is another idea. Perhaps you have some playmates that do not go to our school, or who are not in this room. Suppose you tell them about trying to make sunshine everywhere and every day. I am sure they will be glad to know about it. Perhaps you can get them to help you to make your other little friends have a "Sunshine Club." Try again to-day to make many persons happy and cheerful. Think now whom you are likely to meet. You will go to the store for mother, to the butcher, or grocer, or baker. You may be sent on an errand to some neighbor. Perhaps one of your friends is ill; he may be lonesome and you have forgotten all about him. Think now what you can say and do to make any of these happy and cheerful.

Practice:

1. When I go to the store I will speak pleasantly to the storekeeper.
2. I will visit my sick friend and cheer him by showing him my picture book or my toys.

REVIEW

(Recall briefly all you have said about cheerfulness and sum up the month's work.) Here you have been trying for four weeks to learn to be cheerful and pleasant in all you do. Have you learned to make sunshine for others? Did you find it very hard? How do you feel about it now? Did you not feel happy when you tried to be sunny and pleasant? Did you ever notice when the sun is shining into a room where the blinds are down that the sun comes through a small crack or opening? This looks like a long line of light. We call it a "sunbeam." Children like to watch a sunbeam. The sunbeam brightens only one part of the room, while the rest is in darkness. Cheerful boys and girls are often

[1] See suggestion about "Sunshine Calendar," page 160.

called sunbeams, because they bring light and happiness wherever they go. When you waken in the morning the sun shines brightly outside. Some little sunbeams come into your room and shine into your eyes. The bright sunbeams play about your bed and seem to tell you that it is time to jump out of bed. You open your eyes and see how bright everything is; you jump out of bed, wash and dress, and kneel down to say your prayers, and then you run to mother. You feel so cheerful, so happy—all because the little sunbeams shone so brightly on you.

Children ought to be real sunbeams every day and make every one about them as happy as the sunbeams made them happy and cheerful. I shall call you my "little sunbeams" now. When I see so many, sunny, smiling faces it makes me feel happy and I think that Jesus must be pleased with my "little sunbeams" also.

Let us look at our Sunshine Calendar. Who has won the greater number of stars this month? We shall keep the calendar hanging there during the coming month. It will remind us to be cheerful all the time.

> Rainy days and sunny days,
> What difference does it make,
> When little hearts are full of love,
> And all are glad together!

17. POLITENESS

> Politeness is to do and say
> The kindest things in the kindest way.

My dear boys and girls: You have often heard some one sing the beautiful song, "Home, Sweet Home." What a lovely song this is: "Be it ever so humble, there's no place like home!" What is a home? Home is a place where mother and father and children live happily together, where each one tries to make the other happy, where each one does all he can to live in peace, and where all love each other and show this love by helping each other.

Home should be the dearest spot on earth to you. It is there where your happiest days are spent. Father and mother, brothers and sisters live together in your home. Your dear parents work hard that you may have a warm, comfortable place in which you can enjoy yourselves with your brothers and sisters. Did you ever watch the little birds, when, before they are able to fly, the father bird and the mother bird gather food and bring it to their little ones in the nest? How happy the little birds seem! How eagerly they wait for their father and mother! How cheerily they chirp in their cosy nest!

Sometimes it happens that a little bird is greedy or quarrelsome, just like some little boys and girls I know. This greedy little bird wants the whole worm for himself and does not want his brothers and sisters to have a share. Then the other birds begin to quarrel also and before they know what is happening, one little bird falls out of the nest.

This poor little bird is pushed out of the nest and perhaps at the bottom of the tree a sly pussy is waiting for it. Pussy heard all the noise and knew that if little birds in a nest do not agree, one or more will fall out and then she will have a feast. So this poor birdie was caught by the cat and killed because the birds in the nest were selfish and unkind.

How often something like that happens in the home! One little boy or girl is very selfish. Selfish children want everything for themselves. They want the best; they do not care whether others have anything or not. As long as they have what they want, they are satisfied. But these selfish children are not always allowed to have everything they wish. Their brothers and sisters also want a share of the good things and so it happens that children often quarrel. By doing this they make home very unpleasant and mother is often sad when she sees her little boys and girls so quarrelsome and so selfish.

Thinking of Others

You know very well that you cannot always do as you please. If you wish to get along well with others you must learn to be agreeable and pleasant. Do you remember what I told you about making others happy by being kind and pleasant? You recall how cheerful and happy every one at home is when all try to bring sunshine into the house. But to make others happy you will often have to forget yourself, that is, you must first think of others and then of yourself. For example, at table you see something that you like. You wish to have a certain piece of cake or pie, or you would like to have more of a certain kind of food than your mother wishes you to have. If you are polite, you will let the others choose first and then you will be satisfied to take what is left or what your mother or father gives you. If you are polite, you will not take the best of everything. You will let your brothers and sisters also have some of the good things. So it is with other things. A polite child will not want to have all the toys for himself; he will be glad to share them with his brothers and sisters. He will not let all the hard work be done by others, but will be ready to do his share.

A child who loves his parents will take every chance to do something for them. He will be sorry when he cannot help them in any way. He will never get angry because they ask him to do something he does not like to do. He will always speak to them in a respectful tone and will gladly listen to their advice.

A polite child will not grumble or pout when he is not permitted to do what he wishes. Because the father is the head of the family and labors for the support and education of his children, a polite child will honor him and treat him with respect and kindness. He will quickly and cheerfully obey not only his commands but also his wishes. He will do all he can to make him happy and comfortable.

Since the mother bears the greatest share in your training and since she above all others has your welfare at heart, it is only proper and right that you should show her special attention and treat her with the greatest respect and reverence. Therefore, if you wish to be polite you will show your mother every mark of respect and obedience. A polite child will open the door and allow his mother to pass through first. He will pick up any article she has dropped. He will give her the best side of the walk when out in the street with her. He will help her wherever he can; he will carry her packages for her, and in general, will wait upon her everywhere. Even very small children can do these things. If you will always remember the Child Jesus in His home helping St. Joseph and His Blessed Mother, it will not be so hard for you.

You can imagine how the Child Jesus did all He could to help St. Joseph and the Blessed Virgin. How politely He must have treated them at all times. So try every day to treat mother and father as you think the Boy Jesus treated His foster-father and His mother. If you do this you will make mother and father happy. God will bless you in many ways here on earth and after this life will reward your kindness towards your parents with the joys and happiness of heaven.

Practice:
1. I will help father to-day.
2. I will be careful to do something for mother.

> A child should always say what's true,
> And speak when he is spoken to;
> And behave mannerly at table,
> At least as far as he is able.
> *Robert Louis Stevenson.*

18. POLITENESS IN THE HOME

Many children and many older persons too, are very polite when they are with others, but at home they do not seem to think it necessary to be polite. This is a big mistake. If there is any place on earth where we should show our best manners, it is in our own home, among the members of our own family. Brothers and sisters should be kind to each other. If you are kind to your brothers and sisters they will also treat you with kindness. Sometimes little boys and girls are very rude at home. They laugh at the mistakes of others, refuse to help them when they could easily do so, and in many other ways make the home life very unpleasant. Surely such children do not follow the example of Jesus! Think of Jesus often. This will help you to be polite and kind to all at home.

The Golden Rule

Treat your brothers and sisters as you would like them to treat you. Then all will be helping to make your home the happiest and most pleasant spot on earth. Do not forget, then, to be polite at all times and to all persons. Learn to say "Please," and "Thank you." Always ask for things in a polite way. When any one gives you anything, say "Thank you." Do this also when you are with your brothers and sisters. Jesus will be pleased if you help to make your home a place where all are kind and pleasant.

Practice:
1. I will be polite to my brothers and sisters.
2. I will say "Please" and "Thank you" every time I should.

> Let us try to be polite
> In everything we do,
> Remember always to say "Please"
> And not forget "Thank you."

19. GOOD MANNERS IN SCHOOL

We have talked about politeness in the home. You learned that the home is the best place on earth. But if home is to be a happy place, all in the home must learn to treat one another with great kindness and courtesy. When you leave home for the first time, it is to go to school. Here you spend several hours each day. In school you meet many other children with whom you must learn to live peacefully and happily. The schoolroom is like another home with the teacher in the place of your parents. Did you ever hear the "Golden Rule"? It is this: "Do to others as you would have them do to you." I wonder if any little boy or girl can repeat this rule. Can you, Mary? Let us say it together. Right. This is a wonderful rule. No wonder it is called the "Golden Rule." If we followed this rule all our lives we should always be kind and polite, for we want others to treat us kindly and politely. Did any one ever speak politely to you? When you helped mother yesterday she said, "Thank you, Henry." That made you feel grown up, did it not? Well, you can be little men and women now by trying to treat every one just as politely as you can. Of course, there are many things about politeness you must learn, but if you are in earnest and desire to do your best, you will soon learn what children should know about it.

Politeness to Teachers

The person with whom you have most to do in school is your teacher. You have already learned that your teacher takes God's place in your regard and for this reason she should be treated with respect and politeness. When you enter the schoolroom in the morning, quietly close the door, take holy water, reverently bless yourself, then go to your teacher and say, "Good morning, Sister," or "Good morning, Brother." In the afternoon say, "Good afternoon, Sister," "Good afternoon, Brother." Always say, "Yes, Sister," "No, Sister," or, "Yes, Brother," "No, Brother"; or to a priest, "Yes, Father," "No, Father." Never answer merely "Yes" or "No."

Now try to-day to observe carefully these few rules of politeness. Tomorrow I shall tell you more about how you can be polite. Let us play at being polite. John, you may leave the room; then come in and say, "Good morning, Sister." The others will carefully watch if John is doing it right.

Note.—The teacher can arouse much interest in these lessons in manners by dramatizing the various practices she wishes to emphasize. In this first lesson there were several points touched upon, namely, saluting the teacher upon entering the room; when leaving the room after a session, answering "yes" and "no" properly. It is better to drill these actions by dramatizing, than by using a formal drill.

ENTERING THE CLASSROOM

John—Good morning, Sister.
Teacher—Good morning, John.
John quietly goes to his desk, arranges his books and papers.
Teacher—Now children, do you think John did that correctly?
Permit one or two others to try it. Practice leaving the room in the same manner. Explain to the children that when all enter or leave the room together, it is better to answer the teacher's salutation. With smaller children for instance, those in the first and second grades, it is better for the teacher to salute the children first and have them respond, than to require the class to salute first. The reason for this is obvious.

> Hearts like doors will ope with ease
> To very, very little keys.
> Don't forget that two are these,
> "I thank you," and "If you please."

20. GOOD HELPERS IN THE SCHOOL

This morning I noticed quite a number of boys and girls who said politely, "Good Morning,

Sister." How happy it makes us feel, when we greet each other in that manner. What do you mean when you say, "Good morning, Sister"? You wish your teacher to have a "Good" morning, not a bad or disagreeable morning. You wish that she should have a pleasant and a happy morning. But merely wishing teacher a "good morning" will not be enough. Suppose you say very pleasantly to me, "Good morning, Sister," and then throw your books down noisily, or talk to your companions, or disturb the class in some other way. Will that give your teacher a good morning? I am sure it will not.

There are many ways in which children can be helpful to their teacher. Opening and closing the doors quietly, raising the windows at the proper time, passing papers, pencils and other materials, these and many other things will help your teacher. Do not wait to be asked, but be quick to see where and how you can help. Washing the blackboards, emptying the waste paper basket, cleaning the erasers are some other things that most children can do. If you are too small to do some of these things, find something you can do, and do it quickly, quietly and thoroughly. Some children are always ready to help the teacher, while others seem to be afraid to work. A polite child is thoughtful and is always seeking ways in which to help others. He is ever ready to lend a helping hand.

But there are other ways of helping the teacher. Suppose a boy or girl comes late to school every day. Do you think this is helping the teacher? Of course not. Such a boy or girl disturbs the teacher and the class. It is better to be a few minutes early than to be late even one minute. Some children stay away from school without reason. These also disturb the teacher and sometimes they hold back a whole class because they do not know their lessons, and make the teacher lose time in repeating what she had said before.

Some children are always raising their hands and shaking them in the teacher's face, even when she is busy hearing others recite. This is a bad habit and one that children sometimes show even in public. It does not look well when boys and girls are out with their teacher at recess or walking to church, if they begin to shake their hands as soon as something comes to their minds. If something happens that you think your teacher ought to know, walk up to her quietly and tell her, but do not keep on shaking your hand in her face until she tells you to stop. Never interrupt another child when he is speaking to the teacher or reciting his lesson.

To the Teacher:—Pay special attention to the actions of the children during the day. Commend any polite act you may notice. Do not praise the naturally polite or well-trained child too much, but notice and commend any effort made by bashful and timid children. Let any of the above-mentioned suggestions serve for practice during the day.

How to Treat Visitors

Dear children: I am pleased to notice that all of you are trying to practice the little acts of politeness I mentioned to you yesterday. Of course, you must be careful to do these things every day, otherwise you will forget yourselves and become unmannerly. The older you become the more you are expected to practice politeness towards every one. If you are used to these acts of courtesy in your young days, you will not find it hard to act in a polite and pleasing manner when you are older.

It sometimes happens that your teacher is busy with a visitor; it may be a priest, or another teacher, or perhaps some person who wishes to see the work of the class. A polite child will be very careful at these times to act in such a way that the visitor will have no cause to think ill of the class or of the teacher. Therefore, it is rude to laugh, or talk, or make unnecessary noise, or in any other way disturb the order and quiet of the room. If you are near the door, hold it open when the visitor is leaving. If the visitor is a priest, all should rise and salute him.

To the Teacher:—It will be well for the teacher here to drill the children in the customary form of salutation. In some schools the priest is saluted with "Good morning, Father," while in others the usual form is, "Praised be Jesus and Mary." Many schools still observe the beautiful custom of asking the blessing of the priest, "Father, we beg your blessing," or, "Father, please give us your blessing." These are pious customs to some extent falling into disuse, but which it would be well to retain or revive. The teacher should also drill the children here in the manner of receiving visitors. In some schools, visitors are rare, while in others visits are made quite frequently by other teachers and often by the parents of the children or by other persons interested in the work of the school.

> Good little boys should never say
> "I will" and "give me these,"
> O, no! that never is the way
> But, "Mother, if you please."

21. PATIENCE WITH OTHERS

One of the unkind things children often do is to laugh at the mistakes of others. You yourself make mistakes sometimes, do you not? Do you like to be laughed at when you make a mistake in your reading or in spelling? No, of course not. Children are usually fond of laughing. They do not stop to think that they might cause another person great pain by laughing at him. Children are thoughtless and in this way often hurt the feelings of their schoolmates. I have often told you that the best way to remember to be kind and cheerful and thoughtful of others is to think of the Child Jesus. Can you imagine Jesus being rude and laughing at the faults and mistakes of others? Yet Jesus was God; He knew everything better than any one else. Still He did not laugh and make sport of others. If you take Jesus for your model, you will never be unkind and hurt the feelings of any person. Some children are so thoughtless that when they meet a cripple or a child that has peculiar ways of acting, they laugh at him and make sport of him, even calling him names; some cruel boys go so far as to throw stones at such persons. This is very rude conduct and Catholic boys and girls ought not to do such things. Be very careful then how you treat your schoolmates. Remember the Golden Rule. Can you tell me the Golden Rule, Elizabeth? Very well. The next time you feel like laughing at the faults of others, just think how you would like others to laugh at you. A good plan when some one makes a mistake or is guilty of some fault or odd habit, is to put yourself in his place and imagine how you would feel. This will keep you from laughing at him.

The Gift of Sympathy

Try to remember, then, that to hurt the feelings of others in any way is very unkind and rude and that Jesus and the Blessed Virgin will not be pleased with children who do such things. If one of your schoolmates is a hunchback or is deformed in some other way, be careful not to speak about it to him. If you are thoughtful you will play games that this crippled child can also play. In this way he will forget his misfortune and will enjoy himself also. Thank God that He has given you a sound body. Take good care of it. Again I say to you, show your thankfulness to God for your sound mind and body and do not do anything that will harm your health. Make use of every chance to be kind and polite to your playmates who are not strong and healthy. These little boys and girls often suffer much, and are sad because they cannot run and jump and skip about like other boys and girls.

To-day watch carefully over yourselves that you do not hurt the feelings of any one. If you forget yourselves, be sure to make up for it by being more kind and attentive to the one whom you have hurt.

REVIEW

Review the work of training your pupils in politeness. Go over each point carefully and draw attention to the faults most frequently committed by the class. Drill the class repeatedly in the various forms of polite usages, particularly those most frequently called for. By using these forms in play or dramatization the children will not only enjoy them more, but lessons will be more deeply impressed upon them. From time to time repeat these exercises. This done once a week at least, say on Friday afternoons, will serve to recall the lessons on good manners.

> He knocked against me as he passed,
> And almost made me fall;
> But when he said, "Pardon me, please,"
> It didn't hurt at all.

22. KINDLINESS

My dear children: What is the meaning of the word "home?" Home is the place where father and mother and children live together. No, home is more than that. Home is the place where each one loves the other and shows every one great respect and honor. Now that means just a little more than a place to eat and sleep, does it not? Dear children, you will never know what home means till you are away from it, living with people that do not love you, with people that may even wish to harm you. But as long as you live at home with father and mother, brothers and sisters, you are with those that love you as no one on earth loves you. For is it not your dear father who works day after day to make home more pleasant and comfortable? Your father must work every day so that you may have clothes to wear and enough food to eat. Mother works hard all day washing and ironing, cooking and baking, sewing and cleaning for the family. If mother were alone with father she would not have so much work to do. But she is glad that God has sent her children to take care of. She is happy to work all day long to keep the house clean and neat. Father and mother work cheerfully every day because they love you so much. They are working for their children. They want them to have good things to eat and good clothes to wear. They send you to school to learn so that when you are older you may be able to enjoy the wonderful things in the world and be happy doing something to make yourself useful.

But all the work that father and mother do will not make a home if the parents and children do not show their love and respect for one another. Home ought to be the dearest place on earth. It will be so if every one in the family does his part to make it so.

The Happiest Place on Earth

How can you help to make home what it should be? Small as you are, dear children, you can do much to make home the happiest place on earth. What can you do to make others happy? What can you do to make father and mother happy? I know many of you have been trying to help to make home a place where every one is cheerful, kind, and polite. Sometimes you forget yourselves and become disagreeable at home.

You can be polite to every one, you can be kind to others, you can think of their comfort. That is the secret. To make home the dearest place on earth, every one in that home must be kind and unselfish. Treat your parents with honor and respect; obey them cheerfully and do all you can to help them in their work. Be kind and gentle with your brothers and sisters. Polite children will not quarrel, but they will try to be peaceful in their play and help one another in their work and lessons. Be kind also to your grandparents, especially if they live with you. Do not make fun of old people; be quick to do acts of kindness for them.

Practice all the little lessons of politeness you have learned. Never forget to say "thank you," "please," "good morning," to every one at home. Never leave the house without bidding father and mother goodbye. Be careful that you do not make others suffer through your selfishness. Try in every way to be polite, cheerful and respectful, then you will be doing your share to make your home what it should be, "Home, Sweet Home."

Practice:

1. I will be careful to do all the little polite acts I have been taught to do at home.
2. I will not allow any unkind or unselfish act to escape me to-day.

> To do to others as I would
> That they should do to me,
> Will make me honest, kind, and good,
> As children ought to be.

23. KINDLINESS AND POLITENESS ARE TWIN SISTERS

To be kind, you must be polite, for "Politeness is to do and say the kindest things in the kindest way." Although I have spoken of the necessity of being polite I shall speak of it again, for children so easily forget the lessons of kindliness and politeness. A polite boy or girl is one who will never do anything to hurt another. A child who truly wishes to be like Jesus, will always do and say only kind things. Such a child will never be rough in his ways, nor selfish, nor unkind in his actions. A child that tries to follow Jesus will be polite all day long and everywhere and to everybody. Where the children are kind and polite in the home, there every one will be happy and cheerful.

But it is not so easy to be polite in school where there are so many children. Some children are not well trained; other children, perhaps, have no father or mother to care for them; still others are not careful to be kind to the other boys and girls they meet in school. But in this class there should be no child who would not know how to treat others. Remember the Golden Rule. I have mentioned it to you several times before to-day. "Do to others as you would have them do to you." You wish others to treat you kindly, to let you take part in their games. You like those children who do not quarrel about every little thing. You like those children who are neat and clean. You like children who are pleasant and cheerful. "Do to others as you would have them do to you." If you wish others to treat you politely, you must also treat others politely.

Little Ladies and Gentlemen

Now let us see how a polite child would act towards his teacher. A polite child will greet his teacher on entering the room. He will have his lessons prepared and will try to give as little trouble as he can. When he comes to school he will go quietly to his place and will begin his work at once. He will not disturb the other children in any way. He will help his teacher wherever he can. He will take care of his books and keep his desk and the floor about it clean. He will not have soiled or torn books, nor will he spoil them by marking them with pencil or ink. He will keep his hands and face clean. His clothes will always be neat, his hair combed and his shoes polished.

A polite child will treat his playmates kindly. He will not get angry when he does not win in a game. He will not push or crowd others in the cloakroom or when walking in ranks. He will respect the rights of others and not take anything that belongs to another without first asking for it. Eating and chewing is something that a polite child will not do in school. Neither will he whisper, walk noisily, slam doors, or in any other way disturb the quiet of the room.

Such a child will not spoil his desk, or mark the walls, the building or other property. On the playground, he will not get angry and give way to his temper when things do not go as he wishes. He will give in to his playmates whenever he can. "Thank you" and "please" are words that a polite child uses often with his companions.

All day long you have many chances for practicing politeness. In fact, almost everything you do or say has something to do with politeness. Politeness helps to make things go along smoothly. A visitor can tell at once if the children in a class are polite. You may think that it is very hard always to remember to act politely. It will not be hard if you put yourself in the other person's place. What would you wish others to do to you? Do that to others and you will be polite. Remember the Golden Rule, "Do to others as you wish others to do to you."

Practice:
1. I will watch carefully over myself to-day that I do not treat any one unkindly.
2. I will try to treat all as I want them to treat me.

> Children, do you love each other?
>   Are you always kind and true?
> Do you always do to others
>   As you would have them do to you?
>
> Are you gentle to each other?
>   Are you careful, day by day?
> Never to offend by actions,
>   Or by anything you say?

24. THE GOLDEN KEYS

To the Teacher:—For this morning's talk, prepare seven keys, on each of which is printed or written one of the sayings suggested in the poem quoted on page 25. The keys should be large enough to be seen easily. The keys may be made from cardboard boxes and painted with gold or covered with gilt paper. A large key ring also made from cardboard will serve to hold the keys. Some teachers use this poem as a class exercise. One child holds the bunch of keys, another steps forward and selects a key and holds it before the class. The class then recites the appropriate lines. Or, a group of children stands in front of the room, each child holding one of the keys. They recite the poem in proper order, each taking his turn and showing his key as he recites.

Do you see what I have this morning? What are they? What do you think I am going to do this morning about the doors we can open with these keys. John does not think that we can open doors with keys like this, do you, John? Well, we shall soon see about that. The doors that these keys unlock are not doors made of

GOLDEN KEYS

with them? I am sure you cannot guess. Can you read what is written on this key? on this one? the next one? Can you read what is written on the ring? I see you wonder what all these keys mean. For what are keys used? Yes, you are right; to open doors. I shall speak to you wood or iron. They are much harder to open than such doors. These keys unlock the doors of people's hearts. Now, do you see what I mean? Listen to this beautiful poem:

A bunch of golden keys is mine
To make each day with gladness shine.

"Good morning" is the golden key
That unlocks every day for me.

When evening comes "Good night," I say
And close the door of each glad day.

When at the table "If you please,"
I'll take from off my bunch of keys.

When friends give anything to me
I'll use the little "Thank you" key.

"Excuse me," "Beg your pardon," too,
When by mistake some harm I do.

Or, if unkindly harm I've given,
With "Forgive me," I shall be forgiven.

On a golden ring these keys I'll bind,
This is its motto, "Be ye kind."

I'll often use each golden key
And then a child polite I'll be.

Is not this a beautiful poem? Do you think you will remember what the keys mean? We shall later on learn this poem by heart. To-day try to find out how many of these keys you use. Do you say "Good morning" at the beginning of each day? Do you say "If you please" when you ask for something? Do you use the "Thank you" key often? How often do you use the words, "Excuse me," "I beg your pardon?" When you have quarreled with your playmates, do you ever use the key, "Forgive me?" Do you usually say "Good night" to father and mother and brothers and sisters before going to bed? Thinking about these things ought to keep you very busy to-day. In order to help you to remember, I shall hang the keys where all of you can see them.

Practice:

1. I will take great care to-day to use the "Golden Keys" as often as I can.
2. I will watch which key I am not using as often as I ought.

> Do not look for wrong or evil,
>   You will find them if you do;
> As you measure for your neighbor,
>   He will measure back to you.
>
> *Alice Cary.*

25. USING THE GOLDEN KEYS

I am sure most of you made good use of your Golden Keys yesterday. I see some of you have tried to copy these keys on paper. That is a fine idea. Suppose you try for busy work to-day to make a set of keys for yourselves. Perhaps you can make another set to take home. These keys ought also to be used in your home. Perhaps you can show others also how to use them.

To-day I shall read to you another little poem which I wish you to learn. It is not long, and will be easy to remember. It is this:

> Cross words are like ugly weeds;
>   Pleasant words are like fair flowers;
> Let us sow sweet thoughts for seeds,
>   In these garden hearts of ours.

What is the best way to begin the morning? To say your morning prayers. Yes, Henry, that is the best way. Saying your morning prayers is like saying "Good morning" to God. When you meet your parents and the others in the family, what is the right thing to say? Yes, Mary, "Good morning, Father, good morning, Mother." A pleasant "Good morning" means that you wish each one to have a good or pleasant morning. It costs nothing to say this kindly and cheerfully, does it? But it helps much to make others happy. If you have not used this key often, begin as soon as you can to use it and use it every morning. I wonder how many children said "Good morning" to me to-day. How many said "Good morning" to their schoolmates?

The next key is the "Good night" key. When do we use this key? I wonder if there are any children in this room who do not use this key. What a beautiful home that must be where each one uses this key before going to sleep? Do you say "Good night" to Jesus before you fall asleep? Do not forget to use your "Good night" key. Your father and older brothers may have keys which they use to get in at night when the others are already in bed. Now you have a night key also, but it is a "Good night" key. This lets you into the house of sound, healthy sleep.

The third key is used when you ask for anything. "If you please" or "Please" opens many doors. When someone asks you to go on an errand for them and they say, "Please, Harry, take this letter to the mail box for me," you are willing to do as you are asked. Others also like it if you ask them politely when you wish them to do you a good turn. This key should be used particularly at the table when you want something.

The "Thank you" key ought to be used most. How many times in the day you have a chance to say "Thank you" to others. Do not let this key get rusty. Have it ready to use at any minute.

Making Amends

"Excuse me" or "I beg your pardon," I fear is a key that many little boys and girls do not know how to use. Most children forget all about this key. When should it be used? Can any one tell me? Passing in front of a person unintentionally, pushing a person when passing him, and other like happenings, make it necessary to use this key. "Please excuse me" helps to make things go smoothly, when they otherwise might have been disagreeable. Do not pass before others if it can be helped and never push against others.

When you have hurt some one either by a word or by an act, be sure just as soon as you see that you have hurt him, to say "Forgive me, I did not mean to hurt you." This will make the other person feel that you really did not mean to hurt his feelings.

Try to-day to use as many of these keys as you can. Do not, as some grown people do, forget your bunch of keys. Carry your keys with you everywhere and use them as often as possible. Do not let them get rusty.

Practice:

1. I will not forget my keys.
2. I will use my keys as often as I can to-day.

> If wisdom's ways you kindly seek,
> Five things observe with care,
> To whom you speak, of whom you speak,
> And how, and when, and where.

REVIEW

To the Teacher:—As a review to-day, teach the little poem given yesterday. Let the class repeat it until most of the children know it by heart. Call on different children to tell you when they can use the "Golden Keys." Perhaps you can give a number of children two lines of the first poem to memorize and later carry out one or another of the suggestions made at the beginning of the week's talks. Many other plans will suggest themselves.

26. A KIND ACT

One day a poor old man stood at the corner of a busy street playing a violin. His faithful dog was beside him. But the people passed by and did not pay any attention to the man or his music. Few dropped any money into the cap held by the dog. Here and there a little girl or boy passed by but not many of them noticed the poor old man.

It was getting late and the man had not enough money to buy his supper. He looked tired and hungry. A young girl, who had been watching the old man for a while, now stepped up and said, "Please, play that last tune again."

The man started to play it and the young girl sang in a sweet voice the words of the "Ave Maria," "Hail Mary," for that is what the old man was playing. Soon a crowd gathered and the people, charmed with the beautiful singing, dropped money into the cup. When the song was ended the man turned to thank his young friend, but she had disappeared in the crowd.

The old man was now able to buy a supper for himself and his dog and he had enough money to last him several days. Ever after when he played the "Ave Maria," he thanked God for the noble-hearted young girl and asked our blessed Mother to bless her for her act of kindness towards him.

> Be kind and be gentle
> To those who are old
> For kindness is dearer
> And better than gold.

27. KINDNESS TO ANIMALS

How many of you have pets at home? What have you, John? And you, Harry? And you,

Thomas? I see many of you have pets. You have all kinds of pets. Some have dogs, some have canary birds, others have rabbits, or chickens, or cats. But whatever kind of pet you may have, you must treat it kindly. God made the animals for our use. He did not make them to be cruelly treated by people. Children who are cruel towards their pets usually grow up to be mean and cruel towards people. A little boy that takes pleasure in torturing a cat or fly will very likely turn out to be a man who does not care for the feelings of others. He will hurt others by unkind words and deeds.

Animals love people who are kind to them. The saints were always kind to animals. You remember the story I told you about the good and gentle St. Francis. How the birds loved to gather round him and listen to his words! Do you remember the story of St. Francis and the wolf? When St. Francis lived on a mountain all alone with the birds and beasts, they gathered round him while he prayed; they were not afraid of him, for they knew that he was kind. He always called the birds and animals his brothers and sisters.

The Little Flower's Pet

Other saints also have shown great kindness to animals. We read of the Little Flower of Jesus that when she went out walking with her father, her dog always followed her. One day, while they were out walking, Tom, for that was the dog's name, stopped under a tree by the roadside. When the Little Flower's father whistled for him, he would not come. The dog stood there and barked and barked. "Come, Tom has found something and wants you to see it," said the father. So they went back. And what do you think they found? There in the grass they found a little bird which had fallen from its nest. It was too small to fly. It was terribly frightened to see the big dog standing over it. Of course, Tom was too well trained to hurt the little bird. He only wished his master to come and help it. He knew that the Little Flower was fond of birds and was always kind to them. They could not find the nest from which it had fallen, so they took it home with them. You may be sure that the little girl treated her new pet with every kindness.

To-morrow I shall tell you more about the kindness of the saints towards animals. For to-day think how you have been treating your pets. If you have not treated your pets kindly, make up your mind that you will do so from now on. Always remember that God made each animal for some purpose. Animals are creatures of God given to you to help you, not to be mistreated. Be careful to-day to treat your pets kindly.

Practice:

1. I will treat my pet kindly and not neglect it.
2. I will not be cruel to any living thing.

> He prayeth well who loveth well
> Both man and bird and beast.

28. THE HERMIT AND THE LION

The saints always loved animals and treated them kindly. The animals seemed to know this and were never afraid of them as they are of people they know to be cruel. Of all the animals, the lion is one of the fiercest. He is large and powerful and could easily kill a man. Lions are often hunted by men who wish to kill them. Therefore, unless a lion is very hungry he does not come near any human being. This was not the case with a lion about which I want to tell you.

Many years ago there lived in the desert a holy old man who spent his days and nights praying and fasting. He was all alone in this great wild place; there were no people in the desert, only wild beasts. I suppose some of them often came near to the place where this holy man prayed, but seeing that he never tried to hurt them, they were not afraid of him. One day while this saint was in prayer, a lion came up to him. The saint never moved; the lion came nearer and held up his paw. The old man now looked and saw that a big thorn was stuck in the lion's paw. He carefully pulled out the thorn and washed the wound. The lion licked the hands of the man as if he wanted to show that he was thankful to him. Years after this holy man was captured by wicked men who asked him to give up his faith. But he would not do so. Then they condemned him to be eaten alive by wild beasts. They took the man and with many others put him in a big place where wild animals were kept. These animals were very fierce and ready to jump on the first person they saw. One by one the martyrs were killed by these beasts until at last only this old man was left. A fierce lion was let loose, but when he came close to the holy man, he stopped suddenly, and, instead of pouncing on him, licked his hands and feet and was as meek as a lamb. It was the lion which the saint had helped in the desert. He had not forgotten the kindness of this man. What a lesson for you, dear children! Animals never forget a kind act.

Did you ever notice when walking along the street with your companions that some dogs growl when certain people pass them? At one time or another, these people have perhaps treated the dogs cruelly and they never forgot it. On the other hand, dogs will joyfully bark and wag their tails when they see some one who has been kind to them, even if they spoke only a kind word or patted them on the head.

There are many beautiful stories in the lives of the saints showing their love for God's creatures. A person can not love God and hate His creatures. Thus it is that all good people take care to treat animals kindly. The birds and the animals praise God in their own way and are serving Him as He wishes them to serve. Some of them are made to give us food and clothing, others to help us with our work. Be thankful to God for having given us the animals and never in any way hurt any of them unnecessarily.

Practice:
1. I will thank God for having given us the animals to serve and protect us.
2. I will never strike or hurt an animal unnecessarily.

> He prayeth best who loveth best
> All things both great and small.

29. TIT FOR TAT

A boy was one day sitting on the steps before the door of a house. He had a stick in one hand, and in the other a large piece of bread and butter. While he was eating it, he saw a poor little dog quietly sleeping not far from him. He called out to him, "Come here, little dog!" The dog, hearing himself kindly called, got up, raised his ears and wagged his tail. Seeing the boy eating he went to him. The boy held out to him a piece of his bread and butter.

As the dog put out his head to take it, the boy quickly drew back his hand and struck him a hard blow on the nose. The poor dog ran away, yelping, while the cruel boy sat laughing at what he had done.

A man, who was looking from a window on the other side of the street, saw what this cruel boy had done. "I shall teach that boy a lesson," he thought. The man went to the door and called the boy over to him; at the same time he held up a piece of money in his hand.

The boy went quickly over to the man to get the money. "Would you like this?" said the gentleman. "Yes," said the boy smiling. When he put his hand to take the money, the man struck him a hard blow on his fingers with a cane he held behind him. The boy cried out with pain. "What did you do that for?" said he, making a very long face and rubbing his hand; "I didn't hurt you nor ask you for the money."

"What did you hurt that poor dog for just now?" said the man. "He didn't hurt you, nor ask you for your bread and butter; as you served him, I have served you."

> If I ever see,
> On bush or tree,
> Young birds in a pretty nest,
> I must not in play,
> Steal the birds away,
> To grieve their mother's breast.
> *Lydia Maria Child.*

30. KINDNESS TO BIRDS

Some small boys are thoughtless and cruel towards animals, especially towards birds. As soon as some boys are old enough to play with other children, they begin to show their faults. They seem to take great pleasure in causing others to suffer. Sometimes they hurt their playmates by teasing them, at other times they make them bear all kinds of bad treatment. They strike their playmates, they frighten them by telling terrible tales, they dare them to do things which they know are dangerous.

Another cruel thing some boys do is to shoot birds. What a pity to see boys, even small boys, carry air guns or rifles and shoot the poor little birds that do them no harm! Such boys are heartless. They kill birds just for the fun of it. Do you not think that boys who take pleasure in shooting birds for fun are cruel? Many a time a poor little mother bird is shot by a wicked boy and the baby birds in their nest wait in vain for her return. Again it may be one of the baby birds that is killed. How the mother bird calls for her little bird! How she flutters and flies about crying for it! And a cruel, wicked boy has killed it just for fun. Manly boys do not like that kind of sport. To kill a poor, helpless creature just for fun is surely wicked.

There are other boys who like to steal the eggs in a bird's nest. This is cruel. It hurts the birds very much just as it would hurt your parents if someone stole you or your baby brother or sister out of your house while they are away. Therefore, dear boys, if you wish to be manly and fair, you will not hurt a bird in any way. You will treat the birds as your little friends. God gave the birds to us to help us. They help us in many ways. We shall see tomorrow how the birds help us.

There are also some boys that hurt or kill the birds by throwing stones or sticks at them. Often a bird is struck in the wing or on the leg. Sometimes the wing or the leg is broken and the poor bird cannot return to its nest. Such a helpless bird may be found by other cruel boys who torture it still more; or, perhaps, a cat may find it and eat it, or it may die from hunger and thirst. What pleasure, do you think, is there in crippling a poor bird? Once in a while boys find a young bird that has fallen out of its nest, and instead of putting it back, they take it home and treat it cruelly, and after they have had their fun throw it away, not caring what becomes of it.

God's Little Creatures

There are many thousand kinds of insects, worms, and other living things in the world. God made them all. He made each of them for some purpose. Some of these creatures are ugly, others are harmful to us. Some are poisonous; some hurt us by their bite or sting, others by sucking our blood. But most of the insects and other creatures help us in some way or other. You will learn many interesting things about animals, birds and insects as you grow older. For the present, it will be well if you try to be kind to all of God's creatures, no matter what they are. Never wilfully hurt any living thing. Do not torture bugs, butterflies, caterpillars, or worms. If the insect is harmful, it is not wrong to kill it. But never stick a pin through a fly or a butterfly. They feel it just as you would if someone treated you in that manner. If you are kind, you will never give needless pain to any creature. Therefore, you will not torture any animal or bird by throwing stones at it; you will not cruelly torment any insect or make it suffer unnecessarily. Always remember that the saints were kind to animals and all other creatures. Try to imitate them in this. Resolve never to hurt any bird and try to keep others from doing so.

Practice:

1. I will not throw stones or sticks at birds.
2. For the love of God Who made all living things I will not hurt any living creature.

> Hurt no living thing;
> Ladybird nor butterfly,
> Nor moth with dusty wings,
> Nor cricket chirping cheerfully,
> Nor grasshopper so light of leap,
> Nor dancing gnat, nor beetle fat,
> Nor harmless worms that creep.
> *Christina Rossetti.*

31. OUR LITTLE SISTERS THE BIRDS

St. Francis called the birds his "little sisters," for God had made these as well as the Saint himself. God made all creatures for His honor and glory. In imitation of the saints, you must treat all creatures well. What would the world be without the song of the birds? We love the country with its flowers and trees and birds. How merrily they sing from the first hours of the morning till evening sets in. What beautiful feathers they have! God takes care of them; He gives them warm feathers to cover their bodies and protect them from the heat and cold. Why, then, should cruel boys try to kill them? Let us rather thank God for having made these beautiful birds for us. Let us try to show our thankfulness by treating them as our little friends.

One of the prettiest pictures I ever saw was that of a little girl and boy standing in their garden feeding the birds. The boy was scattering some crumbs of bread and the birds were flying about him and the little girl, all the while chirping and fluttering, or sat on the shoulders of the children, and picked the crumbs from their hands. These children had kind hearts. You would like to have such kind-hearted playmates, would you not? Suppose you try to treat the birds kindly and you will soon be as kind-hearted as these children were and the birds will love you as well.

What Children Can Do for Their Little Sisters, the Birds

Now, what can you do for the birds? You can feed them and give them water to drink. In the winter time when the snow is on the ground and everything is frozen, the birds have a hard time to find enough food. Make it your daily practice to throw out some crumbs and suet for them. Put some fresh water into a dish and set it out for the birds. In winter as well as in summer the birds find it hard to get fresh water. Some kind people build houses for the birds and put them up in their yards. Some build baths and drinking fountains for them. How happy the birds are when they find food and drink! They reward their friends by singing their most beautiful songs.

My dear children, if you are not in the habit of feeding the birds each day, start to do so today. You will find much pleasure in it and you will feel that you are pleasing God by treating His birds kindly. Do not neglect this, but keep it up day after day, especially in the winter time when they cannot easily find food and drink. When you do this, think of the goodness of God to us His children. He feeds us every day. He is watching over us day and night that no harm come to us. Be thankful, then, to God for all He has given you and try to repay His kindness by caring for His little birds. Make friends of the birds. Never let a day pass without helping them in some way. If you are old enough to build houses for them, ask father and mother to let you put some in your yard. Then watch the birds and you will learn many interesting and useful lessons.

How a Little Robin Learned a Lesson

One day a little robin became very tired of staying in the nest all day and wanted to fly out just as his father and mother did. But they told him that his wings were not strong enough. The little fellow thought he knew better, and tried to move his wings up and down in the nest. As soon as he thought father and mother were out of the way, he got to the edge of the nest and looked out. The sun was shining brightly and the world looked so beautiful. "I think I can fly to that tree over there; it is not far," said he. So he stretched his wings and started. But he did not get very far. He soon found that his wings were still too weak and he fell to the ground. Just as he fell the father and mother robin came to the nest and they cried out in terror, for they saw a big cat come along the fence. They knew that if the cat saw their little bird she would eat it. So what did they do? The father bird flew down some distance away from the cat and as soon as the cat saw him she went after him. But the father bird flew away a little further and the cat kept after him. This he did several times, until he saw that the mother bird had taken the little one safely to the nest. Then he flew up into the tree and was safe. You may be sure the little robin was glad to stay in the nest as long as his father and mother wished him to.

There are many other lessons you can learn from watching the birds. Learn to love the birds and the other creatures of God and you will always treat them kindly.

Practice:
1. I will never throw anything at birds.
2. I will feed the birds every day.

> The little birds, how sweet they sing!
> Oh, let them joyous live.
> And never seek to take the life
> That you can never give.

32. OUR PETS

I have talked to you about kindness to animals. I mentioned that you can show your love for birds by feeding them and seeing that they are not needlessly hurt by you or by others. To-day I wish to speak to you about showing your kindness to other animals, for example, horses, dogs, and other pets. Not very many people have horses now, for most persons prefer to use automobiles if they can. But once in a while you may meet a man who has a horse. Hucksters, bakers, milkmen, and others still use horses. Of course I know that little boys and girls have little to do with horses. Horses will not harm you if you let them alone. Still some small boys take pleasure in teasing horses, by hitting them on the back or by throwing stones at them. This is not right. Horses have feelings too, and therefore you ought never to strike a horse. Cruel men think a horse will not go without being whipped. Horses that have to be whipped were trained so by a cruel master. A horse need not be whipped if it has been rightly trained, no more than a little boy or girl who is well trained.

Boys and girls often have dogs or cats for pets. Boys particularly are fond of dogs. Yet many boys treat their dogs cruelly. I shall not say much to you about how cruel some boys treat dogs and cats, but I wish to make you understand that it is wrong to hurt any animal needlessly. My dear children, be very careful not to choose cruel boys and girls for your companions. Boys and girls who are thoughtless and unkind to dogs and cats and other animals will grow to be hard-hearted men and women. They will have no pity for others. They will be glad to see others suffer. You do not want to live with such persons, do you? Watch how your playmates treat their pets. A boy who unnecessarily strikes a dog or throws stones at a cat, is not a kind boy. He is one whom you cannot trust.

Too Much Petting

However, I do not mean that you must pet your dogs and cats and treat them like children as some silly people do. God did not intend that. Dogs and cats are animals that are to serve us; but people do wrong that give them the best food and shelter and refuse to help a poor person. Be kind to your pets, but do not spoil them. Always feed your pets properly. Do not neglect to give them fresh water to drink and see that they have a warm, dry place in which to sleep. If your parents object to your having animals for pets, it would be better for you to obey your parents. Probably they feel that you do not know how to take the right care of them. Perhaps when you are older they will allow you to have pets.

Try to treat all of God's creatures kindly. Remember that God made them for your use. Every insect, every bird, even every worm has been created by God for some special purpose. Try to imitate the saints and love all creatures, especially those God has given you to serve you. Never treat any living thing cruelly. The Golden Rule applies to animals also; therefore, treat animals as you would wish to be treated if you were in their place. Often think of Jesus and His kindness to animals. You cannot imagine Jesus harming any animal. He was tender and loving to all creatures.

> Don't kill the birds, the pretty birds,
> That play among the trees;
> 'Twould make the earth a cheerless place
> Should we dispense with these.
> The little birds, how fond they play,
> Do not disturb their sport,
> But let them warble forth their songs,
> Till winter cuts them short.
>
> Don't kill the birds, the happy birds,
> That bless the fields and grove;
> So innocent to look upon,
> They claim our warmest love.

The happy birds, the tuneful birds,
How pleasant 'tis to see!
No spot can be a cheerless place
Where'er their presence be.
Colesworthy.

33. THE GRATEFUL ELEPHANT

An army was on its way up a hill. The large guns, which were very heavy, were drawn by elephants. There was a long line of elephants, one close behind the other. Each had his heavy load to draw. On one of the wagons a soldier was sitting a little in front of the wheel. The man was very tired; he went to sleep, and, at last, fell off the wagon. The wheel of the wagon with its heavy load was just about to go over his body. There was no time to get him out of the way. The elephant next in line saw the danger, but he could not reach the man with his trunk. So he took hold of the wheel, and lifted it up over the body of the soldier, and put it down on the other side. In this way the elephant saved the poor soldier's life.

This man had always treated the elephants kindly. He never allowed any one to strike them. Had he been cruel to them, who knows if the elephant would have saved his life as he did.

Little children, never give
Pain to things that feel and live.

34. THANKFULNESS

For some weeks now you have been learning many new things. You have learned to read and write, you can do little sums, you know many things about our good God, about Jesus, the Blessed Virgin, the angels and the saints. You know how you can love God more and more, how you can please Him by obeying your parents and the teacher. You have learned something about the beautiful world in which we live, about the birds and flowers and trees and the many other lovely things in the world. You have also learned something about being pleasant and cheerful and keeping the sunshine in your hearts and making others happy.

God's Many Gifts

How many beautiful and wonderful things God made for us! We ought to thank God for all His gifts. Let us try to think to-day what some of these gifts are that God gave us. First there is the sun. The sun is one of the greatest gifts God ever gave us. The sun warms the earth and makes things grow. It gives us light and heat. If there were no sun, everything would freeze and nothing would grow. Without it, no birds, fish, flowers, trees, or shrubs could live. Everything would be dark and dreary and cold. So we must be very thankful to God for the great and wonderful sun. Do you remember the story I told you about St. Francis and the little birds? What did he call the little birds? (My little brothers and sisters.) St. Francis called the sun his brother. He wrote about it a very beautiful poem, called "The Song of the Sun." He was very thankful for the light and the heat that the sun gave. Then God also gave us the moon and the stars. They shine by night.

So you see we have many things for which we ought to thank God every day. We ought to be thankful to God that He made all these beautiful and wonderful things in the world for us. Let us try to-day to be thankful.

Practice:
1. To thank God often for the wonderful world He made for us.
2. To show God we are thankful by obeying God's laws better.

For mother-love and father-care,
For brothers strong and sisters fair;
For love at home and here each day,
Father in heaven we thank Thee.

35. APPRECIATING OUR PARENTS

I have spoken of the great gift God gave us when He made the sun and moon and stars for us. But God gave us also other gifts for which we ought to be very thankful. God gave you good Catholic parents. He could have let you be born in some far-away place. In China or in Africa, for instance. In some of these places little children are thrown out on the streets and left to die. There are some people who are very cruel to their children. They do not give them enough to eat, they do not give them clean clothes, they make them work very hard and often beat them when they do not earn enough. Now your fathers and mothers are not of that kind. They work very hard every day so that you may have good things to eat, decent clothes to wear and a cozy home to live in. Father and mother also see to it that you can go to a Catholic school, where you learn about God and the Blessed Mother and angels and the saints.

A Daily Prayer of Thanksgiving

You ought to thank God every day for your kind parents. Ask God to bless them and to keep them for you a long, long time. Some poor little boys and girls have neither father nor mother, and sometimes they have no one else who really cares for them. Oh, how sad these little children are! Just think what it would mean to you, if your dear good mother or father were dead! Pray fervently every day that God may keep your fathers and mothers well. You must be careful to do all you can to help your dear father and mother. Then God will bless you.

Practice:
1. Thank God for giving you such a good father and mother.
2. Pray that God may keep your father and mother for you many years.

> Whene'er I take my walks abroad,
> How many poor I see!
> What shall I render to my God
> For all his gifts to me?
> *Isaac Watts.*

36. THE GIFT OF FOOD, CLOTHES AND SHELTER

Many children do not know how very good God has been to them. They never think about all His gifts. The other day I mentioned to you how kind God was to let you be born of good Catholic parents. He also made the beautiful world with all that is in it for us. But He does many other things for you. The sun and the moon and the stars help to make us happy and comfortable; and besides all this He has made many different kinds of animals and plants that give us clothing and food.

God's Creatures Serve Us

God made the animals for us. Some, like the horse, are to help us in our work; some, like the dog, are to protect us; some, like the cow, serve us for food. Other animals give us clothing: we get wool from the sheep, leather from the skin of cows, fur from foxes. Then there are the chickens that lay eggs for us, and whose meat is so good to eat. Can you mention any other animals that give us food and clothing? Any that help us with our work? Any that protect us? If we did not have all these animals, what should we do? Let us see, what did you have for breakfast, John? Where do we get milk, cheese, butter, meat, etc? Do you wear anything that is made from an animal? (The teacher can here ask many other questions relating to food, clothes, and shelter. Ask the children to tell you what they know about horses, dogs, cats, birds, etc. Draw out the knowledge they have of the usefulness of these animals. Lead them to see that God created all these for man.)

When we see how very kind God was to make all these and many hundreds of other animals for us, do you not think we ought to thank God for the animals He gave us? We will show that we are thankful by being very kind to-day to any animals we may have about us.

Practice:
1. Not to be cruel to our dog or cat.
2. To feed the birds every day.

> It is very nice to think
> The world is full of meat and drink,
> With little children saying grace
> In every Christian kind of place.
> *Robert Louis Stevenson.*

37. THE GIFT OF HEALTH

We have some other things for which we ought to be thankful. Have you ever seen a blind man? Did you not feel very sorry for him?

Did you ever see a man with his arm or leg off? Sometimes little children become crippled and cannot stand upright or walk or run as other children do. They cannot walk as well as you; they cannot run or play ball as other children do, while you are strong and healthy and can run and play as much as you like. Some boys are crippled; they have a lame leg or a humpback; but God made you well and straight. (If there are children present that have physical defects, the teacher can tactfully suggest that they might be a great deal worse; they are at least able to go to school, while some children must always stay in bed.) We ought then be very careful not to do anything that will injure us. Little boys and girls should obey mother and father when they tell them not to climb wagons or trucks, or run in front of automobiles. God may punish them by letting them fall under a street car or be struck by an automobile. Be careful then to-day.

Practice:

1. To thank God that He made us well and strong.
2. To keep away from dangerous things, such as automobiles, street cars, machines, etc.

> I'm glad I own head, hands, and feet;
> Without them I'd be incomplete.

REVIEW

To the Teacher:—As usual sum up the week's work to-day. Praise the efforts made; encourage the children by kind words. Be sure to recall the resolutions from time to time. Make use of every opportunity to impress the lesson upon the children. Use pictures and illustrations wherever you can.

> Whene'er a task is set for you,
> Don't idly sit and view it;
> Nor be content to wish it done;
> Begin at once and do it.

38. THE STORY OF THANKSGIVING DAY

How many know what holiday we shall celebrate soon? What is it, Lucy? Right. Yes, we shall celebrate Thanksgiving Day. What do you think that means? (We get turkey that day.) Yes, but that is not what it means. Can you tell me, Harry? Yes, it means that we ought to thank God for all the good things He has given us.

Many, many years ago people came to America from other countries. At that time there was no one living here but Indians. The Indians lived by hunting and fishing. They did not have farms, they did not plant potatoes, carrots, beets and such things. They ate wild birds and killed deer and caught fish. They did little work. There were no mills or factories or stores. There were big woods, but very few fields. The Indians did not live in houses; they lived in wigwams.

The Hour of Need

Now when the Pilgrims came from England they found it very hard to make a living. They had to work hard. Then they did not have houses, and so they chopped down trees to build homes. Then they did not have enough to eat; so many got sick and died. Some of the Indians were very kind to these people and showed them how to plant Indian corn, and told them where they could find wild ducks and turkeys. This helped the people very much and they got along better. In the fall of that year they made a big feast to which they invited the Indians. They called this a Thanksgiving Feast because they wanted to show God that they were thankful for all His blessings, and they wanted to show the Indians also that they were grateful for their kind help. Turkeys were very plentiful in the woods and forests and the men shot many of them for the feast. That is why even to-day we have turkey for Thanksgiving Day. But, of course, our parents must buy them now.

Every year since then a day has been set aside to thank God for letting grow the fruits and the vegetables and other things. But we must thank God every day and not wait till Thanksgiving Day. God gives us good things every day in the year and we ought to thank Him every day. But on Thanksgiving Day, we ought to thank God very specially for all His good gifts. We will start to-day to show God that we are thankful.

Practice:
1. Saying our prayers before and after meals with great devotion.
2. Thanking mother and father for what they have given us.

> God is great, God is good,
> So we thank Him for our food;
> Through Him we must all be fed—
> Give us, O Lord, our daily bread.

39. THE GOODNESS OF GOD

The early settlers in New England found it hard to keep warm during the cold winter months. They did not have comfortable houses to live in. They built their homes from logs roughly cut and laid on top of one another, with mud between them to keep out the cold. They did not have the walls plastered, or carpets on the floor. They had to make their beds on the floor, they did not have warm and comfortable clothes, and, as I said before, they had very little to eat. Still they worked and helped one another, and finally, at the end of the first year, the corn they had planted in the spring was ripe. Then they found wild birds and animals and fish to eat. The people grew stronger and healthier. Then they made a great feast to show God that they knew it was His blessing that helped them.

We also ought to thank God for the many gifts He has given us. You have comfortable homes. You can sleep in cozy beds. In the winter you have stoves and furnaces to keep your houses warm. Your clothes are warm and you have many good things to eat. Mother and father work hard to make money, so that you do not have to beg and starve. It is God Who gives you all those things through your parents. God makes things grow. He watches over you day and night. He does not allow anything to happen to you that will hurt you. And all He asks in return is that you thank Him for all His kindness and goodness. Now we are going to show God to-day and every day that we are thankful to Him.

Practice:
1. We will not forget our morning and night prayers.
2. We will be kind to others because God is so kind to us.

> When the weather is wet,
> We must not fret,
> When the weather is cold,
> We must not scold,
> When the weather is warm,
> We must not storm,
> But be thankful together,
> Whatever the weather.

40. THE GIFT OF FAITH

Since Thanksgiving Day is so near, we shall once more think of the many things for which we ought to be thankful. First of all, we wish to thank God for letting us be baptized and giving us a chance to go to a Catholic school where we hear about God, His Blessed Mother, the angels and the saints. In school you hear so many beautiful things about your Guardian

THE BAPTISM OF CHINESE BABIES [1]

Angel and about how you can please God. In some countries children grow up without ever knowing anything about dear little Jesus, or about His Blessed Mother; they know nothing at all about a Guardian Angel. Ought you not to thank God often for all He has given you? I think the best way to show God that you are thankful is to work and pray for those children

[1] *With permission of Rt. Rev. Joseph F. McGlinchey, D.D., from "Conversion of the Pagan World."*

Praying for the Heathen

You have been told that in some far-off countries people are cruel to children. In China, for example, little girls are not wanted; so when a baby girl is born, the parents cast it out. Sick go straight to heaven. How would you like to help these poor little Chinese babies get to heaven? You can easily do it. First, you can help by praying for them every day. I will teach you a little prayer you can say for this:

"Infant Jesus, pray for us and
help the poor heathen children."

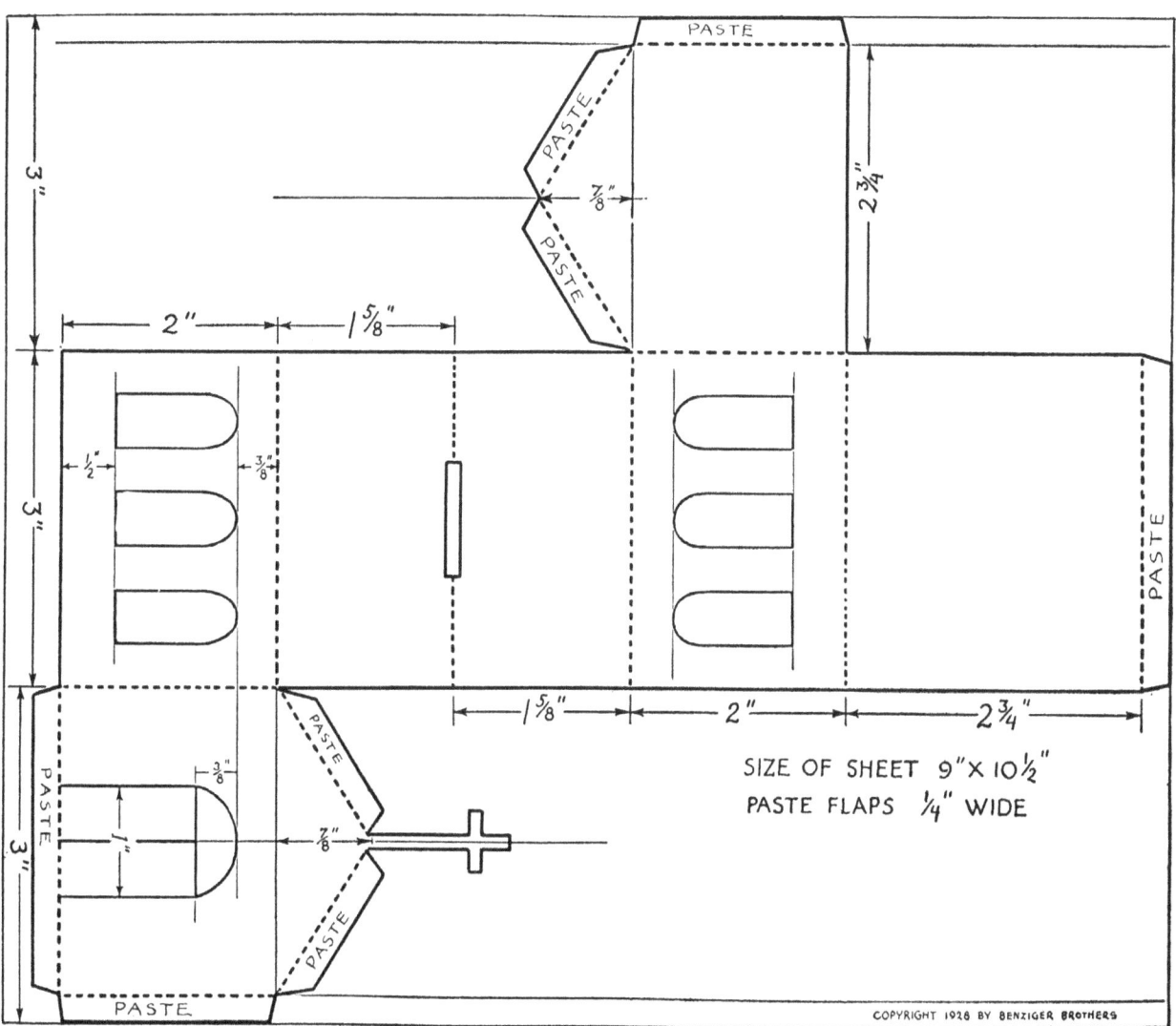

Diagram for a "Mission Bank"

children also and others that are crippled and helpless are cast out and often dogs or wild animals find them and eat them. Now in these countries there are priests and sisters who go around and pick up these little children and baptize them. Many of these poor little babies are no bigger than your dear little baby brother or baby sister at home. When they die they will

Helping the Missionaries

Another way to help these poor little babies is by saving your pennies and sending them to the missionaries. This money helps to buy food and clothing for the poor children. Would it not be delightful to have a little bank in this room, and every time you got a cent or a nickel to put it into the bank? After it is filled I could send it to the missions. Some of you might also ask your brothers and sisters, your uncles and aunts to help you save. Later on I will tell you more about these poor little children.

Church Bank

Practice:
1. I will spend no money for candy or chewing gum, and I will put the money saved in banks for the Missions.
2. I will say the prayer for the heathen children often to-day.

Summer is gone,
Autumn is here,
This is the harvest
For all of the year.

Father in heaven,
We thank Thee for all,
Winter and Springtime,
Summer and Fall.
Lydia Avery Coonley Ward.

To the Teacher:—*Review the talks given during the week. Dwell particularly on making sacrifices for the missions. Here is a good opportunity to instil a missionary spirit. Tell the children stories of the adventures of Missionary Priests and Sisters. The little ones will enjoy hearing these stories. Use this day for that purpose. Use the time to work up a missionary poster.[1] Let the children bring you pictures from missionary magazines. Perhaps you could induce children from other grades to help the little ones to select and cut out pictures. These could be put into a box from which the children might be permitted to make selections for their cut-out picture work.*

God make my life a little light,
 Within the world to glow;
A tiny flame that burneth bright
 Wherever I may go.

God make my life a little flower,
 That giveth joy to all,
Content to bloom in native bower,
 Although its place be small.

God make my life a little song,
 That comforteth the sad;
That helpeth others to be strong,
 And makes the singer glad.

God make my life a little staff,
 Whereon the weak may rest;
That so what health and strength I have
 May serve my neighbors best.
Matilda Betham-Edwards.

[1] For suggestions for a Mission Poster see page 292.

SECTION II

STERNER VIRTUES

1. OBEDIENCE

Necessity of Obedience

To the Teacher:—*Draw out the children's ideas on obedience. What does it mean to obey? To obey means to do what we are asked or commanded to do by those who have authority over us. Discuss with the children the necessity for all persons to obey. Grown people must obey as well as children. Men and women obey the laws of the land. Those who are working for others must do as their employers tell them to do. Father and mother must obey those placed over them. Children must obey their parents. Children must obey their teachers, but the teacher, too, must obey others; for example, the teacher obeys the principal and the pastor, who in turn carry out the orders of the schoolboard; the schoolboard submits to the rules and regulations of the bishop; the bishop does the will of God.*

Example of the Holy Child

To the Teacher:—Place a picture or a statue of the Child Jesus before the class. Show how He, although He was God, obeyed in everything. Frequently tell the children how the little Jesus gladly and promptly did all those things He knew His mother wanted Him to do. Impress upon the little ones that if they wish to please Jesus they can easily do so by obeying promptly and cheerfully.

Obedience to God

By obedience we mean doing what we are told to do by our parents, our teachers and others

THE CHILD JESUS WITH THE TABLE OF THE TEN COMMANDMENTS

who have the right to command us. We have seen that every person, no matter how great and powerful he may be, must obey. Then, too, we know that we must obey promptly and cheerfully. Sometimes you are told to do a thing at once; that means that you are to do it without waiting till you have finished your play. Little boys and girls often think it very hard to obey, but it will be well for them if they learn obedience while they are still young. Later it will be much more difficult.

But first of all you must do what God wants you to do. God made you and placed you in this beautiful world for several reasons; one of them is that He wants you to serve Him here on earth for a while and then after death to be with Him in a lovely place called heaven. If you wish to go to heaven some day, you must do all those things that God expects you to do. Sometimes father or mother promises to give you something if you do what you are told. That is just what God does, and if you do what He tells you, He will take you to heaven where you shall be happy forever. But you cannot be happy in this world nor will you go to heaven when you die if you do not obey God.

You do not feel very happy when you displease mother, do you? A little voice tells you that you were not doing right when you did not obey. You know quite well that you displeased your mother when you disobeyed her. Your dear mother tries to make things pleasant for you at home. She takes good care of you in every way. God acts toward you in the same manner. He is so good to you; He has given you kind parents who love you and work hard for you every day, so that they may give you good food and clothing and a cozy home. There are many children that do not have any of these things. Since God is so good to you, you also must be good to God, that is, you must do all you can to please Him. You can please Him best by doing what He wants you to do.

Practice:

1. I will think of God every time I say my prayers.
2. I will say my prayers with devotion.

   Be obedient! Those who break the rule
   Not only hurt themselves, but the whole school.

2. THE COMMANDMENTS OF GOD

Now what does God want little children to do? God has given rules just as your parents at home and the teacher in school give rules. These rules tell what we ought to do and what we ought not to do. We call the rules that God gives commandments. When you grow a little older you will learn more about these commandments. There are certain things that God expects children to do. God does not tell you about these things Himself, but He speaks to you through those whom He has set over you. Through the Church, God tells you what He wants you to do. The Pope, bishops and priests are the representatives of God on earth. It is their duty to explain the commandments of God and to tell you how you can keep these commandments. God has also given your father and mother and the teacher the right to tell you what He wishes you to do. One of the reasons your parents send you to a Catholic school is that you may learn how to keep the commandments of God.

God Is Present Everywhere

Although you are still very young, you can do many things to show that you want to obey God and please Him. First of all you must pray to Him. When you say your prayers it will help you very much to say them well if you remember that God sees you and that He hears everything you say;[1] He knows what you are thinking. God is with you night and day. You cannot see God, but He sees you all the time. Do not forget this. No matter where you are or what you do, God sees you. So you must be careful not to do anything that will displease God.

Practice:
1. I will remember that God sees me at all times and in all places.
2. When I make the sign of the cross I will think of all that God has done for me.

3. "OF COURSE, GOD IS EVERYWHERE!"

Henry was only a little boy. But he was made of real boy stuff; and boy stuff, you know, is the stuff that boy saints are made of. So whenever Henry was asked by his companions who wished to tease him or by older people who

[1] Cf. "Pictures in the Class Room," poster "God Sees Me," page 259.

did not pray enough to have God always in their hearts, "Do you really think God is watching you now?" he would answer quickly and manfully, "Of course, God is everywhere!"

Yes; God is everywhere. He sees everything we do. When Bernard hid in a dark place to do something bad he thought nobody saw him. But God saw him. So did his Guardian Angel.

Now, one day James and John were playing together, when James asked John to do something wicked. John did not want to; he knew it was wrong. But James kept urging him until at last he was about to give in. Just then he raised his eyes and saw his mother watching them from a nearby window. "I can't," he whispered to James. "Mother is watching me."

Henry was not like Bernard, nor like James, nor like John. He knew that God was looking at him always; so he never did anything he would not have liked God to see. He was made of real boy stuff, you know.

One day Henry was in church with the other children. He knew that God was there as everywhere, and that He was there in a different way, too, in the Blessed Sacrament, as God and Man, under the appearances of the little white Host, looking right at him from the tabernacle. So one day when some other boys made fun in that holy place and whispered to him, he would not join them one bit, but just kept his hands nicely folded and prayed to Jesus to make him a good boy.

Now, who can tell me which was the right kind of a boy, Henry, Bernard, James, or John?

Tell Us Another, Winfrid Herbst, S. D. S.

> When I run about all day,
> When I kneel at night to pray,
> God sees.
>
> When I'm dreaming in the dark,
> When I lie awake and hark,
> God sees.
>
> Need I ever know a fear?
> Night and day my Father's near.
> God sees.
> *Mary Mapes Dodge.*

4. OBEDIENCE TO PARENTS

God gave us commandments in order that we may know what we must do to please Him and to gain heaven. One of these commandments is of very special importance to children. This is the Fourth Commandment which tells us to honor our fathers and mothers. God has given you to your parents that they may teach you to know and love God and do His Holy Will. Parents receive their right to command from God and they must answer to Him for the souls of their children. God Himself does not tell each one of you what He desires you to do, but He wishes you to be guided by your parents. When you obey father and mother you are doing the Will of God, and God will reward you for it. Children who love, honor and obey their parents receive special blessings from God.

How Children Should Obey

To be always and everywhere obedient is not easy. Children often find it very hard to do as they are told to do. Some children obey, it is true, but they do so only because they look for a reward or fear a punishment. This is not the right way to obey. When you obey, you must remember that your parents know what is best for you. Many times you do not understand why you are not allowed to do this or that, or why you should do something you do not like to do. If you had minded when mother warned you not to overheat yourself by running so fast, you would not have caught that cold. If you had listened when mother forbade you to play with that knife or those scissors, you would not have cut your finger. Children do not know what is best for them, but father and mother are older and they have learned many things. You are still very young and must let yourselves be guided by others. Your parents will not expect you to do anything that will be harmful to you. You are therefore quite safe when you obey them. Obey them willingly, promptly, and cheerfully. You obey willingly when you show by your manner that you are pleased to do what father and mother wish you to do. By obeying promptly, I mean doing at once what you have been told to do. You obey cheerfully when you do gladly what has been asked of you. This is not always easy. But a child that is anxious to please father and mother will try to obey in this manner. Such a child will be very pleasing to Jesus and His Blessed Mother.

The Example of Christ

There are many children, and some grown people, too, who find it very hard to do what others tell them. They do not like the word obedience. They think that they need not obey others. They are very much mistaken. Every one must obey; no one is free to do exactly as he wishes. The best example of obedience is found in the life of the Child Jesus. Jesus obeyed Mary and Joseph in everything. Jesus was God and He knew how to do everything in the best way. Yet He never did anything against the wishes of His parents. Always keep the example of the Holy Child before you, especially when you are commanded to do things you do not like to do.

If you want to please the Child Jesus and to follow His example, you will obey father and mother, willingly, promptly, and cheerfully. If you want to obey like Jesus, you must not cry, or pout, or stamp your feet when you are told to go to the store, or watch the baby, or help mother in some other way, but you will go at once and do what you have been asked to do. Some day you will be very glad that you helped your mother by going to the store, watching the baby and doing all those things mother wanted you to do. You will make father and mother proud of you. Above all, Jesus will be pleased with you. He will give you many graces so that you may grow up to be good men and women, and when you die, He will take you to heaven, where you will be happy with Him forever. And now to show Jesus and His Blessed Mother that you mean to please them by being obedient, make the resolution to-day to do some of the following things:

Practice:

1. I will obey mother as soon as she calls.
2. I will stop playing at the time mother wants me to stop.

Once there was a robin,
   Lived outside the door,
Who wanted to go inside
   And hop upon the floor.

"Oh, no," said the mother,
   "You must stay with me;
Little birds are safest
   Sitting in a tree."

"I don't care," said Robin,
   And gave his tail a fling,
"I don't think the old folks
   Know quite everything."

Down he flew and kitty seized him,
   Before he'd time to wink.
"Oh," he cried, "I'm sorry,
   But I didn't think."

Phoebe Cary.

5. "CAN'T I DO SOMETHING FOR YOU, PAPA?"

Marie was a dear little girl of just ten summers. She was kind and gentle to everybody, and her large brown eyes were all full of loving helpfulness. Really, I believe she knew as well as I do that God takes special delight in looking upon boys and girls that are obedient and meek and humble of heart.

Now, this gentleness of Marie's made her so obedient and willing to help that she could read a request in mamma's eyes, or papa's, or sister's, almost any time one was there. She would not even wait to be asked, if she could help it.

One evening when papa came back from work, tired and rather out of sorts, and was sitting at his desk reading the paper, Marie softly went up to his side. Why? Because, you see, her love and her desire to be a little angel of charity and to make others happy sent her there.

Yes; there she stood. Then she lightly touched papa's arm and said, in her soft, musical voice: "Can't I do something for you, papa?"

Papa turned and looked at her. At first he did not understand. He was so tired and worn out. "What do you mean, Marie?" he asked.

"Can't I get you something, or make you comfortable and happy in some way, papa? For I love you so."

Then he understood. This little one for whom he was working so hard wanted to help along by her willingness. His eyes lighted up.

"Of course you can, darling," he cried, as he took her into his arms. "You can give me one big, loving kiss. And I thank God over and over again for having given me the precious girlie that you are, my own Marie!"

Oh, if little people only knew how they can make a heaven out of home by being bits of sunshine, and sweetness, and obedient helpfulness always!

Tell Us Another, Winfrid Herbst, S. D. S.

6. OBEDIENCE TO THE TEACHER

If you wish to learn, you must always listen to your teacher and do what she tells you and in the way she tells you to do it. Do you like to study when the other children make noise? Of course not. And why not? Because it is much harder to study when there is noise. Now you know why the teacher wants every one to look at her when she is speaking and also why she expects all the children to be quiet and orderly when they are studying. It is easy to disturb the whole class. A boy or girl that talks or laughs when the class is trying to study will cause the other children to lose time and miss many important points in their work. It is your teacher's duty to show you how to do your work, but if you do not listen you will not understand what she tells you. Therefore, to learn your lessons well, you will have to do what the teacher tells you.

Why Children Must Obey the Teacher

Last week you were told how your parents take the place of God in your regard. While you are at school the teacher takes the place of your parents. God has also given your teacher the right to tell you what He wants you to do in order to please Him. The teacher helps your father and mother train you and show you how to live in order to please God. Your teacher, then, also takes the place of God for you and it is for this reason that you owe her honor, respect and obedience. It is through the teacher that God wishes to let you know what you must do to please Him and to gain heaven. If you listen well in school, you will learn many wonderful things about God: His Goodness to you; His watchfulness over you; how He cares and provides for you every day of your life. Your teacher will also tell you about the wonderful world that God has created for His children; you will learn about birds and other animals, about trees and flowers, and the many other beautiful things in this big world. Your teacher will also tell you how you can best serve God. She will show you what you can do to be like the Child Jesus.

No Order Without Obedience

The purpose of the school is to train the hearts and minds of the children. The most important duty of the Catholic school is to teach the young to know, love and serve God, to lead good Christian lives. It is also the aim of the Catholic school to teach boys and girls to become good and useful citizens and to be loyal to their country. Every person must rule himself first if he wishes to learn to rule others. It is in school that children must be taught to control themselves. Children must learn to obey the laws and rules of the school. The teacher makes many of these laws. All rules in school are made for the good of the children. For example, the teacher forbids you to speak to each other while she is teaching a lesson. The teacher knows that you cannot give heed to what she is saying if you are talking to your classmates. You may not like this rule, but it is a good one and you ought to keep it. Your teacher also tells you to be kind to one another. Boys and girls that quarrel with others make it hard for the teacher to rule the class. When the teacher makes a rule she has a very good reason for doing so. How pleasant it would be for every one if all the children in the class were obedient to these rules!

When a grown person makes a disturbance on the street, or in some other public place, or when he annoys his neighbors by damaging or destroying their property, he is stopped or arrested and often must pay a fine and make good the damage done. Likewise he is not allowed to injure another person or take what belongs to others. There are laws forbidding such actions and any person found guilty of them is punished. The school is like a little city. If the boys and girls in school control themselves, there will be little disturbance. Children must learn early to control themselves if they wish to live peacefully with others. There are no policemen in school because each child is expected to watch over himself, but if a child does not do this then the teacher must do it for him. This is not a pleasant duty for the teacher. She has enough to do to teach and to help the children with their lessons. The teacher does not need to watch children that watch themselves. Try to make yourself obey the laws made by the teacher and see if you will not become stronger every day in controlling yourself.

The most important rules in school are those which say that you must be in school every day, that you must be on time, that you must be neat and clean, that you must listen to the teacher and study your lessons. Good children will be glad to follow the rules made for the class. These children will learn more quickly than those who try to break the rules.

Practice:

1. I will always listen to what my teacher says.
2. I will be careful not to disturb the class by making unnecessary noise, or by whispering to my classmates.

> If you're told to do a thing,
> And mean to do it really;
> Never let it be by halves;
> Do it fully, freely.
>
> Do not make a poor excuse,
> Waiting, weak, unsteady,
> All obedience worth the name
> Must be prompt and ready.
> *Phoebe Cary.*

> Do at once what you're to do,
> Time quickly passes away.

7. OBEDIENCE WINS GOD'S FAVOR

God desires little children to obey their parents and teachers. God loves those children who do as they are told to do. Do you think He loves those who do not? Do you think God loves children who are lazy and disobedient in school? God loves obedient children. He gives them many graces and blessings. Your teacher takes God's place in your regard. Therefore you please Jesus by obeying all the rules made for the children in school. The more careful you are to listen to the words of your teacher, the more you will learn about the wonderful world, the greatness and goodness of God and the great reward which God has prepared for those who love and obey Him.

Do not forget then, dear children, that everything you do in obedience to your teacher will be pleasing to Jesus. Jesus loves children, but He does not love boys and girls that do not obey those whom He has placed over them in His stead.

Every child in school has the right to certain privileges but at the same time he has certain duties to perform. It is the work of the school to train the children to do their duties as citizens so that they may assist those who govern the state or country by their obedience to the laws of the land in which they live. For this reason, boys and girls are taught to obey the laws of God, for the better they obey the commandments of God the better citizens they become. Children that obey their parents and teachers will necessarily obey others that have authority over them. In like manner, children that make good use of their time and talents will also become good and useful citizens. As you grow older you will understand this better. At present it will be enough for you to know that what you are now doing in school and at home is helping you to prepare yourself to become good citizens of our glorious country.

Practice:
1. I will try to please my teacher by doing promptly and cheerfully what she expects me to do.
2. I will try to like everything that I am expected to do.

> My blessed task from day to day,
> Is nobly, gladly to obey.
> *Harriet McEwen Kimball.*

8. RIGHTS AND DUTIES OF CITIZENS

One of the privileges enjoyed by the citizen of our country is the right to live where he wills, to choose his work, to speak and act as he thinks right. Firemen, policemen, and other officers are hired by the city to protect its people. It is the duty of the firemen to come to the aid of any person whose home or property is threatened by fire. We see policemen walking along the streets day and night. What are they doing? They are watching over us. They are ready to help any one who is attacked by thieves or robbers. They defend people when they are in danger from others. The policeman, therefore, is your friend. He is always and everywhere ready to help and guard you. You ought to respect the policeman and not run away for fear of him. The policemen you see standing at dangerous street crossings are called traffic officers. It is their duty to assist people to cross the streets safely and to watch that automobiles and trucks do not hurt or kill those walking across the streets. Some drivers are very careless and unless policemen were at dangerous places many people would be hurt or perhaps even killed. The city also protects the people against dangerous sicknesses. It provides good water; it keeps the streets clean and in repair; it pays doctors and nurses to look after the health of thousands of school children, and of the sick in the homes of the poor and needy. These are only a few of the privileges that the citizens of our city and our country enjoy.

On the other hand, the citizens must obey and respect the laws of their country. Without obedience there can be no good government. You have learned what your home and the school would be if there were no obedience there. If every one in the family did as he pleased, there would be little order at home. So also in the school; if each child did just as he wished there would be little chance for any one to learn anything. It is the same with the rules or laws made by the government. By the government we mean the men who rule the country. These men are elected by the people to make the laws for them. But all the laws in the world would be of little value if people did not obey them.

But to obey at all times is not easy; there are many laws we do not like, yet if we wish to live happily and peacefully with others we must obey these laws, even if we think they are not good. Those who make the laws usually know what they are doing; they make these laws for the good of our country and for the welfare of the people. Children must be trained to obey while they are still young. Obedience to the laws of the land will not be difficult to boys and girls that have been used to obey father and mother and their teachers. This is why your parents insist so strongly upon your doing what you are told to do. They know what is expected of you later; they know that you cannot become a good citizen unless you learn to obey now.

Self-Control

When speaking of obedience to the school rules I told you that each child must be orderly and quiet in school. It is often necessary for you to move about the room, to pass up and down the aisles, or to form a line. Sometimes when you wish to study your lessons someone disturbs you by making unnecessary noise. Most of the unpleasant things that happen in school or at home are caused by a lack of self-control. What do I mean by self-control? By self-control I mean being able to make oneself do the right or necessary thing without being told. People who do not control themselves do just what they please, without asking themselves whether it is the right thing to do or not. There are many little boys and girls that do just as they please at home, and when they come to school they also think they can do what they like. Is it right to make unnecessary noise in the schoolroom and halls? Why not? Because you disturb others so that they cannot do their work properly. Children that do not learn to control themselves now will cause much trouble when they are grown up. All who disobey the laws of the land do so because they do not control themselves.

Practice:

1. I will respect the rights of others and not take anything that belongs to another without asking him.

2. I will put away all my things and not leave them for some one else to put away.

Obedience is the key to every door.

9. WORK

This morning I have a beautiful picture to show you. It is also an interesting picture. Can you tell me what it means? (The teacher shows a picture of St. Joseph in his workshop with Jesus helping him.) You saw this picture before, did you not? What is St. Joseph doing? How do you know what kind of work he does? What do we call a man that makes houses and tables and other things out of wood? Is Jesus helping St. Joseph? Do you think Jesus liked to work? What makes you think Jesus liked to work? Work is not a disgrace; rather it is an honor, for Jesus and St. Joseph worked. I wonder how many of you like to work? Some are rather afraid to answer that question. I think I know why. It is because you are thinking, "I like to do some kinds of work, but there are some things I do not like to do." Did I guess correctly? I see that I did.

Yes, that is quite true. Most boys and girls like to work, but not many like to do work that is not easy or that they do not like. Boys sometimes do not like to help mother. Perhaps mother tells you to sweep the porch or yard, or help carry out the rubbish. This is not hard work, but it is not the kind of work some boys like. Suppose a little girl is busy with her dolls and mother calls her to watch the baby for a little while. But the little girl does not like that kind of work. She would rather play with her doll than with her baby brother or sister. Or mother asks her to help with the dishes. But the little girl does not like to wash dishes; she would rather do something else. Am I right? Is it not true that it is not because you do not like to work, but because you do not like some certain work?

Little children are usually not really lazy. Watch a number of boys play ball. They run and jump about the field till they are tired and hungry. This is really much harder than work.

Little girls will play house. They wash their dolls' clothes, they iron them, they sweep with their little brooms, and in this way tire themselves out; but helping mother is a different thing.

The trouble is they do not do the work they should do. It is all right for the boys to play ball and other games; there is nothing wrong in the little girls playing with their dolls. But these children should be willing to do something to help make the work of their parents a little easier. Although Jesus did not need to work, for He was God, He did so to give you an example. Boys and girls ought not to be ashamed to help with the housework. It is no shame to help mother wash dishes, or sweep, or carry water, or coal. Jesus, Who was God, did these things.

We All Must Work

Every person in the world must work. Only the sick and helpless are excused. The Pope must work, the bishops and the priests work, your teachers work, the President must work, all men and women must work. No matter who or what a person may be, he must work and often work very hard. There are different kinds of work. Some people work mainly with their hands, like carpenters, mill workers, miners; others work mainly with their minds, such as doctors, lawyers, teachers. All must use the head and hands God has given them to do their work right.

Suppose you do a little thinking to-day about how you do your work. Make use of your time to find out why you do not like to do what you are told to do. Is it because you are lazy?

THE HOLY FAMILY IN SAINT JOSEPH'S WORKSHOP

Or is it because you do not like some kind of work? Some children are so selfish they do not think of helping mother or father. They think only of themselves. Are you one of these? Try to love to do some kind of work. You will then imitate Jesus Who helped St. Joseph. Jesus might have arranged it so that He would not have had to work, for He was God, but He wished to let us know that to work is honorable.

Practice:
1. I will ask myself often: "Do I help as much as I could at home?"
2. I will be careful to do my share of work at home to-day.

> If a task is once begun,
> Never leave it till it's done;
> Be the labor great or small,
> Do it well or not at all.
> *Phoebe Cary.*

10. WORKING UNDER COMPULSION

Some people think work is only a punishment. But this is not so. Work is also a blessing. To many people work, no matter what it is, does not seem hard. This is because they like it. If we like to do a thing we do not find it hard to do. So the best thing for all is to learn to like to do the things they are expected to do. God has given each person a certain amount of talent. By that I mean that every person has received a special gift or ability for some particular kind of work. Think what the world would be if every one wanted to be a carpenter; or if every one wanted to be a doctor. Usually when a person likes to do a certain thing, he finds that he can learn to do it.

Learn to Like Your Work

The first thing to do is to learn to like work. As yet you are too young to know just what kind of work you are best able to do. That will come later after you have passed through school. The important thing for you is to learn to do that work which is expected of you now, in the best way you can. What is expected of little children? Little children are first of all expected to obey father and mother and to do all they can to help to make home pleasant and cheerful. Now they can do this best by doing their share of the work in the home. There are many little things a boy or girl of your age can do. I spoke of these things to you before. No one expects children to do hard work. But surely it is only the right thing for them to learn to do something to help make mother's work a little easier. How many things mother had to do for you all the years before you went to school! Mother had to feed you, wash and dress you, and carry you from place to place for a long time. Even now, how many things mother still has to do for you. Some children cannot keep themselves clean. They cannot wash and dress themselves. I should like you to try this plan. You will find it very interesting. Suppose you begin to-day to count all the things mother had to do for you since yesterday evening. I am sure you will find that mother was kept very busy just with you alone. But suppose there are a few others in your family. How much work mother has to do in a day! And still you think you have much to do. Learn now to like all the work that mother asks you to do. If your mother does not tell you to help her in any way, ask her if you may do something for her. She will be pleased to have you do this. Think how Jesus helped His Mother every day when he was at your age. Try to follow His example.

Practice:
1. I will try to like helping mother.
2. I will do my work without grumbling to-day.

> How doth the little busy bee
> Improve each shining hour,
> And gather honey all the day
> From every opening flower.
> *Isaac Watts.*

11. PREPARING FOR OUR LIFEWORK

Children like to play and spend most of their time playing games. This is quite right, for children need plenty of fresh air and exercise. Children are not expected to do hard work. There is plenty of time for that when they have grown up. Still, children, especially when they are old enough to go to school, are expected to do some work each day. This work consists in helping a little at home, doing what they can to help mother, and in going to school each day and learning their lessons.

Some children find going to school very hard. They forget that school is hard for them simply because they do not try to do their best each day. Remember what I told you about liking your work. Going to school is also work. If you learn to like it, you will find it easy; but if you try to shirk your work, you will find it more difficult each day. Why should children go to school? You expect to grow up to be men and women some day, do you not? You will have to do something to earn money then to make a living. To earn money you must work. As I said before, work will be very hard for those who do not like it, or who do not know how to do it. So you must go to school to learn those lessons which will help you to do your work better later. There are some things every one ought to know, no matter what his work is going to be. Every person ought to be able to read, to write, to do sums, and to speak correctly. These things would be necessary even if he were never to work. When a person can do these things, it will be easier for him to learn other things which he needs for the kind of work he wishes to do.

Your Lesson of To-day Prepares for Your Work To-morrow

From all this you will see that what you do now helps you to get along better when you are old enough to work. This is why those children who do not study now are so foolish. As they advance from grade to grade in school, they will be expected to learn new things. If they have not learned their lessons well in the class before, it will be so much harder in the next class. Each day something new ought to be learned. That is the only way to advance. Your teacher is there to teach you what you ought to learn each day. The best thing for you to do is to try to study what the teacher expects you to study that day.

Here is where the lazy child makes a mistake. He thinks that if he can get out of to-day's work, it will not matter much; but as the days pass by, he finds the lessons growing harder and in the end he is far behind his classmates. Often the teacher makes him do his lessons over, because they were carelessly done; so, after all, he is only making more work for himself by trying to get out of it. The best thing for you to do, is to learn each day's lesson as well as you can. If you find that you do not understand something, I shall be glad to help you if you only tell me. Do all your work in school to-day as though you were being paid for it. You really are being paid for the work you are now doing.

Practice:
1. I will do my work in school to-day in the best way I can.
2. I will try to learn all I can to-day.

> Whatever work comes to your hand,
>   At home or at your school,
> Do your best with right good will,
>   It is the golden rule.

12. THE BLESSING OF WORK

You have seen that every one must work. No one can escape it. God has given each one of us a certain amount of work to do and it is His will that we do it in the best way we can. God has given us talents to learn what we need to know for the work which He has given us to do. We must do our share by using the talents we received from God and learning all that is necessary to make us useful men and women.

Work is a great blessing. Many do not think so, but it is quite true that if we did not need to work, we should not be as healthy and happy as we are now. People who do no work of any kind are usually not well. The body is a machine that must be kept busy. If mother never used her sewing machine, it would become rusty and stiff. If we did not exercise our muscles by work they would become soft and weak. Work keeps us busy. Busy people have no time for useless or harmful thoughts. You know that when you are kept busy with your lessons, or helping mother, you have no time for mischief. Idleness is a dangerous thing for all persons, particularly for children. How many bad thoughts come into the mind of an idle boy or girl! Someone has said, "An idle man's brain is the devil's workshop." This is true. But when a child is busy all day long with doing something useful, the devil cannot enter his mind and heart.

Do the Right Kind of Work

But if work is to help us, it must be the right kind of work. When a man robs a house, he works too, but his work is not honest work; it is not the right kind of work. Generally children are very busy in school. Once in a while, however, I see a boy or girl drawing pictures instead of listening to me, or instead of doing the work they are told to do. This is not doing the right kind of work at that time. Children sometimes help at home with the housework, but they do it so badly that mother has to do it over again. This surely is not doing work in the right way. Much depends upon the way in which you do your work. It does not matter so much what kind of work you are doing, but it does matter how you are doing it. Always do your best. Never do your work carelessly or hurriedly.

My dear children, there is much more I could say to you about working and keeping yourselves busy. But you will learn many useful lessons as the months pass by, if only you try to follow what your parents and your teacher tell you. Do all you can to help at home and in school. Learn well your lessons each day. Never be idle; keep yourself busy with something useful. That does not mean that you should always be working. When you play at the right time and in the right way, you are also doing something useful, for play gives you exercise and will help make your body strong and healthy.

Ask Jesus to help you to do your work well. Jesus knows how hard it is for boys and girls to do certain things. But He is ready to help you if you ask Him. Never forget that Jesus was a boy and that He too, worked just as you do. Often think of how many little helpful things He did for Mary and Joseph. Each time you look at this picture to-day say to Jesus, "Dear Jesus, help me to learn my lesson so that I shall be able to do my work right," or, simply, "Jesus, help me."

Practice:

1. I will ask Jesus to help me to do my work in the right way.
2. I will try to learn my lessons well every day so that I shall be ready to do the work God wants me to do when I am grown up.

> If you find your task is hard,
>   Try, try again.
> Time will bring you your reward,
>   Try, try again.
>   *Alice Cary.*

13. ORDERLINESS

You are still very young and your mother must attend to many things for you. But you can do much to help mother, for instance, by taking care of the books, papers and other things you use in school. The children who do not keep their hands clean will soon have soiled books and papers. If we want to know whether a child is careful or not, we need only look at his books and we shall know at once. A clean child does not have the covers of his books daubed with pictures, or dog-ears on the pages (that is, the pages turned down at the corners), or pages smeared with dirty fingers, or leaves torn out, or the pictures in his reader colored with ink or crayon or pencil.

A Place for Everything and Everything in Its Place

Cleanliness and neatness go together. A clean child will probably be neat in all he does. You should put all your things in their proper places, and not let anything lie about. In school be careful to put away whatever you use and do not allow any small pieces of paper to lie on the floor. Pick up anything you may have dropped and throw all soiled paper into the wastepaper basket.

After you play, pick up your playthings and put them in the place where they are kept. If little girls see any dust or dirt, they ought not wait to be told, but should take a duster or broom and remove the dust.

Remember always to keep your books as neat as possible. Children that love order will have their books covered, will write their name and address on the fly-leaf, and will use a card or a book mark. They will never turn down the corners of the leaves. Careful children will keep their books and papers in proper order in school. At home after play, they will put away their playthings and let nothing lie about for some one else to pick up.

Practice:

1. I will keep my books and desk in order.
2. I will pick up anything that has dropped to the floor.

REVIEW

To the Teacher:—For a review, let the children tell in how many ways they can make themselves useful at home and in school. Make a list of these on the board. It might be a good plan to keep this list for future reference. Call attention to it occasionally. Make a chart listing the common chores children are expected to do at home or in school, and let the children mark this chart for a week or more. Vary the procedure frequently, but try to keep the thought before the children throughout the term.

Suggest to the children to make a booklet, which they might call their "Work Book." In this let them list individually the work they do at home or at school. This is calculated to make them regular in performing their little duties or charges. In some homes where there are several children, the wise mother distributes the work among the children each week, giving each a definite piece of work to do during that week. This develops responsibility and is an excellent means for training young children. Many teachers follow the same policy in their classrooms. They distribute the work in such a way that each child has something to attend to. Children will take a greater interest in their classroom and better order will prevail. At the end of the week, a kind of "check-up" scheme might help to make the performance of these little duties a game rather than work.

Twenty-four hours make a day,
Time for work and sleep and play;
In every week are seven days,
To do God's will and sing His praise.

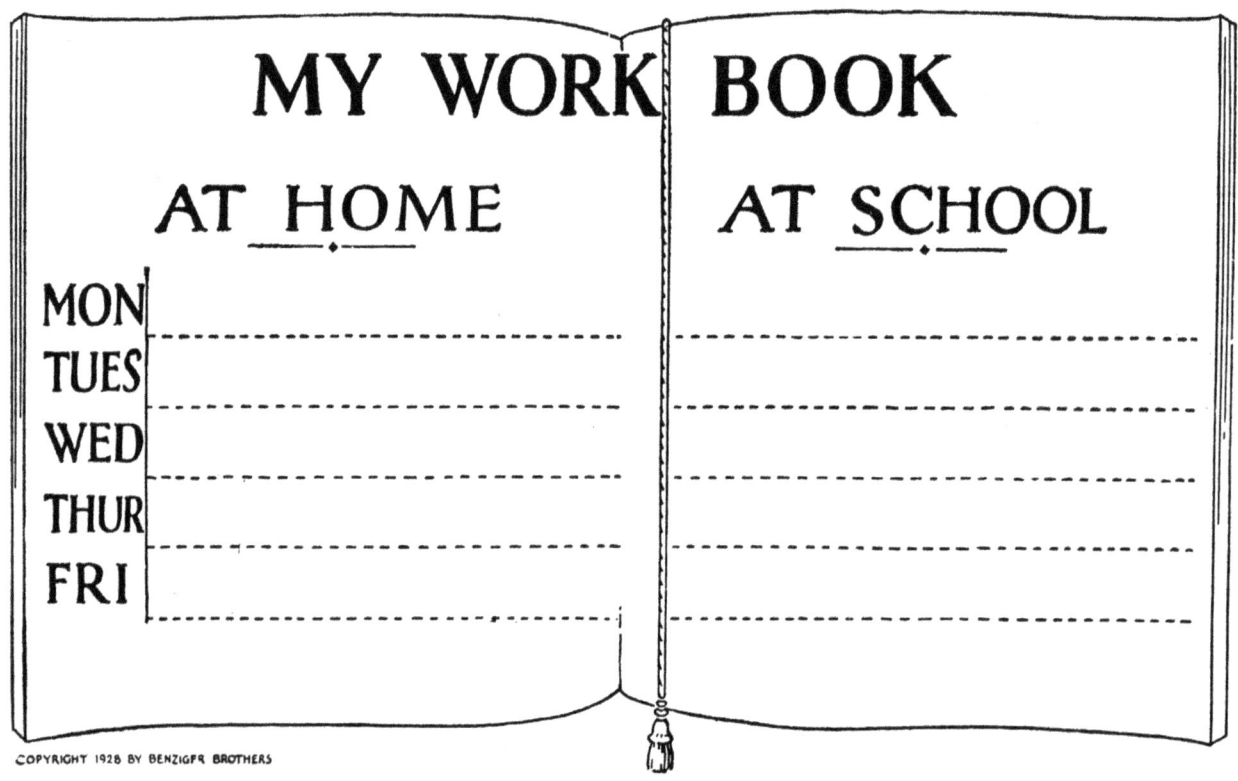

A Work Booklet

14. HELPFULNESS

Dear children: One of the most important lessons that I wish you to learn is that you should love work because Jesus loved it and showed us by His example that work is necessary if we wish to do the Will of God. Each person in the world has a certain kind of work planned for him by God. God, therefore, expects each one to make use of every means possible in order to prepare himself for his life's work. When you like to do a thing you do not find it hard work. So if you wish to make life easier for yourselves, the surest way will be to learn to like doing whatever you are expected to do now. Then work will be easy. Do not think of all you must learn before you are old enough to leave school. You will think that you can never learn so many things. Think only of the lessons you are to study for to-day, and to-morrow's lessons will take care of themselves. When a man builds a house he does not hurry to get the roof on, but he carefully builds the lower part, making it strong enough to bear the rest of the building. If he builds a strong foundation, he will be able to place several stories on top of it and the building will not fall. But if he is in a hurry to finish the work, the chances are that the lower part will not be built solidly and the house will be shaky. So it is with one's lessons. If children hurry to get through school quickly, they will not have the solid foundation of knowledge that is needed for further study. Sometimes they lose a good chance for a better job because they do not know enough to do the work.

An easy way to get used to doing your work each day and doing it well, is to learn to be helpful to others. Little children can do many things to help others. Sometimes boys and girls think they are not good for anything. They forget that they have useful hands which can do many deeds of kindness, a pair of feet which will help them to run errands for mothers or others, eyes that can see for others, and above all a heart that can love Jesus and do many things throughout the day to serve Him and to show their love for Him.

How to Be Helpful to Others

I wish to speak to you about how you can help to make the world more cheerful and how you can help others enjoy greater happiness. I shall begin by showing you how useful you can be in school. You surely want your school to be the best school in the city, do you not? You also want your class to be the best in the school. How can you help to do this? The first way to help is to be punctual in attending school every day. Boys and girls who do not come to school on time are not helping, but hindering the work of the school. When children come to school late they disturb the class. You see how disagreeable it is to those who are on time to wait for the late-comers to get ready for the day's work. Sometimes every one is held back on this account. Many children have the habit of being late for everything. They do not rise as soon as they are called in the morning, and of course, that makes them late for school. Many times children get into the habit of playing on the way to school and so they forget about the time and come when lessons have already begun. If this happens often, these children will form the bad habit of always being late. Some children also have the habit of keeping others waiting till they are ready for the next lesson. When a lesson is over, stop as soon as your teacher tells you and make ready for the next lesson.

If you are in the habit of playing about the streets on your way to school, make it a rule from to-day on, to go straight from home to school and not to stop on the way. By and by you will never be late for school.

Practice:

1. I will be punctual in all I do to-day.
2. I will not stop to play on my way to school.

All true work is sacred.
Carlyle.

15. SCHOOL ATTENDANCE

Another way in which you can help to make your school the best is by coming to school every day. There are some children who come for a few days, then stay away for a while, then return for a short time and again miss a day. Surely such children do not help their school. Rather they are making the school lose its good name. Besides, these children are not learning much and they cannot expect to be sent to a higher grade with the other children. This is a fault that does much to spoil a school or class. When you cannot come to school because you are ill, you are, of course, not to blame if you miss school for a few days or longer. You will have to work to catch up with your classmates, but a child who has had to miss school on account of illness usually tries to make up soon.

Order Is Heaven's First Law

You can help your school by being orderly. Coming into the room quietly, taking care not to disturb your schoolmates by unnecessary noise, not whispering or otherwise annoying the teacher and the class, are means of helping to keep order. Keep your desk and the floor about it clean. Do not throw paper on the floor. Be careful to have everything you use in its right place. Keep the line in going to and from your classroom. Help to keep the school grounds clean by not throwing paper or fruit or other things about—these are still other ways of helping to make your school one of the best in the city.

Having your lessons prepared for each day also helps the work of a school very much. A school in which the pupils are careless in studying their lessons will never be a successful school.

You have been trying to do your best since the day you came to school for the first time. But children forget so easily most of the things I mentioned that I thought it well to speak of these things again. Try to do your best to make your school a good school. This cannot be done unless every child in the school helps. If there are several children who do not attend school regularly or punctually, or who disturb the order of the class in any way, the school will have little chance of being a good school.

Now I know quite well that most of you want your school and your class to be the best. Do all you can in the best way you know how, and you may be sure you are doing your share towards the making of a good school.

Practice:
1. I will help to make my class the best class in the school by doing my best work all day long.
2. I will not spoil the appearance of my school by throwing paper or fruit on the school grounds or on the sidewalks.

> No matter what you do,
> At home or at your school,
> Always do your best,
> There is no better rule.

16. HELPFULNESS AT HOME

Children can help at home in many ways. By being obedient, thoughtful, polite, kind, cheerful and orderly, the home will be made better and all in the home will be happier and more contented. Often children think that just because they are still children there is little that they can do to help others. They say that they cannot earn money, or cook, or wash clothes and iron, or sweep and clean like older folks. Many boys and girls think that all that children can do is play, eat and sleep.

Now let us see how you may really be helpful at home. You can help by keeping your clothes, your books and your playthings in order. By taking care that you do not soil or tear your clothes, you help mother by making her less work. By caring for your books, you make them last a longer time, and thereby you save your parents money. Putting away toys and other playthings when you have finished playing with them also helps at home. How many times mother has to pick up toys, picture books and other articles which you carelessly leave lying on the floor or on the chairs! You are big enough to put away your hat, coat, shoes, books, paper and pencils. You ought to have a place where you can keep the things belonging to you. Can you think how much time and work it would save mother if you were careful about these little things at home? How often it happens that when you are ready for school you cannot find a book or pencil or some other article you need and come to school late on that account.

Ways of Helping

You can be helpful at home in many other ways. Anything you do to help mother, whether it be watching baby, or going on an errand, or sweeping or dusting, is being helpful to mother as well as to yourself. When you help mother you are learning to do something that will help you to get along better in life, for every one is expected to be orderly and useful.

So you see, dear children, when you are doing something to help others you are doing something worth while. What a wonderful thing also to be able to say that you are doing what Jesus did when He was a child! Jesus tried to help wherever He could. You cannot imagine Jesus trying to shirk work by saying that He was tired, or by pretending that He was doing it. No, indeed; Jesus was always looking for something He could do for His Mother and He was happy when He was able to do little things to help her.

When you get home from school to-day, be careful about putting away your school-books. Begin to-day to keep your things in order and never let anything that belongs to you lie about for mother to pick up or put away.

Practice:
1. I will take better care of my books, pencils and paper.
2. I will help mother by putting my playthings away carefully.

> Leave not your work
> Till it is done.
> First do your task,
> Then have your fun.

17. THE SPIRIT OF HELPFULNESS

You have seen how even little children can do much to be helpful both in school and at home. Although you are small and cannot do very hard work, still there are many ways in which a good child can make himself useful. Some mothers say they do not know what they would do if their little boys and girls did not help them. It always pleases me when I hear a mother tell me that her little boy or girl is a great help to her at home. God will surely bless such children. He wants you to do all you can to show your love towards your dear parents. He tells you to honor father and mother. He promises many blessings to the children who show love and respect for their parents. Jesus came upon earth to give you an example of what you should do to show this honor to your parents. Children cannot do great things. You are still too young to go to work to earn money so that father will not have to work any longer. At home you cannot do the hard work that mother does. No one expects you to do these things now. But there are many other ways in which you can help. Boys and girls know very well what they can do to help at home. When you are older you will be able to help more and make it easier for father and mother. But the thing for you to do now is to help wherever you can by doing the little things that even a child can do.

Helping Your Town

Children can be helpful not only in the school and in the home, but they can also do much to help to make better the town or city in which they live. I am sure you are wondering what little children can do to help to make the town better. You can do much to help to make your town the best and cleanest town in the state. How can you do that? We say a town or a city is a fine place when we see the streets and sidewalks clean and free from rubbish and dirt; when the houses are well kept and trees and flowers are carefully tended; when the people respect the rights of others and do not take their property or injure it in any way. A town or a city is good when the people living in it are quiet and orderly.

Now what can children do to help along? As I said before, children can do much to help to make their town or city a good place to live in. How can you help to keep the sidewalks and streets clean? Who can tell me? Yes, by being careful not to throw paper or other rubbish on the street or sidewalk. How can you help to make your street quiet and orderly? Do noisy games disturb the quiet and order of a street? Yes, you are quite right. Some children cause much annoyance to people by loud and rough games, or by throwing stones, or by playing ball where they can easily break windows. People do not like to live in a place where the children are so disorderly and, therefore, if you do these things your town or city or street will get a bad name. Children can play many games that will not disturb the neighborhood. One of the most annoying things in summer evenings is to have children play noisily in the street, screaming and running through people's yards, slamming their gates and otherwise disturbing people. You are not helping anyone when you do things of this kind.

Examine yourself to-day to find out if you are among the children who cause trouble in your neighborhood. If you wish to be a good citizen you must help to make your town or city one of the best in the country. ARE YOU DOING YOUR SHARE?

Practice:

1. I will help my town by playing quietly so as not to disturb anyone.
2. I will be careful not to throw paper on the sidewalk or street.

REVIEW

As a summary use one or two memory gems or short poems to illustrate helpfulness.

> Little deeds of kindness, little words of love,
> Make our earth an Eden like the heaven above.
> *Frances S. Osgood.*

18. TRUTHFULNESS

To-day I shall speak to you about something very important, something that boys and girls should learn while still very young. If this lesson is well learned, it will help to make your life better and happier. I am going to speak to you about being truthful. What does being truthful mean? Can any one tell me? Yes, being truthful means telling the truth; it means not telling lies. Truthfulness is a beautiful virtue. Every person ought to be truthful. How we love a little girl that always tells the truth! What a manly little fellow is the boy that does not lie! Boys and girls that tell the truth at all times will grow to be men and women whom every one will love and respect.

Why We Should Be Truthful

No one thinks much of a person that tells lies. A lie is an ugly thing. A lie is a sin, because by telling a lie, we hurt God. God is truth. He hates everything that is not truth. Therefore God is greatly displeased by untruthfulness. Each time you tell a lie, even if it be only a very small one, you thereby displease God. God hates lying. The devil is called the "father of lies" because he told the first lie.

You see then, my dear children, why you should be careful to tell the truth always. A lie, no matter how small it may be, is a sin, and a sin offends God. God has been so good to you that you should try to please Him in every way you can. If you are careful you will not find it hard to tell the truth. Often think of Jesus during the day. Think what He would do if He were in your place. Jesus was always truthful. He wishes you to follow His example in this as well as in other things.

Many children seem to think it only a little thing when they tell a lie. They do not think of what they are doing when they tell an untruth. I am going to ask you to be very careful to-day and to watch over yourselves, so that if you are tempted to tell a lie, you will not do it. But should it have happened that a lie slipped out before you noticed it, ask Jesus to forgive you. Also promise Jesus that you will try to keep from doing anything that will lead you to commit this sin. To-morrow we shall speak about how children come to tell lies. For to-day, remember that God sees you everywhere; that He knows your thoughts, and that He wishes you to be truthful at all times.

Practice:

1. I will watch myself to-day that I may not tell an untruth.
2. If I have been careless and have told a lie, I will tell Jesus that I am sorry.

> Always tell the truth, my boy,
> Never tell a lie.
> You can keep from doing wrong,
> If you only try.

19. MAKING EXCUSES

You have learned that it is a very bad thing to tell lies. You know that every lie, even a very small one, hurts God and displeases Him. Every lie is a sin. To-day I wish to speak about how little boys and girls happen to tell lies so often and so easily. One reason is because children often make false excuses. Let me try to explain this to you.

Suppose you are playing at home with your little playmate and you suddenly knock over a glass that was standing on the table. The glass falls to the floor and breaks. Your mother told you to be careful not to break anything. Perhaps this glass was the only one of a certain kind she had. Of course, you and your playmate did not mean to break the glass. But when you see the broken pieces on the floor you become frightened, for you know your mother will punish you for your carelessness. So you quickly pick up the pieces and throw them away. When mother comes into the room, you do not tell her about the glass. Soon she misses the glass and asks you where it is. But you say that you do not know. You say this because you know that if you tell mother what happened she will punish you. At last mother finds the broken pieces and then she knows what happened. Now you say that your little playmate pushed you, or that you did not know the glass was on the table. You think that by putting the blame on some one else you will not be punished so much. This is excusing yourself, and if the reason you give for breaking the glass is not the true one, this excuse is a lie, just as it was a lie to say that you did not know where the glass was when mother asked you about it. So there would be two lies and perhaps even more, for each time you repeated the excuse, you would be telling another lie.

Unconscious Lying

You see now how easy it is to get used to telling lies. How often children excuse themselves in this way in order to get out of being punished! It is a bad thing to get used to making excuses for everything. How many times it happens that while playing you throw something down, or you break something. How much better it would be to admit that you did it, without trying to put the blame on some other person! How often it happens that another child is punished for something that you have done because you do not confess that you did it!

Do you not think that Jesus is displeased by such actions? And then, too, sooner or later, the truth will come out, and what will people think of you when they know that you let another be punished in your place? They will call you a liar and they will never believe you again, even should you tell the truth. If you know that a certain child seldom tells the truth, do you believe anything that he says? Surely not. You think that if he told you a lie once, perhaps what he is now saying is also false. There are many other ways in which children tell lies. It is so easy to put the blame on others. But boys and girls who do that, besides telling lies and offending God thereby, also show that they are cowards. Surely there is not a single child in this room who would wish any one to call him a coward.

Be careful, then, to-day in your play not to blame another for what you yourself have done. Tell the truth, even if you should be punished. At least you will not have hurt God. If while playing it happened that you knocked over a glass or some other thing, and broke it, no one could say you committed a sin by doing so, for very few boys and girls break things just for the fun of it. Father and mother may be angry and displeased about it, and may even punish you, still it is far better to tell the truth than to tell a lie. Father and mother will love you all the more for your truthfulness. Remember this, dear children, the truth comes to light sooner or later, and then you will be despised, when others learn that you have not been truthful.

Try to-day not to excuse yourself when you have done something for which you may be blamed or punished. Do this for the love of Jesus and ask our blessed Mother to keep you from telling a single lie to-day.

Practice:

1. I will tell the truth, even if I know that I shall be punished if I admit that I am guilty.
2. I will ask the blessed Mother and my Guardian Angel to help me to tell the truth all day.

> Dare to be true;
> Nothing can need a lie;
> The fault that needs one most
> Grows two thereby.
> *George Herbert.*

20. LYING AND UNHAPPINESS

Children who are always telling lies, whether it be telling lies with the lips or acting lies by pretending to be what they are not, are not really happy. They are always afraid they will be caught. They fear punishment and on this account excuse themselves falsely, yet in the end they are found out and in many cases are punished besides. So it does not help them very much, after all, to tell lies. They cannot be happy, for such children know that they are committing sin. They know that Jesus detests a lie. They know also that the blessed Mother is displeased with them, and that their Guardian Angels will be sad, because they are, on account of their untruthfulness, displeasing to God.

Learn then, dear children, that after all, it is better to tell the truth and to act truthfully and honestly in everything. God will bless you, the blessed Virgin, your Guardian Angels and your patron saints will be pleased with you, people will love and respect you, and you will be trusted by all. This will help to make your life happy and useful, for you will be able to do much good if you are trusted.

Carefully examine yourself this morning to find out if you belong to that class of children that cannot be trusted and must be watched. If you find that you do, then it will be well for you to remember that the Eye of God is upon you all day. God sees you, even if I should not see you. God is ever watching you. To-day I shall place this picture before you as a reminder that no matter what you think or do, God sees you.[1]

[1] Cf. Poster "God Sees Me," page 259.

Pretending to Be

Some children are untruthful, not by telling lies, but by acting lies. Now, you will say, "How can we act a lie?" Many children act lies every day. I shall try to explain this way of being untruthful. You are sitting here before me listening to me. All of you are attentive. Every eye is watching me, and I know that each one is trying his best to learn the lesson I am trying to teach you. Now let us suppose that while I am speaking to you a visitor comes into the room. While I am talking to the visitor, some children think that, since I am not watching them, it is a good chance for them to talk or laugh or waste time. But just as soon as they notice that I am about to turn toward them, they pretend they are busy. This is acting a lie and is just as wrong as telling a lie with your lips. Children that try to deceive me or their parents by pretending they are doing the right thing, are just as untruthful as those that tell a direct lie. Sometimes, while I am explaining a lesson to one group, a boy or girl may think it a good chance to "play off," as we say. This is a bad thing to do. Such children do this so often that at last they get used to it, and so do it without knowing that they are acting a lie. But they will be caught some time and then they will not easily be trusted again. To be trusted by your teacher and your parents is a fine thing. Later on, when you have grown to be men and women, people will respect and trust you also, and you will be happier and more content, because you know you are living according to the law of God.

Practice:

1. I will try to remember to-day that God sees me everywhere.
2. I will not take advantage of my teacher. I will act always as if I were being watched by somebody.

> Dare to do right! Dare to be true!
> The failings of others can never save you.

21. VARIETIES OF UNTRUTHFULNESS

You can be untruthful by pretending to be what you know you are not. There are many other ways in which we may try to make others believe something that is not true. Some of these I have mentioned to you before. Saying a thing when you know it is not true is one very common way and it is called telling lies. As I told you the other day, children are often led into this sin by first having committed a fault, and then telling a lie to hide it. Sometimes children do not at first mean to tell a lie, but they try to hide what they did, then they get tangled up, as it were, and at last end by telling a direct lie. It is better at once to admit a fault than to lie in order to hide it.

Again, some persons are untruthful by telling as certain something of which they are by no means sure. Sometimes mother asks you about something, and you answer "Yes" or "No" without taking the trouble of finding out which is true. Many children form the habit of telling lies in this way.

Talking carelessly also leads to telling lies. For example, some people have the bad habit of making everything greater than it really is. They may be talking about meeting a big dog. A child that is not careful about the truth will tell you that the dog was "a great big dog, almost as big as a pony," or something like that, while in reality the dog was just of an ordinary size. Another way in which little boys and girls sometimes tell a lie is by acting as though they were very sick, while they are really trying to get out of going to school or some work. Often when they do not want to do a thing, they say that it is too hard, or that they cannot do it. This is also lying.

Speaking Untruthfully About Others

But one of the worst faults and one which does a great deal of harm is to tell lies about others. This is a very wicked thing indeed. We may give others much trouble in this way and even cause them to lose their good name. My dear children, it is very important for you to be careful about what you say of others. Always make sure that what you say is true. Then ask yourself, "Is it right?" Sometimes a thing may be quite true, but it may not be right for you to tell it. You will learn more about this when you study the Commandments of God.

From what I have told you, you see it is not easy always to speak the truth, even when you know it. Sometimes you are tempted to lie; this is especially true when you have done something wrong and you think you can escape being punished by telling a lie. How much easier it would be, after all, to confess the truth, for by telling one lie, it often happens that many other lies are added to hold up the first lie. Then, too, you may injure others by lying, which is worse than if we only hurt ourselves. By being careless about the truth, you get the habit of lying and this will make people mistrust you.

There is much more I could say to you about being truthful, but I shall leave the matter for some other time. One thing I wish you to remember is that you must learn to be truthful, just as you must learn to spell or to read or to do sums. Day by day, you must try to speak the truth fearlessly. It will not do for you to give up after trying for a few weeks. You must keep at it every day and soon it will be as easy for you always to speak the truth as it is for you to walk.

Never forget to ask God to help you. Remember that God hates a lie. God is the "God of Truth." When you try to be truthful, God will bless you, people will believe, respect and trust you.

Practice:

1. I will be careful not to make anything greater than it really is.
2. I will not pretend in any way to get out of doing something I do not like to do.

Think the truth, speak the truth, act the truth.

> I must every day
> Be sure that all I say
> Is pure and true.

REVIEW

To the Teacher:—*Review to-day all you said during the week with regard to truthfulness. Dwell especially on guarding against those faults which children are more liable to commit; for example, lying in order to avoid blame or punishment, putting the blame on others, letting others be punished for something they themselves have done, carrying tales, excusing themselves by telling falsehoods. When teaching the Eighth*

Commandment, further opportunity will be given to develop this subject. It will be well to keep a close watch over the children, letting nothing bordering on untruthfulness or deceitfulness pass unnoticed. The good teacher will know how best to approach the child when she notices faults of this kind. She will endeavor by all means in her power to instil a love for truthfulness in the hearts of the little ones and encourage them in every way to practice it in their daily lives. Tale-bearing is sometimes very prevalent among small children. The wise teacher will strive to inculcate a spirit of charity in her pupils and will make it clear to them that she will not tolerate malicious or unkind tales about others. When she finds that some of her pupils are addicted to this fault, she will do her utmost to eradicate it.

She will not listen to every report about others, but carefully investigate the truthfulness of it; frequently she will find it the best to ignore such tales altogether. When the teacher tries to treat all the children alike and does not show partiality, there will be little chance for tale-bearing. The children should know that their teacher is fair and does not permit liberties to some while she restrains others.

22. HONESTY

Some time ago I spoke to you of truthfulness. Now I shall speak about something that is very much like truthfulness, namely, honesty. We use the word honest when we speak of an act or a deed. We use the word truthful when we speak of words. Thus, when a child steals something, we say stealing is dishonest. When he denies that he stole, we say he is untruthful. To be honest means to be just in all our dealings with others and with ourselves. If every person were honest, we should not need policemen to watch our town or city. We should not need so many jails. We could trust every one; we should not need to lock our houses and everything would be safe. What a wonderful thing it would be if every person in the world were truthful and honest!

What is cheating? Is cheating dishonest? What do we call a person that steals? Is every one who is dishonest a thief? There are other ways of being dishonest than by stealing and cheating. Some people are dishonest about their work. Others pretend to be something which they are not. I mentioned this when I spoke about being untruthful. Some people say one thing while they mean another. Others promise to do a certain thing and then do not keep their word. All these are ways of being dishonest.

Dishonesty Is Quite Frequent

Many children act dishonestly. Children may be dishonest in work as well as in play. Your work should always be the best you can do. When you do not do your best work, you are dishonest in a way. Suppose you are asked to wash the dishes for mother. Would you be doing honest work if you did not wash them clean? Or suppose mother told you to go to the store to get a certain article for her. Would it be honest for you to return and say that they did not have what you were sent for, though you never went where you were sent? Or suppose you are helping father and he asks you to go to the house to get something for him, is it honest to say you cannot find it, when you did not even take the trouble to look for it? There are so many ways of being dishonest that children must be very careful not to fall into them. It will be very hard later on to get rid of these faults.

Practice:

1. I will carefully watch over myself to-day to see if I am *inclined* to dishonesty.
2. I will take special care to be exact in doing my work.

<blockquote>There's nothing so kingly as kindness,
And nothing so royal as truth.

Alice Cary.</blockquote>

23. HONESTY IN SCHOOL WORK

Many children are careful about telling the truth; they would not for the world steal; they are prompt to do the work asked of them and yet they may be dishonest. How can this be? Cheating in school is one of the things very few boys and girls think dishonest. They think being dishonest means to steal another person's goods. But they never stop for a moment to think that cheating or copying a lesson from another is also a form of stealing. When you copy an answer from another pupil's paper you are taking something that does not belong to you. Did you ever think of that? When a child looks into his book when he thinks the teacher is not looking, he is also stealing. It is not honest to do such things. Boys and girls that are honest will not do things of this kind, no more than they would take a book or a pencil that does not belong to them.

There is one thing dishonest boys and girls forget. If they cheat in their lessons or in their work in school, they believe they are cheating the teacher. But they are not. They are cheating themselves. How? When they cheat, they are found out sooner or later; then they lose the respect the teacher had for them and she will no longer trust them. Even their classmates will not trust them. Children easily form the habit of cheating when they do not study their lessons. If you were ill, or if something else kept you from studying your lessons, it would be better for you to tell your teacher the truth about it. She will then help you and you will feel happier than if you falsely excused yourself or tried to copy from a companion.

Honesty in Play

It is just as bad to cheat in your play. It is dishonest to cheat in order to win. Always be fair in your games. Never let yourself win a game by unfair means. If you cannot win by playing a fair game, then it is better to lose. Play by the rules of the game. Do not try to get ahead of the others by using unfair means to beat them. If you cheat, no one will want to play with you. If you are honest with yourself and with your playmates you will be loved and respected by all. Then you will know that you are doing the right thing and that God will bless your efforts to please Him by obeying His law, for God forbids all dishonesty.

Rules of Honesty

In order to help you to be honest, I shall give you a few rules that you will find easy to follow. By being careful about these small points, you may be sure that when you are tempted to do dishonest things you will be strong enough to keep from doing them. These points are:
  1. Never take anything that belongs to another without first asking his permission.
  2. If you find anything, no matter what it is, do not keep it; try to find the owner.
  3. Make it a rule always to do your own work. Do not copy from your classmates.
  4. Always do your work in the best way you know how.

I shall explain each of these points to you later. Take care to-day to be honest in all your work. Do not copy or attempt to cheat by looking in your book when you should not do so, or by giving a false reason for not knowing your lesson. Tell the truth.

Practice:
  1. I will not copy from any one.
  2. If I do not have my lesson ready, I will be truthful about it, and not give a false excuse.

24. STEALING

Of course, you all know that when a person takes another person's hat or coat or his horse or automobile, that it is stealing. You know that stealing is an act which is punished even by the law of the land. A man who has stolen an automobile will be fined heavily if he is caught. He may even have to go to jail for a long time. Policemen are busy day and night watching that no one steals another's goods, and they arrest those they catch doing it. But little boys and girls often think that stealing means taking big things. They think it does not matter when it comes to taking such articles as candy, cake, fruits, pencils or paper. But here is where these children make a mistake. There are children that want to have everything they see, and if they cannot get it in the right way, that is, by asking for it, they take it. When once you know that a certain child takes what belongs to others, you do not trust him, do you? You put your pencils and books away carefully so that he may not be able to get them. Taking what belongs to another is not keeping the Golden Rule. Can you tell me the Golden Rule? Good. "Do not do to others what you would not have them do to you."

Let us suppose you have a pretty pencil, or a pencil box, or a new tablet on your desk. Another child, seeing this article, wishes to have it. While you are at the blackboard, this child watches his chance and takes your pencil. Would you not call that stealing? But right here let me tell you how children often accuse others wrongly of stealing. Some children are very careless and do not keep their books, pencils and papers in order. So it happens sometimes that they cannot find their pencil or book. Without thinking, they say, "Some one has taken my pencil, my book." When they look more carefully they find what they thought was stolen. Acting in this way may often cause another child to be accused of stealing. So you ought to be careful about putting your things away properly and never say some one has stolen anything from you, unless you are quite sure the thing was stolen, and not merely lost or misplaced.

Most children do not mean to take things. They see something pretty on another child's desk. They pick it up to look at it. They forget themselves and lay it on their desk and if the other child does not miss it, they think it is all right to keep it for a while. Perhaps they never think about returning the article. Perhaps they break it or spoil it, and all the while they never thing it wrong.

The Habit of Borrowing

Borrowing things from others is also a bad habit. People that borrow much are usually too lazy to do their own work. How often children borrow each other's pencils and knives and books, meaning, of course, to return them later. Many times these articles when returned are found to be soiled or badly damaged. Sometimes the thing borrowed is lost and the borrower does not even think that he is obliged to replace it. Some children get into the habit of borrowing papers and pencils and never returning them. Borrowing is a bad habit and one that grows stronger as the years pass on. A person that has the habit of borrowing soon loses his friends and no one trusts him. Take care not to form the habit of borrowing. See that you have pencils and paper and everything that you need for the day, before you leave home each morning. Then you will not need to borrow anything from others.

Practice:

1. I will try not to borrow anything from my schoolmates. If I must use anything that does not belong to me, I will return it as soon as I can.
2. I will be careful in using articles that belong to others.

Satan finds some mischief for idle hands to do.
Isaac Watts.

25. LOST AND FOUND

I have spoken to you of the evil of borrowing, but I do not wish you to think that borrowing in itself is a sin or is dishonest. It is only when we do not return what we have borrowed, or return it in a damaged condition, that sin is committed. Borrowing often makes people careless about the goods that belong to others. Many other faults lead to dishonesty. Taking articles from another's desk, using another child's toys and carelessly handling them, destroying flowers and trees, cutting or otherwise damaging school property—the desks, the walls, the stairways, and other places—all these and many others like them are faults that will help to form careless habits and will lead to dishonesty.

It happens once in a while that a child finds something that was lost by another. What should he do? Give it back. Yes, if he knows to whom it belongs. But sometimes he does not know; what should he do then? Can you tell me, John? Yes, he must try to find out who lost it. If the article was found in school, he should take it to the priest who will take care to find the owner. If he found it on the street, he may take it to the priest who will take care to find the person who lost it. Or you may tell your parents and they will know what to do to find the person to whom it belongs. You cannot keep anything you found for yourself. It does not matter if the article you found was a knife, a pencil, a ring, or some money. It is not yours; it belongs to some other person and you must try to find the owner and return the article to him.

Keeping Your Promises

There is one other thing I wish to speak about, and that is keeping one's promises. Some children are careless about what they promise. How easy it is when you get into trouble to promise mother that you will not do it again! How quickly that promise is forgotten! Not to keep one's promises is another way of being dishonest. One of the things that makes a man loved and respected is keeping his word. When a man says he will do a certain thing and then sticks to his word, we honor such a man and think well of him. On the other hand, a man that does not keep his word, is looked upon as a liar and a dishonest person. Some children are quick to promise to do a thing, but often very slow in keeping their promises. Before you promise something you ought to think it over carefully; then if you find that you cannot do it, say that you cannot. But once you have promised, you ought to do all you can to keep your word.

Think over to-day how often you make promises. Usually children say, "I forgot," which is another way of saying, "I do not care about my promise." Think it over to-day. You know very well how many promises you make and do not keep. This also is being dishonest and if not corrected will become a bad habit.

Practice:

1. I will carefully guard against making promises that I do not intend to keep.
2. When I promise to do something, I will keep the promise.

> God helps them that help themselves.

> He who does his best, does well.
> *Benjamin Franklin.*

> Lost time is never found again.
> *Poor Richard.*

> What's once begun
> Must always be done.

REVIEW

To the Teacher:—*Review the talks on honesty. If you have noticed in your pupils any marked tendencies to dishonesty, whether it be cheating, copying, lying, or making false excuses, dwell particularly upon faults of that character. In some districts and classes, one form or the other is more prevalent. For example, experienced teachers know that occasionally they get a class that is addicted to copying; another class, to passing papers with answers written on them; another, again, hiding the culprits in any mischief, particularly in the teacher's absence from the classroom. Whatever the prevailing fault, the teacher will wisely direct her talks against it. With a little tact and prudence she will be able to give the children a better attitude in this respect and will have little difficulty in leading them to acquire more desirable qualities.*

> Little children, you must seek
>   Rather to be good than wise,
> For the thoughts you do not speak
>   Shine out in your cheeks and eyes.
>
> If you think that you can be
>   Cross or cruel, and look fair,
> Let me tell you how to see
>   You are quite mistaken there.
>
> Go and stand before the glass,
>   And some ugly thought contrive,
> And my word will come to pass
>   Just as sure as you're alive!
>
> What you have, and what you lack,
>   All the same as what you wear,
> You will see reflected back;
>   So, my little folks, take care!
>
> And not only in the glass
>   Will your secrets come to view;
> All beholders, as they pass,
>   Will perceive and know them too.
>
> Goodness shows in blushes bright,
>   Or in eyelids dropping down,
> Like a violet from the light;
>   Badness, in a sneer or frown.
>
> Out of sight, my boys and girls,
>   Every root of beauty starts;
> So think less about your curls,
>   More about your minds and hearts.
>
> Cherish what is good, and drive
>   Evil thoughts and feelings far;
> For, as sure as you're alive,
>   You will show for what you are.
> —*Alice Cary.*

26. AN HONEST BOY

Richard Graham was the oldest of six children. When school closed in June, Richard or "Dick," as everyone called him, looked for work. Dick was fourteen years old. He was a strong boy and willing to do any kind of work to help his mother. One day, while Dick was out looking for something to do, he walked down Butler Street. While standing at the corner waiting for a chance to cross the street, Dick saw a man drop some money. Dick picked it up and ran after the man. When he caught up with him, he said, "You dropped this money, sir."

The man looked surprised and said, "You must be mistaken, boy. I did not lose any money."

"I saw it drop from your hands as you paid the driver of the taxicab."

"Why, that was at the street corner," said the man. "But why didn't you keep it? No one would have known."

"Because that money is yours, and not mine. I should like to earn some money, but I will not steal it."

This pleased the man and he asked Dick's name, where he lived and what he was going to do. Dick told him that they were poor, that his father was dead and that his mother needed money; that was why he was trying to get work. The man thanked Dick and promised to see what he could do to help him.

A few days later, Dick was called to a big store, where the man gave him work for the summer. He promised to let Dick work after school hours the next year, so that he could help his mother and still go to school.

You may be sure that Dick was glad he had been honest and had not kept the money he had found.

> It is more blessed to give than to receive.
> A good name is better than riches.

27. COURAGE

Dear children: I have spoken to you about being truthful and I tried to show you how often children, by their carelessness in speaking, fall into many faults in this respect. I noticed that most of you tried to keep from telling lies. I am sure you did not find it very easy at first, but by watching over yourselves every day, you found it a little easier each time. It is so in almost everything we do; at first we find it hard, but after a while, it becomes easier and at last we do it without thinking much about it. The beginning is the hardest. To begin well takes courage. I want to speak to you this week about courage and what it means to have courage. When you wish to do something that is a little hard, you must make yourself do it if you wish to get it done. First of all, you must make up your mind that you want to do a certain thing; then you must keep at it and not stop until you have finished what you wanted to do. This is persistent courage.

The Meaning of Courage

I shall write the word on the blackboard for you. C-O-U-R-A-G-E, spells courage. Now say the word after me. *Courage.* Right. Now what does it mean? Courage means not shrinking from doing what is painful or disagreeable. Let me explain it to you. Suppose you are suffering from a toothache. How many ever had toothache? Then you know that a toothache is very painful. How it hurts! You can neither eat nor sleep, so mother says she will take you to the dentist to let him look at the tooth. You fear that the dentist will pull the tooth. How you dread going there! You imagine you feel him pulling the tooth. You know it is going to hurt more then that it hurts now. You make all sorts of excuses for not going to the dentist. All this time you are having great pain in your tooth; but the fear you have of the pain the dentist will give you makes the trouble worse, so that you put it off from day to day. You do not have courage, that is what is the matter. If you had courage, or were courageous, as we say, you would let the dentist pull the tooth, no matter how badly it hurt. It does not take long to pull a tooth and the pain is soon over. Having the tooth pulled is not half as bad as having the pain and thinking about what is going to happen when you go to the dentist. If you at last make up your mind to go and let the dentist pull your tooth, then you are getting up courage.

It is the same with many other things in life. Every one has a great many unpleasant things to do and to bear. Many persons cause themselves useless pain and trouble by thinking much about these things and imagining all sorts of dreadful things that may never happen. If you do not want your life to be spoilt by worrying over the hard things you will one day have to do, you must learn to be courageous. You can train yourself, when a hard or unpleasant thing is to be done, to do it at once and have done with it. Sometimes you hear people say of little boys, "What a little man he is!" What do they mean by that? Being a man, or acting like a man, means being courageous, not afraid to do the right thing; not afraid to do hard and disagreeable things.

I shall tell you more about this to-morrow. Try to-day to find out whether you have courage to do what you know is right. Watch carefully over yourself in order to find out how often you put off doing something you do not like or that you find too hard to do.

Practice:
1. I will watch over myself to-day and see how often I shrink from doing hard things.
2. I will try to make myself do those things first which I do not like to do.

> Whate'er you think, whate'er you do,
> It may be small, but it must be true.

28. COURAGE IN FACING HARD DUTY

You have learned the meaning of the word COURAGE. You know that it means not to shrink or be afraid of doing hard and disagreeable things. You learned also that every one, no matter who he may be, has many hard and disagreeable things to do in his life. No one is spared. The rich man as well as the poor man may have hard and painful things to do every day. The only difference is that some people have the courage to meet the hard things and by earnest work succeed in getting over them, while others always think about all the painful and disagreeable things and in this way make things worse than they really are. Boys and girls must learn as early as they can to get used to taking hold of the hard things and doing the disagreeable things first. We say a person acts manly, or like a man, when he is not afraid of doing difficult things.

Now let us think of some of the unpleasant things children have to do, which require courage to do them in the right way. Most children, especially boys, dread to get up on a cold morning. They lie in bed as long as they possibly can, letting mother call them again and again. They make all sorts of excuses; they think of the cold room, they shiver at the thought of getting out of the warm bed. A little courage would make them jump out of bed as soon as called. After washing briskly in cold water and dressing, they would find themselves feeling much better than if they lazily stayed in bed a few minutes longer. Children that rise as soon as called are usually wide-awake and full of life all day long.

Another very unpleasant duty is learning one's lessons, especially if the lessons are hard. Some children find all kinds of excuses for not studying their lesson! How much easier it would be if they tackled the hard lesson first! Then it would be over. But by shrinking from it, the hard work is only delayed and when you come to school you find matters worse. For if you do not study a lesson when it is given to you, it will be much harder to understand the next lesson. And so it goes on. The lessons get harder every day till you feel you cannot keep up and you just drag along till the end of the year. A little courage the first time would have helped wonderfully. How happy you feel when you have finished something that was hard or disagreeable! You feel that way because you know that you have succeeded in doing something that was not easy to do.

Courage in Playing a Manly Game

How many boys like baseball? How many girls? I see most of the girls like it, too. Would you not feel proud if some great baseball player came to visit you to-day and shook hands with you? You would be so happy and proud you would scarcely be able to wait till you got home to tell father and mother. Why would you be so proud about that? You think great baseball players are great men, do you not? Why? Because they play baseball. Well, you see many boys playing baseball every day in the spring and summer. Would you be so proud to shake hands and speak to them? Not quite so much, would you? You admire a great baseball player more because he has to work very hard to make so many home runs. He must play with men who are also very good baseball players and to beat these men, he must work hard and not give up. It takes courage to do this. Sometimes he does not succeed, but then he must try all the more the next time.

Just as these baseball players had to learn to do all the hard things in baseball before they could become great players, so you must learn to do the hard things that you now have to do before you can expect to become anything worthwhile. It takes great courage to do this. The great ball players and other men and women that have done great things in the world had many hard and painful tasks to do. But by courageously tackling these they succeeded in reaching their goal.

Start to-day to train yourself to do what you have to do, whether it is easy or difficult, in the best way you know how. If you have an unpleasant duty to perform, do it promptly and cheerfully. If you do this, you will find that it is better done and you will be stronger and happier.

Practice:
1. I will do the hard and disagreeable things first.
2. I will not get out of doing what I do not like to do.

29. DARING TO DO RIGHT

It takes much courage to do anything worth while. No matter what it is a person would like to be or to have, some work is necessary. Not everybody likes hard work, but every one knows that to get anything worthwhile, a person must make many courageous efforts. All of us admire and respect people who have done something great. That is why people get so excited when some one wins a game or a race. In the trial the best man wins. We might say that it takes great courage even to try to win. Many persons would probably win a game or a race if they had the courage to try.

You remember the story of the different daring flyers. Why did the whole world honor them so highly? Because they flew across the oceans in their airplanes. Was that something that could easily be done? Most certainly not. It takes a large ship at least five days to cross, going all the time, at great speed. This is very fast even for a ship. It takes most ships a longer time. This will give you some idea of how wide the ocean is. When people are on these ships, they see nothing but water and sky for several days. No trees, no grass, not a piece of ground; only water all around them. Only think, one of these daring airmen flew all alone in his airplane over this great body of water. He had no one to whom he could talk. He had never been across the ocean before. Yet he had the great courage to try to reach the other side. And he succeeded. He had a good reason for trying to do this. It is true there are some boys that like to do daring things. They will jump from a high wall just to show off. Others will climb trees, go swimming in the river when they know it is dangerous, hop on street cars or trucks. This is not being courageous; it is being foolhardy. On the other hand, there have been many men who by their daring have found new lands and new ways to reach other lands. If Columbus had not been daring, he would not have discovered America. These are big deeds, but it takes much courage also to do little things right. Most people in the world never have a chance to do a big thing. Their whole life is spent just doing the small duties of every day life. This also takes courage. A person tires easily of doing the same thing day after day. People get tired doing little things that no one notices. It is because of this that many fail and shirk their duty. We call such people cowards. Boys do not like to be called cowards. But many boys, although they are not afraid, are still cowards, and sometimes very big cowards, too.

Manly Sports

Let us take, for example, a number of boys playing together. They are playing baseball or football or marbles. No matter what the game may be, there are usually some boys found that do not have much training. These boys do not know much about the game but they are always ready to cheat or to quarrel with the others. And when they quarrel they use the name of God in a sinful way, sometimes they curse or use bad words. A courageous boy will not play with such boys. He will tell them to stop using such words and if they do not stop, he will walk away. Do you think that is easy to do? The other boys are sure to call this manly little fellow a coward, or other mean things. It surely takes a great deal of courage to do what every good boy should do at such a time. But it seems a little thing after all when we think of the things great men did. Yet life is made up of small things. How can any one ever expect to show great courage when he neglects being courageous in the little duties of life?

To-day my talk concerned the boys principally. I know every boy wishes to be manly and courageous. Begin, then, to-day to show yourselves little men. This is done, not by going around saying what big things you are going to do by and by, but by manfully doing the little things that come along each day.

Practice:
1. I will examine myself carefully to-day to see whether I have done all the work I was expected to do.
2. When I am given several things to do, I will do the most disagreeable thing first.

Honesty is the best policy.

30. COURAGE OF THE SAINTS

When I spoke to you of the great baseball players and the daring airmen you understood why it is that people admire them so much. There are hundreds of men in the world to-day doing noble deeds. It is not only in big things but also in smaller ones that courage is required. Throughout life there are many occasions to show courage. In suffering, in trouble, in hard work, we find courage necessary. Even though one has been sick a long time, no one gives up the hope of getting well again. So it is also with work. When it is hard or disagreeable, one does not like to do it, but one should have the courage not to give up and let others do his work.

A Family of Heroes

The saints were full of courage. Men, women and even small children suffered much for the love of God. Many of them were put to death for believing in God. Just imagine how much courage they needed when they were told that they should have to die if they did not give up their religion! Some of them were treated very cruelly. In the Bible we read the story of a mother and her seven sons. These were all arrested and thrown into prison. Then the Judge had them brought out and asked them to give up their faith in God. But they said they would rather die than do that. A big fire was made and they were told they would be thrown into it unless they gave up their belief in God. But they were not afraid. The cruel Judge now ordered that the oldest one should be whipped and beaten and at last thrown into the fire. The others stood by and saw their brother's sufferings but they were not afraid. After six had been treated this way, only the youngest boy and the mother were left. The Judge thought he could easily get the boy to give up now. He promised to spare him and give him many fine things if he would do as he asked him to do. But the boy could not be made to give up his faith. Even after seeing how terribly his brothers had to suffer and knowing that he himself would have to suffer the same cruel tortures, he refused to obey the judge. The Judge asked the boy's mother to speak to him and tell him to do as he was told. But this good mother pointed to heaven and told her little son to be true to God and to have courage. She told him that it would be only a little time of suffering here on earth and then he would receive his reward in heaven. And so this brave boy, too, was beaten and tortured and at last burned to death. The mother also was killed and followed her brave and noble sons to heaven. This was real courage. These boys were real heroes, were they not? And there are thousands and thousands of saints in heaven to-day who have reached it because they were courageous and willing to suffer everything for God.

Practice:

1. I will do my duty bravely to-day.
2. I will remember that I am a soldier of Christ and that I must therefore be ready to fight for my Faith.

> Little drops of water,
> Little grains of sand,
> Make the mighty ocean
> And the pleasant land.

31. CLEANLINESS

You have learned that to keep your soul in the state of grace you must be free from sin; in other words your soul must be pure. In like manner, if you wish to keep your body free from sickness you must keep it clean. Cleanliness, dear children, is the first step to health, for many diseases come from dirt. If you want to be cheerful and happy, strong and healthy, then you must keep yourselves clean. Many children, particularly boys, are very careless in this matter. Of course, no one expects a child to be spotless all the time, but there are some children who are never clean. Never forget to wash yourself properly and have a bath at least every week. Never go to school with dirty hands or nails, nor with untidy hair. You may not be able to have fine clothes, but you can keep your clothes clean and neat. There should be no buttons missing, no rents in your clothes, and your shoes should be polished.

I know very well that your mother sees to it every morning that your face and hands are washed and your hair combed, your shoes cleaned and your clothes in order. But you are big enough now to help yourself. Boys and girls of your age ought to be able to wash themselves and to brush their hair and polish their shoes. You are not expected to mend your clothes if they are torn; you are still too small to do that. But you can help mother very much by trying to be careful not to tear them. When a button comes off, tell mother about it right away, so that she can sew it on before you go to school or out to play.

Keeping Out of Puddles

Children that are neat and clean bring honor to their families, to their teachers, and to their school; while those that come to school with soiled hands or faces, with hair in disorder and torn clothes, with dusty or muddy shoes, bring shame upon themselves and their families. It is a very pleasing sight to step into a classroom and see the bright, clean faces of happy boys and girls. We think at once that these children must have good mothers, for when the hands and faces are clean, the clothes also are usually neat and clean. When we see a child with dirty hands and face, with hair tousled, clothes torn, and soiled shoes, we at once blame the child's mother. Sometimes it is not the mother's fault. Many times naughty boys will step into puddles of water just for fun, or climb trees and fences when they are wearing good clothes. Some little girls will play in dirty places and get themselves and their clothes so soiled that it will be hard for mother to clean them again. Always be careful to keep yourself as clean as you can. After school, put on an old suit or an old dress, then you can play without fear of spoiling your clothes. Mother will not mind it so much if you soil or tear an old suit or an old dress. To-day be careful about your hands and faces. Wash them as often as necessary. Do not go to the table without first washing your hands.

Practice:

1. I will wash my hands as often as necessary.
2. I will be careful not to touch anything clean with soiled hands.

A full bath more than once a week.
Brushing the teeth more than twice a day.
Sleeping long hours with the windows wide open.
Drinking as much milk as possible but no tea or coffee.
Eating some fruit and green vegetables every day.
Drinking at least four glasses of water every day.
Playing out of doors a part of every day.
A bowel movement every day.
Mary E. Spencer, "Health Through the School Day."

32. KEEPING YOUR SKIN CLEAN

If you examine the skin on your arms closely, you will notice that it is full of little holes. These holes are called "pores." You cannot see many of these, but there are thousands of them all over your body. These holes, or pores, are the ends of tiny pipes just under the skin. These pipes are to carry away water which is called perspiration. When you run or exercise, you perspire freely. This water is not pure, clean water, but it is waste water and the body must get rid of it, if it is to be healthy.

If these pores are closed up, the water cannot come out, of course, and frequently this causes diseases. As you grow older, you will learn many interesting things about your body. But even now you can learn how to take the proper care of it, especially of the skin. The waste matter that forms in your body day by day must be carried off in some way. If it is not carried off, poison will form and the body will become diseased. You see, then, that it is very important to keep these pores open.

Frequent Baths

Now you know why it is so necessary to wash often, not only your face and hands but the whole body. Use plenty of soap and water and wash yourselves thoroughly. Never fuss when mother tells you to take a bath. Did you ever notice the little birds take a bath? How they plunge into the cold water, and they seem to enjoy it, too. Children could learn a lesson from the animals. Most of them like to keep themselves clean and do so whenever possible. The cat keeps herself clean by washing herself with her tongue. How often, too, she washes herself in a day!

Remember if you wish to be healthy, you must be clean; if you wish to keep yourself clean, you must wash often and thoroughly.

Practice:

1. I will wash my hands and face thoroughly to-day.
2. I will not cry or run away when mother wants me to take a bath.

Cleanliness is next to godliness.
Francis Bacon.

33. KEEPING YOUR TEETH CLEAN

Dear children: I have spoken to you of the need of keeping your skin clean by washing it thoroughly with soap and water from time to time. Having a clean skin will mean that your body will be stronger and that you will not become ill so easily. There are many diseases that are spread by unclean skin. Dirty hands are often the cause of people getting ill. Clean people do not catch sickness as quickly as dirty people. But there are persons who are very careful about keeping the outside of their bodies clean, yet sometimes neglect a very important point, namely, keeping the teeth clean.

There are several reasons why the teeth should be treated with care. Dirty teeth are not pleasant to look at. No one likes to look at a person whose teeth are yellow. We see some boys and girls who keep their hair neatly brushed, whose clothes are clean, whose eyes are bright, and whose skin is clear, but whose teeth are so dirty that one feels like telling them to brush them.

The teeth are very useful. It would be hard to get along without good teeth. God has given us our teeth that we may be able to chew our food properly. Each person grows two sets of teeth; the first teeth are sometimes called the "baby teeth." They begin to show when the baby is about five months old. By the time a child is seven or eight years old, the "baby teeth" begin to decay, that is, they wear out, and the second set takes their place. The teeth cause much pain when they once begin to decay, but with proper care the teeth may last as long as a person lives. The reason why so many grown people have trouble with their teeth and sometimes must even have all their teeth taken out, is that they did not take good care of them when they were children.

Why Teeth Decay

Unclean teeth decay or wear out quickly. When we eat, little pieces of food lodge in the teeth, and unless the teeth are brushed often, this food will remain there and cause decay. Decaying teeth cause the breath to become bad and no one cares to be near a person whose breath offends the sense of smell. Decayed teeth also lead to sickness. Many diseased people would be well to-day, if they had taken the right care of their teeth. But it is too late for them now, and to cure them, it is sometimes necessary to pull out all the teeth. This is not very pleasant. Besides, having toothache is very painful. I am sure some of you have had toothache at one time or another. Do you remember what pain your teeth caused you? Probably you could not sleep all night, and kept your mother awake on account of it. Eating too much candy hurts the teeth; cracking nuts breaks the hard covering of the teeth, and when this is broken, food will stick in the cracks.

How can you keep your teeth and your mouth clean? The teeth should be brushed every day and the mouth should be rinsed often. How often should the teeth be brushed? The teeth should be brushed after every meal or at least two times each day. I wonder how many brush their teeth every day! How often? How many have tooth brushes? How many use them? Do you know how to brush the teeth? They should be brushed up and down. Can you show me the right way to brush the teeth? Warm water and a good tooth paste will help to keep the teeth and the mouth clean.

I shall speak to you again of the care of your teeth; but if you remember to brush your teeth at least twice a day you will do much towards keeping them from decaying.

Practice:

1. I will carefully brush my teeth to-day.
2. I will rinse my mouth to keep it clean.

> Sing a song of cleaning house
>   With many pearly teeth;
> Look above and then below
>   Our room is most complete.
> When the door is opened
>   The pearls begin to say,
> "You see we're brushed both morning and night
>   And free from all decay."

Mary E. Spencer, "Health through the School Day."

REVIEW

How many brushed their teeth this morning? How many rinsed their mouths? Good. I see also that most of you have been careful to have clean hands and faces. I see boys and girls whose hair is neatly brushed. How have you taken care of your books this week? Now I am going to look for the cleanest hands and fingernails. Raise your hands. I see many clean hands and nails. You are not old enough to keep yourselves as clean as you should and your mother must look after you every day, but there are some things that even the smallest children in school can do to make themselves clean and so help to keep well and strong. I shall mention a few of these things: come to school every day with clean hands and face; brush your teeth every day; keep your hair brushed; clean the nails after washing the hands. Children can keep their clothes neat and tidy by hanging up their coats and hats as soon as they come in. They can keep their shoes clean by trying to find the clean places on the street crossings, so as not to step in the mud.

Clean children will always remember:

1. Never to throw paper on the floor, or sidewalks, or playground.
2. To help their teachers keep the school clean and beautiful.
3. Never to wet the fingers in the mouth in order to turn the leaves of books or to handle cards.
4. Never to put pencils in the mouth.
5. Never to spit on the floor or sidewalk.
6. Never to write with chalk on any building or fence.
7. Never to scratch desks.

> Little Bo-Peep has lost her teeth,
>   And this is the tale about them;
> Had she brushed them each day,
>   As the "Health Rules" say,
> She needn't have been without them.

Mary E. Spencer, "Health Through the School Day."

To the Teacher:—Lessons in health are a part of the regular course in most schools; for this reason, it has been thought sufficient here to take up the matter of cleanliness in a general way. Every teacher will find helpful material on this subject in "Health through the School Day" by Mary E. Spencer. There are also many excellent suggestions given in the various school journals and teachers' magazines in regard to the formation of health habits. These will furnish a variety of exercises that will enable the teacher to impress the value of cleanliness in relation to health.

I brush my teeth three times a day,
And three hours outdoors I play,
Eleven hours I sleep at night,
And wake up when it's bright,
And healthy and strong am I;
Vegetables and fruit I eat, but never pie.

Boys and girls should not drink tea,
But milk and cocoa, if strong they'd be.

B is for Bedtime, which should be at eight,
You'll never feel well if you go to bed late.

Mary E. Spencer, "Health Through the School Day."

SECTION III

SELF–CONTROL

1. SELF-CONTROL

Dear children: What is the meaning of the word self-control? I think the easiest way to explain this to you is to say that it is the power to make oneself do at all times what one knows to be right and reasonable. It is a very important habit, for without it people could not get along with each other, nor could they do the things which they find hard and disagreeable. Self-control is more necessary than to know many things, for it would be of very little use to a person to know much, if he could not make himself do what he knows to be right.

Runaway Ponies

One day a little boy was riding along the street in a small cart drawn by a pair of beautiful ponies. All at once a naughty boy standing near the curb, struck one of the ponies a heavy blow. This frightened the ponies so much that they started to run away at breakneck speed. The little boy in the cart was so alarmed that he lost hold of the reins. He would probably have been hurt badly, had not a man run in front of the team and brought them to a stop. The little boy was not strong enough to control the ponies when they became frightened. In like manner, we are sometimes carried away by our passions, because we have not enough self-control to hold them in check.

By controlling a thing, then, we mean being able to make it do what we wish it to do. A man, for instance, sits at the wheel of an automobile. By turning the wheel he can make the automobile turn to the right or to the left just as he pleases. We say he controls the automobile, and when he cannot guide the wheel properly we say he has lost control. Have you ever watched the motorman on a street car? Did you notice how he makes the car go or stop, just by turning a wheel or moving a handle? An engineer on a train guides the cars over the tracks by turning certain wheels and by pulling certain handles. We say he controls the engine, if he can make it go slow or fast, and bring it to a stop just when he wishes.

A horse that has shaken off the reins runs wildly about and may cause serious harm. When a motorman loses control of his car, it may leave the tracks and run into people or automobiles along the way. Often much damage is done when this happens. You can also imagine how much harm is done when an engineer loses control of his engine. Suppose the engine is going down a hill and the engineer cannot control it. The train will go faster and faster and finally, when it comes to make a turn, will leave the tracks, causing the cars to fall over on their sides. Or again, two trains may run into each other, smashing the engine and the cars, killing or injuring many people. Every year hundreds of people are killed in this way. Often these accidents could be avoided if the engineer were able to control the engine at the right time.

To-day I want you to think about what would happen in the world if no one tried to control things. Watch carefully to see how many times an accident might happen if somebody did not take care to control things.

Practice:

1. I will try to notice to-day how much control helps to make things safe for us.

2. I will watch over myself to find out how much I need control.

> Work while you work, play while you play;
> That is the way to be cheerful and gay.

2. NECESSITY OF SELF-CONTROL

Did you notice anything yesterday for which it was necessary to have some kind of control or check? What did you see, John? and you, Henry? I see you used your eyes very well. But I wonder how many tried to find out how often they had to control themselves. I see a number of you did. That is very well. When you were doing that, you were controlling yourself, too, because you made yourself do something you did not wish to do.

Now just what happens to the horse, the street car and the train when they are not controlled, will also happen to people if they do not keep themselves under control. Every person must learn to manage himself. If he does not do so, he will cause much trouble to himself and others. All of us have certain feelings and desires that make us think, say, and do many things that we ought not to think, say, and do. To keep ourselves from thinking, saying, and doing things which we know are not right, we must keep ourselves in check, that is, we must hold ourselves back when we feel like doing these things.

I am sure you are thinking, "What must I hold back?" When mother wants to hold you back, she takes you by the arm, does she not? Now, you cannot do that with yourself, can you? You cannot hold yourself back in just that way, can you? So there must be some other way by which you can hold yourself back, check yourself or, as we say, control yourself.

Control of the Senses

How do you learn to know things? By seeing, hearing, feeling, tasting, and smelling. What do we call these? How many senses have you? Can any one name them for me? It is our senses that we must learn to manage or control, if we wish to make ourselves think, do and say the right things.

Somebody has said that our senses are like horses. Horses must be trained if they are to be useful. This training must be done while they are still young. Perhaps you have heard people say, "You can't teach an old dog new tricks." What do you think they meant by this? Yes, if we wish to teach a dog tricks, we must teach him while he is young. It is the same with children. It is easy for them to learn many things while they are young, which they would not so easily learn if they were older. So you see why I am speaking to you of learning self-control now. The best time to learn it is before you begin to form bad habits. Once you have a bad habit, it will be hard to get rid of it and put a new one in its place.

Watch over yourself carefully to-day so that you may know in what you must learn to control yourself.

Practice:

1. I will watch carefully in order to learn in what regard I most need to control myself.
2. I will pick out one fault which I will try to control to-day.

> Every gentle word you say,
> One dark spirit drives away.
> *Virginia Harrison.*

3. SELF-CONTROL IN CHILDREN

To-day I shall try to show you how necessary it is for you to begin early to control yourselves. Every person in the world must control himself if he wishes to live in peace with himself and others. Here are some questions which will help you to find out what you must do in order to learn to control yourself. Do you like to think bad things of others? Do you like to think of wicked things? Do you say unkind things to others or about them? Do you get angry easily, or do you strike others? Are you greedy in eating, especially of candy, cake or other sweets? Do you usually try to take the best of everything for yourself and leave the worst for others? If you do any of these things, then you know that you must start at once to learn to control yourself. You must learn to rule your heart so that it will love the right thing. You must learn to control your will so that it will help you do what you know to be your duty.

Self-Control Is Our Protection

People who do not learn to control themselves are liable to eat too much and too greedily; they eat and drink what they like, whether it is good for them or not. Sometimes little children act very greedily about their food. They eat just what they like, and as much as they like. If they had self-control, they could make themselves keep from eating what they know will hurt them and make them ill. Another bad habit which those who cannot control themselves have, is over-sleeping. Boys and girls that find it hard to rise as soon as they are called in the morning should learn to overcome their laziness. Rude and quarrelsome children lack self-control. They want their way in everything and pout and grumble when they do not get it. Such children never learned to control themselves or they would sometimes give in to their playmates and respect the rights of others. Some children get angry very easily and strike those with whom they quarrel. They quickly show that things do not please them. Many children do not like to work and they do all they can to get out of it. For such children it is very necessary to learn to make themselves like to do their share of the work, for they will have to work some time or other whether they like it or not. You see now that the lack of self-control causes much trouble to every one. Every one keeps away from a person who cannot control himself. No one cares to be friendly with those who cannot give in to others.

Since there are many things in a day which you must do whether you like them or not, it is a very wise thing to learn as early as you can to do them cheerfully. Then you will have reason to feel that you are doing the best you can and at the same time you will learn to control yourself. Begin to-day to practice control over yourself. Keep yourself in check, just as you would a horse that is trying to get away from you. Hold back when you feel like doing something you know you ought not to do.

Practice:
1. I will ask God to help me with His grace to control my bad habits.
2. I will pick out one fault to-day which I know gives me trouble and I will try to control it.

> Every gentle deed you do,
> One bright spirit brings to you.
> *Virginia Harrison.*

4. CONTROLLING OUR THOUGHTS

To learn to control yourselves, my dear children, it will be well to begin to keep your thoughts in order. What you think is as important as what you do. For first you think about a thing; then you do it. Many times you keep thinking about something so long that at last you cannot keep from doing what you have been thinking about.

Everything we do is first in our thoughts. Before you make a thing, it must be in your thoughts. For this reason your thoughts must be carefully watched, so that they will lead you to do the right acts. Thoughts are like little seeds. If we wish to grow beautiful flowers, we must put the seeds of beautiful flowers into the ground. If we wish to raise corn or wheat, we must put corn or wheat into the ground. So it is with our thoughts. If we wish to do kind deeds, we must first plant the seeds of kindness in our thoughts. If we wish to be obedient, pure, patient, and cheerful, we must first have thoughts of obedience, purity, patience and cheerfulness in our hearts.

Sometimes we have good thoughts, but because we are busy about other matters we do not give them a chance to grow into good deeds. Perhaps when you come home from school, the thought may come into your mind that you will be obedient to mother that day; you will not wait for her to ask you to help to wash the dishes or go to the store. But when you get into the house, you notice your doll or some other plaything, and at once you begin to play and forget all about the good thought you had. If you wish to do a kind act you must keep thinking about it. That is why I tell you so often to think about doing this and that, because if you think about it often you will usually also do it. People who think much usually also do much.

The Uselessness of Idle Thoughts

You see, dear children, that thoughts are very important. If your thoughts are to lead you in the right direction you must learn to control them well. Some children, particularly lazy children, spend their time thinking about many things they would like to do. They think about what they would do if they were rich, or if they had this or that; they think sometimes about bad things; they let their thoughts run wild, just as you may have seen frightened horses run, going here and there and everywhere without knowing where or when to stop.

To control your thoughts, you must take care not to let them go from one thing to another. If you are thinking about your work, keep thinking about it till you must do something else. Never let your thoughts stay on wicked things. Thoughts are sometimes like butterflies. Did you ever watch how they fly from one flower to another, never staying long in one place? Butterflies are very careful not to get on anything that would soil their pretty wings. You ought to do the same when bad thoughts come to your mind. Do not let your thoughts stay on these things but control yourself quickly and think about something good. Think of God, of His goodness to you; think of Jesus and His Blessed Mother; think of your Guardian Angel, your patron saint and the other saints. Think only good and beautiful thoughts and you will do only good and beautiful deeds.

Practice:

1. I will think only of beautiful things to-day; of God, His angels and His saints.
2. I will try to keep my thoughts pure and holy.

REVIEW

To the Teacher:—Repeat to-day the important points stressed in the talks on self-control. Illustrate by telling a suitable story. Let the children suggest ways to control themselves, especially in their thoughts. Use the memory gems you deem most appropriate.

They say that God lives very high;
  But if you can look above the pines
You cannot see our God; and why?

And if you dig down in the mines
  You never see Him in the gold;
Though from Him all that's glory shines.

God is so good, He wears a fold
  Of heaven and earth across His face,
Like secrets kept, for love, untold.

But still I feel that His embrace
  Slides down by thrills, through all things made,
Through sight and sound of every place.

As if my tender mother laid
  On my shut lids, her kisses' pressure,
Half-waking me at night and said,
  "Who kissed you through the dark, dear guesser?"

              Elizabeth Barrett Browning.

5. CONTROLLING OUR WORDS

The control of our words is in a way even more important than the control of our thoughts. A thought may remain in the mind for a long time and finally be forgotten. But a word once spoken is gone forever. You cannot call it back. Sometimes you will find it very hard to keep away angry thoughts, but you can at least keep from speaking angry words. The tongue seems to be only a little thing, but it can do much harm. If some one speaks unkindly to you, you feel it for a long time after. Many children say they would rather take a whipping than a scolding, because a whipping is soon over while a scolding is not so easily forgotten. How much harm is done when a person says something about another that is not true! You may say it is only a little thing to say this or that. But little things often cause great troubles.

One day a party of men were passing through a forest. One of them lighted a cigarette and thoughtlessly threw the match into a pile of dry leaves. That night a great fire broke out. It burned for many days and was put out only with great difficulty. Thousands of trees were destroyed. All this was the result of so small a thing as a match.

SELF-CONTROL

The Tongue Is Like a Fire

St. James says that the tongue is like a fire. Just as the little match set the whole forest on fire, so often a small word sets many hearts on fire. Anger and many other evils come from words carelessly spoken. Suppose you tell an untruth, perhaps in tale-bearing. Maybe you told a companion what another said about him. This child may go home and tell what was said to his parents. The parents of both children may have been friends, but now on account of your tale-bearing they may become enemies. The bad feelings caused by your words may last for years and lead people to hate each other in their hearts. And you say a word is only a little thing!

An impure child may say just a few short words whereby he teaches his companion to commit a horrible sin. This child may tell others, and God alone knows how many other sins may follow this first one caused by only a few words.

My dear children, after thinking about the great harm a word can do, will you not try to be truthful and careful about what you speak? Will you not try to control your tongue, to keep it in order, to stop it from saying that unkind word? You must not let your tongue say just what it pleases. Think before you speak. Although you are still very young, you must learn to hold your tongue in check. Here is a good rule which will help you to control your words:

> If you want an honored name,
> If you want a spotless fame,
> Let your words be kind and pure,
> And your tower shall endure.

Practice:

1. I will learn this rule and try to keep it.
2. I will watch over my tongue to-day that I do not say any unkind words.

> Two eyes and only one mouth have we;
> The reason, I think, must be
> That we are not to talk about
> Everything we see.
>
> Two ears and only one mouth have we;
> The reason is very clear—
> That we are not to talk about
> Everything we hear.
>
> *Mrs. E. R. Stoddard.*

6. HOW TO CONTROL THE TONGUE

Speaking at the wrong time and in the wrong place is a lack of self-control. Where are you not permitted to speak unless it is necessary? Yes, in church. Do little children always remember this? And in school also, it is forbidden to speak when it is not necessary. At home children speak when they wish. If something comes into their minds, it must be said at once. But this cannot be permitted in school.

A Helpful Rule

Here is a rule which will keep your tongue from saying unkind things. It is the rule of the three gates. Now what are these gates? The first one is, "Is it true?" The second, "Is it kind?" The third, "Is it necessary?" When you want to tell something about another, use the first gate and ask yourself, "Is it true?" Very often it will not pass this gate, for when you stop to think, you find perhaps that after all it is not true. But suppose it passes through the first gate, then try the second, "Is it kind?" Here is where you ought to stop. It is never kind to speak about the faults of others unless you wish to help them to correct themselves by telling their faults to their teachers or parents. So your words seldom pass through this gate. Now suppose you try the third gate; you will often find that what you wanted to say is not necessary and therefore had better not be said.

Practice:

1. When I am tempted to speak about others I will think of the three gates.
2. I will be careful of what I say about others.

> Guard, my child, thy tongue,
> That it speak no wrong;
> Let no evil word pass o'er it,
> Set the watch of truth before it.

7. THE CONTROL OF OUR TEMPER

If it is so necessary to control unkind words, how much more necessary is it for children to avoid bad words, as well as cursing and swearing. Some children learn to use words of this kind very early. Before they start school, even before they can say their prayers, they have learned to use such words. What a pity that is! How sad it must make Jesus feel when He sees little children whom He loves so dearly use such ugly words! Think also, when Jesus is laid on your tongue in Holy Communion, how you should try to keep your lips clean and pure! You know that when you receive Jesus in Holy

has a temper? Do they show it by their looks? Did you ever see an angry person? How did he act? How did he talk? Were you afraid of him? Why? Sometimes people get so angry that they become sick. So anger is a very bad thing, is it not? Some people get angry so easily, one never knows when they will give way to their temper. Anger is like poison; it makes people act as if they were insane.

THE THREE GATES TO CONTROL THE TONGUE

Communion, you receive Him really and truly, so that when the Sacred Host touches your lips, it is Jesus touching your lips. How pure you should keep those lips! Nothing sinful should ever pass them. Think often of this and it will help you to keep from saying unkind, untrue, or bad words.

Did you ever hear people say a certain person has a temper? Sometimes even little babies show a bad temper. How do you know that a person

Ready to Fight

Do children ever get angry? Yes, some children show early that they have a bad temper, which, if they do not learn to control in time, will make them suffer much later. Some boys get angry so easily that they are always ready to fight. How often little boys begin a friendly game, but before long they quarrel over some little thing and end by throwing one another down and striking one another. If these boys had control over themselves they would not do this. Some children cannot play a single game without starting to quarrel. You do not like to play with such children, do you? But suppose you are the one that does the quarreling? Then you must begin at once to learn to hold your temper in check and not to allow your anger to show itself. It is a good plan to say an Our Father or to count ten before speaking when you are angry. Try it. Ask Jesus to help you to be meek and humble. Repeat this prayer frequently, "Jesus, meek and humble of heart, make my heart like unto Thine." To be meek means to be ready to give in to others when it is not a sin. To be humble means not to be proud about the good we think we have. If you are meek and humble, you will have little trouble getting along with others.

Practice:

1. I will try not to lose my temper to-day when playing with others.
2. When I have given way to anger, I will, as soon as I notice it, ask Jesus to forgive me.

> How many deeds of kindness
>   A little child can do,
> Although it has so little strength
>   And little wisdom too!
> It needs a loving spirit
>   Much more than strength to prove
> How many things a child can do
>   For others, by its love.

8. UGLINESS OF BAD TEMPER

Most people like children, but no one cares for a child that is ill-tempered and disagreeable. Let us see to-day how a bad-tempered child acts so that after seeing his conduct you may not want to give way to your temper again.

A child with a bad temper will not allow any one to contradict him. If a bad-tempered boy is playing with his companions and it happens that it is hard to tell which side made a winning point, the bad-tempered boy will get angry when something is said against him or his side. It may be only a very small thing, yet this boy will argue and call ugly names until the whole game is spoiled. The game then breaks up and this boy goes home. There he comes into the house, throws down his cap, and acts in a very disagreeable way. His mother asks him what is wrong, but he answers her with a growl. For this he is corrected, and then he gets angry again, slams the door and runs out of the room. At meal time he is still angry; he does not speak, but pouts and so makes those around him unhappy. At last he goes to bed, still angry; his prayers are said in a hurry; he does not think about his faults; he forgets to ask God's pardon for them; and so he finally goes to sleep only to wake up the next morning to start the new day with a feeling that no one cares for him, that every one is trying to make life hard for him.

Blaming Others

Now, of course, you see what a very foolish fellow this boy is. He is ready to blame every one else for that which he himself, by his bad temper, caused. Had he learned to control himself, he would not get angry so easily over such little things. Think how disagreeable such a child makes himself everywhere. And as he grows older matters will always become worse, unless he gets sense enough to hold down his bad temper.

What I have said just now about boys is just as true about girls. Girls ought to be more gentle and quiet, but how often we find little girls flying into a fit of bad temper, because they are not allowed to do just as they please. What an unpleasant thing it is to have ill-tempered children at home!

Now there are some children who say that they cannot help it if they have a bad temper. They hear father or mother say it is their disposition. You certainly can help it; and at your age it is rather easy to correct your faults. The older you grow, the harder it will be to control your temper. The first thing which will help you to control your bad temper is to realize that you have it; the next step is to make up your mind that you will not allow it to get the best of you; and the third is to ask Jesus daily to make your heart like His. When you feel yourself getting angry say at once, "My Jesus, help me. My dear Mother Mary, help me to control myself." Ask your Guardian Angel and your patron saint to help you.

Practice:
1. I will not allow myself to show bad temper at home to-day.
2. I will get rid of my bad temper while I am young.

> Kind hearts are the gardens,
>   Kind thoughts are the roots,
> Kind words are the flowers,
>   Kind deeds are the fruits.
>
> Take care of your garden,
>   And keep out the weeds;
> Fill, fill it with sunshine,
>   Kind words and kind deeds.
>   *Alice Cary.*

REVIEW

To the Teacher:—*Review the talks on temper and self-control. Dwell particularly on those faults which you notice are more prevalent among the children in your class. Help the children by wise suggestions to overcome themselves. Praise their efforts. Encourage them to persevere in spite of their repeated falls. Keep up a spirit of kindly interest in them and you will be rewarded by their earnest response and willingness to overcome their bad habits. By so doing you will not only teach the children to live peaceably with others but you will help to lay the foundation of peace in this nation as well as with the people of other nations. Early lessons in peace may be given by the teacher in the first and second grades by inculcating those sound principles of right living which govern the maintenance of peace. The most effective means at the command of the teacher at the present time is to awaken in little children the feeling that the good or bad habits acquired by them now will serve to make their relations with others more pleasant or more disagreeable, as the case may be. Therefore, the teacher must exercise great watchfulness over her pupils and promptly check and repress any tendencies that would lead to the acquisition of habits destructive of peace and harmony. Such bad habits are: 1. Manner of handling toys. A child who slaps his toys will likewise slap his playmates. 2. The kind of games the children choose. If they prefer rough games, in which the striking of others, the use of force and brutal strength predominate, you have an indication of the domineering and overbearing character which will eventually lead to many disagreements and quarrels. Try to induce the children to play games which emphasize the friendly feeling, rather than that of the brute conqueror. Skill, and not brute strength should decide the victory. "Play Fair" is a splendid motto and one that every Catholic teacher should keep before the minds of her pupils. If she can impress this lesson upon their tender minds, she is doing much towards laying the foundation of future peace among nations. Let us bear in mind the words of the Savior, "Peace be unto you."*

> Little children, love each other;
>   Show true love to great and small,
> Love your father and your mother,
>   And love God most of all.

9. CONSCIENCE

Since your conscience helps you to keep in the right path to heaven, you surely ought to be thankful to God for giving you this help. But you must do more than that. When you have a fine watch, you must keep it in good order if it is to be of any use to you. How do you keep a watch in order? First of all, you must use it. Of what good would the finest watch in the world be if you locked it up and never used it? Then you must wind your watch regularly. If you did not wind your watch every day, it would soon stop. Thirdly, your watch must be cleaned now and then, for dust will get into it and then it will lose time. And fourthly, your watch must be set, that is, its hands must be turned to the right time.

Now just as a watch must be kept in order, so also must your conscience be treated. First of all, the watch is made to tell time; it keeps on ticking all day long, telling the hours, the minutes and the seconds all day long without stopping. But if you leave your watch at home, it does you no good, although it may still keep on ticking. So it is with your conscience; it points out to you the good to be done and the evil to be avoided; but if you do not listen to it, of what good will it be to you? It will be as useless as the watch locked up in a drawer. God has given you a conscience and He wishes you to use it. Suppose your uncle gave you a beautiful watch, and you would not use it for fear it might be broken. Would your uncle like it if he heard that you do not use it? It is the same with God. God knows that you need something to tell you what is right or wrong. Now if you do not listen to your conscience, if you go right ahead doing just as you please without caring whether it is right or wrong, then you displease God.

The Reward of a Good Conscience

People are always ready to trust a person who does the right thing because it is right no matter what may be the cost. Therefore, dear children, listen to your conscience. Obey the little voice that tells you not to do a certain thing. Obey this conscience when you are with others and you feel that what they are doing is not right. Dare to do the right thing. No one wishes to be called a coward. But you will be a coward before God and His saints if you are afraid to do the right thing because others may laugh at you. How often does it happen that children will do bad things, just because their companions call them cowards for not joining in mischief.

One day a boy named Henry asked his mother to let him go to the river with some other boys. His mother said that he might go, but that he should not go into the river to swim. Henry coaxed her to let him go in swimming, but his mother would not let him, for she knew the river to be dangerous. Henry left the house pouting and joined his playmates. After playing in the sand for a while, one of the boys said, "Let's take a swim in the river." The other boys gladly agreed, but Henry said he could not go, because his mother had forbidden it. The boys laughed and made fun of Henry, calling him a coward and a baby. Poor little Henry was tempted to go in swimming in spite of his mother's warning. He thought he could take just one swim; his mother would never find it out. But the little voice in Henry's heart kept telling him over and over, "Do not go, do not go." While Henry was thinking about what he should do, the other boys took off their clothes and jumped into the river, calling to Henry to come along. But Henry listened to the little voice and called to them, "No, I won't go in." Hardly had he said this when he heard a loud cry and looking towards the place from which it came, he saw one of the boys sink. The others, instead of trying to help him, swam to the shore, picked up their clothes and ran away. Henry called for help, and soon some men who were working on a boat near by, rowed out to where the other boy was last seen, but they could not find him. A few hours later his body was found. Was Henry a coward? Certainly not. He was a brave little fellow who had learned to listen to his conscience.

If you are tempted to-day to do something wrong, listen at once to your conscience which tells you not to do it.

Practice:

1. I will do what I know is right because it is the right thing to do, and not because I shall be punished if I do not do it.
2. I will not let myself be coaxed to do anything which I have been forbidden to do.

10. DAILY EXAMINATION OF CONSCIENCE

Your watch must be wound every day if you wish to keep it in good order. Your conscience also must be attended to every day, if you wish to keep it working well. What is it that you must do? You must each day examine your conscience. You have heard this before, when I told you about preparing for confession. Each evening before you go to bed, think over the faults and sins you have committed during the day and try to be sorry for them. The most important thing in the examination of conscience is to find out why you did this or that wrong. If you take care always to find out what made you do this or that, you will find it easier to conquer your fault. Never forget therefore to examine your conscience each evening, for if you neglect to do this, your conscience will go to sleep and you will not feel its sting even when you have committed greater faults.

The Help of Confession

The third thing to do to keep a watch in good order is to have it cleaned now and then. So also your conscience needs to be cleaned now and then, because sin stains it. This is done by confession. You may be ever so careful about your watch, yet little bits of dust will get into it, which, while they may not always cause the watch to stop, will hinder it at least from working right. So with your soul even though it be not soiled by mortal sin, yet it will on account of little faults be covered, as it were, with dust and dirt. A good confession will help to brighten it up again and you will be able to hear its voice as well as before.

The examination of your conscience each night and the cleaning of your soul by a good confession are two points that I wish you to remember well. To examine your conscience will not take a long time; just a few minutes a day. And if you carefully examine your conscience each day, it will not be hard for you to know what to confess. As I told you before, a very important thing to remember in examining your conscience is to find out what caused your faults; for if you can find out that, you will the more easily be able to get rid of those bad habits which cause you to fail.

Practice:
1. I will never omit to examine my conscience before I go to bed.
2. I will try to find out why I got angry, or was disobedient, or did any other deed that my conscience told me was wrong.

> It is well to be wise and great;
> 'Tis better to be good.

11. REGULATING YOUR CONSCIENCE

A watch must tell the time exactly if it is to be of any value to you. So it must be regulated or kept regular, which means that it must be made to tell the time exactly, running neither too fast nor too slow. Some watches tell only the hours and the minutes, while others tell the seconds also. How many children can tell the time? Does the clock in our room tell the seconds? Do all watches tell the seconds? How many seconds are there in a minute? How many minutes in an hour? How many hours in a day? Some consciences are like those clocks or watches that tell only the hours and the minutes; they tell only of the big faults, the mortal sins. You must not have a conscience of that kind, for you must be able to know even the smallest fault. Some children seem to think if a thing is not a great sin, it may be done. In small as well as great things your conscience should help you. If you wish to have peace and joy in your heart, keep your conscience clean.

Four Things Necessary

Often think about your conscience as a watch and remember that it ought to be kept in order if you are to have the best use of it. Remember the four things necessary for this: First, to obey your conscience; secondly, to examine it every day; thirdly, to clean it by going to confession often; and lastly, to keep it in order, that is, to see that your conscience tells you all your faults, small as well as great. Again, I ask you to remember that you are followers of Jesus. For as such you try to lead a life as pure and holy as His life was.

Be very careful, then, so to keep your conscience in order that it will tell you even your slightest faults. A good conscience will help you to be active in doing good; it will tell you to do the things that will make others happy.

Practice:
1. I will keep my conscience in order by always listening to it.
2. I will obey my conscience when it tells me to do a good act.

> All that you do,
> Do with your might.
> Things done by halves
> Are never done right.

REVIEW

To the Teacher:—*Use this day to review the lessons on conscience. Make every effort to induce your pupils to examine their consciences every night. Lead them to form the habit of finding out what causes their faults. The teacher must be careful not to form a false conscience in her pupils. There is some danger of this when you stress certain faults too much. Train the consciences of your pupils so that they will be able to use them as trustworthy guides which will warn and advise them in the various situations confronting them in their daily lives.*

12. A CHILD'S CHRISTIAN DAY

All life is made up of single days. If we look at the year as a whole, it seems a very long time, but if we think of it as made up of single days it will not seem so long. In the same way, if we make a resolution to be obedient, kind, unselfish and polite during the whole year, it will seem a hard task indeed; but if we resolve to be

GUARDIAN ANGEL AND CHILD

obedient, kind, unselfish and polite for just one day, that will not be such a great task.

If each day is well spent, our whole life is right and well arranged, full of happiness and blessings. How should a Christian child spend the day? A Christian child ought to have a fixed rule for the day. This beautiful poem tells how you should begin the day:

> When I wake bright at morning light,
>   And new begins the day;
> I put away the dreams of night,
>   Sit up, and then with all my might
> I bless myself and say:
>   "O God! I offer up to Thee,
> My soul and heart, Thine own to be;
>   And all I do or hear or see,
>   And all my work and play."

A Child's Rule of Life, Rt. Rev. Msgr. Robert Hugh Benson.

Directly you awake make the sign of the cross. Then rise at once and dress yourself and when you are ready, kneel down and say your morning prayers with your mind and heart fixed on God.

> "Then when the clock strikes (more or less)
>   Or when it's time for me,
> Get up, and wash myself, and dress,
>   (Observing not to make a mess)
> And all with modesty;
>   Put on my clothes and brush my hair,
> My shoes and stockings; and take care
>   To do it tidily.

A Child's Rule of Life,
Rt. Rev. Msgr. Robert Hugh Benson.

Never forget to say a prayer to your Guardian Angel, nor to make the "good intention." Say: "I offer up all this day to Thy greater glory, my God." Here is another poem that tells you what to do:

> "And then before I go away,
>   I kneel down on the floor
> And bless myself again and say
>   The prayers I'm told to, every day,
> Sometimes a little more.
>   At least Our Father, Hail Mary,
> The "I Confess" and "Glory Be,"
>   At least . . . unless more time there be,
> As I have said before.

A Child's Rule of Life,
Rt. Rev. Msgr. Robert Hugh Benson.

Help of the Guardian Angel

I shall tell you something that happened in a country far away from here, to show you that you ought never to forget to say your morning prayers. In a small town there lived two little boys, who were good children. They never forgot their morning and evening prayers in honor of their Guardian Angels, and if it happened that one of them did forget, the other was sure to remind him of it. One night their father, who slept in the room next to theirs, heard a loud noise. Quickly he jumped out of bed, struck a light, and hurried into the children's room, where he saw, to his great terror, that part of the ceiling had fallen just between the two little beds. At once he snatched up the younger boy in his arms, woke the elder one, and left the room as fast as he could with both of them. Scarcely had he done so, when the whole ceiling fell in. You may be sure the boys never forgot the prayer to their Guardian Angels for the rest of their lives. Thus you see, you ought never to forget to pray to your Angel Guardian to protect you during the day and night.

Practice:
1. I will ask my Guardian Angel to protect me to-day.
2. I will make the sign of the cross as soon as I awake each morning.

> I wish I could see the bright angel,
> Who walks all the day by my side.
> I wish I could say to him "Thank you,"
> For being my guard and my guide.

13. SPENDING YOUR DAY WELL

I shall tell you another story something like the one I told recently which will also show how our Guardian Angels protect us.

One fine Sunday evening in summer the mother of a family was, as she thought, the only person left at home in a lonely farmhouse. Her husband and children had gone out. After a while she thought that she would take a little walk in the fields, but as she was getting ready she felt a great fear. She went out nevertheless; but before she had gone a hundred yards she felt as if something were dragging her home again, and so, though she could not tell why, she went back. She entered the sitting room; it was empty. She looked through all the bedrooms, the kitchen, the cellar; nothing seemed wrong. But when she drew near the stable, she found her ten-year-old daughter playing on the top of an old well, which at that moment was caving in. Needless to say, she pulled her away at once, and the mother said to the trembling child: "Annie, you have to thank your Guardian Angel for my coming."

Here you see another case where the Guardian Angel protected this little girl.

Daily Mass and Communion

Whenever you can, go to Mass and receive Holy Communion, for by so doing you bring a blessing upon the whole day. Then go to school and learn your lessons. Do them cheerfully, for if you do not learn when you are young, you will find it hard to do so when you are old. In school, listen attentively to your teacher; do all you can to learn your lessons every day. After school, hurry home as soon as possible, and see if there is anything you can do to help your father and mother. If they do not need you, you may enjoy a good game with your playmates, but be careful that you do nothing wrong at play.

Prayers Before and After Meals

Never sit down to table without saying grace. If you think about the many thousands of children that are starving in some parts of the world, you will be satisfied with whatever food your mother sets before you. Do not pick out for yourself the best, for that would show selfishness and would be displeasing to Jesus. There is no time and place where selfishness shows itself so much as at the table. Children, and even older persons, may be very polite at other times, but when they sit down to eat, they often forget themselves and act very rudely.

After meals thank God for the food He has given to you. A little boy said to his mother one day: "Why do we have to thank God for what we have just eaten? Didn't we buy it at the store? And does not father earn the money we pay to the storekeeper for the things we get?" Of course, this little boy did not think. He forgot that God allows all kinds of fruits and vegetables to grow for us; he forgot that it was God Who gave his father the health and strength to work for his family. He did not remember that it was God Who made the animals from which we get food and clothing.

Try, then, to be thankful to God for His great care for you. While you have enough to eat, and probably more than enough, thousands of poor little children are dying of hunger every year. Say your prayers before and after meals with great devotion and never sit down to table or rise from it without saying grace. No matter where you are, or with whom you eat, do not be ashamed to say grace before and after meals.

One day a little girl and her father were out for a walk. It was a very warm day and soon they became tired and thirsty. They came to a restaurant, and, as it was near noon and they did not intend to return home until later, the father made up his mind to have dinner there. There were several people seated at the tables in the dining room when they entered. They sat down at a small table and the father ordered something to eat. The waiter brought the food and set it down before them. All at once, a clear voice was heard saying grace. The room became so quiet that you could have heard a watch tick. Every one turned to look in the direction where the little girl stood. But she continued her prayer till she had finished; then she sat down and ate her dinner. The people were pleased with the piety of the little girl and many a one felt ashamed of himself, for there were some in that dining room who did not think of asking God to bless their food, because they were afraid others might laugh at them. This little girl did not forget to pray, although she was in a strange place and among strange people. Try to-day to say your prayers before and after meals with great attention.

Practice:
1. I will say my prayers before and after meals with devotion.
2. I will thank God for all His gifts to me.

> Each little flower that opens,
> Each little bird that sings,
> God made their glowing colors,
> God made their tiny wings.

14. CONDUCT AT TABLE

Yesterday I spoke to you about thanking God for His many gifts to you. I mentioned only a few of these wonderful gifts of God. You can remember many other things, I am sure, that God has given to you. You have learned something about them during the few months you have been in school. God made all these things for you and He wishes you to use His gifts in the right way. So when you are at table, it will be well for you not to be greedy in eating and drinking. Children sometimes eat so fast that they do not give the food a chance to be properly chewed. Many become impatient if they are not served at once. Some boys and girls always look for the best. All these things are faults and sooner or later will cause trouble. If you are careful to eat only the right kind of food, and in the right way, you will grow to be strong and healthy. Then you will have a better chance in the world, for a strong and healthy body is necessary if you wish to work well and enjoy life. Many people are ill because they did not take the proper care in eating and drinking when they were young.

Sharing Your Good Things

I should like to tell you about something else that will help you spend the day well. It is to share with others the good things that have been given to you. Many times you have a chance to give an apple or an orange or a piece of cake or candy to a child that does not get these things at home. In some homes the father is sick and cannot work. Then the children very often do not have enough to eat. You may have more than enough. Would it not be pleasing to Jesus if you shared what you have with these poor children? Sometimes also you can deny yourself something that you really do not need. For example, you have had a very good dinner; you enjoyed it and you ate heartily. At the end of the meal mother brings the dessert, some cake or pie. Now you know quite well that you have no need of the cake or the pie and that you could very well do without it. Suppose you say to yourself, "For the love of Jesus I will not eat much of this cake or pie." That is what we call denying ourselves. During the day you will have many a chance to deny yourself. There is no more pleasing way than this to help you to be like the child Jesus, for that is what Jesus did all His life. He denied Himself so that we could enjoy the great happiness of heaven in the next world. This will help you to live free from sin, for a child that thinks of giving up his will and his pleasure in eating and drinking, will often think of pleasing God and therefore will have little or no time for bad thoughts or wicked deeds.

Practice:
1. For the love of Jesus, I will to-day deny myself in eating.
2. I will share some of my food with a poor child.

> The best things of all,
> All others above,
> Are your home and your mother,
> And your dear mother's love.

15. HOW TO END THE DAY

During the day, a Christian child will try to do all he can to please his parents, his teachers and all who have any authority over him. He will also try to live peacefully with his brothers and sisters at home. A child that wishes to follow Jesus will treat his playmates as he would wish to be treated by them. He will not quarrel, nor fight nor strike any one; neither will he damage the property of others or cause any disturbance by loud and noisy games. The dutiful child will not go with bad companions; he will be careful not to use the name of God in vain. But if it should happen that he has offended God during the day by doing something wrong or by disobeying a command of God, he will quickly show that he is sorry for it.

> If Satan tempts me in my ease
>   When I'm in company,
> I don't go down upon my knees,
>   But quickly so that no one sees,
> I sign myself and cry:
> "Lord! save me from this wicked sin,
> And keep me safe both out and in
>   From harm and misery."

This little poem tells you what to do when the thought comes to you to do something wicked. Make the sign of the cross at once. You do not need to do this so that others see you; you can turn aside, and you can say to yourself, "Lord, save me!"

At the end of the day, kneel down and thank God for keeping you safe during the past day. Never go to bed without saying your prayers. Say a special prayer to your Guardian Angel; thank him for watching over you during the day. Pray also to St. Joseph for a happy death. Many a child has died suddenly during the night. St. Joseph is the patron of the dying and he will get you the grace to die well. Every night before you go to bed ask yourself, "How have I spent this day? Did I please God to-day? Did I do anything to displease Jesus and His Blessed Mother to-day?" I shall read another poem for you. This will show you how to end your day:

> So, when the day is done at last,
>   Before I go to bed;
> When all my work and play is passed
> I kneel again, shut both eyes fast,
>   And lowly bow my head.
> I cross myself again, and pray,
> That all I've done that's wrong to-day
> May by Christ's Blood be washed away.

My dear children, say every evening: "St. Joseph, obtain for me the grace of a happy death." Then undress yourselves modestly, and when you are in bed make the sign of the cross, and say some little prayer, so that your last thoughts in the day may be given to Jesus. Here are some beautiful prayers that you should learn by heart:

> Now I lay me down to sleep,
>   I give my soul to Christ to keep;
> Wake I in the morn, or wake I never,
>   I give myself to Him forever.

> God keep the house from roof to floor,
>   The twelve Apostles guard the door
> Four great angels round my bed
>   Two my feet and two my head.
> Matthew, Mark, Luke and John,
>   Bless the bed that I lie on.

> Here I lie for to sleep;
>   I give my soul to God to keep.
> And if I die before I wake,
>   I pray to God my soul to take.

REVIEW

To the Teacher: It might be well as a review to teach one or more of the little verses given in the morning talks. Children love poetry and can easily memorize selections of this type. Review the week's work.

> In the morning when I waken
> With the cross I sign myself,

And say "Jesus, Mary, Joseph,
I give you my heart and life."
Then when dressed I kneel devoutly
And I say my morning prayers;
With the cross I ask a blessing,
Both before and after meals.

When 'tis evening, kneeling humbly,
My night prayers I say to God;
Then my conscience I examine,
And ask pardon for my sins,
When in bed I think of Jesus,
And my arms fold like a cross,
And say: "Jesus, Mary, Joseph,
I give my heart and life."

With this prayer each work I'll offer;
"Jesus, I do all for Thee";
"Jesus, Mary, Joseph, help me,"
In temptation my cry be.
From occasions that are sinful
And bad company I'll fly;
Than offend Thee mortally,
Dearest Lord, I'd rather die.

Should I ever thus offend Thee,
I will ask without delay
Thy forgiveness;—in confession,
If I can, I'll humble be,
Telling all without concealment,
To the priest as though to Thee.

SECTION IV

THE LIFE OF CHRIST

1. THE FEAST OF CHRISTMAS

My dear children: It does not seem so very long ago since you came to school for the first time, does it? How many lessons you have learned since the first day you came to school! You can now read and write, you can add a few numbers, you know how to spell many words, but—and this is most important of all—you have learned beautiful things about God, the Blessed Mother, the angels and the saints. Every day you can learn something new; if you are careful to observe the rules made by your teacher, you will soon be able to do many other things that will help you in later life.

We have now come to the month of December. Can any of you spell the name of this month? Does any one know what feasts we celebrate during the month of December? Can you tell me, Albert? (Christmas.) Yes, that is one feast. There is another great feast we celebrate during this month. Who can name it? I see, no one can tell me what that is. I will tell you. It is the feast of the Immaculate Conception of the Blessed Virgin Mary. That is a very hard name to remember, is it not? I shall tell you something about this feast in a few days. There is still another beautiful feast in the month of December, one that ought to interest children very much. This is the feast of the Holy Innocents. I shall also tell you something about this feast soon.

The greatest feast of the month is the feast of Christmas, the Birthday of Jesus. On your birthday mother usually bakes a cake to show that she has not forgotten the day on which her little boy or girl came into this world, for of course, very few other persons are interested in your birthday. When the birthday of a person is celebrated by many people, we know that that person must have done something to make these people honor him in this manner. You have heard about George Washington's Birthday, I am sure. Perhaps you have also heard of the great Abraham Lincoln. We shall celebrate the birthdays of these men in February. Washington and Lincoln have done much for our country and although they are dead many years, each year on the day of their birth, the people of the United States show them great honor and respect. In many cities all stores, factories and schools are closed, so that people may have time to show their love for these great men.

Christmas is the Birthday of our Lord. Jesus was born on this day in a stable near Bethlehem; a little town far away from here. Jesus was born about nineteen hundred years ago, but people still show their love and respect for

Jesus by keeping this day as a great holiday. I am sure most of you know the story of the Birth of Jesus. I shall tell it to you again, so that you may know it better and can see for yourselves how much the sweet Infant Jesus must have loved us all to come down from His beautiful home in heaven to live on earth.

2. WHY JESUS CAME DOWN UPON EARTH

I have told you that Jesus appeared upon this earth on Christmas Day. I know that many of you are asking, "Why did Jesus come into this world, when He had such a beautiful home

THE INFANT JESUS IN THE CRIB

Practice:
1. I will think of how much Jesus loves me.
2. I will learn as much as I can about Jesus.

> Jesus on his Mother's breast,
>   In the stable cold,
> Spotless lamb of God was He,
>   Shepherd of the fold.
>   *Christina G. Rossetti.*

in heaven?" Yes, that is something you ought often to think about: "Why did Jesus come down upon earth?" None of us would want to leave a cozy, comfortable home to live in a poor cold stable, would we? We would not like to leave a place where we could have everything we wanted, to go to some other place where we should have very little. In heaven the angels served Jesus and adored Him and showed Him every honor. On earth, he was treated very unkindly by most people, was made to suffer cruelly and at last was nailed to a cross on which He died. What was it then that made Jesus come down from heaven to earth? It was His great love for us. Jesus loved us so much that He wanted us with Him in heaven to enjoy the wonderful sight of God and the angels and to live with Him forever.

Do you remember the story of Adam and Eve? On account of the sin they committed, heaven was closed and no one could enter it. When our first parents were driven out of Paradise, God promised that He would send a Redeemer Who would save mankind. Jesus, the second Person of the Blessed Trinity, as you learned in your Catechism a short time ago, became a little Child and was born on the first Christmas night. In this way He became a man, that is, He began to live just as other people live. He came into this world, a poor helpless little baby. Although He was God, He did not talk or walk, or help Himself in any way, because He wanted to be just like all other little babies. So you see, Jesus was once a tiny baby just as you were. His mother had to feed Him, clothe Him and take care of Him just as your mother takes care of her little baby at home.

Now you know that it must have been very hard for Jesus to be so small, so poor, so cold and so helpless. But Jesus did all this out of love for us. He did it because He loved you so much. Does not this fill you with shame because you do not do much for Jesus? Jesus gave up everything for love of us. Do you ever give up anything for love of Jesus? I am sure you never thought about that, did you? There are many things you could give up to show Jesus that you love Him. One of these things is your own will. What do I mean by that? I mean this: Sometimes you are playing with your playmates and mother calls you to go to the store for her. Of course, you would rather keep on playing, but if you go at once when mother calls you, you are giving up your own will and your act is pleasing to God.

Practice:
1. To-day I will often think why Jesus came down upon the earth.
2. I will show my love for Jesus to-day by giving up my will in something.

> I prayed to Jesus, oh so hard,
>   To bring me Christmas morn,
> A little baby brother, like
>   Himself when He was born.
>
> But Christmas came, and Jesus said;
>   "I cannot find another,
> And so I've come My very Self
>   To be your little brother."
>   *John Francis Quinn, S.J.*

3. UNSELFISHNESS OF JESUS IN THE CRIB

When you visit the Crib in church on Christmas Day, you will see the figure of a little baby lying in a poor stable. There is not even a bed in this place and the little baby has no warm clothes to wear, nor a blanket to cover Him. How we should thank Jesus, when we think that He loved us so much that He came upon earth from His beautiful home in heaven to live poorly and unknown and to suffer and die for us! Again I ask you, "Why did God come down from heaven?" God came down because He loved us and wants us to enjoy the happiness of heaven after we die. After the fall of Adam and Eve, no one could enter heaven, unless a Savior would come to redeem us from our sins. Jesus was born in a poor stable and lived a poor life and died a cruel death in order to atone or make up for our sins.

When you think about the many sufferings Jesus had to bear you will not grumble at every little pain or trouble you have. Jesus, the little child lying in a poor stable was God, and He suffered willingly for your sins. That is why you, who are God's creatures and who have often offended Him, should also willingly suffer for your own sins. Jesus did not think of Himself. He did not cry and say, "Why should I suffer like this? I did not do anything wrong. Let those suffer who do wicked deeds." Jesus was unselfish. He thought of you and me. He thought of all the people who had ever lived.

He thought of all who then were living and of all who would ever live in this world. He thought of the many millions and millions of souls who would never see God and never enjoy the beauties of heaven if He did not come down upon earth.

There are so many people in this world who think only of themselves. A person who lives only for himself and does not care what happens to others, if only he has everything he wants, is called a selfish person. Selfishness is one of the meanest faults a person can have. It is selfishness that causes people to cheat and steal. A person who cheats or steals hurts some other person by taking what belongs to him. But the selfish person does not care about that. All he cares for is to have the money or the goods which he takes from some one else. He wants what others have and so he takes it in any way he can. It is selfishness also that makes a man a drunkard. A man who drinks too much does not care for any one but himself. Such a man may have small children at home who have hardly enough to eat; but he cares only about himself, he is happy only when he himself has what he wants. It is selfishness also that makes some people so mean and stingy that they are unwilling to help others. People of this kind do not help the poor and the sick. They seem to have no heart. When others suffer pain, they do not concern themselves about it. They say "It is none of my business." Is this the way Jesus acted? Surely not. Are such people following the example of Jesus? Again, we must answer, "No." You see, dear children, that selfishness is a very bad fault. We do not like to live with people who are selfish.

Practice:

1. I will watch over myself and correct my selfishness.
2. I will be careful to treat others as I would wish to be treated by them.

> Baby Jesus smiling sweet
> On Your Mother's knee,
> I am opening wide my heart,
> Won't you come to me?

4. THE SELFISHNESS OF SOME CHILDREN

I have spoken to you of the bad fault we call selfishness. You do not like selfish people, do you? You like people who are kind to you. You like men and women who are cheerful and happy and who try to make others happy also. But I am sorry to say there are some children, even boys and girls as young as you, that are very selfish. What does selfishness mean? It means living for one's self without any regard for others. I shall try to show that selfish children are not really happy.

You do not like a playmate that does not share what he has with others. Did you ever see a boy that goes off by himself to eat his candy or cake so that he does not have to share it with his friends? Did you like such a boy? You thought it was a mean act, did you not? Did you ever do such a thing? If you did, then you know that it was a selfish deed. There are children who take more than their share of the good things at home and in school. These children think only of themselves. They forget that to take more than they have a right to, is to take it away from some other person. Again, there are children who take fruit or candy or other things from their playmates. A greedy boy may see another child have something he would like to have. It may be a ball, or a piece of candy, or some cake or fruit. The greedy boy waits till the other is not looking, then he roughly grasps the ball or whatever it may be and runs away. He is selfish as well as greedy. Greedy children are never liked by any one. No one cares to give a greedy child anything for they know he will not share it with others.

There is one bad habit that some children have and that is shoving others in order to get the first place. I have seen children who never can wait till it is their turn for anything. If the teacher tells them to form rank, these selfish boys and girls are sure to try to push ahead of every one and take the first place. A child that is always pushing for the best in everything, without regard to others, shows very bad manners and is classed as selfish. A polite child will not be selfish, for he will always have before him the Golden Rule, "Do to others as you would have them do to you."

The faults we have been speaking about are very disagreeable and we do not like to see children that allow such faults to become habits. But these faults are hard to overcome. Children that always want the first place and the most and best of everything, children that do not like to share the good things they have with their playmates, do not find it very easy to be big-hearted and kind and generous. If you are very anxious to get rid of these bad faults, ask Jesus to help you. Jesus gave you an example of unselfishness. Jesus wanted to share the good things He had with us. That is why He came into the world. Even when He was but a small child, He suffered so that we could enter heaven. He was satisfied with all that Mary, His Mother, and His foster-father, St. Joseph, gave Him. He was pleased to be able to do without some things, if by so doing He could help some poor person.

Now, dear children, I know you will want to be a little like Jesus. By being satisfied with what you have, by willingly sharing your toys and your food and other things with your brothers and sisters and playmates, you will show Jesus that you wish to follow His example.

Practice:

1. To show Jesus that I wish to be like Him, I will share any good things I have with my playmates.
2. I will give in to my playmates when we disagree about something.

> What can I give Him,
>   Poor as I am?
> If I were a shepherd
>   I would bring a lamb,
> If I were a Wise Man
>   I would do my part,
> Yet what can I give Him?
>   I'll give Him my heart!
>   *Christina G. Rossetti.*

REVIEW

To the Teacher:—Review the principal points in the work of the week. Selfishness is such an ugly fault that the teacher must use every means to eradicate it from the hearts of the children entrusted to her. Selfishness characterizes the present age. It is the source of great unhappiness in later life, making a man disagreeable and even hateful in the eyes of his companions. It is well for the teacher to study this fault and to strive to assist her charges in conquering it.

The spoiled child is one of the biggest problems the teacher has to face in her effort to train the child to unselfish and generous conduct. There are many ways of spoiling a child. One of the commonest is by fulsome flattery and by infusing a silly pride into the mind of the child with respect to fortune, family, good looks, or mental abilities.

Letting a child have his own will in all things is another way of spoiling him. Stubbornness, temper, and disobedience are the result of such training. Children that have never learned the meaning of self-denial and self-control will develop into self-centered men and women.

Too great tenderness, frequent caressing, the gratifying of every whim, receiving attention because of witty remarks, amusing acts, good looks or pretty clothes—it is these things that spoil the heart of a child and make him a prey to self-conceit. Pride and sensuality are the very root of selfishness. Therefore, the wise teacher will watch for early symptoms of these tendencies. Selfishness does not usually manifest itself all at once; it is developed little by little, until it becomes second nature to the child.

The primary teacher is often confronted with the problem of redeeming the spoilt children of indulgent or indifferent parents; but she must not be discouraged, for the child, as a piece of plastic clay, in the hands of a skilled artisan, will allow himself to be formed according to her ideals.

Let the teacher do all in her power to develop generosity in the hearts of her pupils. Generosity is the antidote against selfishness. A good heart is the source of all generosity. Let the teacher devise ways for the practice of generosity. Suggestions have been given in the work of the preceding days. Review these practices from time to time and praise any sincere efforts made by the children. Frequently recall the lesson of unselfishness taught by the Infant Jesus from His Crib in the stable of Bethlehem.

> Hearts are joyous, cheerful;
>   Faces all are gay;
> None are sad and tearful
>   On bright Christmas day.
>   *Father Abram Ryan.*

5. THE FRIEND WHO IS WITH US ALWAYS

Once upon a time a good Sister who lived in the convent with St. Teresa said to her, "Oh, my dear mother, how I should like to have lived in Palestine in Our Lord's time! How I should like to have looked upon His beautiful face and listened to the music of His heavenly voice! Oh, I am sure that could I have been with Him there I should have become a saint!"

"But, dear Sister," the Saint answered sweetly and wisely, "You could not have been with Him every day. Martha and Mary were with Him only from time to time you know. But now you can really be with Him every day; you may speak with Him whenever you like; for He is with us day and night, year in and year out, in the Blessed Sacrament. Surely, we are more favored than were the people of Palestine, even though we do not see Him visibly present."

A Child's Faith in Jesus

Then the good Sister saw what a mistake she had made. She was ever after happy in the presence of Jesus.

I remember there was a little English boy who had learned the lesson of the Real Presence exceedingly well. He had heard that Jesus was present in the Blessed Sacrament, and he believed it with his whole heart.

One day he came to church all alone to ask the Savior for something. He entered the sanctuary, climbed up on the altar, and kneeling at the little tabernacle door he rapped gently and asked, "Are you there, Jesus? They told me often You are in this little house here."

No answer came, "Jesus must be asleep," he murmured. "I will quietly awake him."

Again he rapped. "Are you there, Jesus? Oh, speak to me! I believe in You and I love You with my whole heart!"

Then Our Lord could not longer resist the touching plea of this innocent little soul. A voice came from the tabernacle, "Yes; I am here, dear child. My love for you keeps Me here always. What can I do for you to-day, My little brother?"

"O Jesus," sobbed the boy, delighted that he had been heard, "my father is not a good man. Make him good, and he will serve and love You."

And the Prisoner of Love answered, "Dear child, do not weep; I will grant your prayer."

And, surely enough, the next day that father went to church, made a good confession, received Holy Communion, and was ever afterwards a model Catholic.

Oh, how our dearest Jesus in the Blessed Sacrament loves us! How ardently He desires us to come to Him! Oh, if men knew how He loves them and how His Heart rejoices when they believe in His love. They believe in it too little, too little!

Tell Us Another, Winfrid Herbst, S. D. S.

> Sleep, little baby, sleep,
> The holy angels love thee;
> And guard thy bed, and keep
> A blessed watch above thee.
> *Christina G. Rossetti.*

6. PREPARATIONS MADE THROUGHOUT THE WORLD FOR CHRISTMAS

Dear children: As we are coming nearer and nearer to the feast of Christmas, we notice everywhere signs of the approaching festival. Perhaps mother promised to take you to the city to show you the big stores with their wonderful toylands and the many brilliantly lighted windows of the various shops. Probably you have already visited these places. Wherever you go, you see signs of Christmas. Christmas bells, holly wreaths and many other gay ornaments are used to decorate the stores and windows. At home mother is busy cleaning the house; every room, every corner is swept. What does all this mean? Why so much preparation? Why so many glittering ornaments everywhere? Christmas is coming, the great feast is near. That is the answer. The birthday of Jesus is coming and people are preparing to celebrate it.

But how few people in the world think of what Christmas really means. Many of them think only of making money by selling things to be used as gifts; for weeks, even months before Christmas, hundreds of persons are busy making toys and ornaments to be used at Christmas time. These people are preparing, not to celebrate the birthday of the Savior, but to make money. Others are thinking only of the pleasures they will have on that day. They are making great preparations so that they may give their friends and relatives gifts; they are thinking also of what gifts their friends and relatives will have for them.

To little boys and girls and to all good Christian people, the feast of Christmas means more than a time to give and receive gifts. To them it is a reminder of the greatest of all gifts that the world has ever received, Jesus Himself. Jesus gave Himself to us on the day He came into the world. He comes into the hearts of His loving children each time they receive Holy Communion; He comes into your hearts each time you earnestly wish Him to come to you. You see that you ought to prepare your hearts well so that when Jesus comes to you on Christmas day, He will find your heart a beautiful place, pure and clean and ready for Him.

Just watch how carefully your dear mother cleans the house for Christmas. She wants everything to be spotless and shining. So, too, your heart ought to be pure and clean, that is, free from sin. Jesus will love to come into the hearts of those children who try to be obedient, kind, pure, and simple. Now is the time for you to begin preparing your heart for Jesus. When Mary and Joseph arrived in Bethlehem, they could find no other shelter than a poor stable. I hope that when Jesus comes to you on Christmas morning, He will find your heart ready for Him and that you will not turn Him away from you. I shall speak to you about how to prepare your hearts for the coming of Jesus. Try to be attentive and careful to do what you can to let Jesus know that you wish Him to come to you. Say often during the day the following little prayer:

"O dearest Jesus, come into my heart, and make a good and pious child of me! My heart is small, and no one shall come into it, but Thou, my dear Jesus! Come, O Jesus, into my heart and make it all Thine!"

Practice:

1. I will learn this prayer and say it often during the day.
2. I will carefully watch over myself that I may not hurt Jesus by any unkind action to-day.

> Infant Jesus, meek and mild,
> Look on me a little child;
> Pity mine and pity me,
> Suffer me to come to thee.

7. A CHILD'S PREPARATION FOR CHRISTMAS

You have learned that all people who truly love God prepare their hearts for the coming of Jesus on Christmas Day. Many people do not think of Jesus and what He did for us when they make ready for Christmas. They are thinking only what pleasure they can get out of the feast, what gifts they will receive and what they will eat on that day. Jesus loved us so much that He came from His beautiful home in heaven to live and suffer and die upon earth for the love of us. He became a little child to teach us that we must always have hearts pure and innocent like those of little children.

But it is a sad fact that there are many children to-day who do not know anything about the dear Infant Jesus and what He did for us. These children have never heard anything about God and His goodness and kindness towards us. You have been so fortunate as to have parents who are sending you to a school where you can learn many things about God, His angels and His saints.

Let us think now about what you can do to

make your hearts ready for the Infant Jesus. If you had been living at the time when our Blessed Lady and St. Joseph were looking for a place of shelter on that cold winter's night and they had come to your house, would you have refused to let them in? How proud you would have been to give them your own room, your own bed! I am sure you would gladly have given your warm clothes to the Blessed Mother for the Infant Jesus. You would have been willing to wait on the Blessed Virgin and serve her and the little Baby Jesus. I am sure when you heard the story of the Birth of Jesus for the first time, you felt sorry that you were not

SAINT JOSEPH SEEKS SHELTER FÓR THE BLESSED VIRGIN IN BETHLEHEM

living in Bethlehem, for you would gladly have given Jesus a warm and comfortable shelter.

You can do this even now, though Jesus is no longer a little child. How can you give Jesus shelter? By giving Him your heart as a resting place. Jesus is God. He can come into your heart, and He will come into your heart if you ask Him to do so. Even if you have not yet been allowed to receive Jesus in Holy Communion, you can receive Him into your heart in another way. You must earnestly wish for Jesus to come to you and He will come into your heart.

To-morrow I shall tell you how you must prepare your hearts for the coming of Jesus. Often think of Jesus to-day and ask Him to help you make your heart ready for Him. He will be pleased to help you if you ask Him. Ask also the Blessed Mother to help you. She surely knows what Jesus wants, for she prepared everything for His first coming into the world. St. Joseph also will be glad to assist you. In all your thoughts to-day keep Jesus ever before you.

Practice:
1. I will often think of Jesus Who will soon come into my heart.
2. I will ask the Blessed Mother to help me to make my heart ready for Jesus.

> As we watched at dead of night,
> Lo! we saw a wondrous light;
> Angels singing "Peace on earth,"
> Told us of the Savior's birth.

8. PIOUS EXERCISES IN PREPARATION FOR CHRISTMAS

The teacher will find it helpful to suggest pious exercises to the children in preparation for Christmas. Great care should be taken not to stress these too much for fear that a false notion of piety may result. Such practices as the following will stimulate pious thoughts and lead the little ones to perform acts of virtue during the day:

During the first or second week of December, have the boys build a stable in a conspicuous part of the room. Let them put some straw on the floor of the stable and place the stable in such a position that a few steps may be built leading up to it. Chalk boxes, boxes made of cardboard, or blocks of wood may be used for steps. On the lower step place two sheep, one for the boys, the other for the girls. If their conduct for the day has been satisfactory, the sheep representing them is placed a step higher. If on a succeeding day, the behavior has not been good, the sheep is put down a step. The boys and girls will vie with each other to see whose sheep will first enter the stable.

The plan may be varied according to the number of children in the class. One sheep to represent a part of the bed on which the Infant Jesus is to rest. Explain to them that by saying these prayers devoutly they will please the Infant Jesus as much as if they were making a real bed for Him.

A Bed for the Holy Infant

Bedstead ... 10 Holy Masses
Mattress .... 10 Acts of Obedience

Model for a Christmas Crib

might be used to represent the children in each row. Give one child charge of moving the sheep, and, to make the scheme more effective, use the first few minutes each morning to record the result of the efforts of the previous day. This latter might prove more effectual than attending to it at the close of each day's session, for it will recall the resolution more vividly.

Another practice that appeals to most children is the following: Ask the children to make a little bed for the Infant Jesus. Tell them they can do it by offering prayers, each prayer

Spring ..... 10 Acts of Kindness
Sheets ...... 10 Acts of Contrition
Blankets .... 10 Acts of Unselfishness
Pillows ..... 10 Acts of Longing for Jesus

The teacher may add other furnishings and acts and also substitute other practices for those here suggested.

The following practice is a favorite with many primary teachers: Arrange two piles of straw on a table or stand, or near the crib. Tell the children that for each good work performed for the love of the Infant Jesus they may carry a wisp from these piles to the crib and place it in the manger. Again the teacher may suggest the various acts, for example, kindness, unselfishness, obedience.

> Angels at the foot,
> And angels at the head,
> And like a curly little lamb,
> My pretty babe in bed.
> *Christina G. Rossetti.*

9. JESUS' LOVE FOR PURE HEARTS

Dear children: You have made up your minds that you will think about Jesus coming into your hearts. I hope you have said the little prayer you learned because it will help you to remember to keep your heart pure for Jesus. Would you wish to ask Jesus to come into a heart soiled by faults and sins? I do not think so. You want your heart to be spotless. Jesus loves pure hearts. Jesus is the Spotless Lamb, and the best way to please Him is to try to keep your hearts pure for Him.

"Blessed are the clean of heart, for they shall see God." Jesus said these words one day when He was speaking to the people. He meant to let them know what a great thing it is to have a pure heart. How can you keep your hearts pure? You can keep your hearts pure by not letting any stain of sin be on them. Every sin that you commit leaves a stain on your soul.

Your heart may be poor, that is, you may not have many great gifts to offer Jesus, because you are still small and cannot do great things, yet you can have a pure heart, and you have many chances to practice virtue, that is, you can often make your heart rich in grace by being more obedient, more kind, more pure and holy. Your soul was made clean on the day of your baptism. On that day you became a child of God. Your heart was pure and bright. There are many children who try to keep their hearts pure for Jesus. But should you have had the unhappiness of committing a big sin, your soul can become pure and bright once more. How can this be done? By going to confession. You must say to God: "Lord, I am very sorry because I have offended you. Forgive me, I will never do it again."

You must just tell the priest what sins you have committed. The priest takes the place of God in the confessional. This has been explained to you before. God knows all things. He knows also what you have done, but He wishes you to tell the priest. He wishes you to tell him that you are sorry and that you never want to commit sin again. After doing this, your heart will once more be pure and ready for Jesus.

Practice:
1. I will tell Jesus how sorry I am that I ever committed a sin.
2. I will ask Jesus to keep my heart free from sin.

> Infant Jesus! Bethlehem's wonder!
> Mary's Babe! My God, my All!
> By Thy manger, can no wanderer
> Vainly on Thy mercy call.
> *Eliza Allen Starr.*

10. JESUS' LOVE FOR KIND HEARTS

When Jesus was born, His dear Mother wrapped Him in swaddling clothes and laid Him in a manger. What is a manger? Many of you have never seen a real manger. Have you ever been in the country to visit your uncle or aunt on the farm? If you were, you have probably been in the stable and noticed that the cows and horses have their food put in a sort of box. This box is either nailed to the wall of the stable or stands on legs like a table. This is what is called a manger or crib. Now in the stable in which Jesus was born, there was, of course, no bed. So the Blessed Virgin laid the little Infant in the crib or manger. There was some hay or straw in this manger, for there were some animals in the stable. You would not think hay or straw very soft for a bed, would you? At home mother has a soft mattress in your bed; then you have warm blankets with which to cover yourself. But Jesus did not have any of these things. A crib with a little hay or straw and swaddling clothes were all He had. But He was satisfied with this little. He was happy because by suffering for us He could open heaven again and redeem the souls of the just.

How can you give Jesus a warm bed and a comfortable place in which to rest? By making your heart pure and by filling it with thoughts of love and kindness. Little children can do a great deal of good by being kind. If people are unkind to you, do not try to have them punished but be very kind to them, and soon they will love you, and be very sorry that they hurt you.

We must remember that Jesus loves all and came into this world to save all; so if we really love Him, the best way to show it is to love and be good to all His creatures, even to animals. We must remember that animals feel pain, as they suffer when people treat them rudely. Some children take pleasure in hurting poor dumb animals, such as dogs and cats. It is very sad to see such children take delight in tormenting God's creatures. How grieved their Guardian Angels must be! A child that is cruel to animals will be cruel to other children and very likely grow up to be a very cruel and cowardly man or woman.

Try to remember that Jesus loves a kind heart, and that the more you treat others kindly, the more Jesus will love you. Some time ago, I spoke to you of the ways in which you can show kindness to others. Your parents, your brothers and sisters, your playmates, all with whom you live or with whom you have something to do, should be treated kindly. Do you remember what the Golden Rule says? "Do to others as you would have them do to you." Keep this Golden Rule and your heart will be a warm and loving place in which Jesus will love to rest.

Practice:
1. I will be very careful to keep the Golden Rule to-day.
2. I will treat animals kindly. If I do not have a cat or dog at home, I will be kind to the little birds and put out some water and suet or crumbs for them.

REVIEW

To the Teacher:—*The points in the talks on Christmas may be amplified if the teacher judges it necessary to stress one or other of the virtues in which the children may be lacking. The teacher will notice a marked difference in the classes as they come to her year after year. It should be the teacher's aim to discover the faults and weaknesses of her class and by a judicious and tactful treatment of the virtues opposed to them, lead them to the love and practice of these virtues.*

Sum up briefly the qualifications that a child should possess in order to be pleasing to Jesus. Hold these ideals before the children as a mirror in which they may behold themselves. Stress the beauty of virtue, rather than the ugliness of the opposite vice.

Dear Little One! How sweet Thou art;
  Thine eyes how bright they shine.
So bright they almost seem to speak
  When Mary's look meets Thine!

When Mary bids Thee sleep, Thou sleep'st;
  Thou wakest when she calls;
Thou art content upon her lap,
  Or in the rugged stalls.

When Joseph takes Thee in his arms,
  And smoothes Thy little cheek,
Thou lookest up unto his face
  So helpless and so meek.

Yes! Thou art what Thou seem'st to be,
  A thing of smiles and tears,
Yet Thou art God, and heaven and earth
  Adore Thee with their fears.
         Father Faber.

11. THE CHRIST CHILD

St. Anthony's statue is just lovely, isn't it? And we find it in so many, many churches. Now, I wonder who can tell me why it is so very lovely? Why, because almost always the Infant Jesus is in his arms, or clinging round his neck, or patting his cheeks. Happy St. Anthony! One time, you see, someone peeped into his room on the sly—and saw the living Christ-Child thus caressing the dear Saint. Wouldn't you like to hold Him in your arms, too? Of course! Well, you really do. He gives Himself to you, enters right into your heart even, every time you receive Holy Communion.

But whenever I see St. Anthony's statue I think of a beautiful story. There once lived a very holy man. His name was Boniface. And it happened, as it may happen to any of us, that he became very sick. You know how lonely we often get when we must lie in bed day after day in suffering. Boniface, too, got lonely.

So one day he complained gently to the Blessed Virgin. Holy people, you know, realize that God is everywhere; and hence they speak familiarly to Him and His dear Mother and the saints whenever they like—and they like it often, just as we ought to like it often. "Dearest Mother," he said, "I'm so lonely here with nobody to visit me and keep me company."

And what do you think happened then? Oh! something wonderful! The gracious Virgin herself appeared to him, carrying her little Jesus, wrapped in swaddling clothes, in her arms. She went right up to the bed and placed her precious burden at the holy man's side. Then the Christ Child, with His own tiny hands, pulled away the cloth that covered His face. And Boniface gazed upon the beauty of Jesus. Oh, what sweet company he had then! He was no longer lonely.

How beautiful was Jesus? Ah, I cannot tell you! Not even the tongues of angels could describe Him. As beautiful as heaven—no, more beautiful. So sweet and charming and fair to look upon was that Babe that Boniface cried out in rapture: "Oh, if in Paradise there were nothing else but that blessed face, it were worth while to suffer all tribulation, that we might gaze upon a countenance so glorious!"

Now, in the Sacred Host we see that same dear Jesus, only with the eyes of faith. And

St. Anthony Embracing the Child Jesus

in Holy Communion He is not only placed at our side, but is given to us to hold for a while in close embrace. So whenever you see the Host in the priest's hand and hear him utter these holy words, "Behold the Lamb of God!" you must say, "Dear Jesus, I believe that You are in Your Sacrament of Love; I believe it as firmly as if I really saw You with my own bodily eyes."

Then one day you will see Him in heaven, as He actually is; and He will be "Your reward exceeding great."

Tell Us Another, Winfrid Herbst, S. D. S.

> Beautiful angel!
> My guardian so mild,
> Tenderly guide me,
> For I am thy child.

12. MARY AND JOSEPH ON THEIR WAY TO BETHLEHEM

My dear children: Christmas, the birthday of Jesus, is coming nearer and nearer. Soon Jesus will knock at the door of your heart and ask you to let Him in. Will your heart be ready? Will you be able to give Jesus a place to which He can come? That all depends upon you, my children. You remember the story of the birth of Jesus.

After the angel told the Blessed Virgin that she was to be the Mother of God, Mary and Joseph lived in Nazareth for some time. But they could not remain in this quiet little place very long, for soon they had to go to Bethlehem, because the King ordered that all his people should be counted. This King wanted to know how many people belonged to him. Thus every family had to go to the town to which they belonged. Mary and Joseph started out for Bethlehem. This was a long trip to make, especially in those days when there were no automobiles or trains. However, Mary and Joseph did not complain. They knew it was the will of God that they should go to Bethlehem. Mary and Joseph give us a good lesson herein. They were told to do something which was hard to do. They had a cozy little home where they lived happily together. Mary knew that Jesus would soon come into the world and she would have been happy to have Jesus born in her little house, where she could take the best care of Him. Instead of this, she had to go to a place where she was not sure about finding a house or even a few rooms in which they could live.

From Mary we can learn to be obedient to the laws of the country. God gave the King who ordered Mary and Joseph to Bethlehem the power to rule over his people, and the people had to obey the commands given them. We have no king in our country, but we have a President, who rules over the people. Our President carries out the laws made by the men elected by the people. These laws may not please everybody, but nevertheless, it is the duty of every good citizen to obey. I spoke to you about these things before, and I mention them again here, because Mary and Joseph also obeyed the law, although it meant much suffering to both of them, not only because of the long and weary trip from Nazareth to Bethlehem, but particularly on account of the Infant Jesus, Who was soon to come into this world.

Jesus, too, wished to show us by His example that He loved to suffer for us, and, in order to make it easy for us to understand how much He loved us, He willed to be born poor. There are always more poor people in the world than rich, and so Jesus wanted these poor people to feel that He came into the world like one of them. Jesus was even poorer than most other poor children. Because His Blessed Mother and His foster-father St. Joseph obeyed the command of the King, they were forced to seek shelter in a stable on the very night in which Jesus was to be born.

You can follow the example of Mary and Joseph by obeying the laws made for the town, or city or country in which you live. Most of these laws, of course, concern the grown-up people. But some of them are for children also. Since I spoke to you about these things before, I shall ask you to tell me what some of these laws are. Can any one tell me a law that concerns children? (Let the children mention a few of these laws, for example, respecting the rights of others, not damaging others' property, keeping the sidewalks clean, obeying the rules of health, of safety, and the like.)

To-day, then, to please the Infant Jesus

Whose birthday is soon coming, try to observe these rules better than you did before. Think over now which laws you do not keep. Little boys and girls forget easily; that is why some of you are not careful about how you behave on the streets, and often deface people's houses and hedges, or disturb others by noisy games.

To-day, obey promptly and willingly in order to imitate our dear Mother Mary and St. Joseph who made the long trip to Bethlehem in obedience to an order given by the King.

Practice:

1. I will be careful not to use chalk on houses or to run on people's lawns.
2. I will to-day observe at least one health rule better; for example, sitting and standing erect.

> What lovely Infant can this be
> That in the little crib I see?
> So sweetly on the straw it lies,
> It must have come from Paradise.
> *Father Faber.*

13. THERE WAS NO ROOM FOR THEM IN THE INN

When Mary and Joseph arrived in Bethlehem, they found the small town quite crowded. Joseph went from house to house to ask for shelter, but everywhere he was told, "We have no room." What a great sorrow this was to St. Joseph. For himself he did not mind, but he felt very sorry for the Blessed Mother. It was getting dark and they had to find some place in which to sleep. It was also getting cold, and on this night Jesus was to come into the world. Mary and Joseph felt very sad as they walked out of the town and made their way towards a stable. Now, you know, dear children, that no one goes to a stable to sleep unless he can't find a place elsewhere. How would you feel, if you were driven out of your home and had no other place to go? Of course, you would be glad to find shelter even in a stable. But a stable, at its best, is a very poor place for people to live in. It may be quite comfortable for animals, but it is not a place where people could stay long.

In this stable there was not a chair, nor a table, nor a bed. There was no place where a fire could be made. Everything was rough and cold. It was the only place to which Mary and Joseph could go, and although they were tired and sad, they thanked God for the shelter.

While listening to this story, I am sure, many of you have been thinking, "I wish I had lived in Bethlehem at that time. I would have given Jesus my warm little bed." "He could have had my room." "The Blessed Mother and St. Joseph could have lived at our house." "Were there no little boys and girls in Bethlehem that night? Didn't they know about the Infant Jesus and His Blessed Mother?"

My dear children, the people of Bethlehem did not know that Jesus was coming to them that night. It is true, many of them had heard about the Messias that was to come. But they imagined that He would come as a rich and powerful king. They never dreamed that He would be poor and lowly.

Yes, dear children, I am sure that most of you wish you had lived in Bethlehem at the time Jesus was born, so that you could have given Him shelter. But you have the same chance now, if you make use of it; you can give Jesus a better place than a stable to live in when He comes to you on Christmas Day. Keep your heart pure, be kind to others, obey father and mother and your teachers, do all you know Jesus expects you to do and your heart will be a pleasing resting place for the dear Infant Jesus. Prepare your heart well. Do a good act whenever you have a chance. Be kind to the poor, pray devoutly, study your lessons as well as you can, and in everything you do or say, try to please Jesus. Then you will not be like the people of Bethlehem who said to Joseph, "We have no room."

Practice:

1. To do a kind deed as often as a chance offers to-day.
2. To make a special effort to keep my heart pure to-day.

> When the hour of death is nigh,
> Then may Mary, standing by,
> Take me in her arms to die,
> Sweet, Holy Child.

14. THE SHEPHERDS HASTEN TO THE CRIB

When Mary and Joseph reached the poor stable just outside the town, they found there an ox and an ass quietly eating the hay put before them by their master. Some of the hay was lying in a crib. A crib is a sort of box in which the food for animals is placed. When

THE ADORATION OF THE SHEPHERDS

Jesus was born, Mary, His Blessed Mother, laid Him in this crib. What a poor bed that was for the little Child!

That night some shepherds were watching their sheep in a field near by. It was very quiet out there in the dark. All at once they heard beautiful singing. Then the sky became bright and suddenly a beautiful angel appeared. Just imagine how surprised the shepherds were! The angel spoke to them. He told them he had wonderful news for them. He told them that in a stable near Bethlehem Our Lord had just been born. Imagine how happy the shepherds were on hearing this! They had heard about the Messias Who was to come to redeem the human race. And now He was here. They were to see Him, for the angel told them to go to the stable and there they would find a little child lying in a manger. That little child was Our Lord. You may be sure the shepherds hurried to the stable. When they reached it, they found the Child just as the angel had told them. The shepherds were very happy. They knelt before the crib and adored the Infant, for they knew that this little Baby was truly the Son of God, Who had become man to redeem the world. Then they gave Him little presents.

Now, can you tell me, what would you have done if you had been with the shepherds when they went to the stable that night? What did the shepherds give to the little Baby? Why do you think people give presents on Christmas Day? When you visit the crib in church, what does it make you think of? What should you do when you kneel before the crib? You should offer Jesus a present. But what could you give to the little Infant? What should you offer to Jesus when you visit Him? Your heart. That is right. Offer Jesus your heart. Say to Him: "Jesus, holy Child, come to me. Help me to be a good child. My heart is small, but take it, dear Jesus, I give it to you. It is yours." Oh, how pleased Jesus will be with your present! He wants your heart. Give it, then, to Jesus. Let Jesus take it and live in it, so that you may be as happy as the shepherds were when they saw our dear Lord on the first Christmas night.

But when you give some one a present, you do not give something that is old or torn, or soiled, do you? No, indeed. People usually buy the best they can; they wrap it carefully in fine paper and tie the package with gayly colored ribbon. How do you think your heart looks? Is it clean? Is it fit to be given away as a present? Is it perhaps soiled by sin? Then you had better make it pure once more by going to confession, by letting our dear Lord know how sorry you are, that you have allowed your heart to become stained by sin. Tell Jesus that you are sorry that you have hurt Him by your sins and He will wash your heart and make it pure and holy once more.

Try to-day, then, to do all you can to get your heart ready to give to Jesus as a present. Keep it free from everything that will soil it. Offer your heart to Jesus frequently during the day. Say to Jesus, "Take my heart, dear Jesus, and make it pure like Thine."

Practice:

1. To say often to-day, "My Jesus, I offer you my heart."
2. To avoid everything that might soil my heart.

> Merry, merry Christmas,
> May the coming year
> Bring as merry a Christmas
> And as bright a cheer.
> *Father Abram Ryan.*

15. LONGING FOR JESUS

Everybody wishes to be happy on Christmas. Christmas is the happiest day in the year, because on that day Our Lord was born. On Christmas day, Jesus came to free us from sin and to open the gates of heaven again. For many years, the pious people who lived on earth had been looking for the coming of the promised Redeemer. Do you remember that when God drove Adam and Eve out of Paradise, He promised to send a Redeemer Who would come from heaven to earth to save all mankind? This Redeemer, Who is also called the Messias, had just now come upon earth, but very few people knew it. The first people to know about the birth of Jesus were these poor shepherds. The King did not know about the coming of the Messias. Neither did any of the rich people that lived in that country. Only a few pious men, the shepherds, were called by God to visit Our Lord. Why were these men called? These poor shepherds were good men who longed for the day when the Messias was to come. They often spoke about the promised Redeemer. They tried to lead holy lives so that they would be worthy one day to see the Savior of the world. They prepared themselves all their lives, although they were not sure they would live to see the Messias.

You, my dear children, know that Jesus will come to you. If you wish to receive Him into your hearts, you must make your hearts ready for Him. How can you do that? You do not wish to ask Jesus to come to you if your heart is soiled by sin, do you? Certainly not. In order to receive Jesus, your souls must be pure. When you were baptized your souls became holy.

Be careful, then, my dear children, to keep your hearts pure and holy for the coming of Jesus. Allow nothing to enter your hearts that would not please Jesus. Ask Jesus to help you. Ask our Blessed Mother to help you. She knows just what kind of a heart you should have ready for Jesus. Ask your Guardian Angels to help you. Now try very earnestly to-day to prepare for the great feast.

Practice:

1. I will tell Jesus often to-day that I am sorry I ever offended Him.
2. I will watch carefully to-day to keep my heart free from sin.

> A carol of joy! a carol of joy!
> For the glorious Christmas time;
> While the heavens rejoice and the earth is glad.
> Let the merry bells sweetly chime.

> Oh! happy spirit, angel bright!
> Beside me ever stay;
> Watch o'er me throughout the shadowed night
> And guard me through the day.

16. THE CHRISTMAS CLOAK

Jennie came home from school crying. It was only a few days before Christmas at that. Surely, no time for tears.

"What are you crying for, Jennie?" mother asked anxiously.

"Oh, mother, Marie has clothes so much nicer than mine," sobbed the girl.

"Now, Jennie, aren't you ashamed of yourself?" mother said, surprised. "Is that the way to be a good girl, thinking about nice clothes even when you are in church? Your clothes are neat and warm, and you always have enough. What more do you want? You must thank God for taking such good care of us. And don't forget that Marie's father is rich. He can afford to buy her more expensive garments. But you know father has to work hard every day to support us. While we have a comfortable home to live in and healthy food to eat, and warm clothes to wear we should be grateful to God—and bless Him for keeping father well and strong. Really, Jennie, it is very naughty for you to be dissatisfied."

Just then mother saw Elsie Prull walk down the street. "See," she said, "there's Elsie. What a poor, thin cloak she wears! She is just shivering from the cold. But it's the best she has; for she is poor and her mother has been sick for a long time. And you, who have everything you need, and more, even, are crying out of envy. Jennie, do you think God likes that?"

Now Jennie was really a good girl. So she saw at once how wrong it was for her to act in such a way. Then, too, there was Elsie—she pitied Elsie.

"Mother," she said suddenly, "I'm sorry I acted so thoughtlessly. I'm quite ashamed! And, mother—you know I have an extra cloak upstairs. It's warm and heavy and still good. Won't you let me give it to Elsie, please?"

How happy mother was to hear that! Now her darling was a darling indeed. "Of course, you may," she said. "Though we haven't much, we must not forget those who have even less."

At once Jennie hastened over to Elsie's home, a bundle under her arm. It was the cloak. Oh, how happy Elsie and her poor sick mother were! They were so happy that they cried.

That night Jennie had a dream. "Oh, mother," she cried the next morning, "what a lovely dream I had last night. I dreamt I saw the Christ-Child, just as He came to us the first Christmas night. Oh, He was so sweet and dear! He smiled upon me and stretched out His arms for me to come and kiss Him. And, mother —He had on my cloak—the one I gave to Elsie." Jennie's eyes were moist with emotion and her voice trembled.

"See, Jennie, thus Jesus rewards you. Thus He shows you that what you do for others in His name you do for him."

A few days later Christmas came. Under her beautiful tree Jennie found an extra large box. What could it be? She opened it. "Oh, mother," she cried, "see what the Christ-Child brought me! a cloak, just like the one I gave away, only all new! Oh, mother, it's just as though I gave it to Jesus, and He gave it back much nicer than before."

And in church that day, kneeling before the crib, Jennie whispered, "Dear Baby God, now I know that whenever we do anything for You, You do still more for us. I am going to do so much for You. I am going to try to make others as happy as You have made me."

17. DRAMATIZING THE STORY OF CHRISTMAS

To the Teacher:—If you have carried out some of the pious exercises suggested on page 2 you will probably find it helpful to dramatize "The Adoration of The Shepherds" as outlined on page 91 of the section of dramatizations. Let the children as far as possible arrange by themselves both the crib and the dramatization. Your pupils will reveal a surprising amount of initiative in this matter if left to themselves. And the more spontaneous their actions in putting up the crib or in dramatizing the story of the shepherds, the more educative will the exercises be. What really counts here as everywhere else in education is not what the teacher does for her pupils, but what she gets her pupils to do for themselves. While the tots are busy working on the crib or in rehearsing the story of Bethlehem, their little hearts will be glowing with love for Him who became as one of them that He might redeem us all, and their souls will thus be turned into warm and cozy beds for the reception of the Savior on Christmas Morn.

> Sing high, sing low,
> Sing to and fro,
> Go tell it out with speed;
> Cry out and shout,
> All round about,
> That Christ is born indeed!

18. THE WISE MEN GO TO VISIT THE CRIB

My dear boys and girls: Let us go back today to the crib and see what happened after the shepherds came to adore the Holy Child. God also wished the people who lived far away from Bethlehem to hear about the birth of Jesus.

He told Wise Men in the East to watch for a new star. This new star was to tell them that a Savior was born. When they saw the star they were glad, for they knew that Jesus, the Savior, was born. They said: "We must go to see this new-born King of the Jews."

They knew it would be a long journey, for the new King was to be born in Judea, where the Jews lived. But they did not care for that. They were willing to travel many miles through deserts and marshes and over hills and mountains to see the Savior. They were not afraid were willing to suffer everything. Now, my dear children, when you hear the story of the three Wise Men, does it not make you feel ashamed that you do not visit Jesus in the tabernacle oftener than you do? How hard you find it to rise early in the morning to be on time for Mass! How often you pass by the church without even thinking of our dear Lord all alone, waiting for some one to visit Him! You think it too much to walk a few squares to church; the Wise Men traveled for days and weeks. You have only to leave your home for a short time; you

THE WISE MEN GO TO VISIT JESUS

of losing their way. The star would guide them on the right way. So three of these Wise Men started for Judea, and the wonderful star went before them and showed them the way.

I said before that the Wise Men were willing to go away from home to visit the new-born Savior in Judea. They were not afraid. They left everything behind, their home, their wives, and their children. They were going to a strange country. They would meet people whom they did not know. These people might not be friendly; perhaps they might even do them harm. But all this did not frighten the holy men, and they went cheerfully on their journey. They wanted to see Jesus. That is why they do not forsake father and mother and brothers and sisters when you go to church, while the Wise Men left all their dear ones, not knowing if they would ever see them again. Does not this make you feel ashamed? Could you not try to be a little like these holy men? Could you not visit Jesus oftener? Try to-day at least to visit Jesus in the tabernacle each time you pass the church. Stop in for just a few minutes. Go to the front of the church and kneel down before the altar-rail. Tell Jesus how happy you are that you can visit Him. Ask Jesus to bless you. Ask Him to help you in your work. Such a visit will take only a few moments.

To-day, then, imitate the Wise Men by visiting

Jesus as often as you can. Remember that Jesus is waiting for His little boys and girls. Think of the Wise Men coming so far to see Jesus and thank our dear Lord for making it so easy for you to visit Him.

Practice:

1. To visit Jesus in church on my way home from school, and also before school this afternoon.
2. While in church to ask Jesus to bless me and to thank Him for calling me to Him.

> A star, you know,
>   Made three kings go,
> Unto the sacred shrine,
>   In which was born,
>   On Christmas morn,
> Our God and Lord divine.

> See amid the winter's snow,
> Born for us on earth below,
> See the tender Lamb appears,
> Promised from eternal years.
>
> Hail, thou ever-blessed morn!
> Hail, Redemption's happy dawn!
> Sing through all Jerusalem,
> Christ is born in Bethlehem!
>
> "Say, ye holy Shepherds, say,
> What's your joyful news today?
> Wherefore have ye left your sheep
> On the lonely mountain steep?"
>
> "As we watched at dead of night,
> Lo! we saw a wondrous light;
> Angels singing 'Peace on earth,'
> Told us of the Saviour's birth."
>
> Teach, oh teach us, holy Child,
> By Thy face so meek and mild,
> Teach us to resemble Thee
> In Thy sweet humility.
>
> Virgin Mother! Mary blest!
> By the joys that fill thy breast,
> Pray for us that we may prove
> Worthy of the Saviour's love.
>
> Hail, thou ever-blessed morn!
> Hail, Redemption's happy dawn!
> Sing through all Jerusalem,
> Christ is born in Bethlehem.

19. THE WISE MEN IN BETHLEHEM

After a long journey the three Wise Men reached Judea. They thought the Savior would be born in Jerusalem, the great city. When they arrived in that city they went to the palace of the King and asked: "Where is the newborn King of the Jews? We have seen His star in the east and have come to worship Him."

Now when the King heard this, he was filled with fear. He was not pleased to hear that a new King was born. He called together the wise men of the city and asked them where the promised King of the Jews was to be born. They told him the new King was to be born in Bethlehem. King Herod told the three Wise Men to go to Bethlehem and look for the newborn King and then come back and tell him where the child was, for he also wished to go and worship Him.

In a little while the three holy men were in Bethlehem. Joseph and Mary were filled with wonder when they saw these good men. The Wise Men knelt before the little Jesus and prayed. They also gave Him costly presents. Mary thought about the words of the Angel telling her that her child was the Son of God, the Savior of the world. How wonderful it was that these strange men, coming from so far should know that Jesus was God, and that He was truly the Savior of the world!

After the Wise Men had spent some time in Bethlehem visiting the Infant Savior and speaking to Joseph and Mary, they at last had to think about returning home. This made them feel very sad. They would have liked to remain there forever. They could not tire of looking at the divine Child. Yet they had been away from their country so long that it was necessary for them to return. You can imagine, my dear children, how it grieved these holy men to leave Jesus and Joseph and Mary.

So it ought to be with you when you visit Jesus in church. You ought to be sorry that you must leave Him. You ought to stay with Him as long as you can. Of course, Jesus does not expect you to remain with Him day and night. However, you can think of Him often and pray to Him even when you are with others. You do not need to fold your hands when you pray in this way. Just think of Jesus. Wish that you were able to see Him. Whisper a little prayer. For example, say:

> Jesus, day by day,
> Lead us on life's way.

Or you might say some other little prayer you know. Jesus will be pleased with you if you do this. He will receive such prayers with as much pleasure as if you had visited Him in Bethlehem with the Wise Men.

The Wise Men Teach You a Lesson

During the time the three Wise Men were in Bethlehem they spent as much time as they could in the company of Jesus. They did not go around seeing the town or making friends with other people. No, they came so great a distance to see the Infant Jesus and they made good use of this precious time. Do you always spend the time in church well? How often it happens that children laugh and talk and look about while in the presence of Jesus. Such boys and girls do not seem to know that Jesus is in the tabernacle waiting for His children to speak to Him. How sad Jesus must feel when He sees such children; they do not go to church to visit Jesus. They do not make good use of their time. How many times Jesus would bless them if they asked Him to do it! How many times Jesus would help them to be good, if they told Him that they needed help!

Be careful, then, each time you visit Jesus in church, to behave properly. Do not look about to see what others are doing. Think of Jesus there in the tabernacle watching you and waiting for you to ask Him for His gifts and graces. Each time you go to church try to think of the three Wise Men visiting the Infant Jesus in Bethlehem. Imagine you are with them. How well you would be able to pray if you always thought of this!

In your visits to Jesus to-day, try earnestly to behave in such a way as you imagine the Wise Men acted. Therefore:

1. Be as devout as you can when you are in church;
2. Imagine that you are one of the Wise Men and act as you think they acted in the presence of Jesus.

Little Jesus, wast Thou shy
Once, and just so small as I?
And what did it feel like to be
Out of Heaven, and just like me?
Didst Thou sometimes think of *there,*
And ask where all the angels were?
I should think that I would cry
For my house all made of sky;
I would look about the air,
And wonder where my angels were;
And at waking 'twould distress me—
Not an angel there to dress me!
Hadst Thou ever any toys,
Like us little girls and boys?
And didst Thou play in Heaven with all
The angels that were not too tall,
With stars for marbles? Did the things
Play *Can you see me?* through their wings?
And did Thy Mother let Thee spoil
Thy robes, with playing on *our* soil?
How nice to have them always new
In Heaven, because 'twas quite clean blue!

Didst Thou kneel at night to pray,
And didst Thou join Thy hands, this way?
And did they tire sometimes, being young,
And make the prayer seem very long?
And dost Thou like it best, that we
Should join our hands to pray to Thee?
I used to think, before I knew,
The prayer not said unless we do.
And did Thy Mother at the night
Kiss Thee, and fold the clothes in right?
And didst Thou feel quite good in bed,
Kissed, and sweet, and Thy prayers said?

Thou canst not have forgotten all
That it feels like to be small:
And Thou know'st I cannot pray
To Thee in my father's way—
When Thou wast so little, say,
Couldst Thou talk Thy Father's way?—
So, a little Child, come down
And hear a child's tongue like Thy own;
Take me by the hand and walk,
And listen to my baby-talk,
To Thy Father show my prayer
(He will look, Thou art so fair),
And say: "O Father, I, Thy Son,
Bring the prayer of a little one."

And He will smile, that children's tongue
Has not changed since Thou wast young!

Francis Thompson.

20. THE FLIGHT INTO EGYPT

King Herod told the Wise Men to come back after they had found the Child Jesus. He said he wanted to go and worship the new-born King. But this wicked King did not tell the truth. He wanted to kill this little Child, for he did not want any one else to be King. He waited for the Wise Men to return, but they did not come back. Why did they not return? Because God did not wish little Jesus to be put to death. An angel came to them and told them to go home another way, so that Herod would not find out where the Child was.

Of course, Herod was very angry when he learned that the Wise Men had gone home without telling him where the new-born King was. He said to himself: "I will find the Child anyway and kill Him." He called his soldiers and told them to go to Bethlehem and hunt all the little boys that were less than two years old, and kill every one of them. In that way, he thought, the Child Jesus would surely be put to death.

The Holy Innocents

Just think, dear children, what a terrible thing that was. Imagine how the cruel soldiers entered the homes and tore the dear little ones from their mothers' arms in order to kill them. These poor mothers fell on their knees and begged the soldiers to spare their children. Many of the mothers cried out, "Kill us, but spare our babies!" Others cried, "What have our poor little babies done to King Herod!" But the wicked men did not spare any of them and soon the town was filled with the moaning and weeping of the heart-broken mothers. These little boys died for Jesus. They were the first ones to give up their lives for Him. The feast of the Holy Innocents is celebrated in remembrance of the little boys who were killed that day by the soldiers of the wicked King.

But the little Jesus was safe. God sent an Angel to Joseph to tell him what the wicked King was about to do. He told Joseph that he was to take the Child and His mother and flee to Egypt at once. There they were to stay until the cruel King died. Joseph got ready as quickly as he could. He did not complain at being awakened in the middle of the night. He did not say to himself: "I can wait till the morning. That will be time enough." No; at once he called the Blessed Virgin and the Child Jesus. He told Mary what the angel had said. Mary, too, was very sad. It made her heart heavy when she heard that Herod wanted to kill her little Boy. But Joseph and Mary obeyed at once. What a noble example these two holy persons give us! It surely was very hard to

THE FLIGHT INTO EGYPT

leave their little home and go to a strange country where they did not know any one. Sometimes you complain when father or mother or your teacher tell you to do something that is hard. At such times, you will do well to think of Joseph and Mary leaving Bethlehem in the middle of the night to go to Egypt!

When you look at this picture (show a picture of the Flight into Egypt) think of Joseph and Mary leaving their home at dead of night. Mary held little Jesus close to her breast. It was a very long journey across the hot and sandy desert, and they must often have been tired and hungry and thirsty. In the desert it was very hard to get fresh water to drink. After traveling all day they had to sleep on the sand at night.

How many times you complain when mother asks you to go to the store or to do other errands for her. You say it is too hot or too cold. You grumble because you do not want to stop playing. Suppose Joseph and Mary had complained when they were told to go at once. What would have happened to Jesus? They did what God wanted them to do and they did it at once. You do not always know what your parents or your teachers have in mind when they ask you to do something for them. It may be for your own good. At any rate it will be better for you and it will make them happier, if you go at once, without showing that you do not like it. When you find it hard to do as you are told, think of the Flight into Egypt. Often look at this picture and remember what it means. Jesus will be pleased with you if you follow the example of Mary and Joseph.

Think now in what way you can imitate Mary and Joseph to-day.

Practice:

1. I will to-day obey quickly whenever I am commanded to do something.
2. When I find it hard to do a thing, I will think of Mary and Joseph with the Infant Jesus leaving their home to go to a strange land.

> Jesus, teach me how to pray,
> Suffer not my thoughts to stray,
> Send distractions far away,
>   Sweet, Holy Child.
>
> Let me not be rude or wild,
> Make me humble, meek, and mild,
> Pure as angels undefiled
>   Sweet, Holy Child.
>
> When I work or when I play,
> Be Thou with me through the day,
> Teach me what to do and say,
>   Sweet, Holy Child.

21. THE HOLY FAMILY IN EGYPT

We have seen that the Child Jesus had to suffer much even while He was very young. Although so small that He still had to be carried, He suffered when His mother and St. Joseph had to take Him from His cozy bed and hurry with Him to Egypt. That was a long, hard trip to make. The roads were rough and the donkey on which Mary rode with Jesus in her arms may have stumbled often as they hurried along the way. The journey certainly was not in any way as comfortable as riding in a street car or train or automobile. When your parents take you along on a trip they try to have everything as comfortable as may be. The journey to Egypt was long and hard. When the Holy Family arrived in Egypt, they found no one whom they knew. They were among strangers. Joseph had to look for work in order to support his dear ones. We can imagine the Child Jesus playing about the house, and when He was older trying to help His Mother in little things. We can see Him running to meet St. Joseph at the end of the day's work. Perhaps He carried his tools.

Here I have a very beautiful picture showing St. Joseph, the Blessed Mother and the Boy Jesus spending the evening together in their home. See, how happy they are! We can imagine that they are speaking of their home in Nazareth. Mary and Joseph are wondering when they may return. Those years spent in Egypt must have seemed long and weary. Yet Joseph and Mary were very happy also, for they had with them Jesus, the Son of God. "When Jesus is with us all is well," said a holy man. And truly, Jesus was always with Mary and Joseph. They were among strangers in a country far away from all those whom they knew and loved. But they had their Holy Child. I am sure that Jesus did all He could to make Mary and Joseph happy. He tried to please them in every way. He helped Mary with the work about the house; He assisted Joseph in his workshop as soon as He was old enough to do so. He was so obedient, so cheerful and so happy that it was not possible for Mary and Joseph to grieve about being away from their own country. With Jesus, even Egypt was heaven to them. Without Jesus, Bethlehem would be as a dreary desert.

Now, my dear children, I am sure many of you often wished you had lived in Egypt at the time Our Lord was there as a little boy. I am sure you would have done everything you could to make Him feel at home there. How would you like to have had Him for your playmate! You would have been glad to share all your toys

When you look at this picture, remember that even on this very day you can enjoy the company of Jesus, just as Mary and Joseph did long ago. Try to think of Jesus as a little Boy, just about as old as you are now. Think of what He did at the time; how He spoke to His Mother, to His foster-father St. Joseph; how He treated His little playmates; how kind and cheerful He was to all whom He met. Can you not try also to do these things?

THE HOLY FAMILY IN EGYPT

with Jesus. You would not have allowed Him to be lonely. How happy you would have been to speak to the Blessed Virgin and St. Joseph!

But you can enjoy the company of Jesus even to-day in all your games, in all your work and play. Jesus is with you, if you keep your hearts pure. If you obey your parents and teachers, if you do all you are expected to do, Jesus will be with you all through the day. You can visit Him many times; you can speak to Him as often as you wish. You can speak to His Blessed Mother and to St. Joseph. Think of Jesus in all you do and say, and you will be just as close to Him as if you had been one of His little playmates in Egypt.

Practice:

1. I will act as I imagine Jesus would act were He in my place.
2. When I play, I will imagine Jesus among my playmates.

Dear Infant Lord, we bend the knee,
And give our children's hearts to Thee.

REVIEW

To the Teacher:—*If you used the pictures suggested during this week, arrange them in convenient places around the room. Some teachers hang the pictures too high. Place them low enough for the children to examine closely. Let the children discuss the subjects of this week's morning talks. Get them to tell the story. Draw them out. Let them relate their experiences in carrying out the suggested practices. Perhaps they may be able to suggest others.*

A plan which has been very helpful is to procure smaller pictures for the children and at the end of the week or at the end of the month, permit them to make a booklet in which to paste these pictures. They might write a sentence or two about the pictures. By having the children take these pictures home the interest of the parents in their children's school work is increased. Often the children will tell the story to father and mother, and in this way long-forgotten memories of childhood days may recall careless parents to a sense of their duty.

> Sleep, Jesus, sleep,
> Upon Thy Mother's breast;
> Great Lord of earth and sea and sky,
> How sweet it is to see Thee lie
> In such a place of rest!

22. THE BOY JESUS AT HOME

Dear children: You have been learning so many wonderful things about the Child Jesus that some of you might begin to think Jesus was not a real boy. An Angel came to tell Mary that the little Child who was to be born to her was the Son of God. A large number of Angels appeared in the sky at His birth. A wonderful star led the Wise Men to Bethlehem. An Angel appeared to Joseph to tell him to take Jesus to Egypt. Afterwards an Angel told Joseph when to return to Judea. Angels guarded Him everywhere, and although He was often in great danger, God carefully watched over Him that no harm should come to Him. These were such wonderful things to happen to a little child that it is not surprising if you should think that Jesus was perhaps not a real boy.

But Jesus was much like other boys of His age. He grew, little by little, as other boys do. He worked for His foster-father, helping him by going on errands or carrying small pieces of finished work to the people for whom they were made. He was good and kind to all, and everybody liked Him.

After Mary and Joseph returned from Egypt they went to live in Nazareth. Their house was small, for they were poor. You see that Jesus as a Boy did not have many and expensive toys. Often little boys and girls are very disagreeable because they do not have the playthings they wish to have. They are not satisfied with what father and mother give them. Jesus was satisfied with everything His parents gave Him. He thanked them warmly for their gifts.

As Jesus grew taller and stronger, He helped Joseph with his work. He would carry the wood for him and help him in every possible way. Jesus would take the water pitcher to the well for His Mother, for in those days people did not have the water running in pipes through the house as we have to-day. The neighbors noticed that Jesus was always gentle and mild, and ready to oblige others. His parents had only to speak to Him, and he hurried to obey their wishes, even in the slightest things.

The Example of Jesus

Now stop a moment, and see in how far you are like Jesus. Do you help your mother at home as much as you are able? Or do you make more work for her? Do you help father sometimes when he works about the house? Or do you run away when you know father or mother wants you? Do you think Jesus did anything like that? Surely not. Jesus did all He could to help His parents. He wanted to give you an example. Jesus was God. He did not need to obey Mary and Joseph, for He was greater than they. But He wanted to show you that you must obey your parents and those placed over you in everything that is not sinful. This evening, before you go to bed, carefully examine your conscience about how you obeyed father and mother to-day. Jesus gladly did all He was told to do. He did not even wait to be told. When He knew His mother or St. Joseph wished something to be done, He did it without waiting to be told. How it ought to put some children to shame, when they think how disobedient they are, how crossly they answer their parents, how slow they are to leave fun and play when they are asked to run on an errand or deliver a message. Children know that father and mother love them dearly, but they are too small to understand the reason why they expect them to do many things. Learn to-day, then, to be gentle, loving and kind to your parents. Do not grumble when you are asked to do anything for them. And when you are older, when you have grown to be men and women, it will always make you happy to know that you tried to please your parents for the love of Jesus.

Practice:
1. I will make father and mother happy by obeying promptly and cheerfully.
2. I will learn to please father and mother by doing what I know I ought to do without waiting for them to tell me.

> Why do bells for Christmas ring?
> Why do little children sing?
> Once a lovely star
> Seen by shepherds from afar,
> Gently moved until its light
> Made a manger cradle bright,
> There a darling Babe lay
> And its Mother sang and smiled,
> "This is Christ, the Holy Child."
> Therefore, bells for Christmas ring,
> Therefore, little children sing.
>
> *Eugene Field.*

23. THE CHILDHOOD DAYS OF JESUS

Not much is told us of Jesus when He was a Boy. This is to show us that a good child lives quietly in his home, being loving and obedient. Jesus sets you an example in everything. We know that Jesus was so much better than other children, that He was obedient to His Mother, dutiful to St. Joseph, gentle and unselfish with other children, kind to their pet animals.

St. Elizabeth, the cousin of the Blessed Virgin, had a little boy six months older than Jesus. This little boy grew up to be St. John the Baptist, about whom you will learn many things. Jesus often played with His little cousin; they dearly loved each other. They had pet lambs, and played with them, for the lambs were fond of Jesus and little John. Would you not like to have been one of the little pets of Jesus?

Jesus loved to pray. Often He would steal away to pray in some quiet spot. Mary and Joseph were happy to have so good and pious a Child and thanked God every day for letting them live with Jesus. I wonder if your father and mother are also happy to have you. I wonder if they are so pleased with you that they thank God for having given you to them.

Perhaps they are sad because you are naughty, disobedient, cross and selfish. Maybe your parents are glad that God gave them a good child, one that is loving and kind; a child that tries to please them in every way. Do you think you are one of the children whose parents thank God every day for giving them such a good boy or girl? Or are you one of those that make their parents sad and unhappy? Examine yourself very carefully about this, and try from now on to bring as much happiness to your father and mother as the Child Jesus did to Mary and Joseph.

Jesus Prepared Himself for His Life Work

The Boy Jesus studied, learning His tasks as other children do, without wasting any time. He worked hard to please His teachers. He was making ready for the work that God intended Him to do when He grew up. God also wants you to prepare yourselves well for the work He wishes you to do when you are grown to be men and women. Some of the little boys here may one day be priests. Would not that be a wonderful thing! To be a priest is the greatest thing in the world, for a priest has the power of calling God from heaven to the altar. A priest is like another Christ. He has charge of the sacraments, he can help souls to get to heaven. My dear boys, pray every day that God may call you to the priesthood. Study hard now, so that one day you may be ready to work for God by saving souls. Some of the little girls in this room may one day be Sisters. This, too, is a wonderful thing. A Sister can do much to save souls for God. Just think how much good you could do if you were a Sister. You could speak of God to little boys and girls. You could tell them many beautiful things about Jesus, His Blessed Mother, the angels and the saints. So, my dear girls, you also should pray very hard that God may give you the grace to work some day as a Sister teaching others to know, love and serve Him.

But not all of you will be priests or Sisters. God does not call every one to lead or teach others. God expects that you do your share in the work of the world. We need good men and women who will give a good example in the world, just as the Child Jesus lived in this world in order to give you a good example. You may become doctors, or lawyers, or business men; the girls may become teachers, or stenographers, or mothers of families. For this, all need to be ready. Now is the time to get

"O dear Jesus, Who wast once a child like me, make me more like Thee every day."

Practice:

1. I will say this prayer often during the day.
2. I will try to have Jesus before my eyes all

JESUS AT STUDY

ready. If you learn your lessons well as children, it will be easy to learn the bigger things later on.

How happy you are to know that when you study, or work, or play, or whatever else you do, you are doing just what the Boy Jesus did at your age. You should try to live as He lived, and be kind, gentle, loving and obedient in all things. Ask Jesus for the grace to be like Him. Ask Mary to help you that you may be children who wish to be like her Son. Often say this little prayer:

through this day, so that I may copy His actions in everything I do.

> Sweet Babe of Bethlehem,
> Hail, Mary's little One!
> Hail, God's most Holy Son,
> Sweet Babe of Bethlehem.
> *Father Faber.*

24. JESUS AT NAZARETH

To-day I shall show you two pretty pictures. This one shows the Boy Jesus studying His lessons.[1] The Blessed Virgin is teaching Him. See, He is telling His Mother something that He learned during the day. His Mother is listening to Him. What a pleasure it must have been for the Blessed Virgin to listen to Jesus. How pleased she was to see her dear Boy learning so well. Do you think that your mother can be as well pleased with you? Do you tell your mother what you learned in school? I am sure your mother will also be delighted to know that you are trying your best to learn your lessons every day. I shall put this picture here so that you can easily see it. When you look at it, think of Jesus telling His Mother about His lessons and try to be as diligent as He was so that your mother, too, may be pleased with you.

The other picture is also a pretty one. Here we see Jesus and His Blessed Mother in their garden.[2] Mary is working while Jesus is tending the flowers. He is carrying water for them. See the beautiful flowers. Can any one tell what kind of flowers these are? (Point to the different flowers.) The Boy Jesus was never idle. His Mother helped Him to study, but when she was busy with the housework, Jesus helped her. He ran errands; He brought her what she needed; He fetched water; He did all the small, helpful things that a good child can do for his mother. Sometimes when they were working together like this they sang beautiful songs; they praised God by singing hymns and psalms. What a happy Mother and Child!

I wonder if your mother is happy when she

JESUS HELPING HIS MOTHER

[1] This picture is contained on page 9 of "The Wonder Days" by Marion Ames Taggart.

[2] This picture is contained on page 11 of "The Wonder Days" by Marion Ames Taggart.

has you at home with her. How pleased she would be to have her little boy or girl run errands, bring the things she needs, or help her in many other little ways. I spoke of this to you before. Perhaps you have become a little careless about helping mother. There are so many things that a boy or girl of your age can do. You can play with the baby to keep him quiet while mother is preparing a meal, you can help mother wash the dishes, you can pick up things that have fallen on the floor; and there are many other ways of helping so that it will not be hard for a good child to know what he can do to help.

I shall place this picture here so that you may often look at it. Let it remind you about helping your dear mother as much as you can. If you do this, you will make your mother happy and you yourself will receive God's blessing. God blesses the children that treat their parents with great love and respect. Never forget the example Jesus gave you. He obeyed His parents in everything! He tried to please them in every way He could; there was nothing He would not do to help His mother and St. Joseph.

To-day again, I wish to remind you about doing something to show your dear parents how much you love them.

Practice:
1. I will watch for a chance to help mother in her work at home.
2. I will do the work mother gives me in the best way I know how.

25. JESUS GOES TO THE TEMPLE WITH HIS PARENTS

I notice that you are interested in the pictures I showed thus far. They are very pretty, are they not? These pictures remind us of the Savior of the world, Who became a little child, lived on this earth just like other children, and gave us an example that as He has done, we also should do.

We learned that Jesus lived at home with His Blessed Mother and St. Joseph just as other children live with their parents. But Jesus was more loving, more gentle, more obedient than other children. Jesus was God then just as He is now. He knew all things, yet he studied His lessons in order to do the will of God. Jesus knew that when He grew up to be a man He had a great work to do. For this He must get ready. He remained quietly in His home, helping His parents, sometimes playing with His little cousin John and all this time He was kind, gentle and obedient.

Jesus grew like other boys. When He was very small, He played in St. Joseph's workshop, picking up the shavings and trying to use the tools lying about. You know that St. Joseph was a carpenter. Most boys like to play at being carpenter. They like to hammer and saw and build little houses. Now when you do this, think that Jesus also at one time did these things. But as he grew older he helped St. Joseph with his work. He carried the wood, helped to build houses and make furniture. When the work was finished, He often carried it to the people for whom it was made.

When a Jewish boy reached the age of twelve, he was looked upon as almost a man. He could choose his trade and was now obliged to go on the great feasts to visit the temple at Jerusalem. You may be sure that most boys felt very important then.

You go to church every Sunday. This is not a great task for you. Perhaps it is only a short walk. If, however, you have a long way to go, there are street cars and automobiles in which you can ride. In a short while you are at church.

It was not so when Jesus was a boy. There was a place in His town where people gathered every week to worship God. This place had a queer name. It was called a synagogue just as the churches where the Jews worship are called to-day. To this place Jesus often went with His parents.

Several times a year the Jewish people went to Jerusalem to celebrate the great feasts. That was a long trip. It took some people three or four days to make the trip. Once a year Joseph and Mary made this trip. They did not take Jesus along with them until He was twelve years old, because the journey was so long and they feared He was not strong enough. But as soon as He was twelve years old, He was obliged by law to go to Jerusalem just as all other boys of that age. You can imagine that Jesus talked about this trip for weeks before, much as you would if you were to go away on a long trip.

The Journey from Nazareth to Jerusalem

At last the day came for them to start. Other people from Nazareth went also and there were many people on the road from Nazareth to Jerusalem. Some rode, others walked. Joseph and Mary walked, as did also the Boy Jesus. But it was a pleasant trip for Jesus even if He had to walk. He enjoyed the green fields, the hills and the mountains and the beautiful river. He thought of His Heavenly Father, Who watched over all creation and thanked Him for His wonderful works. Each evening, the travelers rested out in the open or stopped, if possible, at an inn. Then the journey was continued once more until they finally arrived at Jerusalem. This was a large city, but the most wonderful part of it all was the big temple. This temple was made up of a great number of rooms; it was not like our churches, although it was a place where people came to pray.

Like a real boy, Jesus was interested in all that was going on. He listened in wonder to the teachers of the law. These men were gathered in a large room, where they read parts of the Scriptures and then talked about what they had read. Jesus loved to stay here and listen to what these men had to say. Each time He came to the temple with His parents He hurried to this room. He not only listened to what the men said, but He began to ask them questions. Sometimes these learned men asked Jesus questions and they were surprised at the answers He gave them.

At last the days of the feast were over. The people prepared to leave Jerusalem and return to their homes. In the evening they were to meet and camp for the night. (The children were allowed to go with either the men or the women. So it happened that Mary thought Jesus was with Joseph, while Joseph thought He was with Mary.) But Jesus did not leave Jerusalem with His parents. This was a strange thing for Jesus to do, you will think. Yes, it surely was, but since Jesus was God, He wanted to give an example of how we should be willing to leave everything for the love of God.

The Child Jesus Is Lost

When Mary and Joseph found that Jesus was not with the people that came down from Jerusalem, they looked for Him everywhere. They

THE BOY JESUS IN THE TEMPLE

returned to Jerusalem. But they could not find Him. For three days they searched. You can imagine how sad and sorrowful the Blessed Virgin and St. Joseph must have been. They had no idea where He could be. They then thought of the temple. They went from room to room and at last found Him in the midst of the learned men. Here Jesus was listening to them and asking them questions.

Jesus was only a boy, yet these learned men were listening with the closest attention to what

He was saying. As soon as Mary and Joseph saw Jesus they were filled with joy; but Mary, thinking of the sorrow and suffering she and St. Joseph had had, during the three days, said to Him, "Son, why has Thou done so to us? Behold, Thy father and I have sought Thee sorrowing." You see the Blessed Virgin had suffered too much to forget at once. But Jesus answered: "How is it that you sought Me? Did you not know that I must be about My Father's business?"

By these words Jesus meant to remind His mother that He came into the world to do the work that His Heavenly Father had given Him to do. But when Mary called Him, He went away with her obediently. This is to show you that a child's first duty is to obey, for thus he serves God best.

Our dear Savior liked to be in the temple. It was the place where God was truly worshipped. People came here from all parts of the country in order to worship Him. The temple was the house of God. Jesus was God. Why should He not wish to stay there? Surely He loved this place and would have liked to remain there always. Yet as soon as Mary came to take Him home with her, He went at once, willingly and cheerfully. He did not plead to be allowed to stay just a little longer.

A MOTHER'S QUEST

"And not finding Him, they returned into Jerusalem seeking Him." (St. Luke, II, 45.)

>Have you seen my little Love
> Going by your door?
>Off he flew, my little Dove,
> And my heart is sore.
>
>You would know my little Boy,
> Dressed in white and brown.
>How my heart o'erflowed with joy
> As I wove His gown.
>
>You would know Him from His hair,
> All of raven hue;
>You would know Him anywhere,
> Once He looked at you.
>
>Oh, if you should see my Own,
> Seeking out His home,
>Tell Him how my joy has flown
> As the streets I roam.
>
>Lead Him in beside thy hearth,
> Bid Him there remain;
>Tell Him, though I search the earth,
> I will come again.
>
>And if hungry He should be,
> Give Him of your bread;
>If He nod so wearily,
> Make His little bed.
>
>Woman, if you see my Boy,
> Oh, to Him be kind!
>You will have the fullest joy—
> Lo, 'tis God you'll find.

Songs for Sinners, Hugh Francis Blunt.

REVIEW

To the Teacher:—*Review the week's morning talks, getting the children to tell you what they have remembered. Let each child tell you what impressed him most in the life of the Child Jesus. During this week three pictures were used. If you have these in small sizes, let the children make booklets and paste them in. A sentence or two written below the pictures will help the children to remember what you told them.*

Again Jesus gives boys and girls a lesson. Do you like to go to church? Do you love to visit God in His house? How often boys and girls go to church only when they must go. Sometimes they do not go even when they are sent. They play in the streets and even outside the church without going in. Jesus remained three days in the temple to teach little children and older people, too, that they should be glad to go to the house of God and remain there for some time in prayer.

Like the Boy Jesus, whom you see in this picture (show the picture, "Christ in the Temple,") you, too, ought to be glad to go to church and to stay there for some time. I spoke of this to you before. You made up your mind then that you would visit Jesus as often as you passed a church. Do this every day, if you can. When you have more time, stay a little longer with Jesus. Do not leave without asking Him to bless you and help you in your lessons. Ask Him to make you a good child, loving, kind and obedient as He was.

Practice:

1. I will gladly visit Jesus in church.
2. I will remain a little longer in church, if I have time.

"Lord, teach us to pray!"
Once when Jesus used to be
Living here like you and me
Good men asked Him this, and He
Taught them how to pray.
They were great big men, I know,
Couldn't say "Our Father," though;
But I've learned it all; and oh,
Listen while I pray.

L. M. Wallace.

26. THE SUFFERINGS AND DEATH OF OUR LORD

During the three years that Christ spent teaching the people and preaching to them, He did much good and worked many miracles. Do you know what a miracle is? A miracle is something so great that no one but God could work it. For instance, you learned from your Bible that one day Jesus changed water into wine. Can any one do that? If people want to make wine, they must have grapes or some other kind of fruit from which to make it; and then it takes a long time before it is wine. But in this miracle Jesus turned the water into wine all at once. He healed the sick, cured the lame and the blind, and even raised the dead to life. Now you would think that all the people would love Jesus for the good He did. But there were many who hated Him, because Jesus told the people what was wrong and what they must avoid to get to heaven, and some of these men, not willing to do what Jesus said, began to hate Him. They tried in every way to set also the other people against Him. Jesus knew all this, yet He was kind and gentle and kept on doing good. But the more good He did, the more these bad men hated Jesus.

You remember the twelve Apostles who helped Jesus to teach the people. These men were very poor and they were not learned. Most of them had been fishermen; but when Jesus called them they went at once and left everything to follow Him.

Judas Sells Our Lord

Now there was one among these Apostles, Judas by name, who was not following his conscience which told him he was doing wrong. Judas was a miser. Do you know what a miser is? Yes, a miser is a man who likes money so well that he does not use it, but keeps it and always tries to get more. A miser will do anything to get or keep money. This Apostle did not like it when people gave money to Jesus, for Jesus at once gave it to the poor. Judas was angry with Jesus because He gave all the money away. So what did he do? Dear children, you will hardly believe the horrible thing that this wicked man did. Judas went to the bad men who hated Jesus and asked them, "What will you give me if I deliver Jesus of Nazareth up to you?" Just think, Judas wanted to sell Jesus to these bad men! Can you think of anything more horrible? Judas loved money so much that he was willing to sell his Master to these wicked men who wished to put Him to death. Oh, I know you do not think anything so wicked possible. But that is what sin leads to.

See, dear children, Judas had this bad fault: he liked money too much. Had he listened to his conscience, Judas would never have done so monstrous a thing. But Judas did not listen to his conscience. He shut his heart to his good angel; he listened to the devil. You see now, how necessary it is for you to watch and be careful about little things. Judas did not all at once think of selling Jesus. He began by keeping back a little money here and a little there. He was not honest. When Jesus told him to give anything to the poor, Judas grumbled and kept some of it back. Then when Judas heard that the Jews wished to catch Jesus, the idea came into his mind of going to them and asking what they would give him if he told them where they could find Jesus.

Be careful, dear children, about your small faults. If these are not stopped, they will soon grow larger, and who knows what they may lead you to do? Pray often to Our Lord, asking Him never to let you act as Judas did. Ask our blessed Mother to help you to be true to Jesus always.

Practice:

1. I will listen to the voice of my conscience so that I may overcome my faults.

2. I will think of the horrible deed of Judas and will pray that I may never hurt Jesus by being so ungrateful.

> O! Sacred Cross! O Holy Tree!
>   On which my Blessed Savior died,
> Teach my poor heart the mystery
>   Of my Redeemer crucified.
> Cross of my Savior! Sacred Sign!
>   Lead from sin to grace divine.
> *William, Cardinal O'Connell.*

27. THE SIN OF JUDAS

Yesterday I spoke to you about Judas and the horrible sin he committed. You learned that Judas did not listen to his conscience when it told him not to love money so much. You saw how small faults grow until sometimes they lead to great sins. Now let us see to-day what Judas did after he talked with the men who wished to kill Jesus. You see these men were afraid to arrest Jesus in broad daylight for they feared the people would come to help Him. Jesus had cured many from sickness and had been kind and gentle with sinners. So when Judas came and said he could tell them where they might catch Jesus without the people knowing of it, these wicked men were very glad. They offered Judas thirty pieces of silver, which would be about nineteen dollars in our money. Just think, children, to sell our dear Lord for a small sum of money!

Then Judas told them where Jesus usually spent the night. He said the Apostles would be asleep and Jesus would be praying in the Garden of Olives. He himself would meet them there and show them where Jesus was. Then they asked him how they would know Jesus, and Judas answered, "Whomsoever I shall kiss, that is He; lay hold on Him and lead Him away carefully." Again, think what a dreadful thing Judas was going to do! He would kiss Jesus as a sign that He was the man they wanted. With a kiss he betrayed His Master. A kiss is a sign of great friendship and the wicked Judas used it as a sign to betray Jesus!

Do you think that men and women ever act as if they were friendly to Jesus and then turn traitor to Him? Yes, indeed, they do this when they receive Holy Communion with a mortal sin on their soul. Oh, yes; they are sometimes so careless about preparing for Holy Communion that they do not confess all their mortal sins. Perhaps they hide one sin that they are afraid to tell the priest. The devil tells them that the priest will scold them, or that he will think they are wicked. So they do not tell all the big sins and receive Jesus into their wicked hearts just as Judas gave Jesus over to the bad men who hated Him. Ask Jesus, dear children, never to let you do such a horrible deed. Examine your conscience carefully each night, and especially before going to confession, then you need never fear that you will act as Judas did.

Practice:
1. I will never go to bed without having examined my conscience well.
2. I will pray that I may never make a bad Communion.

> Jesus, hanging on the Cross,
>   Tell me, was it I?
> There are great big tear drops, Lord,
>   Did I make you cry?
> I have been a naughty child,
>   Naughty as can be;
> Now I am so sorry, Lord,
>   Won't you pardon me?

28. THE LAST SUPPER

Dear children: After Judas agreed to meet the Jews in the garden to show them where to find Jesus, he snatched up the money they gave him and put it into his purse. Then he went back to the place where Jesus and the other Apostles were. He hid the money carefully for he did not want any of them to know what he had done. But Jesus knew all that had happened. He tried to catch Judas' eye to make him sorry. But Judas kept his eyes turned away from Jesus. He did not want to look at his Master's face. Jesus would have forgiven him his dreadful sin, if he had only told Him that he was sorry. But the heart of Judas was like stone and he kept his secret to himself.

The Apostles now sat down to supper and Jesus spoke kindly to them about many things.

He told them that one of them was to betray Him that very night. He said this so that Judas might still have time to tell Jesus that he was sorry. The other Apostles were surprised when they heard this. They asked Our Lord, "Is it I, Lord?" But Judas was silent. He pretended that he did not know anything about it. Our Lord then told his Apostles that He was soon going to die and that this was to be His last supper with them. At this supper He blessed bread and wine and told them to eat and drink of it, for it was His Body and Blood. This was their first Communion.

Judas then went out of the room, for he wanted to get to the garden before Jesus and the other Apostles arrived there. He did not stay to make a thanksgiving. Often you see people running out of church almost as soon as they have received Holy Communion. These people do not stay to give thanks to Our Lord.

After a while Jesus left the supper room and went into a large garden filled with olive trees. The Apostles were very tired and they soon fell asleep. Jesus left them and walked away a little distance and then knelt down to pray. While he was praying, He saw before Him all the horrible sins that were ever committed or that would be committed till the end of the world. These sins pressed so heavily upon Him that He sweat blood. You know that when you are very much frightened your whole body becomes cold and water is pressed out of every pore of your skin. But Jesus' agony was so great that the very blood was forced through the veins and trickled to the ground. For three hours He prayed and suffered in this way. How our dear

"Is It I, O Lord?"

Lord must have prayed for us that night! He knew all the sins each one of us would ever commit. He asked His Heavenly Father not to punish us for them, but to punish Him. He prayed that He might not lose us His children through sin. Oh, if you only thought often of the suffering Jesus bore for you that night! How it would help to keep you from sin. Ask Jesus again and again to help you with His grace never to hurt Him again by sin.

When God comes down each day to dwell,
　With hearts He loves the most.

I wish I were the chalice fair,
　That holds the blood of Love,
When every flash lights holy prayer,
　Upon its way above.

I wish I were the little flower
　So near the Host's sweet face,
Or like the light that half an hour
　Burns on the shrine of grace.

THE LAST SUPPER

Practice:
1. I will think of the suffering of Jesus in the Garden and ask Him to give me the grace never again to hurt Him by sin.
2. I will thank Jesus for giving His Body and Blood in Holy Communion.

　　I wish I were the little key
　　　That locks Love's Captive in,
　　And lets Him out to go and free
　　　A sinful heart from sin.

　　I wish I were the little bell,
　　　That tinkles for the Host,

I wish I were the altar where
　As on His Mother's breast,
Christ nestles, like a child, fore'er
　In Eucharistic rest.

But oh! my God, I wish the most
　That my poor heart may be
A home all holy for each Host
　That comes in love to me.
　　　　　　　Father Abram Ryan.

29. JESUS IN THE HANDS OF HIS ENEMIES

During the three hours that Jesus prayed and suffered in the Garden, the Apostles were sleeping a short distance away. Jesus had to suffer all alone. When He came and found them sleeping, He said to them, "Could you not watch one hour with Me?" Then He told them to get ready, for the enemy was near. At midnight Judas came with a band of men carrying lanterns and clubs and ropes. Jesus went to meet them. Judas now went to Jesus and kissed Him. At this sign the men came up and roughly took hold of Jesus and dragged Him away. The

THE AGONY IN THE GARDEN

Apostles were frightened. They went away. And so Jesus was in the hands of His enemies, and the Apostles who had been His friends were not there. Do you not think that must have hurt our dear Lord very much? Here He was among His enemies who were anxious to kill Him. Where were now the brave Apostles, the men who had followed Jesus so gladly and so proudly when the people ran after Our Lord to make Him king?

See, dear children, what happened to Our Lord. There was God standing amidst these wicked men. Why did the angels not come down from heaven to help Him? Jesus did not wish to be freed from His enemies. He wished to suffer and to be put to death. And why did He wish to die? Jesus wished to die for us. He came upon the earth to save us. It was through bitter sufferings and a cruel death that He wished to open heaven for us again. You remember the promise made to Adam and Eve after they were driven from Paradise? God promised them a Redeemer. Jesus was the Redeemer. Jesus loved us so much that He desired to suffer everything and was ready to die a terrible death so that heaven would once more be open to mankind.

Dear children, think often about the sufferings of Jesus. When you consider that Jesus suffered so much to save your souls, how thankful you ought to show yourselves. You will do well to examine your conscience. Do you ever think of what Jesus did for you? Do you ever thank Him for coming into this world, a poor helpless little child? Do you thank Him for the example He has given you of living a poor life and being obedient to His parents for so many years? Do you try to please Him even in small things? Do you try to follow His example by being obedient, kind and unselfish as He was?

Think about these things to-day and offer Jesus your heart. Tell Him how sorry you are that you ever hurt Him by sin. Tell Him that you will try from now on to do everything you know He desires you to do. Thank Jesus every day for suffering so much for you.

Practice:

1. I will often think about what Jesus suffered for me.
2. I will tell Jesus how sorry I am that I hurt Him by my sins.

> For sins of mine that made Thee bleed,
> For selfishness with those in need,
> For all of wrong in word or deed,
>   My Jesus, mercy!
>
> For those who will not love Thee, Lord,
> Who wound Thy heart and hate Thy word,
> Whose mean acts pierce Thee as a sword,
>   My Jesus, mercy!

REVIEW

To the Teacher:—Try to inspire the children with a great devotion to Jesus suffering from the ingratitude of men. Make them see how painful it was to His Sacred Heart to be deserted by those to whom He had shown so much kindness. Lead the children to comfort our dear Lord by their love. Tell them they should often offer their little hearts to Him. Teach them the following prayer: "Jesus, how many drops of blood did You shed for me in the Garden? I know you saw my sins there. I wish I had never sinned. Please let me comfort You by loving You always."

30. THE SIGN OF THE CROSS

Although most children upon reaching the school age know how to make the sign of the cross, it would be well for the teacher to have the class make it several times in unison with her. She should make sure that all the pupils make the correct motions and pronounce the words clearly and with devotion. Teachers who have any difficulty in teaching their pupils the sign of the cross will find it helpful to adopt the method explained in detail in "The Catechists' Manual."

31. THE LESSON OF THE PASSION

I have often told you that Jesus came into this world to give us an example. What lesson does Jesus wish to teach us in His bitter sufferings on the night of His capture? Jesus wishes to teach us that we must bear patiently our little sufferings. People do not treat us as badly as we deserve. We have done so many things to hurt Jesus, we have disobeyed the law of God so often, that it is only just that we also should have to bear something for our sins. Jesus was God; He had done nothing but good to all. He healed the sick and helped the poor. He took pity on sinners and treated them with great gentleness. Yet he had to bear such great pains and sorrows. Should we not be willing to bear something for the love of Jesus when He bore so much for us? Let us try to remember this when anyone hurts us. How often you are hurt when one of your playmates leaves you to play with other children! You feel deeply hurt, do you not? You say, "I am not good enough for Mary any more. All right, when she wants me to play with her again, I will not do it." Boys have baseball teams. One side has a good player but the other side coaxes him away. Now if you were the captain of your team, you would feel hurt and perhaps call this boy a traitor, because he helps the other side to play. Perhaps you may even begin to fight on account of it. And Our Lord allowed Judas to betray Him to His bitterest enemies and He did not complain. Jesus was God; He could have caused all His enemies to have been struck dead on the spot, but He did not do it. He was willing to bear all for us. Try, then, in your quarrels, to think what a very small thing your trouble is compared to what Jesus had to endure. And Jesus was innocent, and you are not always free from fault.

Jesus Is Taken to Pilate

I have talked to you about some of the sufferings our dear Lord had to bear for our sins. I told you about the horrible sin of Judas in selling Our Lord to the wicked men who wished to put Him to death. I told you also of the agony Jesus suffered in the Garden when He sweat great drops of blood. Then about how Jesus was arrested and dragged by the soldiers from the Garden and how the Apostles became frightened and ran away, leaving Jesus alone in the hands of His enemies.

Jesus was now led to the Judge. This Judge was the Governor of the country. His name was Pontius Pilate. You say that name in the Apostles' Creed, "suffered under Pontius Pilate." The bad men wanted to force this Judge to put Jesus to death. But he would not do so, for he could find nothing wrong that Jesus had done. They dragged Him from one judge to another that night, giving Jesus no rest. Can you imagine how our dear Lord must have looked, when He was pulled along the streets by these cruel men? Remember that He sweat blood during the frightful agony in the Garden and that His clothes must have been sticky with it. Jesus had long hair and a beard such as the men wore in those days. The soldiers and the other wicked men pulled Jesus about not caring how much they made Him suffer.

His clothes were torn, His hair was tangled and His holy face was covered with dirt. These bad men spit in His face, they struck Him and laughed at Him and mocked Him in every way. What terrible sufferings Jesus had to bear that night! Think what pain and sorrow Jesus must have felt when He thought of His Apostles. One of them, Judas, sold Him to these bad men, the others ran away and left him alone. His dear Mother was not near Him. Not a friend did Jesus have by Him during that long night. Every one about Him during that long night hated Him and tried to show his hatred by making Him suffer the most horrible things.

Practice:
1. When my playmates leave me to play with others, I will not grow angry about it.
2. When someone hurts me, I will think of all Jesus had to bear, and will try to bear my sufferings patiently.

Dear Jesus, we shall make
A sweet bouquet for You,
Of all our thoughts and words
And everything we do.

The Little Flower's Love for her Parents, Sister M. Eleanore, C. S. C.

32. JESUS IS SCOURGED AND CROWNED WITH THORNS

Jesus was dragged from one place to another on the night He was arrested, and everywhere He was mocked and laughed at. By that time it was morning. Surely, one would think, now the people to whom Jesus had been so good will hear about His state and come to help Him. But what did happen? The people gathered in the streets to see and hear what was going on. The leaders of the Jewish people went among them and made them turn against Jesus and ask that the Judge should condemn Him to death. This frightened Pontius Pilate, for he was afraid of the people. To please them he ordered Jesus to be beaten with whips as if he had been a robber or a murderer. They dragged Our Lord away, tore off His clothes, tied Him to a post, and whipped Him so hard that the flesh was torn and the blood poured out. Jesus was bruised and cut from head to foot and His whole body was dripping with blood. During this dreadful scourging, as it is called, Jesus did not complain, but prayed for His enemies. Even while they hurt Him so cruelly, Jesus prayed for those who caused Him all these pains.

But the wicked men were not satisfied with beating Jesus till His whole body was covered

BEHOLD THE MAN!

with wounds. After this painful scourging, the soldiers led Him to another place and there they put a crown made of sharp thorns on His head. They pressed this crown deep into His head, so that the blood flowed freely. They next put an old purple cloak on His shoulders and made Him sit down. Then they knelt before Him and mocked Him saying, "Hail, King of the Jews!" Some of these wicked men struck Jesus on the head and in the face.

Bear Your Sufferings Patiently

My dear children, do you realize now how much Jesus loved you? Think of the sufferings He bore for you. The terrible scourging and the dreadful crowning with thorns were so painful that it is a wonder Jesus did not die at once. Still He did not complain. He prayed for those who hurt Him. He asked His Heavenly Father to forgive them. What a lesson for you, dear children. Do you forgive those who hurt you or who try to do you harm? Or do you try to get even with them by paying them back in the same way? Learn from Jesus to bear all insults patiently and freely forgive those who hurt you in any way. You will never have to bear what Jesus suffered. You are not called upon to lay down your life for Jesus as the martyrs did. Still you have many chances to bear small sufferings for Jesus. In your dealings with your parents, your teachers, your classmates and others, there will always be something that you do not like. Why not try to imitate Jesus by silently bearing these small troubles? Keep quiet about them. Tell no one but Jesus and He will help you to become a saint through the small trials and crosses He sends you now and then.

Practice:

1. When I have to suffer anything from others, I will try to bear it quietly and not complain.
2. If any one hurts me, I will pray for him.

> Dear Jesus, make me think of Thee
> Through all the busy day,
> That when I work and when I play,
> I may from sin keep free.

Little Flower's Love for the Holy Eucharist, Sister M. Eleanore, C. S. C.

33. PILATE CONDEMNS JESUS TO DEATH

After the dreadful scourging and crowning with thorns, Pilate showed Jesus to the people. He thought they would be moved to pity, if they saw Jesus now. But the leaders of the Jews had stirred up the people against Jesus. They forgot all the kindness Jesus had ever shown them. They were blinded by their hatred of Him and when they saw Jesus standing before them bleeding and crowned with thorns, instead of pitying Him, they shouted "Crucify Him!" This meant that they desired Him to be nailed to a cross. Could you imagine a more cruel punishment! To nail a person to a cross was a horrible torture. Only great robbers and murderers were crucified. So these wicked people wished to see Jesus nailed to a cross. They wished Him to suffer yet more. They were like wild beasts let loose. The more blood they saw, the more they longed for.

Pilate was a coward. I told you before, dear children, that when Jesus was first brought to Pilate, he found that Our Lord had done nothing wrong. But to please the Jewish leaders and because He was afraid of the people he had Jesus beaten with whips. Now the people wished Jesus to be nailed to the cross, and Pilate, being a coward, told the people to do as they liked with Jesus. See what it is to be a coward! Pilate's conscience told him that Jesus was a good man. He wished to free Jesus, but he was afraid the people would not like it. He did not listen to his conscience and so at last he gave up Jesus to be nailed to the cross.

Cowards Are Not Respected

Do you wish to be like Pilate? Surely not. Pilate was a coward, was he not? He knew Jesus was not a bad man. He knew Jesus was something more than a mere man. Pilate did not wish Jesus to teach him the truth. He shut his heart to the little voice that told him that he was doing wrong. He wished to please the people. He did not wish to lose his job. See what cowards are ready to do for what they think will make them happy! Do you think Pilate was happy after he gave Jesus to the Jews? Indeed he was not. Did the people like him better after he let them have their way? They did not, for some time later he had to give up his place and died in disgrace. That is what he gained by acting the coward. To-day the name of Pilate, like the name of Judas, is hated by all good people. Judas was a traitor, for he sold His best friend. Pilate was a coward, for he was afraid to do what he knew to be right.

People do not respect traitors and cowards. You will be better loved if you always do what you know to be right.

Practice:
1. When others laugh at me and make fun of me for doing right, I will ask Jesus to make me strong and not to let me be a coward like Pilate.
2. I will be faithful in keeping my promises to Jesus.

O Jesus, sweet Jesus, O Jesus Divine,
My life and my death unto Thee I resign;
Every action of mine shall Thy patronage claim
For whatever I do shall be done in Thy name.

34. JESUS ON THE WAY TO CALVARY

Now that the Jews had Jesus in their power, they did all they could to make Him suffer. They brought a heavy cross, laid it on His bleeding shoulders and forced Him to drag it through the streets. They made Him carry it up a hill. This hill was called Mount Calvary. Our dear Lord could hardly walk; He was weak and smarting from His many wounds. But most of all His Sacred Heart was sad because of the sins committed by the people. On his way to Calvary Jesus fell several times. Each time the cross fell heavily upon Him. The men beat Him cruelly and pulled Him up again. While on the way to the place where He was to be nailed to the cross, Jesus met His Blessed Mother. What great sorrow she must have felt when she saw her dear Son so terribly wounded and bleeding, with a heavy cross on His shoulders! How she longed to wipe the sweat and blood from His holy face! How she would have liked to help Him carry that heavy cross! But the rough men pushed her away. She followed Jesus on His way to Calvary and remained with Him to the end.

Will you not also have pity on the great sufferings of the dear Mother of Jesus? Do you remember what the holy man Simeon told her in the temple: "A sword shall pierce thy heart?" The sharp pain which Mary felt when she saw Jesus wounded and covered with sweat and blood did pierce her heart. You know, dear children, how it pains your dear mother when you are sick. Mother has no rest night or day as long as one of her children is suffering. So the Mother of Jesus suffered with Jesus. Ask the Blessed Mother to make you feel pity for the sufferings of Jesus. Promise her that you will always remember what Jesus suffered for you.

The Sorrowful Mother

The Death of Jesus

When Jesus reached the top of the hill, they pulled off his clothes and along came pieces of His flesh that had stuck to His garments. The blood started to flow again. They laid Him on the cross and nailed His hands and feet to it. Can you think of anything more cruel, dear children? These bad men took long nails and drove them through His hands and feet. The blood squirted into their faces and on their arms and hands, but these cruel men did not feel any pity. Jesus felt the pain very much. His Blessed Mother heard the blows of the hammer and it was as if they were striking her heart. Oh, what dreadful pain our dear Lord suffered! The nails held Jesus tight to the cross. What pain He felt again when they raised the cross and let it fall into the hole dug for it! The openings in His hands and feet were made bigger by the weight of His body. For three long

THE DEATH OF JESUS

hours Jesus hung on the cross. His Mother stood under it, but she could do nothing for Him. She had to listen to the mocking and laughing of the wicked Jews. Now they were glad they had Jesus out of their way. Now He could no longer tell them that they were wicked. He was dying on the cross.

Think of Mary standing for three hours under the cross watching every movement Jesus made. How she longed to help Him! If she could only give Him a drink! He was so thirsty. Blood filled His eyes; His hands and feet were bleeding. His whole body trembled with pain. Standing with Mary under the cross were Mary Magdalen and St. John, one of the Apostles. At last, Jesus cried out in a loud voice, "Father, into Thy hands I commend my spirit." His head fell on His breast. Jesus was dead.

Showing Our Love for Jesus Crucified

Now, dear children, see how much our divine Savior loved you, what sufferings He bore in order to save your souls. He could not have done more for you than give up His life. And such a death as He had! The most painful death any one can ever suffer! Do you wonder now why the martyrs were so glad to die for Jesus? Do you see now why the saints tried to lead such holy lives? Is there nothing that you can do to show Jesus that you love Him and that you are thankful to Him for what He suffered for you? Yes, there are many ways in which you can show your thankfulness to Jesus. You can show your love to Jesus crucified by obeying the commandments of God and of the Church, by loving His Blessed Mother and by being willing to suffer something for His sake. What can you suffer? Think of all the pains Jesus suffered. In His sacred head, His hands, His whole body, what great pains He bore! When you have a headache or a toothache or some other pain, think of Jesus hanging on the cross, and offer up your little pains to Him. If your pains were ever so great, Jesus suffered still more than you.

My dear children, there is much more I should like to tell about the sufferings of Jesus, but I shall have to wait till another day. Often look at your crucifix and tell Jesus how sorry you are that He had to suffer so much. Remember also that each time you commit sin, you are doing to Him what the wicked men did who crucified Him. You do not want to scourge Jesus, or strike Him, or mock Him, or nail Him to the cross, do you? Be careful, then, that you do not commit sin. Every time you sin you crucify Jesus again. Pray hard each day that you may keep from sin.

Practice:
1. I will keep a crucifix near me so that I may often think of the sufferings of Jesus.
2. I will ask the Blessed Mother to help me love Jesus so much that I shall never offend Him again by my sins.

>Dear Jesus, all I have to Thee I give;
>I am content if I for Thee may live.

The Little Flower's Love for her Parents, Sister M. Eleanore, C. S. C.

35. THE LESSONS OF THE CROSS

My dear children: You have been so attentive to me while I spoke to you of the sufferings and death of our dear Lord, that I know you will try to please Jesus by often thinking of what He did for you. We call the death of Jesus the Sacrifice of Calvary. Some of you may have been thinking that had you been in Jerusalem when Jesus was crucified, you would have done something to show that you loved Him. You are angry with the Apostles for leaving Jesus to suffer alone. You hate the wicked men for treating Jesus so cruelly. You despise the people for forgetting all that Jesus had done for them. Perhaps among those that called the loudest, "Crucify Him!" were some whom Jesus had cured. You would have made your way through the crowd and have stood near the cross with Mary. But you forget that you have a chance to show Jesus even now how much you grieve over His sufferings and death. The Apostles were frightened and ran away when Jesus was arrested. They were weak and cowardly. But after the death of Jesus when the Holy Ghost came down upon them they were filled with courage and were ready to suffer anything for Christ. All of them except St. John died a martyr's death. But how about your courage? Are you ever cowardly when asked to follow Jesus? Are you not sometimes ashamed to be obedient to your parents because some of your playmates may tease you about it? **When you are playing with your companions** and mother calls you to come home, do you not act as though you did not hear her, because the others may tease you? Examine your conscience and see how cowardly you act at times. But try now to follow the example of the Apostles and be brave. Do your duty no matter what it may cost you.

Our Sins Crucify Jesus Anew

You hate the wicked men for treating Jesus cruelly. What do your sins do to Jesus? Your sins crucify Jesus over again, that is, by committing sin you hurt Jesus as much as did these cruel men when they beat Him with whips and nailed Him to the cross. If you do not wish to be like these bad men, be careful to keep from committing sin.

You think the people in Jerusalem were very ungrateful, do you not? But how about the ingratitude you show to Jesus? The people whom Jesus helped, those whom he cured, and especially those whom he called back to life, certainly should have been grateful. Some of them no doubt were; but most of them forgot Jesus. Some of you may forget what Jesus has done for you. How many graces did not Jesus give you! From the very beginning of your life Jesus has given you graces without number. Count them if you can. You were born of good parents, you received Baptism and were made a child of God, you are sent to a Catholic school, you have the grace to go to confession and to receive Jesus in Holy Communion, and thousands of other graces. Are you grateful? Do you thank God for these graces? Or are you like the people of Jerusalem? Do you forget all Jesus has done for you as soon as the devil whispers something into your ear? Be careful, then, dear children lest, while you blame these wicked people, you yourself do the same evil thing.

Practice:
1. I will be patient when I must suffer any pain.
2. I will be grateful to Jesus for all He has done for me.

>Dear Jesus, take my heart and let it be
>A little holy altar just for Thee.

THE STATIONS OF THE CROSS

HOW TO MAKE THE STATIONS

You can say the Stations by yourself in a little while. Go to the altar steps. Kneel down, make the Sign of the Cross and say an Act of Contrition. Then go and *stand* in front of the first station. Make a genuflection and say: "We adore Thee, O Christ, and bless Thee. Because by Thy holy Cross Thou hast redeemed the world." Then *look* at it. Think of Jesus suffering for you. Be sorry for your sins that made Him suffer. Then go to the second and the following stations and do the same. However, at the twelfth station, instead of standing, *remain kneeling*. After you have gone to all the fourteen stations kneel down at the altar steps again and say one Our Father, Hail Mary, and Glory be for the intention of the Holy Father.

The Stations tell the story of Our Lord's passion. Each Station is one part of His sacred passion.

Jesus Is Condemned to Death

The First Station: We see Jesus before a judge. The Jews want Jesus put to death. The judge knows Jesus had not done wrong, but he is afraid of the people. So he says Jesus must be crucified.

Jesus Is Made to Carry His Cross

The Second Station: Our Lord has to carry His own cross up the hill on which He will be crucified. Soldiers take Him and put the cross on His shoulders.

Jesus Falls the First Time

The Third Station: Jesus falls under the cross. It is so heavy.

Jesus Meets His Blessed Mother

The Fourth Station: Jesus passes the place where the Blessed Virgin stands in the crowd waiting to see Him. They look at each other with great love and tenderness but do not speak.

Simon Helps to Carry the Cross

The Fifth Station: Jesus is getting so weak, the soldiers fear He will die on the way. They make a man named Simon help Him carry the cross.

Veronica Wipes the Face of Jesus

The Sixth Station: A Roman lady is in the crowd looking at Jesus. She runs out and dries the blood and sweat from His face and He thanks her by leaving a picture of His holy face on her veil.

Jesus Falls the Second Time

The Seventh Station: For a second time, Jesus falls under the weight of the cross.

Jesus Speaks to the Women of Jerusalem

The Eighth Station: Good women weep to see Jesus suffer so much. Jesus comforts them.

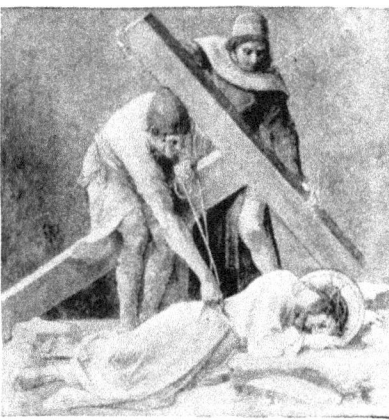

Jesus Falls the Third Time

The Ninth Station: Our Lord's strength is nearly gone. He falls again.

Jesus Is Stripped of His Garments

The Tenth Station: Jesus reaches the place where He is to be crucified. The soldiers tear His garments from Him, breaking open all the wounds on his body.

Jesus Is Nailed to the Cross

The Eleventh Station: They throw Jesus on the cross, and nail Him to it, with one nail through each hand, and another through each of His feet. Then they raise the cross, putting one end in the ground.

Jesus Dies on the Cross

The Twelfth Station: Jesus hangs on the cross for three hours, and then dies.

Jesus Is Taken from the Cross

The Thirteenth Station: His friends take Jesus down from the cross and put Him in the arms of His blessed Mother.

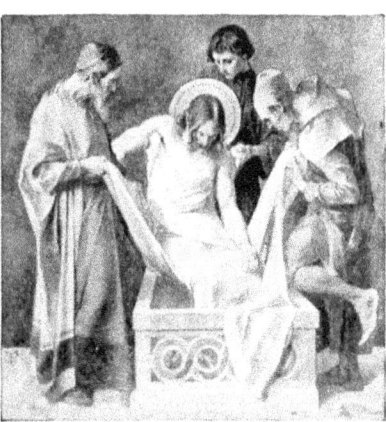

Jesus Is Laid in the Tomb

The Fourteenth Station: The same friends take him to a tomb which is inside of a great rock. They wrap Him in fine linen and bury Him.

36. THE WAY OF THE CROSS

To the Teacher:—*In the second grade, the teacher may find it expedient to teach the children the Way of the Cross. To do this most effectively, let the children bring cut-out pictures of the Stations, or, if they cannot procure these, let them use the pictures from illustrated catalogues. Paste these on heavy cardboard and arrange them on the sand table as suggested in the chapter on sand table projects. Some teachers mount large pictures of the Way of the Cross which they hang on the walls, low enough for the children to examine. These pictures are inexpensive. Another plan followed by some teachers is to let the children make Station Booklets. Pictures for these may be cut out of old magazines or catalogues, or complete sets may be purchased at little cost. If you have a large picture of the crucifixion, display it in a conspicuous part of the room during these talks on the Passion. An excellent help to teach children the "Way of the Cross" will be found in Father Finn's "Boys' and Girls' Prayer Book," pages 175-206. Cf. Bibliography, page 298.*

SECTION V

THE BLESSED SACRAMENT

1. THE SANCTUARY LAMP

When your mother took you to church when you were small, do you remember what it was that you noticed first? (You will receive a variety of answers. Some will say the windows, others the altar, still others the statues, pews. Some will remember the sanctuary lamp, the light before the altar.) Perhaps many of you wondered why a lamp is hanging before the altar. This lamp, my dear children, is kept burning day and night all the year round. It is never allowed to go out. Like the wonderful star that led the wise men to the crib, so this light leads to the altar of God, to the place where Jesus stays here on earth. The sanctuary lamp, as it is called, burns there before the altar to tell every one who comes into church that Jesus is truly there in the Tabernacle.

Dear children, you come to church almost every day, some of you a few times in the day. Do you ever notice the light burning there before the Tabernacle? Did it ever come to your mind that your heart ought to be like the sanctuary lamp, ever burning for the love of Jesus? At night time when it is dark in church, this light looks like a star. It is the bright star that points out to all the way to Jesus in His Tabernacle. This sanctuary lamp says to you, "Dear children, come to Jesus, come to Jesus."

Jesus is hidden in the little house on the altar. You have already learned the name of the little house. What is it called? Yes, it is called the Tabernacle. There is a small door to this Tabernacle, and behind it is the gold cup or ciborium in which the Blessed Sacrament is kept. When the Wise Men following the star came to the stable at Bethlehem, what did they find? Yes, they found the Baby Jesus, lying in a crib. So also when you come to go to church, and follow the sanctuary lamp, you will find Jesus in the Tabernacle. You cannot see Jesus as the Wise Men saw Him in Bethlehem; but Jesus is there as truly as He was in the stable at Bethlehem when they adored Him. Now He is in church under the form of bread. He lives in the Tabernacle and rests in a gold cup or ciborium. Sometimes the priest opens the Tabernacle and takes out the little white Host and puts it into a gold case called ostensorium. Then He raises it and blesses the people with it. This is called Benediction. Jesus is there in the white Host, really and truly, although you can see nothing but the Host.

When you come to church, look at the sanctuary lamp and think of it as the star of Bethlehem. Let it lead you to the Tabernacle where Jesus lives. Kneel before the Tabernacle and adore Jesus as the Wise Men did. Offer Him your heart. Tell Him to take it and make it like to His own. Ask Him to keep it ever pure, and never to let you soil it by sin. Say to Jesus, "Dear Jesus, I believe it is really You living in the Tabernacle. Come into my heart." Each time you see the sanctuary lamp, say,

"Dear Jesus, let me be like the light always burning for love of Thee."

Practice:
1. I will try to be like the light before the altar, and live for Jesus all day.
2. I will try to keep my heart pure, so that it may be a little Tabernacle for Jesus when He comes to me in Holy Communion.

> Jesus, Jesus, come to me;
> Oh, how much I long for Thee!
> Come Thou, of all friends the best,
> Take possession of my breast.

2. THE WISDOM OF A LITTLE GIRL

One day Florence was given a beautiful crucifix as a present. On the cross was a nice, though very heart-breaking, figure of the crucified Christ.

"Now, Florence," said her daddy, "to show me how pleased you are with the crucifix, you must tell me the difference between the figure of Jesus hanging on the cross here and the dazzling white Host the priest holds up for adoration during Mass."

Quickly came the answer—an answer that made daddy prouder than ever of his precious girlie, "When I look at the figure on my cross, daddy dear," she said, "I see Jesus and He is not there; and when I look up at the little white Host I do not see Jesus, but He is there."

"You darling!" said daddy, as he took her into his arms.

Tell Us Another, Winfrid Herbst, S. D. S.

> Lord Jesus, King of Paradise,
> Oh, keep me in Thy love;
> And guide me to that happy land,
> Of perfect rest above.
> *Father Faber.*

3. THE VERY GREATEST ACT OF LOVE

Now, dearest, I am going to tell you the sweetest story to be found in the whole wide world. Oh, yes; you have heard it often. Of course you have! But it never grows old; it never loses its charm. It's about the greatest act of love, about the greatest gift that was ever given to man, about the Holy Eucharist. You know what the Holy Eucharist is. Surely you do! If I were to ask you, you would tell me at once that it is the dear Sacrament which contains the Body and Blood, the Soul and Divinity of our Lord Jesus Christ, under the appearances of bread and wine.

You have many times heard how much Jesus loved us. You know how Adam and Eve, our first parents, shut the gates of heaven by their disobedience, so that no one could get in. When the loving Savior saw this, He was moved with compassion. He made up His mind to open those heavenly gates again. So he became Man. He came down to the earth, was born at Bethlehem of the Blessed Virgin Mary, lived at Nazareth, spent three years among the people, and then suffered and died upon the cross. You see, His Father had told Him that if He would do all this He would reopen for us the gates of heaven. So He came and did it. Wasn't that good of Him? Could any act of love be greater?

Yes; there was something greater still. And Jesus, Whose love for us, His dear children, is infinite, did that something more sublime. It was not enough for Him to die for us. True, He wanted to ascend to heaven and open its gates for us, but at the same time He wished to remain with us on earth; for it is His delight to be with the children of men. So He instituted the Most Holy Sacrament of the Altar in order that though leaving us, He might yet remain in our midst and give Himself often to each one of us. This is the very greatest act of love. Only God could have thought of anything like it.

It was on the night before he died, at the Last Supper, that Jesus gave us the priceless gift of His own Self. It happened in Jerusalem, in an upper chamber. The twelve Apostles were with Him. Imagine you see the room, with its lofty ceiling, its slender columns, its oriental tapestry. The Savior is seated at the table; around Him are the twelve. His garments are very poor, like those of the Apostles. But Oh! His face is so beautiful, so full of love. An atmosphere of infinite tenderness seems to surround Him. A heavenly gentleness fills the room.

And now Jesus takes bread in His **holy** and

adorable hands; He raises His eyes to heaven; He blesses the bread; breaks it, and gives it to His expectant Apostles. And Oh! how sweet are the words that fall from His divine lips. "Take ye and eat," He says. "This is My Body." Then He takes the wine and blesses it and gives it to them. And again sacred words break the hallowed stillness of the supper room. "Drink ye all of this," He says. "This is My Blood which shall be shed for the remission of sins. Do this for a commemoration of Me." Jesus has instituted the Holy Eucharist, Holy Communion, the Holy Mass. He has ordained His Apostles priests.

Look at those happy Apostles. They are kneeling around Him. They have received their First Holy Communion. What peace, what joy, what heavenly bliss fills their hearts! They had been filled with sadness at the thought that He would leave them; but now they know that He will abide with them forever; for He has instituted the Blessed Sacrament. It is the very greatest act of love.

Dare we, then, doubt the love of Christ for each one of us? Never! We must trust Him absolutely; we must come often to rest confidently in His Eucharistic arms. Jesus once said to a holy soul: "It is certain that a hundred sins offend Me more than one alone; but if this single sin is distrust of Me, it wounds My heart more than one hundred others, because distrust wounds My Heart to its innermost core. I love men so much!

Tell Us Another, Winfrid Herbst, S. D. S.

4. THE SACRED HEART OF JESUS

Dear children: The beautiful month of June is set aside to honor the Sacred Heart of Jesus. The Heart of Jesus is filled with love for all

THE APOSTLES RECEIVING THEIR FIRST HOLY COMMUNION

creatures. Why do we honor the Heart of Jesus? We speak of the Heart of Jesus, because the heart is the seat of love. When we want to show that we love a person much, we say we love him with our whole heart. For this reason we honor the Heart of Jesus. Jesus loves us so much that He has given the last drop of His Blood to save us. After his death on the cross, a cruel soldier pierced His holy Side with a lance. The Heart of Jesus was opened and water and blood flowed from it.

Have you ever seen a picture of the Sacred Heart? What did you see? Yes, you saw Jesus pointing to His Sacred Heart. By this is meant that if we wish to love Jesus and please Him, we must learn to know and love His Heart and all that it means to us. The Heart of Jesus is meek and humble. In that beautiful prayer which I taught you, "Jesus, meek and humble of Heart, make my heart like unto Thine," you ask to be meek and humble like Jesus. You have learned what it means to be meek and humble. The Heart of Jesus teaches you that to be praised by people is not the greatest thing to be desired. It is far better to be praised and

THE SACRED HEART OF JESUS

loved by God. Sometimes people make great mistakes; they praise a person for doing something which to them seems good, but which to God is wicked and sinful. How foolish it is to be pleased when others praise us for doing what we should not do!

What the Heart of Jesus Teaches Us

The Heart of Jesus is mild, that is, quiet and peaceful. Is your heart mild? Do you treat others gently? Do you not sometimes speak sharply to your companions and playmates? Are you rough in your actions? How often children burst out into anger when they do not get what they want, or when they cannot have everything their own way! Proud and vain children are not imitating Jesus. Jesus was meek and humble. When the bad men treated Him so cruelly He did not get angry with them. When they pulled Him about from place to place, He went with them meekly and calmly. He did not threaten them with eternal punishment. He could have struck them dead on the spot, but He wanted to bear insults in order to show us how we should act when we are mocked and insulted by others.

Try to have a great devotion to the Heart of Jesus. Jesus knows what children have to bear. He is willing to help you if you only ask Him. His Heart is filled with pity for your faults and failings, and He is ever ready to help you to become meek and humble. Often say the prayer, "Jesus, meek and humble of heart, make my heart like unto Thine." Try to think of the love the Heart of Jesus has for you. When you are tempted to do something wrong call on the Heart of Jesus to help you! "Heart of Jesus, help your little child!"

During this month, try to do something each day in honor of the Sacred Heart. Whatever you do, do it all for the honor and love of the Heart of Jesus. Offer all you do and say to the Sacred Heart and then one day when you come to die, Jesus will take you and keep you in His Heart, where you will have joy and rest forever. Ask the Sacred Heart of Jesus to bless your father and mother, your brothers and sisters, and your teachers and classmates. Ask the Heart of Jesus to help you with your lessons; ask Him to make you a good child, obedient, pure, gentle and kind. Never let a day pass without doing something to honor the Sacred Heart.

Practice:
1. Often in the day I will say a prayer to the Sacred Heart.
2. I will offer all I do to-day to the Sacred Heart of Jesus.

Heart of Jesus, I adore Thee;
Heart of Mary, I implore Thee;
Holy Joseph, pure and just,
In your aid I put my trust.

5. HONORING THE BLESSED SACRAMENT

Jesus is present on the altar in the Blessed Sacrament and remains there in the Tabernacle day and night. He lives among us. He is ever waiting for us to come to visit Him. He is ready to give us His graces and blessings. He looks at each one of us as we come into the church. He waits lovingly for us to ask Him for anything we need. Oh, what a great pleasure it ought to be for us to visit Jesus in the Tabernacle! When we are asleep, Jesus is still watching over us. He never sleeps. He never tires. But, oh, how often his Sacred Heart must feel sad and lonely! During how many hours of the day there is no one in church! And the lonely nights! No one thinks of Jesus, perhaps, all night long. And still Jesus remains on the altar. He loves us so much that He promised to remain with us till the end of the world.

How should you treat Jesus in the Most Holy Sacrament of the Altar? When you visit some one, you first bid him the time of the day. You say, "Good morning," or "Good afternoon." When you visit Jesus in the Tabernacle, you ought also to greet Him. Since Jesus is God, the right thing to do as soon as you enter the church is to get on your knees and adore Him. Which way should you turn? Towards the Tabernacle, of course. How little some children think what they are doing when they turn their backs to the altar when they kneel down? If they thought of Jesus living in the Tabernacle they would look towards it and then kneel down facing it. Children ought to be careful how they kneel down. In kneeling down, let your right knee touch the floor. We call this making a genuflection. Some boys and girls are very careless about making genuflections. Do you think they would be, if they thought of Jesus waiting for them in the Tabernacle and watching them as they kneel down?

When you kneel, make the sign of the cross and say, "Jesus, for Thee I live, Jesus for Thee I die, O Jesus, I am Thine in life and in death." Then enter your pew quietly and speak to Jesus. Do not sit down at once. Some children sit down as soon as they get into the pew. Do you not think that you ought to say something to Jesus first? You do not sit down as soon as you enter a house. When you think of Jesus present in the Tabernacle, you will not look around and talk or act in an unbecoming way. You are in God's own house; you ought to behave respectfully in His presence. As long as you are in church, do not forget that you are in the presence of Jesus. You have learned what you should say to Jesus when you are in church. Never let yourself be led to talk to others unless it is necessary.

Before leaving the church, you should bid Jesus "good-by"; this you do by genuflecting again. When you visit people, you surely do not run out of the house like an unmannerly child. Why, then, should you do it in church, in God's own house? Did you ever see children run out of church as if it were on fire? Do you think such children remembered where they were? Be careful not to be among those who run out of church. Walk out slowly and quietly. If you love Jesus, you will visit Him often in church. This would not take much time.

Jesus knows that you must go to school or that you ought to be at home. But you often pass the church during the day. How easy it would be to step in for just a few minutes and tell Jesus that you love Him. Sometimes you will find no one else in the church. Then you will be all alone with Jesus. All alone with Jesus! Think what that means! Jesus is there ready to listen to you; you can tell Him all your little troubles. How pleased He will be to hear you tell him that you love Him, that you are sorry that you ever hurt Him; that you wish to please Him more every day! And when you ask Him to help you, He will be ready to give you many graces and blessings.

Thank God every day for having given Himself to you in the Blessed Sacrament of the Altar. Visit Jesus often in the church. Receive Holy Communion as often as you are permitted. If you have not yet received your

First Holy Communion, ask Jesus to help you to prepare your heart for His coming. You will soon have this great happiness.

Practice:
1. I will be careful to greet Jesus when I go to church.
2. I will spend the time in church in talking to Jesus.

> The church is big, so dim, so still,
> Where Jesus stays all day,
> I think you must be lonesome, Lord.
> I'll slip inside and pray.

6. "WE DON'T TALK IN CHURCH!"

Alice was only a girlie. But she was very good. If she hadn't been I wouldn't be writing about her now.

One Sunday she knelt in church during Mass, saying her prayers from her little prayerbook. During the Holy Sacrifice a richly dressed lady came in and sat down at Alice's side. She was not a Catholic, so she did not kneel at all, but just sat and watched what was going on.

Everything that took place at the altar, the priest in his sacred vestments, that altar with its lights, the ceremonies, the altar boys in their cassocks and surplices, was strange to her. She was puzzled. Soon she became so curious that she bent over and whispered to Alice, asking her what it all meant. And now just see what a very good girl Alice was.

She wanted to be polite. So she took her pencil and wrote on the flyleaf of her prayerbook the words, "Please, we don't talk in church." This she showed to the lady.

Was the lady angry? No; and she did not say another word. But she thought to herself, "This church must be a holy place. It is not like our Protestant churches. There must be something sacred and wonderful about this religion. I'll have to find out more about it."

So she went to see a priest. Then she took instructions and became a Catholic.

Who made her a Catholic? Alice, by her good example and without saying a single word, preached the little sermon that did the great good work. And her reverence for the Holy Mass and the Blessed Sacrament prompted her to preach it.

Now, isn't it true that children can be God's apostles if they only want to?

Tell Us Another, Winfrid Herbst, S. D. S.

7. THE SAINTS AND THE BLESSED SACRAMENT

Dear children: Many times during the year you have been told to follow the example of the saints. The saints loved God above all things in this world. They tried to please Him in everything they did. They showed their love for Jesus in many ways. Some of them, like the martyrs, gave their lives for Jesus. They were killed for their love and faithfulness towards Him. Others, such as the saints in the wild deserts and in lonely caves, spent long hours each day in prayer and fasting. Others, again, served God in caring for the poor, the sick, the crippled, and the orphans. Others spent their lives in doing just ordinary things. But each and every one of them had a great devotion to Jesus in the Blessed Sacrament. Even as children, many of the saints showed such great love towards Jesus in the Blessed Sacrament, that it is no wonder they became so holy and pleasing to God.

Saint Imelda

I mentioned several of these saints to you before. Can any one name any saint who showed special love towards Jesus in the Blessed Sacrament? Yes, that is right, Blessed Imelda; St. Paschal Baylon, the Little Flower of Jesus. Little Imelda from her babyhood was very fond of talking to Jesus and Mary. She was a holy child; she seemed always to be among the angels. Often when she was playing with her little friends she would disappear. Then after searching for her for a while, people usually found her kneeling before a little altar which she had arranged in her room. When she was so small that she had to be carried, she liked nothing better than to be taken to church by her mother. Many children cry when they are in church, for they do not understand Who it is that lives there. But little Imelda, even as a small baby, knew that Jesus was in church. She watched the altar the whole time and never turned away from it. Her mother had trouble to take her away. As she grew older, she loved Jesus in the Blessed Sacrament more and spent much time before the altar. You remember how she died after receiving her first Holy Communion. What a beautiful example this dear saint is to you! Think how you can imitate her.

Saint Paschal Baylon

St. Paschal Baylon so loved the Blessed Sacrament that he, too, found it hard to go away from the altar. You remember how, while yet unable to walk, he crawled to church and there was found by his parents before the altar. He often ran away from his mother to go to church, and when, on account of the danger of being hurt in the streets, he was forbidden to go to church alone, he cried bitterly. Little Paschal never tired of speaking to Jesus while he was in church. When out in the fields with his sheep, he would turn to the place where he knew the Blessed Sacrament was kept and speak to Jesus. How often our boys could imitate this saintly boy! Many times you pass a church and you would have time to visit Jesus if you only thought of it. Instead of playing noisy games around the church and disturbing the people who are praying there, it would be better if you visited Jesus for a few minutes. Boys ought never pass a church without raising their caps to salute Jesus living there in the Blessed Sacrament.

The Little Flower of Jesus

Another saint we mentioned before is one who lived not many years ago, the Little Flower of Jesus, as she is called. She, too, had, even as a little child, a great devotion to Jesus in the Blessed Sacrament. One day she was out walking with her nurse. It was Sunday afternoon. Little Thérèse was not yet old enough to be obliged to hear Mass on Sundays, but the nurse took her to visit Jesus in church every day. On this Sunday afternoon it began to rain while they were out walking. They turned back to the house, but little Thérèse remembered that she had not yet visited Jesus that day. So she ran into the hall and grasped her hat and out into the rain she went. She did not bother about getting an umbrella. All she thought about was that she wanted to see Jesus in His church. The nurse went after her and brought her back into the house. Little Thérèse cried hard, for she said she had to go to church to visit Jesus. When you hear these stories of the saints, who even as very small children loved Jesus in the Blessed Sacrament and spent long hours before the Tabernacle, it surely ought to make you feel ashamed that you are so careless about visiting Jesus. Make up your minds now that you will try to visit Jesus oftener during the day.

But now, my dear children, you will have a fine chance to show how much you really love Jesus. Vacation is close at hand, and then you will not need to go to school for nine or ten weeks. Nor will you be able to go to church as often as before. Perhaps then you will forget all about Jesus in the Blessed Sacrament. Of course, you know that you must hear Mass on Sundays and holydays, but I am very much afraid that many of you will not think of Jesus lonely and watching for his dear little boys and girls who came so often to visit Him while they went to school. Will you leave Jesus all alone this summer? Or will you try to be faithful little friends? Do you think you could visit Jesus at least once a day in vacation? Of course, if you live far from the church and the way is dangerous, Jesus will not expect you to come to the church. But some of you live quite close to His church. Some of you may pass it several times in a day.

But whether or not you will be able to visit Jesus in the Tabernacle often during this summer, there is one thing I want to tell you. In the summer time, some of your parents take you away with them, where there is no church. Then they have to miss Holy Mass on Sundays. When you hear your parents make plans for the summer, be sure to remind them of getting a place near a church, so that all can go to Mass and receive Holy Communion often. You can do much good by reminding your parents of this. When you visit your relatives, find out as soon as you can where the church is, and visit Jesus in the Blessed Sacrament when you can.

Be very careful, then, dear children, how you spend your vacation. Do not forget Jesus in the Blessed Sacrament. He is there in the Tabernacle in the summer as well as during the other seasons of the year. It is never too hot or too cold for Jesus. Do not neglect to say your prayers. Oh, how sad it is to find that boys and girls who have been so good and pious all through the school-year forget during vacation everything they learned about prayers and loving God. Keep your heart free from sin. Watch with whom you go. Stay away from bad companions. Remember that Jesus is watching you. The Blessed Virgin, your Guardian Angel, and your Patron Saint are also watching you. Be just as obedient to your parents, just as kind and gentle with your brothers and sisters and your playmates as during the school year. Never forget your morning and evening prayers.

Think often of Jesus and place yourself in His Sacred Heart so that He may keep you free from all sin during this vacation. May God bless you, my dear little ones, and keep you safe and sound till school opens again!

Practice:
1. I will follow the saints in my devotion to Jesus in the Tabernacle.
2. I will often visit Jesus in the Tabernacle.

> I know who is hiding
> In the wee white Host.
> Jesus there is biding
> He whom I love most.
> *Father Faber.*

8. "I AM NOT POOR!"

It seems that nobody really likes to be poor, except those who are poor for Jesus' sake; and they like it because it makes them more like Him. Then, of course, in Him they have all riches. But not only they; all of us are rich in Him especially in Holy Communion. If we have Jesus, you know, we have God; and in God we have everything.

I remember there was a boy living near Vienna some time ago whose name was Godfrey. But he could no longer go to church and school; he could no longer run about in the free, fresh air with his companions; he was sick, very sick. And he would never get well again, the doctors had said. Poor little fellow!

Poor little fellow! I should say not! Listen. Do you hear the tinkling of that little bell? It announces the coming of Jesus in the Blessed Sacrament. God's priest is bringing Godfrey Holy Communion as Viaticum.

With eyes full of heavenly happiness the suffering boy receives His great God, the gentle Savior, Jesus. Then he closes his eyes in quiet, heartfelt prayer. He is one with God, his all. For more intimate is the union between the soul and Jesus in Holy Communion than that of two pieces of wax that have been melted together.

Some time later his mother arrived. She had been hastily called from far away, for her Godfrey was at a boarding school. With a mother's soft touch she placed her hand on the hot feverish brow of her darling boy, now dying—but dying in the arms of Jesus, where we all want to die. "My poor, poor boy!" the mother sobbed with breaking heart.

Godfrey heard. He opened his eyes. There was in them the light of that other and better world for which we live.

"Oh, mother dear," he whispered contentedly, "I am not poor. I am rich—O so rich! Mother, I have Jesus!"

> Come to me sweet Savior,
> Come to me and stay,
> For I love Thee, Jesus,
> More than I can say.

SECTION VI

THE BLESSED VIRGIN AND THE SAINTS

1. DEVOTION TO THE BLESSED VIRGIN

Next to our dear Lord and Savior, there is no one whom we should love and honor so much as Mary, the Mother of God. The Blessed Virgin Mary is truly the Mother of God. God loved her so much that He chose her to be, after Jesus, the highest being on earth. To be the Mother of God is surely a wonderful grace. And the Blessed Virgin Mary was so pure and holy that God chose her to be the Mother of the Redeemer.

Why the Blessed Virgin Is Honored So Highly

I have often spoken to you of loving and honoring the Mother of Jesus. Jesus Himself, although He was God, obeyed Mary in all things. He loved her dearly and showed her every honor. Now we cannot please Jesus better than by showing His Blessed Mother our love and honoring her as Jesus wishes us to honor her.

When some one speaks well of your mother and tells you that you have a good mother, you are pleased, are you not? Certainly. It pleases you to hear some one say good things about your mother. When your little friends come to your house to play, you are glad when they treat your mother with kindness and respect.

Jesus, too, is well pleased with those who love His Blessed Mother. Jesus wishes us also to look on the Blessed Virgin as our mother. When He hung bleeding upon the cross, He lovingly turned to St. John and said, "Son, behold thy Mother." Jesus meant by this that St. John was to look on Mary as His own mother. But Jesus thought also of the thousands of children who would come into the world after His death, and by the words He spoke to St. John, He gave to all of us Mary as our loving Mother. Therefore, love and honor the Blessed Virgin, dear children. She is your heavenly Mother. Your mother at home does everything she can to make you happy. Day and night she works for you. So also Mary, your heavenly Mother, shows at all times her great love for her faithful children.

St. Theresa's Love for the Blessed Virgin

The great St. Theresa lost her earthly mother when she was still very young. She knelt before the statue of the Blessed Virgin and said to Mary: "Now, that my dear mother has been taken away from me, I choose you as my mother. Be with me always; teach me especially how to love Jesus more." And when St. Theresa had any troubles, she knelt before the statue of the Blessed Virgin and told her needs to Mary. You know, of course, dear children, that the statue of the Blessed Virgin is not the Blessed Virgin, but only an image of her, just as you may have a photograph of your mother. You can talk to the picture as if you were speaking to the one whom it represents. So St. Theresa spoke to the statue as if the Blessed Mother were really there. The Blessed Mother, of course, could hear her prayers, for she is in heaven and Jesus has given her the power to hear the prayers of those who love her.

The surest way to get to heaven is through the Blessed Virgin. For this reason, she is called the "Gate of Heaven." This means that if you have a great devotion to Mary, if you try to love and honor her, you will always try to lead a good life, which is the way to heaven.

Remember, then, to think of Mary, the Mother of God, as your mother also. She is never tired of loving you and praying for you. She watches over you and obtains many great favors from Jesus for you. Do all you can to show this dear Mother that you love her and that you wish to be her child always. Love Jesus, her divine Son, and follow His example, and your dear heavenly Mother will look on you also as her child.

To show your love to our Blessed Mother and

to honor her in your home, ask your mother to-day to allow you to make a small altar in your room. Place a picture or a statue of the Blessed Virgin on it, and keep, if you can, some flowers before it. Say your prayers each day before your altar. Sometimes you might also bring other children to pray before this altar. Sing a hymn to the Blessed Virgin and in every way you can show her your love and devotion.

Practice:
1. I will to-day think of Mary as my dear heavenly Mother.
2. I will try to lead others also to love the Blessed Virgin.

> Holy Mary, Mother mild!
> O sweet, sweet, mother!
> Hear, O hear, thy feeble child,
> O sweet, sweet, mother!

2. MARY'S SPECIAL LOVE FOR CHILDREN

Almost all men and women love children. There are a few people who do not love them, either because they have never been with children, or because the children they know are cruel and wicked. You cannot blame some people for disliking children, because bad boys and girls tease and annoy them and make them suffer much on account of their mean and thoughtless actions.

But, as I said before, that is not usual. Most people love children. How much more reason have you to know that the Blessed Virgin has a special love for children. She loves them because they are still pure and innocent. She loves them because they love Jesus and try to please Him in all they do.

Now, if Mary so loves children that she takes a special interest in them and cares for them in a particular manner, it is only just and right that children ought to love and honor Mary more than all the other saints in heaven. You ought, then, do all you can to show your love for this dear Mother. Young as you are, you can show this by your thoughts, your words and your actions. Learn to follow the Blessed Virgin in her thoughts, words and actions, that so you may imitate her example. For if any one was pleasing to Jesus, it surely must have been His Blessed Mother. She was so holy that she never committed a single sin. Indeed, Mary was free even from original sin, as you learned long ago.

The best way for you to follow the Blessed Virgin is first to learn something about how she spent her days as a child and later as the Mother of Jesus. This will show you how you must act in order to please God Who was so greatly pleased with Mary that He selected her to be the Mother of His Son.

Practice:
1. To-day, I will ask the Blessed Virgin to help me to love Jesus more.
2. I will think of the love the Blessed Virgin has for me.

> Mother Mary! at thine altar,
> We thy little children kneel!
> With a faith that cannot falter,
> To thy goodness we appeal.
> We are seeking for a mother
> O'er the earth so waste and wide,
> And from His Cross our Brother
> Points to Mary by His side.
>
> Mother Mary! to thy keeping
> Soul and body we confide,
> Toiling, resting, waking, sleeping,
> To be ever at thy side;
> Cares that vex us, joys that please us,
> Life and death we trust to thee;
> Thou must make them all for Jesus;
> And for all eternity.
>
> *Father Faber.*

3. CHILDHOOD OF THE BLESSED VIRGIN

The parents of the Blessed Virgin were St. Joachim and St. Anne. They were pious people who served the Lord faithfully. They had one great sorrow, however; they had no children. They passed their days in prayer and good works. Day after day they asked God to send them a child, and at last God heard their prayers and sent them a lovely little girl. They named this child Mary. Mary's parents were not rich. They had to work for a living. They lived quietly and peacefully in their little home. How happy St. Anne must have been! Mary was so beautiful and at the same time so obedient, so sweet-tempered, so cheerful and kind that she never gave her Mother a moment's trouble.

THE BLESSED VIRGIN AND HER PARENTS

Before Mary was born her parents promised to give her to God. So while the little Mary was three years old, her parents took her to the temple and there they offered her to God. Although Mary was still so young, she understood quite well what that meant. It meant that she now gave herself entirely to God. She knew that God had done great things for her; so she was willing to give herself to Him, that He might do with her just as He liked. Can you imagine, my dear children, how the little child must have looked when she offered herself to God? With her hands folded, her face bright and happy, she went up the steps to the temple. Her parents watched her proudly, yet with not a little sadness. For they knew that they must leave their dear little child there in the temple. They thought of how sad and lonely their home would be without her.

And the little Mary, do you not think that she also felt sad at leaving her dear parents? Certainly Mary's heart must have been filled with sadness at parting from her good parents. But she knew that God would take care of her parents and console them.

See what a beautiful example the Blessed Virgin gives you here! As soon as she was old enough to understand what she was doing, she gave her heart and soul to God. It is true that most children do not understand things so early as Mary. When you were three years old you did not understand much about God and what you owed Him. But you are old enough now to understand what God wants you to do. He does not want you to leave your parents now to go to serve Him, but He does want you to give Him your heart. "My child, give me thy heart," Jesus says to you often. Are you willing to give your heart to Him? What does it mean to give your heart to Jesus? It means that you think and act only for Jesus; that you live for Him alone. Thus in all you do, in all you speak, think of pleasing Jesus. Please Him in everything and you will give your heart to God as the little Mary did when her parents took her to the temple.

Practice:

1. I will offer my heart to God to let Him do with it as He desires.
2. I will try to live only for God, by doing all for Him.

Mary, Mother of my God,
Be my mother fair,
Guard my little soul from sin,
Keep me in your care.

4. THE LIFE OF THE BLESSED VIRGIN IN THE TEMPLE

Yesterday you heard how the parents of Mary brought her to the temple when she was still very young. It must have caused them much sorrow to leave their only child and go home without her. But they knew she was in a good place and that God wished her to serve Him there. In those days when people promised their children to God, they took them to the temple at Jerusalem. This was a very large building, or rather, a group of buildings. I spoke of this temple when I told you about Jesus going there when He was twelve years old. In this temple there were pious men and women who educated the children brought there to serve God.

As Mary grew older she spent her time in prayer, work and study. She prayed especially that God might give her the grace to see the promised Redeemer, for she knew from her studies that He was soon to come into the world. Day after day she worked, making the beautiful garments the priests of the temple wore. With other little girls of her age she studied her lessons, which were chiefly learning the Sacred Scriptures. The Scriptures were the writings of holy men who had foretold the coming of the Savior. Mary also joined her companions in their games and plays. In many ways she was just an ordinary little girl. But she was so pure, so holy, so sweet and lovable that there was no other girl there quite like her.

Dear children, picture to yourselves the Blessed Virgin in the temple. There she was far from her dear parents, among strangers. Why was she away from her dear mother? Because her parents had made a promise to give her to God. Was Mary sad and peevish about leaving her home and living among strangers? No, indeed, she went gladly, for she knew she would be where God wanted her. What a lesson for you, my children. Are you also glad to go to the house of God, when God wants you to be there? Do you like to go to church? Or do you belong to those children who find all sorts of excuses to get out of going to church? None of you are expected to stay in church always; you will be there only a short time. Can you not try to imitate the Blessed Virgin by loving to go to church for holy Mass, for Benediction, or to make a short visit to Jesus? Try to-day to follow the example the Blessed Virgin gave you and please God by gladly going to church when you can.

Practice:
1. I will try to go to church when I can.
2. I will offer to God all I do to-day and ask Him to take my heart and make it pure and holy.

Though many things I soon forget,
This one thing holds its place,
May I learn it as a little child,
"Hail Mary, full of grace."

Petals of a Little Flower, trans. by Susan L. Emery.

REVIEW

To the Teacher:—*Devotion to the Blessed Virgin always appeals to little children. Therefore, do all in your power to cultivate in the hearts of your pupils a true and sincere devotion to our Blessed Mother. Strive to induce them to look upon Mary as their model in everything. Appeal especially to the little girls to imitate the purity, the charity, the gentleness of Mary. Remind them occasionally to ask themselves frequently: "What would the Blessed Virgin do in my place now? How did she treat her companions? How did she do her work? Did the Blessed Virgin complain when she was asked to do something she did not like to do?"*

To help to foster greater devotion to Mary, erect a little altar on which a statue of the Blessed Virgin is placed. Permit the children to decorate it. Teach them that the small sacrifices they make are like beautiful flowers offered to their heavenly Mother. Teach them how to make small sacrifices, for instance, to curb their tongues, to refrain from an unkind word or deed; to do a kind act; to be more obedient at home; to live peaceably with others.

During the day call attention to the loving care Mary exercises over her children and so inspire them to ask Mary's help when they find their lessons hard or when they are tempted to evil. Remember that the more childlike and sincere a devotion you can instill into the tender hearts of the children at this age, the more solidly and fervently the love of our Blessed Mother will flourish in their hearts in later years.

> Mary—our comfort and hope—
> O may that word be given,
> To be the last we sigh on earth—
> The first we breathe in heaven.
> *Adelaide A. Proctor.*

5. THE BLESSED VIRGIN OUR MODEL

The Blessed Virgin was the most beautiful of all children, Jesus alone excepted. This was as it should be. Mary was to be the Mother

THE IMMACULATE CONCEPTION

of God. God, therefore, made Mary the loveliest being who ever lived or ever would live. When speaking to you of the beautiful temple in Jerusalem, I probably did not mention that it was most richly built and decorated. Nothing was too good to be used in this temple. All the ornaments were of gold and other precious metals. Did you ever notice at holy Mass that the sacred vessels used by the priest are of gold? The vestments the priest wears when saying holy Mass are richly made, and everything about the Tabernacle is of the finest material. Again I say, this is as it should be. Nothing is too good or too expensive for Our Lord. In the same way, since Mary was to be the Mother of God, it was only right that she should be the purest and most holy being on earth. Long ago you learned that God kept Mary free from even original sin. We call this her Immaculate Conception.

On account of her great virtue Mary is your model in everything. She did everything she had to do in the best way. What do I mean when I say Mary is your model? When I wish you to learn to write a letter or a word, what do I do? I first write it on the blackboard or on paper for you. Then you watch how I do it, and after this you look at what I have written and try to copy it.

Each time you make a letter or write a word you look at mine to see how nearly correct you have copied it. My letter or word is your model. Just in the same way, you ought to use the Blessed Virgin as your model. You do not expect to copy the letter or word I made for you just as well as I did; for you feel mine ought to be better, since I am much older than you, and have written so many of these letters and words before. So it is with copying the virtues of the Blessed Virgin. You cannot expect to be just as pure, holy, obedient, gentle and kind as the Blessed Virgin was, for God gave her special graces; but by copying her, you may be sure that you are learning to do all these things in the way God desires you to do them.

To follow the example of the Blessed Virgin, you must often think about her. It will not be hard for you to know how she did her work, for you can easily picture to yourself how she did everything in the most perfect way. Your conscience will tell you plainly how you should obey father and mother; how you should treat your brothers and sisters, how you should keep yourself pure in thought, word, and action. If you follow your conscience, you will be sure to be on the road to heaven. Learn to imitate the Blessed Virgin in your daily life and you may be sure, dear children, that in this way you will become more and more pleasing to God. Ask the Blessed Virgin to help you to become a good child. Ask her to help you to get rid of your bad habits and faults. Pray to her often to make you pure and pious. Never forget to pray to her every time you need help. Mary, like a good mother, will gladly help you, if, like her, you do all you can to prepare your heart for Jesus.

Practice:
1. I will be obedient to-day as I know the Blessed Virgin was.
2. I will to-day keep my heart free from all sinful thoughts in imitation of the Blessed Virgin who was so pure.

> At morn, at noon, at twilight dim,
> Maria, Thou hast heard my hymn.
> In joy and in woe, in good and ill,
> Mother of God, be with me still.
>
> *Edgar Allan Poe.*

6. MARY'S PURITY

To follow the Blessed Virgin in her virtues you must, as I said yesterday, know what it was that made her so pleasing to God. One of the greatest graces the Blessed Virgin received from God was that of purity. Purity is cleanliness of heart and soul. It was on account of her immaculate purity that she was selected to be the Mother of God. Mary was so pure that not even the slightest stain of sin was on her soul.

One of the first things, then, that you should imitate is the purity of the Blessed Virgin.

How can you do this? First, by keeping your heart clean, that is, by keeping it free from sin. Telling lies, saying unkind words, thinking bad thoughts—all these soil the heart. But above all you must keep your soul free from those sins which would make you especially displeasing to God; I mean bad thoughts, words and actions. Never say or do anything that you would not like to say or do before your Guardian Angel, or when your mother is near you. Listen to the voice of your conscience. It will warn you when you are in danger of doing anything to soil the purity of your soul. Keep your heart clean; never let anything bad or wicked get into it. To keep your heart clean and free from evil, be careful with whom you go. Do not play with children who speak of bad things. Never let any one tempt you to do an action which you know is sinful. Run away at once when you are with those who are not careful about what they say.

Pray every day to the Blessed Virgin and ask her to help you to lead a pure and holy life. For this intention say every day, as long as you live, three Hail Marys, in order to receive the grace of always keeping yourself pure. Often say, "Dear Mother Mary, keep my heart free from sin." Never go to bed without asking your heavenly Mother to keep your heart and soul for Jesus.

Practice:
1. I will often say to-day, "O Mary, conceived without sin, pray for us who have recourse to thee."
2. I will watch over my speech to-day that nothing I say may stain my soul.

> Dear Mother Mary,
>   As we kneel,
>   To thy goodness
>   We appeal.
>
> Guard us, dear Mother,
>   Through the day,
>   In all our work
>   And all our play.
>
> When darkness comes
>   The day to hide,
>   May we still feel thee
>   Close beside.

7. HUMILITY OF THE BLESSED VIRGIN

Another virtue that the Blessed Virgin possessed was that of humility. Humility means being humble, and being humble means to know ourselves as we really are in God's sight. When we are humble we will not think ourselves better than others, even when we know that we are prettier, have more money, or wear better clothes. These things should not make a person proud.

Take a lesson from the Blessed Virgin. As

you learned before, she was the loveliest being God ever created. Was she proud on account of her beauty? Oh, no! She praised God for giving her such wonderful graces, but she never for a moment thought herself better than others. She was obedient to her parents, kind and gentle to her companions, pure and holy in all her actions. Did she ever look down on her little friends in the temple and brag about anything she had? Sometimes we find children vain about their pretty faces or good clothes! Some children brag about what they have at home, their toys, their fine house, and other things. These things are nothing to be proud of; rather should such children thank God for letting them enjoy these gifts.

The Gifts of God Should Not Make Us Proud

Other children look down on their classmates because they have more talents, can learn and understand their lessons better. Again I say such children have no reason to be proud, for a good mind is the gift of God. Perhaps they are not making the best use of the talents God has given them. If God has given you talents to learn, He wants you to use the talents. If you are lazy and do not study your lessons, God will not be pleased with you. If God has not given you many talents, He will be quite satisfied if you make good use of what He has given to you.

Never be vain, then, because you are more beautiful than others; do not think yourself better because you wear finer clothing, have richer parents or more talents than your companions. These things do not count before God.

Do you not think, dear children, that if God looked upon riches, a fine house, pretty clothes, and fine food as wonderful gifts, He would have given the Blessed Virgin all these things? Would He not have given her the finest home to live in, rich and beautiful clothes to wear, servants to wait on her, and everything that would help to make her life easy and comfortable? Instead He gave her the most wonderful gifts of the heart and mind, and in great humility she thanked God for all. To show her gratitude she made use of her many graces to live a life of great holiness and purity; and so she became worthy to be made the Mother of God.

Try then, dear children, to imitate the Blessed Virgin in her humility. Although you are still small, many of you have perhaps sometimes allowed yourselves to feel proud about what you thought made you better than your playmates. True, it is not being proud to know that God has given you many good qualities, but you should thank God for these. You ought never on that account think yourself better than others. Ask the Blessed Virgin to help you to be humble so that you may in this way please Jesus and become more like Him.

Practice:

1. I will not think myself better than others on account of my talents or other gifts.
2. I will often say this prayer: "Jesus, meek and humble of heart, make my heart like unto Thine."

> "Hail Mary," lo, it rings
>   Through ages on;
> "Hail Mary," it shall sound,
>   Till time is done.
>   *Adelaide A. Proctor.*

8. KINDNESS OF THE BLESSED VIRGIN

Although God had given Mary more graces than to all other human beings, Mary was not proud of them. Nor did she ever think herself better than any one else. She lived quietly and peacefully with her companions. She never thought of putting herself above them, of telling them that she knew better than they how to do things. She never quarrelled with any one. Most often when children quarrel it is because one of them wants to show that he knows what is best or that he is the strongest. Of course, that is being proud. Some children cannot bear it if others get ahead of them in any way. When this happens, they try by all kinds of mean, sly acts to beat the others. It is right, of course, to try to get ahead in your lessons. It is even quite well for you to try to beat your schoolmates, but it is not right, when they get ahead of you, to say that they cheated. It is not right for you to try by dishonest means to beat them. Some children are so proud that they will do almost anything to win. This is not imitating the Blessed Virgin.

The Blessed Virgin was also kind and gentle to all. You can imagine that among the girls in the temple there were some who did not always treat their companions politely. Just as in school there are children who are unkind and even rough in their manners, so there were also among her companions some with whom it was hard to get along. Now, how do you think the Blessed Virgin treated these girls? Did she treat them roughly also? Did she speak unkindly to them? Did she try to keep away from those whose ways did not please her? You cannot imagine the Blessed Virgin doing any of these things, can you? Why not? Because you know that she was kindness and gentleness itself. You know that she was always kind and loving towards all.

It is not easy, I know, for you to get along well with some children. Some boys and girls are rough; they are ever ready to quarrel. Learn to be as kind and gentle to these as you know the Blessed Virgin would be if she were here. Be ready to do a kind act for them. Show them that you love them. Treat them as you would wish them to treat you. Remember that if you wish to show our Blessed Mother that you love her, you must learn to act as she did in all she had to do. Remember that she gave you an example that you must follow if you wish to please her.

Show your love and devotion to Mary, then, dear children, by copying her kindness and gentleness. Treat all with whom you live kindly for the love of your heavenly Mother. Mary will reward you for this by helping you to love Jesus more every day. Often ask her to help you. Say to her, "Dear Mother Mary, help me to be humble; help me to be kind and gentle as you were."

Practice:
1. To show my dear Mother Mary that I love her, I will treat my classmates kindly to-day.
2. I will not be rough in my manners towards my playmates to-day.

Mother Mary, keep my soul
Pure from every sin,
So my little Lord will smile
When He enters in.

REVIEW

My dear children:

The Blessed Virgin is a good and kind Mother. She loves you so much that she is willing to help you in every way. She wishes you to come to her, to visit her altar in church, to pray before her statue or picture at home. She asks you to tell her your little troubles. She will take you to Jesus.

Do you remember how Blessed Herman Joseph went to pray at her altar every day? And how our Blessed Mother helped him? She was so pleased with the little boy's devotion, that she stooped down to receive the apple he offered her. All the saints had a great devotion to the Blessed Virgin. Many of them gave their whole lives to teaching others to love her.

In the life of the Little Flower, St. Thérèse, we read that when she was yet quite small she lost her mother. Her mother died when Thérèse was about four years old. When she was ten years old, she became so ill that everyone thought she was going to die. Her sisters prayed before a statue of the Blessed Virgin which was in the room where Thérèse lay. All at once the statue seemed to become alive and looked so sweetly at the sick girl that it seemed as if heaven itself were opened. Thérèse became well and ever after thanked the Blessed Virgin by loving her dearly and giving herself entirely to Jesus.

All the saints had a great love for Mary. It was she who helped them to become saints. My dear children, try always to show a great love to the Mother of God. Do something in her honor every day. Never let a single day pass without having imitated one or other of her virtues. Especially follow her in her purity and never let anything bad soil your heart. Visit her in church, pray to her before your little altar, ask her to bless you and to keep you for Jesus.

Do this, dear children, not only during the beautiful month of May. Do it always. Do it every day of your lives. Have special devotion to our Blessed Mother on her feasts and on those other days especially set aside to honor her. One day of every week, Saturday, is her day. Likewise two months of every year, May and October, are for her special honor. The Church has many prayers and devotions in her honor and as you grow older you will learn them. Offer yourself, body and soul, to your Blessed Mother in heaven and you may be sure that one day you will live with her divine Son Jesus. Pray every day, "O Mary, my Mother, make me thy child."

> Mother of Mercy, day by day
>   My love of thee grows more and more;
> Thy gifts are strewn upon my way,
>   Like sands upon the great sea-shore.
>
> Get me the grace to love thee more;
>   Jesus will give if thou wilt plead;
> And, Mother! when life's cares are o'er,
>   Oh, I shall love thee then indeed!
>
> Jesus, when His three hours were run,
>   Bequeathed thee from the cross to me;
> And, oh, how can I love thy Son,
>   Sweet Mother, if I love not thee?
>
> *Father Faber.*

9. DEVOTION TO THE SAINTS

My dear children, you know that on the first day of November the Church celebrates the feast of All Saints. Many people spend the evening before this great feast in parading the streets and doing all sorts of silly things. They say they are celebrating Halloween. But very few of them know what Halloween means. You remember what I told you about Halloween. Halloween means the "Eve of All Saints."

You have often heard me speak about loving and honoring the saints. What do we mean by this? The saints of God are the special friends of God. Now, when you have a little friend you want others to be kind to your friend and you are pleased when others like him also. So it is with God. The more we honor His friends the more we please God.

What Is a Saint?

A saint is a person who is holy; and as sanctifying grace makes one holy, all who are in sanctifying grace are holy. But usually, when we speak about saints we mean the souls in heaven. All of us hope to be in heaven some day. It is for this that we are on this earth. You remember the question in the catechism, "Why did God make you?" And the answer, "God made me to know Him, to love Him, and to serve Him in this world, and to be happy with Him forever in the next world." By the next world we mean heaven. You see then, dear children, that God expects each one of us one day to live with Him and His saints in that beautiful place called heaven.

We Do Not Adore the Saints

The saints in heaven do not need our help, but their prayers for us are very powerful with God. Since the saints are such dear friends of God, we ask them to intercede for us with God, for He will not refuse the prayers of His special friends. We do not adore the saints. We adore God alone, but we honor the great men and women whom God Himself honors. God likes us to honor His saints and have them plead for us. God grants us many favors through the saints which we might not have received, if we had asked alone. You have heard father and mother say they are going to pray to St. Anthony for something; or they are saying prayers to St. Joseph. When someone at home is ill, mother tells you to pray to the Blessed Virgin. Now, what does it mean to pray to the saints?

What the Saints Do for Us

When we pray to the saints we ask their help and prayer. We know that the saints can hear us, because they are with God, Who lets them know what takes place on earth. How do we know the saints will help us? The saints will help us, because they are members of the same Church and because they are our brothers and sisters. God is our Father, the Blessed Virgin our mother, and the saints and angels are our brothers and sisters. We are like one big family where all try to help one another.

Practice:

1. I will think of the saints to-day as often I can.

2. I will try to learn something more about the saints.

> Do your best, your very best,
> And do it every day;
> Little boys and little girls,
> That's the wisest way.

10. HONOR DUE TO SAINTS

We honor the Blessed Virgin more than any other saint, because she is the Mother of God. The Blessed Virgin is greater and higher than all others, except God alone. Since she is the Mother of God, she is the most perfect and the most powerful of all creatures. For this reason, you should do all you can to foster a great devotion to the Blessed Virgin. Mary is also your Mother. If you ask her to help you, she will, like a good mother, come to your aid. Above all try to please the great Mother of God by keeping your heart free from sin. In this way you will become a special friend of the Blessed Virgin and she will help you and protect you every day of your life.

How We Honor the Saints

We can honor the saints in many ways. We can ask their help and prayers; we can honor them by celebrating their feasts; by venerating their statues and pictures, by bearing their name, by singing hymns in their honor, and most of all by trying to live as they lived. Now we shall see how little boys and girls can honor the saints.

First: You can ask their help and prayers. Even little children need help from the saints. Many things happen in your lives which are hard to bear. For example, there is a little girl whose mother has been ill a long time. No one seems to be able to help her. The doctor comes every day and gives the mother medicine. But that does not help much. Or perhaps the family is even too poor to have a doctor. The poor sick mother suffers much pain. The little girl would like to help her mother, but she does not know what she can do. Little children cannot do very much, but they can pray. So this little girl can pray to the Blessed Mother. She can ask this loving Mother to ask Jesus to make her mother well again.

Many times, also, boys and girls need help to make them good children. For some it is very hard to obey. Other children get angry very quickly and quarrel with their playmates. Still other boys and girls often say bad words or do evil deeds. They would like to get rid of these faults and bad habits, but they are not strong enough to fight the temptations. You also need help from the saints. You have many faults and bad habits that you would like to get rid of. Suppose you ask the saints to help you. They were once as small as you. They had to fight hard, too, to overcome their bad habits. So they will be glad to help others to fight against sinful thoughts, words and deeds. See what powerful help we can obtain by praying to the saints! Resolve to pray every day that the saints of God may help you to gain heaven.

Practice:
1. I will honor the Blessed Virgin to-day by being obedient to my mother.
2. I will ask the saints to help to make me a good child to-day.

> The boys and girls who do their best,
> Their best will better grow,
> But those who slight their daily tasks,
> They let the better go.

11. CELEBRATING THE FEASTS OF SAINTS

Another way to honor the saints is to celebrate their feasts. You have learned that every day we celebrate the feast of some particular saint or saints. But there are so many saints in heaven that we can not celebrate their feasts one by one. So the Church has set aside one day in the year on which we think of all the saints. We call this feast "All Saints Day." This is a great feast. That is why all Catholics must go to church to hear Mass on this day. Every day we are put in mind of some special saint. That is why we paste pictures on our calendar in school on some days. As little children cannot remember the names of so many saints, we pick out only the names of the greatest saints or of those that have a special interest for children. Some of these saints were very young when they died. Blessed Imelda was only about eleven years old. St. Agnes died at the age of fourteen. She died a martyr's death. St. Thérèse, or the Little Flower, as she is commonly known, even while only a small child loved God so dearly that He soon called her to heaven. I shall tell you many interesting stories of these dear saints during this year. If you are attentive you will learn how these saints, who once were boys and girls like you, became such great friends of God and were rewarded by Him for the pains they took to please Him.

The saints are worthy of our love and respect because they are God's special friends. By their holy lives they have won for themselves this great honor. What made the saints so holy? The saints were people like ourselves. Once they were little boys and girls like you. In fact, many of the saints in heaven are children who lived holy lives on earth and when they died, although they were yet only children, were rewarded by God by being taken to heaven. Some of the saints, when they were as old as you are now, showed that they wanted to become great saints and did everything they could to please God. Blessed Herman Joseph, about whom you will learn more later, used to spend much of his free time in church praying. He had a special devotion to the Blessed Virgin. He told her all his troubles. Herman's parents were poor, and the little boy often had to go barefooted, even in cold weather. Once, when he told the Blessed Virgin about this she spoke to him and commanded him to lift up a certain stone and there he would find money with which to buy shoes.

Blessed Imelda was a young girl about eleven years old when she died. While still very young, little Imelda loved to visit the church. She had one great desire. She longed to receive Jesus in Holy Communion. In those days little boys and girls were not permitted to receive Holy Communion until they were at least about twelve years old. Imelda used to look at the tabernacle and then she would tell Jesus how much she longed to receive Him into her heart. One day, while the Sisters with whom she stayed, were receiving Holy Communion, one of the little white hosts, which you know is Jesus, left the hands of the priest, flew to Imelda and remained in the air above her head. Little Imelda was kneeling in her place, praying so devoutly that Jesus might come to her, that God heard her prayer. The priest left the altar, went to Imelda and gave her Holy Communion. Imelda was so happy, that when the sisters came to call her after a while, they found her dead. She had died of joy.

Practice:

1. I will, like Blessed Herman Joseph, visit the statue of the Blessed Virgin to-day.
2. I will ask Blessed Imelda to pray for me that I also may receive Jesus into my heart in a worthy Communion.

> Am I growing better?
> Teacher, can you say
> I am growing better—
> Better every day?

12. A BOY SAINT

During the year I shall tell you many other stories about the saints and what they did to show their love for Jesus and His Blessed Mother. Now I shall relate to you just one more example.

In a far-away land there lived a little boy named Paschal Baylon. That is a very odd name, is it not? When Paschal was so small that he could scarcely lisp the names of father and mother, he was already able to pronounce the holy names of "Jesus" and "Mary." These were the first words his good mother taught him. It was a pleasure to see him make the sign of the cross and fold his tiny hands in prayer. One fine Sunday morning when Paschal was not yet two years old, his mother carried him to church. When the priest raised the Sacred Host at Elevation, the little child did not take his eyes off it. During the whole Mass, his eyes never wandered from the altar. From this time on, little Paschal felt a great devotion towards the Blessed Sacrament and every chance he had, he visited Jesus in His tabernacle.

THE BLESSED VIRGIN AND THE SAINTS

One day, while Paschal was still very young, he could not be found anywhere. His father and mother searched high and low but Paschal was not to be seen. They were very much troubled and went to their neighbors to ask their help in searching for him. The poor mother ran through the streets crying out, "Have you seen our little Paschal? He has left home and we do not know what has become of him. O goodness! Suppose the gypsies should have stolen him!"

The gypsies were people who often stole little children and carried them away. But no one had seen little Paschal. After hours of searching, the mother suddenly felt herself impelled to go to church. How great was her joy and happiness when she found the child lying on the altar steps, his bright blue eyes fixed on the tabernacle and so earnestly gazing upon it that he did not notice his mother coming near him. He had crawled on hands and feet to church, for he was still too small to stand upright and walk. Just think of it, dear children, a little child to crawl to church! This little boy grew to be a great saint. He is known for his great devotion to Jesus in the Blessed Sacrament.

Now, my dear children, I see you were all very much interested in these stories. You will learn many beautiful things about the saints of God while you go to school. You see that to be a saint is not so very hard after all. By keeping the commandments of God and by trying to live as you know Jesus and His Blessed Mother would like you to live, you will also one day become saints. Keep your souls free from sin, or if you have committed a sin, make it clean again by a good confession, and you will be a saint.

Try to-day to think often: "I want to be a saint." Ask Jesus to make you a saint. Ask the Blessed Virgin to help you to become holy. Pray to your Guardian Angel that He may protect you from all sin so that you may one day be with him in heaven. Do not forget to ask your patron saint to protect you in a special manner. Your father and mother gave you the name of a saint in order that you might have some special saint in heaven who would pray for you and whose example you might follow.

Practice:
1. I will often say to myself to-day: "I want to be a saint."
2. I will pray to my patron saint to-day and I will try to learn something about his life so that I may follow his example.

> Children, for your parents' love,
> Give them honor due;
> Let your care their solace prove.
> He who sees you from above
> Shall brightly smile on you.

REVIEW

As usual we recall the principal points of the week's morning talks. Impress upon the children that God wishes them to become saints. Proceed as follows: Let us honor and love the saints in heaven, for by doing this we shall honor and love God. Often remember that God wishes you also to become saints, for that is the reason why He called you to be Catholic boys and girls. You can become a saint if you really want to. All the holy men and women now in heaven, all those whom we honor as saints of God, were once boys and girls like you. One of the main reasons why you attend a Catholic school is that you may learn how to live so that one day you may be taken to heaven, there to be happy forever in the presence of God and in the company of the saints and angels.

Resolve to learn all you can about the lives of the saints, especially your patron saint. Try to please your holy patron by doing all you can to keep the commandments of God and by imitating your patron saint as well as you can. When you are older and able to read, try to get books that tell you about the saints. Ask your mother to tell you about the life of your patron saint. Ask her to tell you stories about the saints. You will like to hear them over and over again, for I am sure you will be delighted to know what God's friends have done to please Him so that you may follow their example and also become one of His very dear friends.

To help you become a saint promise to do the following: To receive Holy Communion often. (If the children have not yet received Holy Communion, teach them to make a Spiritual

Communion.) Frequently during the day say, "My Jesus, all for Thee!"

13. PROTECTED BY AN ANGEL

In a certain city there is a narrow street—so very narrow that one man could almost reach across from side to side. In this street there stood, some years ago, an old, rickety wall that threatened to fall at any time. It happened one day that a woman was passing through this street, leading a little girl of five by the hand. When they had come to within a few paces of the wall the child stopped, and stared before her. Her mother called out to her: "Come on, dear. What ails you?"

But the child remained as if rooted to the spot, and did not stir.

"Why, what's the matter? Come on," repeated the mother, in a tone of some vexation.

But lo! suddenly there was a fearful crash, and the clouds of dust filled the air. The old wall had fallen; and if the mother and child had gone only a few steps further, they would have probably been crushed.

Pale as death with fright, the mother snatched up her child and ran toward home. There she knelt down with the little one before a crucifix, and thanked God with an overflowing heart for their preservation. Then she again asked the child what caused her to stop in the middle of the street. The latter replied by asking:

"Didn't you see anything, mamma?"

"See what, dear?"

"Oh, that beautiful man, all white, with a long bright dress! He stood right in front of me, so that I could not go on."

When the mother heard this a shudder of holy fear ran through her. She took up her child and kissed her, with tears in her eyes saying:

"O happy child! It must have been your Good Angel you saw. Thank him with all your heart, and never forget what you owe to him."

> Dear Angel! ever at my side,
> How loving must thou be,
> To leave thy home in heaven to guide
> A little child like me!
>
> Thy beautiful and shining face
> I see not, though so near.
> The sweetness of thy soft, low voice
> I am too deaf to hear.
>
> Yes, when I pray, thou prayest too;
> Thy prayer is all for me.
> But when I sleep, thou sleepest not,
> But watchest patiently.
>
> *Father Faber.*

SECTION VII

THE CHILD APOSTOLATE

1. LITTLE APOSTLES

When Jesus was going about the country teaching the people how to get to heaven, He was helped by twelve men. These twelve men were called the Apostles. (At this point the children might read pages 25, etc., of "Our First Communion," by Rev. W. R. Kelly, treating of Our Lord and His Apostles). These Apostles were to do the work of Jesus after He ascended to heaven. Can any of you name an Apostle? The Apostles followed Our Lord wherever he went. All day long they helped Him. They stayed with Him at night and did whatever they could to make the people love and follow Jesus. These men were to teach others to know and to love and to serve Him with all their hearts. Did you ever think that you, too, could be an apostle? I hear you say, "How can I be an apostle? I cannot preach or teach." Yes, my dear children, you can be an apostle. You may not be able to preach as the priests do, or teach as the Sisters are doing. You can preach and teach in another way. But you say, "How can I do this?" I shall tell you how.

Good Example Teaches Others

One day St. Francis, of whom I spoke to you many times, asked one of his Brothers to go with him to the city to preach. The Brother agreed, and they set out. After walking through the city for some time, St. Francis returned home. During the whole time not a word was spoken. When they reached home, the Brother asked St. Francis: "When are we going to preach?" St. Francis answered, "We did preach." But the Brother showed surprise and said, "When did we preach?" Then St. Francis said, "When we passed through the city with downcast eyes we preached to the people, for those who saw us were made to love God more by our conduct."

So you see one way to be an apostle is to give a good example to others. People know that you are Catholic children when they see you coming out of a Catholic school. You do not give a good example when you run noisily out of the building, while shouting and pushing one another. When you talk back to mother, you are not giving a good example to your brothers and sisters. Your conduct in school, on the street, on the playground and wherever you go is seen by others. If it is good, you will lead others to be good also, for they will know that it is your love for God that makes you good.

Think in how many ways you can be an apostle and try to remember that you can do more good by example than if you were able to preach or teach.

Practice:

1. I will watch over my conduct to-day so as to give a good example to my playmates.
2. I will be respectful towards my parents and teachers in order to lead others to be respectful towards them.

> A little child may have a loving heart,
>   Most dear and sweet,
>   And willing feet.
>
> A little child may have a happy hand,
>   Full of kind deeds,
>   For any needs.
>
> A little child may have a gentle voice,
>   And pleasant tongue,
>   For every one.

2. UNSELFISHNESS OF THE LITTLE APOSTLES

You cannot be an apostle if you are selfish. Selfishness is a mean fault. You are selfish when you keep everything to yourself and are not willing to share what you have with others. Selfishness is not fair. There is nothing you can do without the help of others. You need the help of others from morning till night. You receive from others the best they have. Your father and mother give you so many things that it would take a long time to count them all. In school your teacher helps you to learn what she has learned. Others help you by working in the field, others by making clothes, still others by digging in mines, and so on, till you find that if you were not helped by others you would starve and die a miserable death.

You cannot say then to others, "I don't need you," for you do need help from them. Just as you need help, it is necessary for you to give help. Here is where so many children make mistakes. They are ever ready to take from others, but are very unwilling to give help. This is selfishness.

Now if you wish to help others, if you want to do good to others, you must become "Little Apostles." You cannot be an apostle if you are selfish. You must, therefore, avoid selfishness. You must be willing to share as much as you can the good things you have. Now what good things have you that you may share with others? You have so many good things at home, in school and in the world outside that it is easy for you to find something which you can share with others. I have many times spoken to you about sharing your toys and books and other things with your brothers and sisters. Of course, I do not mean that you must allow them to use them roughly or break your toys and tear your books. You know very well what I mean, do you not?

Sharing with Others the Gifts Received from God

But sharing these things is not the only way of being apostles. Indeed, that is only a very little part of being an apostle. You must give to others some of the good things you have received from God. For example, God gave you the grace of being baptized, of being reared by Catholic parents to be good Catholic children. You have the grace to know Jesus, His Blessed Mother, the angels and the saints. You have learned much about heaven and the joys and happiness which you will one day find there. Here are some wonderful gifts you can share with others. If you wish to be an apostle, you must learn to give others a chance to know about the goodness and mercy of God and the way they can reach Him. But I shall tell you more about this later.

Practice:

1. To-day I will share my good things with others.
2. I will be careful to give a good example to my playmates.

> Daughter of the Father!
> Lady kind and sweet!
> Lead us to our Father;
> Leave us at His feet.
>
> Jesus! hear Thy children
> From Thy throne above;
> Give us love of Mary
> As Thou wouldst have us love.
> *Father Faber.*

3. GRATITUDE OF LITTLE APOSTLES

God has given you many graces and blessings. In return for all these He expects you to show your thankfulness by doing His holy will and by doing all you can to make others love Him and serve Him faithfully. It might be well for you to think again of some of the graces and blessings you have received from God. We easily forget what we owe to God and we live on thoughtlessly from day to day without ever so much as thinking that God gave us our life and that He has the power to take it from us when He wishes.

The greatest grace you received was the one that made you children of God. What grace is that? Baptism. Through Baptism you were cleaned from original sin and made children of God. Without Baptism you would never be able to enter heaven. What a wonderful gift of God Baptism is! How you should thank God for it. The next great gift God gave you and the most wonderful of all is the Blessed Sacrament. What a truly wonderful gift it is! Jesus is present day and night in the Tabernacle. In Holy Communion He gives Himself to you as your food. His sacred Body and Blood strengthen you on your way to heaven. Is not this something for which you ought to be very thankful? Then there is the Sacrament of Penance or as we usually call it, confession. When your soul is stained by sin, it is made pure and clean once more if you make a good confession. How good God is to you! He knows that it is very hard to live in this world without committing sin, so He has given you many helps to aid you to fight against sin. In confession and Holy Communion you have wonderful helps. How thankful also you ought to be that you can visit Jesus in the Blessed Sacrament, that you can speak to Him as often as you wish, that you can ask Him to help you to lead a good life.

Many Graces and Blessings

Besides these graces you have many others; among them I might mention the great blessing you have in your good parents. God gave you good Catholic parents whose whole life is spent in working for you and doing all they can to make you a good Catholic child and a useful citizen. They send you to a Catholic school so that you might learn about God and how to serve Him best. In school you have the opportunity of learning many beautiful things about the Blessed Virgin, the Mother of God. How many lovely things you have learned about the angels, especially your Guardian Angels! How delightful for you to know that day and night one of God's messengers is watching over you! And then the friendship of the saints in heaven and their interest in you, is not that also a great grace? Truly, dear children, if you only remembered these gifts of God and thought about them more frequently, how much more holy your life would be!

But I started out to tell you why you ought to be apostles. It is not enough to be thankful to God for all the blessings He has given to you. What more can you do? When you have a very dear friend, a friend who is very good to you, a friend who loves you much and does all he can to please you, a friend who wishes you to be happy and contented, you talk about him to your companions and playmates, do you not? You tell every one how good and kind this friend is to you, what he has given you, what he does for you. You are pleased when others admire your friend. You are happy to know that your playmates also love your friend and think well of him. Is this not true?

God is your best friend, is He not? He is good and kind to you, and no one else, not even your dear parents, love you as much as He. Should you not also try to get others to love Him? What can you do to make others know and love Him? Small as you are, you can do much to lead others to love him. If you loved God as much as you ought, would you not want others also to know and to love Him? Would you not want others to know how good He is? Would you not be pleased to see that your parents, relatives and companions also loved and served God?

Do you know now why you ought to be little apostles? Do you think you ought to be satisfied that you yourself know, love and serve Him without wishing that every one else in the world should also know, love and serve Him? To-day think over the many reasons there are why you should be an apostle and then it will not be very difficult for you to begin at once to work for the honor and glory of God.

Practice:
1. I will think often to-day about all that God has done for me.
2. I will ask God to give me the grace to help others to love and serve Him better.

> Lord Jesus, King of Paradise,
> Oh, keep me in Thy love,
> And guide me to that happy land
> Of perfect rest above.
> *Father Faber.*

4. HOW TO BE LITTLE APOSTLES

To-day I shall speak to you about how you can be little apostles. I am sure you will be surprised to learn that this is easy. Nothing hard is required of you. If you wish to be a little follower of Jesus and one of His apostles, you can begin right in your own home. You have no idea how much good children can do in their homes. Father and mother are always interested in their children, and so when a child loves Jesus very much he will speak of Jesus at home and tell father and mother all he learned about Him that day. So also the child will be glad to tell at home what he heard about the dear Blessed Mother, and the angels and the saints. He will tell his parents how all can please God by living good lives, by keeping the commandments and by often receiving Jesus in Holy Communion. Parents are pleased when they notice that their child has been so attentive. Perhaps your parents will take a greater interest in their prayers and go to church on week-days because you have been telling them about the great blessings Jesus gives those that come to visit Him in His Tabernacle. Do you see how much good you can do? Is not this being an apostle?

The Boy Apostle

Once there was a little boy whose father never went to church. Day after day he went to work and in the evening when he came home he was too tired to listen to his boy tell him about school. This made the little boy very sad, for he loved his father dearly and wanted to tell him about his First Communion which he would soon receive. A day or two before his First Communion, the little boy came running home joyfully to his mother to tell her how happy he was because he had just made his first confession. That evening, the father was more tired than usual, and after supper he sat in the rocking chair to read his paper. Our little boy waited for a while, then he quietly crept up to his father's chair and smiling pleasantly said to him: "Papa, O Papa, I've some good news to tell you."

The father looked up from his paper and seeing the boy looking so happy, asked him: "Well, what is the news?"

"Papa, I've been to confession to-day, and oh, I'm so happy! And Papa, you know

Father Brown said I am allowed to receive Jesus in my heart next Sunday. Won't that be fine?"

"That surely is good news," said the father.

"Papa, I want you to give me something for my First Communion," said the boy. "I don't want any money. You can give me something better than that."

"What is it then?" asked the father.

"Please, papa, will you go to Mass with mamma and me on Sunday and receive Holy Communion? It would make me so happy."

The man was quiet for a minute and then said, "Yes, my child, I shall give you that joy. I want to thank God, too, for having given me such a good boy."

This little boy was a real apostle. Do you think his father would have gone to church, if he had not asked him? See what good children can do!

Father and mother often have many troubles. You can help them with your prayers; you can ask God to help your parents. Think over to-day what you can do to help your parents to love God better and to get to heaven.

Practice:
1. I will pray for my parents that God may give them the grace to get to heaven.
2. I will try by my good example to lead my parents to love God more.

> How sweet it is to feel, dear Lord
>   That thou wilt surely see
> Each work, or thought, or act of mine
>   That may be done for thee!

REVIEW

Review the morning talks and the subject of the little apostles. Let the children tell you in how many ways they can be little apostles at home. Dwell at some length on the influence children have over their parents. Encourage them to tell their parents the stories they heard in school about God and the saints.

> My God! how wonderful Thou art!
>   Thy Majesty, how bright!
> How beautiful Thy mercy-seat
>   In depths of burning light!

> Yet I may love Thee, too, O Lord,
>   Almighty as Thou art,
> For Thou hast stooped to ask of me
>   The love of my poor heart.

> No earthly father loves like Thee,
>   No mother half so mild
> Bears and forbears, as Thou hast done
>   With me, Thy sinful child.
> Father Faber.

5. LITTLE MISSIONARIES

Many missionary priests, brothers and sisters leave their homes each year to work in China, Africa and other heathen countries. These missionaries save thousands of souls. You are too young to go away from home, but you can be apostles and missionaries even if you cannot go to countries far away from here. You can be little missionaries in your own home, in school, and wherever you may happen to be. (The reading by the children of the story, "The New Apostle" in "Our Sacraments," by Rev. W. R. Kelly, page 108, etc., will be found helpful here.)

People love children. Your parents love you dearly and would do anything to please you. So it ought not be hard to be a little missionary to your parents, for they will gladly listen to you when you speak to them of God. Suppose you talk about God and His angels and saints, to your grandparents, to your uncles and aunts when they visit you. Show them your pictures, the little books you have made. They will be pleased to listen to you and maybe you can get them to love Jesus more and to serve Him better.

But there are also others to whom you can be apostles and missionaries. In your neighborhood there are many children; some of these may not know about Jesus and His blessed Mother. Perhaps all they know about God is to use His holy name in the wrong way. What a fine chance this is for you to be a missionary! In your play you may sometimes be able to say a word about holy things and tell your companions how wrong it is to use the name of God in the wrong way. You can speak of Jesus' love for us; how He loved to be with children. You can show your companions your pictures and explain their meaning to them.

Many children do not know that they have a Guardian Angel. Speak to these children about the angels. Tell them they are sent by God to watch over His children. Oh! how many beautiful things you can talk about to your playmates! Think how pleased Jesus will be with you, if you do this. Sometimes you can also tell the stories you heard in school. Perhaps a little girl does not go to your school and did not hear these stories. She may go home and tell them to some other children and these will learn something more about Jesus and the saints. And what an apostle you will have been! How pleased Jesus will be with His little helper! Try to see in how many ways you can make your playmates think and speak of Jesus. In your plays and games remember that you can do much good by keeping in mind holy thoughts. This will help to keep you from committing sin and will also make you happier.

Practice:

1. In my games with my playmates to-day I will try to tell them of something of God and His saints.
2. If possible, I will speak of the Guardian Angel to my playmates.

> Sweet Saviour, bless us ere we go;
> Thy words into our minds instil;
> And make our lukewarm hearts to glow
> With lowly love and fervent will.

6. BOYS AS MISSIONARIES

What I said yesterday was meant particularly for the girls. Boys can also be little missionaries, and I believe they have more chances for being so than girls. Let us now see how they may be little missionaries. When several boys are together they usually grow rough and quarrelsome and before long, if there is one among them who does not know how to keep down his temper, a fight is started. Here is a chance for the little missionary to step in. Often he will be able to stop a fight by telling those that are fighting that it is wrong, or by trying to keep on playing or by starting another game. Sometimes the boys that are watching make those that fight keep it up. Some boys are always glad to see others quarrel. Sometimes they start the trouble by daring a boy to whip another one. This is not being an apostle. If you wish to do the right thing you will try to do what you can to stop a fight and if you cannot stop it, you will walk away and show that you do not like it. If all the boys in this class would do that, there would be very few fights about the school or on the playground.

Another chance to be apostles is when you hear boys of your age using bad words, cursing or swearing. Here again the best way to show that you do not like it is by trying to stop this kind of talk. If the boys are older than you, it will be better for you to walk away at once. Your playmates will soon notice that you do not like to hear such talk and they will respect you for your courage. At the same time you are an apostle, for some of the boys will see that their conduct is wrong and that they are displeasing God by doing such wicked things.

There are many other ways in which boys can help their friends to get to heaven. I spoke to you about setting a good example. When your classmates see you are reverent and well-behaved in church, when they see that you are attentive in school, careful about keeping the rules, kind, and polite to others, they will follow your example. See, my dear boys, what fine missionaries you can be right here among your classmates. You can save many souls by praying for them; you can help many to live better lives by giving a good example. A good boy is like an apostle preaching to others and teaching them to know and love God.

Thank God every day that He has called you to be His little apostles. Ask Him to make you love Him more and more every day so that you can bring souls to Him. Ask Jesus to help you be apostles all through your lives. Ask Him especially to give you the grace of giving yourself to Him entirely, and, if it be His holy will, to let you one day be a priest working for the salvation of souls.

Practice:
1. I will pray that God will help me to know how I can win others for Jesus.
2. I will do what I can to keep others from committing sin.

7. KIND CHILDREN ARE LITTLE MISSIONARIES

All through the day you can do much to help others to love God more and to serve Him better. One other way to help is to be patient with the faults of others. You may have to live with children who are cross and ill-mannered, or you may live in a neighborhood where the children are rude and use bad words. You may visit your little cousins and find them selfish and impolite. You may meet people who are rough in their ways and have no respect for God or the saints. What can you do? You can be patient. You can be quiet and not begin to quarrel with the children with whom you live. You can try to be peaceful with those who like to quarrel. You can show that you do not like to listen to bad words, and best of all, if you find that you cannot do anything to stop this kind of conduct, you can pray for these children and ask God to give them the grace to know that they are displeasing Him and to help them to be better. Scolding about them or speaking of their faults to others will not help.

Remember that you also have many faults which others must bear patiently. You cannot expect other children to be better than you yourself are; if you find it so hard to be good, others also find it so. Therefore, it is better for you to try to be yourself what you would like your friends and playmates to be. If you cannot make yourself be obedient, kind and polite, surely you cannot expect that you can make others so.

Good Example Leads Others to Do Good

After all, the best way for you to try to lead others to love God more is to show by your example what a Catholic child should be. If you are always obedient to your parents at home, then your brothers and sisters will copy your example. If you treat your playmates kindly and if you try to be peaceful with all, you will not have to tell others what they should do. They will see your conduct and will try to imitate you. If others see you behave well in church, on the street and everywhere, it will not take long for them to notice this and they will be led to do as you are doing.

Remember what I told you about St. Francis; you do not need to open your mouth to preach a sermon. Your behavior is a sermon to all who see you. Try, then, above all things to do what you know a good child ought to do. Try to act in a way that you know Jesus would like to have you act. Try to follow His example, that others seeing in you a little follower of Jesus, may learn through you how to please Him and to love Him more and more each day. In this way you will be a real apostle and will help Jesus to save many souls.

Practice:
1. I will not get angry when others do not please me.
2. I will ask Jesus to let me follow His example in all I do.

> All things bright and beautiful,
>   All creatures great and small,
> All things wise and wonderful—
>   The Lord God made them all.
>
> Each little flower that opens,
>   Each little bird that sings—
> He made their glowing colors,
>   He made their tiny wings.
>
> The purple-headed mountain,
>   The river running by,
> The morning and the sunset,
>   That lighteth up the sky.

8. THE APOSTOLATE OF PRAYER

There is still another way in which you can show that you are true missionaries of Jesus, and it is a way which you can follow each day, in every place and with every one. It is to pray for others. You must pray for one another. Our Lord Himself taught us a beautiful prayer. How our Lord taught the "Our Father" to the Apostles is beautifully told by Rev. W. R. Kelly in "Our First Communion," page 25. (Cf. Bibliography, page 299.) Do you notice that in this prayer we say "*Our* Father" not "*My* Father"? By this He meant to teach us that we all are children of one Father Who is in heaven. Now for whom must you pray? First of all, of course, for your dear parents. Ask God to bless

OUR LORD TEACHING APOSTLES TO PRAY

your father and mother and give them the grace they need to make their boys and girls good Catholics. Ask God to keep them well and strong for many years. Then pray for your brothers and sisters. Pray for your grandparents and other relatives. Next you must pray for your teachers. Ask God to bless them and give them the strength to teach little children to know Him, to love and serve Him. Pray also for your classmates that they may live as good Catholic boys and girls should live.

In your prayers, do not forget the Pope, the Bishops and Priests. The Pope needs your prayers, and little children can help him much by asking God to give him the grace to lead his people to God. Pray especially for your Priests. Pray for the Priest to whom you go to confession. Ask God to help him to lead many souls to heaven. The Holy Souls in purgatory also need your prayers. Who knows but that some one whom you love dearly, is with them.

Perhaps there are children in this room whose father and mother are dead. How much you should pray for them! Pray for the dying. Every day thousands upon thousands of people die. Many of these die suddenly; they fall dead, or are run down by automobiles. How many people are living in mortal sin, who, if suddenly called out of life, would be lost forever. Pray that God may give every sinner the grace of being sorry for his sins before he dies. Think what graces you would receive if by your prayers even one soul would be saved from hell. Pray for those in mortal sin. Pray especially for those children who are tempted to commit their first mortal sin. Ask God to keep them from it.

In your prayers also remember the sick, the crippled, those in trouble, the orphans, the poor, especially those who do not know that to be poor and afflicted is a sign that God loves them.

Pray for those who do not know God; for the millions of pagans who have never heard of the true God. Pray for the missionaries in faraway lands, the Priests, Brothers and Sisters, who have left their homes and their country to work for these souls. Pray for the many children who do not know about Jesus, His dear Mother, the Angel Guardian, and the Saints. Your prayers may help to convert some of these. Pray also for those who know God, but do not serve Him.

Now you see how many persons you can help with your prayers. Pray especially when you are at Mass. Jesus desires you to ask of Him many things for others. He will hear your prayers. If you have received your First Holy Communion and are permitted to go to Holy Communion often, do not forget after each Holy Communion to pray for all these intentions. That is the best time of all to pray. Jesus said, "Ask and you shall receive." So, my dear children, try to be little apostles, helping Jesus to win souls for heaven.

Practice:
1. I will not let a day pass without praying for the heathen children.
2. I will pray every day for my parents.

Very good is God to me;
Look where I may, His gifts I see;
The food I eat, the clothes I wear,
Are tokens of my Maker's care.

REVIEW

To the Teacher:—The talks on Little Missionaries will furnish the teacher an opportunity for instilling into the hearts of the little ones a missionary spirit. Tell them how they can, although they are very young, help to win souls for Jesus by their prayers. Encourage them to make small sacrifices, such as saving the money they have for candy to give to the missions. Teach them the merit of sacrifice for others.

As for prayers for parents and relatives, if the teacher is aware that the parents of any of the children are careless in the performance of their religious duties, she may stress this in her talks, without, however, making any direct reference to any one in particular. In a general way she might tell of instances where parents have been brought back to God by the prayers of children. Strive to form in the children the habit of offering all prayers and good works each day for a special intention. Remind the children of the intention each time they pray or begin a new task. For instance, say to them: "To-day, dear children, let us offer all we do for the conversion of the heathen children; for the prevention of at least one mortal sin; for the dying; for those children whose parents do not send them to Catholic schools." How much good a teacher can do by accustoming the children thus early to offer their works and prayers to God!

PART TWO
CLASSROOM PROJECTS
DRAWING—CONSTRUCTION WORK—DRAMATIZATION

PART TWO

SECTION I

SCHOOL CALENDARS—FEASTS—SPECIAL DAYS

1. SCHOOL CALENDARS

The calendar for each month may be drawn on the blackboard, on cardboard, or on plain paper. Cardboard has been found serviceable where little blackboard space is available. If the calendar is made of cardboard, it will enable the pupils to help in its construction. Black cardboard is easily obtained; or black paper may be pasted on heavier paper; sometimes cardboard that has been used for other purposes may be covered with black paper and will serve the purpose quite well. Likewise a piece of ordinary paper painted black is excellent for the purpose. For the background white water-color, chalk or crayola may be used. The children can cut out suitable pictures from magazines and paste them on the calendar. Rule off a space for all dates. The days are to be numbered as they occur; this will stimulate interest in the work. The child that writes the best figures should be chosen to insert the date in the proper space. As the important feasts occur, pictures illustrating them may be pasted in the space for the date. This work can be made very attractive and interesting. In the first month it will be well for the teacher to write or print the names of the days of the week at the head of the proper columns; later the children will be able to do this.

How to Make the Calendars

Use cardboard of about 22 x 28 inches for the calendar. Rule off about two-thirds of the space for the dates. With chalk, white drawing pencil or crayola draw the background. The sketches on pages 161-187 serve as suggestions. Any simple scene illustrating some phase of the month's work in school will answer the purpose. The calendar is then completed by pasting pictures of children, trees, flowers, in the proper places. The children will like to do this work and it will give them early training in poster work. Space for the dates should be left vacant, and the filling in of the proper date should be made part of the morning exercises. As suggested before, the child whose figures are the best should as a rule be chosen to insert the date. This will stimulate interest in writing figures and the children will try to make their figures better than they would without this incentive. The alert teacher will find many other ways of using the calendar to best advantage. The sketches given will suggest other ideas for constructing the monthly calendar; elaborate drawings, however, should be carefully avoided. The simpler the sketches, the greater the utility. Simple outlines will appeal to the child at this stage of school life. Familiar scenes will attract, while strange sketches and objects will confuse the mind of the child. The blackboard calendar may be made and used in the same manner, but pasting pictures will sometimes mar the surface of the board, and it is somewhat difficult to remove the pictures after the month is over. Cardboard calendars have the further advantage over the blackboard calenders inasmuch as they may be handled more easily and can be transferred from one part of the room to another.

2. SUBJECTS FOR POSTER CALENDARS

The following suggestions (see pages 161-187 for illustrations for various calendars) may be helpful in constructing poster calendars for the school year:

September

Special Event in the Month—Opening of School

As September is the month when school begins, the opening of the school year might be illustrated in the calendar for September. For background draw the sky, some trees and grass. In the foreground draw a school, showing children on the way to school. Show that it is a Catholic school. The trees, the schoolhouse and the children may be represented by cut-out pictures.

Religious Dedication of the Month—Month of the Holy Cross

To bring out this feature make the Cross the central object in the picture. Show a group of children surrounding it. The Cross may be shown as part of an outdoor scene, or it may be pictured in the schoolroom, hanging on the wall, for example, the teacher pointing to it and explaining its meaning to the children.

October

Special Event—Columbus Day

A poster picture of the landing of Columbus and the planting of the Cross is easily made. Let the children cut out Indians, boats and trees. The figures of Columbus and his men may be cut from old histories or magazines. Make the planting of the Cross prominent.

Religious Dedication of the Month—Month of the Guardian Angels

This may be represented in many ways. Construct a poster showing children engaged in play and their Guardian Angels watching over them. Or, show children crossing a dangerous place being protected by their Guardian Angels. A playground or a street scene may easily be drawn and the figures of the children and the Guardian Angels cut out and pasted on.

November

Special Event—Thanksgiving Day

Bring out the religious motive in this picture. Show this in one of the following ways: Draw a landscape scene with a church prominently placed; men, women and children are on their way to church to assist at Holy Mass in thanksgiving to Almighty God for all the gifts and graces received. At the bottom of the picture write or print the words: "WE GIVE THEE THANKS, O ALMIGHTY GOD."

A second way is to show a family grouped about a table. Father, mother, and children are saying grace. The same inscription may be used for this picture.

Religious Dedication of the Month—Month of the Holy Souls

Carry out this theme by drawing a view of a cemetery. Show the Cross around which a few graves are grouped. Below the picture write or print the words: "ETERNAL REST GRANT UNTO THEM, O LORD."

By means of pictures cut from catalogs or magazines show a priest saying Holy Mass. The words "ETERNAL REST GRANT UNTO THEM, O LORD," should be written below this picture.

December

Special Event—The Birth of Jesus

Draw the stable of Bethlehem and cut out pictures of Jesus, Mary, Joseph, the shepherds, sheep, and angels. This poster picture is easily made.

Religious Dedication of the Month—Month of the Holy Child Jesus

Show the Infant Jesus with His Blessed Mother. This idea may be carried out in many ways. Let the children suggest different pictures that may be made. Many of the

Christmas pictures will give you ideas of representing the Child Jesus as an infant.

January

Special Event—The Three Wise Men Adore Jesus

This is an interesting subject and one that can easily be constructed with cut-out pictures. Let the children draw or cut out pictures of the Wise Men and their camels, and arrange to show the journey of the three Kings to Bethlehem.

Religious Dedication of the Month—Month of the Holy Childhood of Jesus

Show Jesus as a child surrounded by other children. Or, Jesus may be shown playing with St. John, or with a lamb.

February

Special Events—Candlemas Day, St. Valentine's Day

Draw or construct the prison of St. Valentine. Under this write or print the words, "COURAGE" or "BRAVERY."

Draw or cut out the figures of several boys dressed in cassocks and surplices carrying candles for the Candlemas procession. Instead of this poster the children may construct a cage with two doves to represent the offering made by the Blessed Virgin on the feast of the Purification.

Religious Dedication of the Month—Month of the Holy Family

Let the children cut out pictures to show the Holy Family at Nazareth.

March

Special Event—St. Patrick's Day

Show St. Patrick explaining the mystery of the Blessed Trinity with a shamrock. Let the children cut out shamrocks and make a border around this month's calendar.

Religious Dedication of the Month—Month of St. Joseph

Show St. Joseph in his workshop assisted by the Boy Jesus. Let the children cut out carpenter's tools and decorate the poster with them.

April

Special Event—The Resurrection of Christ

Let the children cut out trees and arrange them to represent the garden in which the Holy Sepulchre was located. Show the tomb of Jesus. Cut out a picture of the risen Savior and paste it on the poster.

Religious Dedication of the Month—Month of the Passion and Death of Jesus

This may be illustrated by showing the three crosses on the top of Mount Calvary. The children may tear the paper to represent Calvary. The crosses are made of white paper and pasted on the hill.

May

Special Event—The Ascension of Our Lord

Cut out a picture of the Ascension of Our Lord. Draw a suitable background and paste the picture in place.

Religious Dedication of the Month—Month of the Blessed Virgin

Represent the Blessed Virgin surrounded by a group of small children. Any other picture of the Blessed Virgin may be used for this calendar.

June

Special Event—The Feast of Corpus Christi —The Feast of the Sacred Heart

If the feast of Corpus Christi is the subject of the calendar show a monstrance around which a number of children are grouped. If the feast of the Sacred Heart is selected as the theme show a picture of the Sacred Heart surrounded by a number of children.

Religious Dedication of the Month—Month of the Sacred Heart

Instead of the usual picture of the Sacred Heart of Jesus, arrange a poster representing Jesus surrounded by small boys and girls. Jesus shows His divine Heart to the children. Below the picture write or print the words, "MY CHILD, GIVE ME THY HEART."

3. A SUNSHINE CALENDAR

The calendar may be constructed in a manner similar to what was suggested above. The dates however should be marked with yellow chalk or crayola to represent "sunshine days," or a yellow disk cut out and pasted in the space for the date might be used to represent "sunshine days." In case the latter method is used, the date can be written on this disk with chalk or crayola of a different color. Count those days "sunshine days" in which all the children have succeeded in keeping a clear record. To stimulate greater interest in the calendar, print a capital B in the upper section of the block for the date on days when the boys have a clear record. Similarly, a letter G in the lower section will show the days when the girls have made a perfect score. In the space allotted to Saturday print a large B and in the space allotted for Sunday a G. At the end of each week count the number of days the girls have had good records and put as many gold stars in the spaces for Sunday. In the same manner the boys' weekly record may be marked. At the end of the month count the totals. A motto or a slogan printed on the chart will add to its effectiveness. For this the following are suggested: "Be Cheerful," "Cheerfulness," "Smile," "Keep Smiling," "Keep the Sun Shining," "Sunshine Every Day."

The Chart of Holy Joy

The result of each week's record may also be placed on a separate chart, called "The Chart of Holy Joy." Use a large sheet of cardboard, of any suitable color. In the center paste a large picture of the Christ Child. Above the picture, draw the sun. Let the rays of the sun fall about the head of Christ. Cut-out pictures of smiling children grouped about the central figure, add to the interest. The lower third of this chart may be ruled into two rows of blocks, each row to represent a week for the boys and girls respectively. In these blocks mark in large figures the total numbers of stars gained by the boys and girls in a given week. Transferring the totals from the calendar to this chart will prove interesting and exciting to the children and will stimulate them to greater endeavor to keep cheerful and pleasant throughout the day. Other ways of marking will suggest themselves. The main object is to create and maintain interest in the practice of cheerfulness. A motto like the one from St. Paul, "Rejoice in the Lord," may be placed on the chart.

Other subjects will suggest themselves to the teacher. Let the children help to plan the calendar.

If the teacher wishes to use a set of calendars that feature the religious dedication of each month and that may be used for coloring, she may procure a series of school calendars designed by Sister Mary Aurelia, O. S. F. These calendars are prepared for school use and may be used for coloring with crayon or water color.[1]

4. MODEL FOR CALENDARS

The calendars illustrated on the following pages will serve as models for cardboard or blackboard drawings either made freehand or reproduced by means of a pantograph. These calendars may also be used by the children as copies from which they may construct cut-out pictures for their individual use, should the teacher so desire.

5. DAYS OF SPECIAL INTEREST IN THE LOWER GRADES

September	Date
Labor Day	
The Nativity of the Blessed Virgin Mary	8
The Most Holy Name of Mary	12
The Exaltation of the Holy Cross	14

[1] Published by the Abbott Educational Company, 1603 Michigan Avenue, Chicago, Ill.

SCHOOL CALENDARS—FEASTS—SPECIAL DAYS 161

September Calendar—Opening of School

September Calendar—Month of the Holy Cross

October Calendar—Landing of Columbus

October Calendar—The Month of the Guardian Angels

SCHOOL CALENDARS—FEASTS—SPECIAL DAYS

November Calendar—Thanksgiving Day at Church

166 PRACTICAL AIDS FOR CATHOLIC TEACHERS

November Calendar—Thanksgiving Day at Home

November Calendar—Month of the Holy Souls

PRACTICAL AIDS FOR CATHOLIC TEACHERS

November Calendar—Month of the Holy Souls

December Calendar—The Birth of Jesus

December Calendar—Month of the Child Jesus

SCHOOL CALENDARS—FEASTS—SPECIAL DAYS 171

January Calendar—The Wise Men Adore Jesus

January Calendar—Month of the Holy Childhood

SCHOOL CALENDARS—FEASTS—SPECIAL DAYS 173

February Calendar—Candlemas Day Procession

February Calendar—Presentation of the Child Jesus

SCHOOL CALENDARS—FEASTS—SPECIAL DAYS 175

February Calendar—St. Valentine in Prison

February Calendar—Month of the Holy Family

March Calendar—St. Patrick Preaching on the Holy Trinity

March Calendar—Month of St. Joseph

APRIL CALENDAR—THE MONTH OF THE CRUCIFIXION

April Calendar—The Resurrection of Our Lord

May Calendar—Ascension of Our Lord

May Calendar—Month of the Blessed Virgin

June Calendar—Corpus Christi

June Calendar—Feast of the Sacred Heart of Jesus

SCHOOL CALENDARS—FEASTS—SPECIAL DAYS 185

June Calendar—Month of the Sacred Heart of Jesus

G	MON	TUES	WED	THUR	FRI	B

A Sunshine Calendar

The Chart of Holy Joy

The Seven Sorrows of the Blessed Virgin
Mary (also celebrated on the Friday after
Passion Sunday) 15
St. Michael the Archangel 29

October
The Holy Guardian Angels 2
St. Thérèse, the Little Flower of Jesus 3
St. Francis of Assisi 4
Feast of the Most Holy Rosary of Our Lady 7
Columbus Day 12
St. Theresa 15
St. Raphael the Archangel 24

November
All Saints 1
All Souls 2
St. Elizabeth of Hungary 19
The Presentation of the Blessed Virgin 21
Thanksgiving Day

December
St. Nicholas 6
The Immaculate Conception of the Blessed
Virgin Mary 8
The Birth of Our Lord Jesus Christ 25
The Holy Innocents 28

January
New Year—The Circumcision of Our Lord 1
The Most Holy Name of Jesus (Sunday
between Circumcision and the Epiphany) 6
The Epiphany of Our Lord 6
St. Sebastian 20
St. Agnes 21
St. Francis de Sales 29

February
The Purification of the Blessed Virgin Mary 2
St. Blase 3
St. Valentine 14

March
St. Patrick 17
St. Joseph 19
St. Gabriel the Archangel 24
The Annunciation of the Blessed Virgin
Mary 25
Bird Day

April
St. Isidore 4
Bl. Herman Joseph 7
The Resurrection of Our Lord
Arbor Day

May
Blessed Imelda 12
St. Paschal Baylon 17
Mother's Day
Memorial Day 30
The Ascension of Our Lord

June
St. Anthony of Padua 13
Flag Day 14
St. Germaine Cousin 17
St. Aloysius 21
St. John the Baptist 24
Corpus Christi
The Feast of the Sacred Heart of Jesus

SPECIAL DAYS

From time to time special days have been set aside by custom or by law to commemorate important events in the history of our country or to pay tribute to the memory of outstanding leaders of the nation. These days should be observed in the schools by appropriate exercises. These exercises may consist of songs, recitations, dramatizations, the making of posters and special projects. In the primary grades the programs should be brief and simple.

Suitable material for the observance of Lincoln's Birthday, Washington's Birthday and Memorial Day may be found in school journals and magazines. Suggestions are presented here for the observance of those days to which a religious significance may be attached. Among these may be numbered Columbus Day, Thanksgiving Day and Mother's Day.

These programs are to be considered as merely suggestive. Others may be planned by the teacher. If the pupils are permitted to assist in the planning and arranging of the programs, they will take greater interest in the projects.

Labor Day

This holiday occurs so early in the school year that the teacher in the first grade has no opportunity to prepare for it. The second grade teacher, however, may be able to arrange for a brief exercise to be held on the Friday preceding Labor Day (if school has opened before that date) or on the Friday following it. Explain to the class the dignity of labor and the necessity for each person to do some kind of work. Tell them work is honorable. Show them a picture representing Jesus helping St. Joseph in the carpenter shop.[1] Jesus worked; the blessed Virgin worked; St. Joseph worked. All persons must work.

Arrange the children in groups. Let each group represent a trade or an occupation. Let the children briefly tell about the work done by the people engaged in that trade or occupation. For example: We are carpenters. Carpenters build houses. Carpenters make tables and chairs. Let a child tell the story of the picture showing Jesus helping St. Joseph.

Columbus Day

During the month of October the teacher will, of course, place special emphasis on the life and achievements of Columbus. For the children in the second grade a reading lesson on Columbus will be interesting. Let them cut out and color Indians, trees and wigwams. Let them make boats for the sand table. They may write short sentences about Columbus. Let them dramatize events in the life of Columbus.

First grade children should be told the story of Columbus and then let them dramatize it. Use the sand table to show the landing of Columbus and the planting of the Cross. Columbus Day is a day of great significance to Catholics. Therefore, Catholic schools ought to observe this day in a fitting manner. The following program offers suggestions for the second grade:

PROGRAM FOR COLUMBUS DAY

SONG .... "America"...... Sung by the class
DRAMATIZATION. "The Discovery of America," *Little American History Plays for Little Americans.* By a number of children
STORY ...."Christopher Columbus." Told by the children
SONG ...."Hail Columbia." Sung by the class

Halloween

Children consider Halloween one of the most enjoyable holidays of the year. The Catholic teacher ought not allow this day to pass with-

[1] Cf. picture, page 46.

out telling her pupils the original meaning of the feast in order to encourage them to observe it in a fitting manner. Some time before Halloween she should talk to the children about the meaning of the word. Halloween means "All Hallow Eve," or "All Saints Eve."

Observe the day by letting the children stage a little celebration in the classroom in honor of the saints. This festival might be arranged in the following way: For several days preceding the feast, tell the children something about their patron saints. Let them bring pictures of the saints. These may be mounted on sheets of construction paper and the name of the saint printed below the picture. Instead of printing the names, the children might cut out the letters. Try to get as many pictures of the saints as possible. Pictures from discarded religious goods catalogs, old calendars or magazines will serve admirably for the purpose. On Halloween let the children assemble in groups in a convenient part of the room. Then let the children who bear the same name form one group. Let one child begin the story of the saint and the next one continue it, and so on till all in the group have had a turn.

Each of the other children may hold the picture of his patron saint and tell the story. The children who do not bear a saint's name may be chosen to tell something about a familiar saint whose story may not have been related by any other member of the class.

The teacher ought to do all in her power to show the children that damaging the property of others, disturbing the peace of their neighbors by noisy celebrations is not honoring the saints. Remind them of their duties as good citizens. Teach them to observe the feast in a more becoming manner, by spending the evening at home. Telling or listening to stories, enjoying games, cracking nuts and making candy are harmless diversions and will not in any way interfere with the comfort and rights of others.

Thanksgiving Day

Call attention to the purpose of the feast several days before. Tell the story of the First Thanksgiving Day. Ask the children to think of all the things for which they ought to be thankful. Remind them of the many gifts they have received and are daily receiving from God. Teach them to be thankful for all the graces and blessings they have received from Him. Let the children make Thanksgiving Booklets.

PROGRAM FOR THANKSGIVING DAY

SONG—"Dearest Lord, We Thank You," *Catholic Education Music Course, First Year*, Justine Ward.. Sung by the children
STORY—"The First Thanksgiving"..Told by a child
DRAMATIZATION—"The First Thanksgiving," *Little American History Plays for Little Americans*..By the class
RECITATION—"We Thank Thee," *Loretto Series, Language Busy Work*, Vol. I, page 106..By a child
RECITATIONS—"Thanksgiving Rhymes"..By several boys and girls
SONG—"The Father's Love," *Catholic Education Music Course, First Year*, Justine Ward..Sung by the class

Christmas

Christmas is the feast dearest to the heart of a child. But there is great danger in the preparation for the observance of this feast that the real significance of it may be overlooked. Begin early in December to tell the story of the Birth of Jesus. Emphasize the lesson of God's boundless love for His creatures. Let the children make a sand table project showing Bethlehem. Illustrate on the sand table the adoration of the shepherds and the coming of the Wise Men. Help the children to make booklets and posters.

PROGRAM FOR CHRISTMAS

SONG—"A Welcome to Jesus," *Catholic Education Music Course, First Year*, Justine Ward..Sung by the class
STORY—"The Birth of Jesus"..Told by a number of children
RECITATION—"The Childhood of Jesus," *Catholic Nursery Rhymes*, Sister Mary Gertrude, M. A. By a child
SONG—"Why?" *Catholic Education Music Course, Second Book*, page 68 .... By the class
DRAMATIZATION—"The Adoration of the Shepherds" By a number of children
RECITATION—"Dear Little One" By several children
RECITATION—"Sweet Babe of Bethlehem"..By a child

SONG—"When Christ Was Born," *Catholic Education Music Course, First Year*, Justine Ward.. Sung by the class

Holy Week

Some special program ought to be introduced during this week to commemorate the events connected with the Sacred Passion and Death of Our Lord Jesus Christ. On the Monday in Holy Week arrange some exercises in which all the children can take part. Tell the story of the sufferings and death of Jesus. Speak of the joy and the glory of the Resurrection of Our Lord. Sand table work, booklets and posters will help to impress the lesson.

PROGRAM FOR HOLY WEEK

SONG—"Stabat Mater" (English words) Sung by the class
RECITATION—"The Sacred Passion of Our Lord Jesus Christ," *Catholic Nursery Rhymes*, Sister Mary Gertrude, M. A................Several children
STORY—"The Way of the Cross". Told by the children
RECITATION—"The Child on Calvary"....By a child
SONG—"It Is Love," *Catholic Education Music Course, First Year*, Justine Ward. Sung by the class
RECITATION—"Contrition" ....By a child

Mother's Day

This day is usually observed on the second Sunday in May. However, the teacher should set aside some day during the week before for its observance in school. This day will afford a splendid opportunity to impress upon the children their duty towards their mothers. Let the children take an active part in planning the program. The following may prove helpful:

PROGRAM FOR MOTHER'S DAY

SONG—"The Mother's Prayer," *Catholic Education Music Course, First Year*, Justine Ward..Sung by the class
RECITATION—"We Thank Thee".........By a child
DRAMATIZATION—"Jesus Blesses Little Children" By the class
SONG—"Little Robin, Never Fear," *Catholic Education Music Course, First Year*, Justine Ward.. Sung by the class

Teach the children to make a spiritual bouquet for their mothers. This will be an appropriate gift. For this purpose let them make a booklet; cut out and paste on the cover the letters M O T H E R, or TO MY MOTHER. On the inside page draw or cut out a suitable flower. If the children can do so, let them write or print on the petals the names of the prayers they have offered. These booklets are very attractive when decorated with some simple designs or tied with brightly colored ribbon.

pictures from last year's calendar useful in constructing this year's calendars.

The Nativity of the Blessed Virgin Mary—September 8

The first notable feast of the month is the *Nativity of the Blessed Virgin Mary*. Call it "Our Blessed Mother's Birthday." Children will understand this better. Birthdays are memorable days in the lives of children. This feast will give the Sister an opportunity to lay the foundation for a childlike devotion to our Blessed Mother. Incidentally it also offers an occasion to impress upon the plastic minds of the child the duty of love and gratitude he owes his earthly mother. Tell the children about the great love and tenderness the Blessed Virgin has for us, her children. Have them do some kind act in her honor to-day. Also tell them how they will please our Blessed Mother by being very kind and obedient to their mothers;

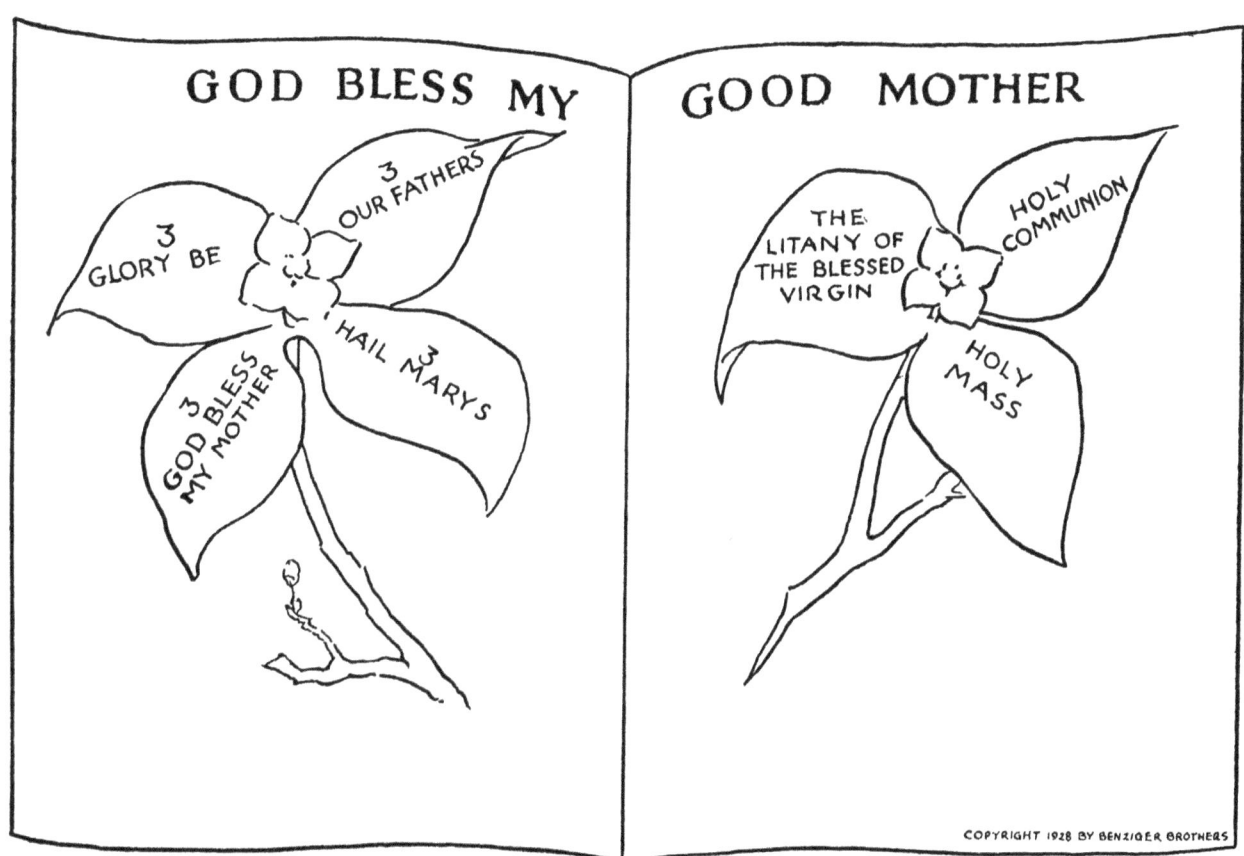

A Booklet for Mother's Day

6. FEASTS OF THE CHURCH

SEPTEMBER

There are few days in this month to interest very young children. Valuable material, such as pictures and illustrations, may be found in old religious calendars, especially in ecclesiastical art calendars. The teacher will find the for instance: to come as soon as mother calls; to go to the store without waiting to be told two or three times; to watch the baby, so that mother may finish her work. The little ones will be glad that they can do something so simple to please the Blessed Virgin; it will serve to remind them of the great love and devotion of their mothers, how they ought to show their gratitude to mother for all she is doing for them every day.

After this talk, let one of the children paste in the calendar space for September 8th a picture of the Blessed Virgin. For this it is usually advisable to choose a child who has been particularly attentive and diligent, though sometimes it might serve as a mark of confidence for an unruly child. Make this a part of the morning exercise. If the feast should happen to fall on a day when there is no class, do it the day before; *do not omit it under any circumstance.* Always have this done before the feast rather than after. At the end of the talk propose some definite practice for the day. During the day recall it from time to time.

Practice:
1. To help mother to-day by doing what I am told without grumbling or pouting.
2. To think of the Blessed Mother in heaven and to remember that she wants me to please her.

The Feast of the Most Holy Name of Mary— September 12

Coming so soon after the feast of the Nativity of Our Lady, this feast may serve as a review of what you told the children of the Blessed Mother before. Recall again the love and care of the Blessed Virgin for us, especially for those who try to please her. Remind the children again of all their own mothers are doing for them. It will likewise be opportune to say something about the love and respect we should have for the holy names of Jesus and Mary. It is surprising how many little boys and girls say these names without the least thought of what they mean. In many homes the name of God is used in quarrels and the little children soon imitate the bad example of their elders. The teacher will do well to take note of this. If there are little girls in the class who bear the name of Mary, call attention to it. Impress upon them the great honor they have in being named after the Mother of the Child Jesus.

THE HOLY CHILD JESUS AND HIS BLESSED MOTHER

Tell them how very careful they ought to be, so that the Blessed Virgin may always be pleased with her little namesakes in the school.

Practice:
1. To salute the statue of the Blessed Virgin as I pass it to-day.

2. Every time I look at a statue or picture of the Blessed Virgin, to try to remember that she is my mother also.

If you have a statue or a picture of the Blessed Virgin, put it in a conspicuous place on her feasts; decorate it; place flowers and candles before it. Teach the little ones to say indulgenced ejaculations. Father Finn, S. J. calls them short prayers blessed by the Church. Ecclesiastically approved simple forms of such indulgenced ejaculations are contained in "Boys' and Girls' Prayer Book," by Father Francis J. Finn, S. J. Tell them to talk to their Blessed Mother just as they would talk to their own mothers. Teach them to ask the help of the Blessed Virgin in all their little wants. Paste a picture of the Blessed Virgin in the proper space on the calendar.

The Feast of the Exaltation of the Holy Cross—September 14

Since the month of September is dedicated to the Holy Cross, the teacher will have occasion to explain the meaning of the Cross to the children frequently during the month. Briefly relate the touching story of Our Lord's sufferings and His death upon the Cross. The teacher must tell the story in such a way as to make the children feel the significance of the Cross. She must make her talk animated; she must use simple yet forceful words; she must bring home to the little hearts the great truths of our holy religion; but this the teacher cannot do unless she puts her whole heart and soul into the work. The children must be able to see from the teacher's manner that what she says comes from the bottom of her heart, that the teacher herself is deeply moved by the great sufferings of Our Lord.

Use this feast to instil a great reverence for the crucifix; have the pupils make the Sign of the Cross with the utmost devotion. Call their attention to the meaning of the crucifix. Show them a crucifix. Teach the children to kiss it reverently. Ask how many of them have crosses or crucifixes at home. If they have none, tell them to ask mother or father to get one and put it in their bedrooms. Holy pictures, crucifixes, holy water fonts, and other pious objects are often wanting in modern Catholic homes. It is through the children that we may hope to revive the beautiful custom of having these devotional articles in Catholic homes.

The Feast of the Seven Sorrows of the Blessed Virgin Mary—September 15

(Also celebrated on the Friday after Passion Sunday)

Even very young children can, in some measure, realize the pains and sufferings of others. The feast of the *Seven Sorrows of the Blessed Virgin Mary* will give the teacher another opportunity to impress upon the tender little hearts of her pupils the love and devotion they should have towards their dear Mother in heaven. Show them that God did not spare even His own Mother, but sent her many pains, sorrows and sufferings. From this we learn that, if we wish to go to heaven and enjoy great happiness there, we must be willing to suffer many things here on earth for the love of God. Children will sometimes hear their mothers or other persons say: "Why does God send so many sufferings to me? I go to church often, I say my prayers, I try to do what is right, yet God sends me nothing but sufferings and trouble." Impress upon the children that the great happiness God will give us in heaven is worth all the sufferings and troubles and pains that we bear here on earth, and that the more we suffer patiently here, the greater will be our happiness in heaven.

Relate briefly the story of the Seven Sorrows of the Blessed Virgin. They are as follows: the Sorrow (1) at the prophecy of Simeon; (2) at the flight into Egypt; (3) having lost the Holy Child at Jerusalem; (4) meeting Jesus on His way to Calvary; (5) Standing at the foot of the Cross; (6) Jesus being taken from the Cross; (7) at the burial of Christ. The tender hearts of the children will be moved to deep sympathy. Bring home to their minds also the many pains and troubles their dear mothers must undergo in rearing their children, how they suffer when they are ill, and when they disobey commands. This will teach the pupils sympathy for the sufferings of others.

Practice:

1. To be particularly kind and attentive to mother to-day.

2. To do something very special to give her pleasure.

Enter into details as to what they might do. Guard particularly against *general* resolutions; be specific each time.

The Feast of St. Michael the Archangel— September 29

By this time the children will have learned something about the angels; in the story of the

ST. MICHAEL

fall of the angels they will have heard about St. Michael; They will remember how he called out to the bad angels, "Who is like God?" The story of St. Michael and the bad angels will thrill the little ones; the boys particularly will be fascinated by the tale of the fight and the victory over the bad angels. Use this story to appeal to their sense of fair play; make clear to them how much they owe to God Who made them as well as this lovely world in which they live. Show how wicked we are when we refuse to obey God. Call attention to the many times little boys, and sometimes little girls also, say bad words or even curse words. Sometimes they play with children who use bad words and do bad deeds. God does not like this. If they wish to be like St. Michael, they will try to check these children when they say bad words or do bad deeds; and if they cannot stop them they should go away and not play with them again.

This feast will offer an opportunity to impress more deeply upon the children the reverence with which they should pronounce holy names and the veneration they should have for holy things. St. Michael fought with the bad angels. He shows us that we should not allow wicked persons to lead us to do bad things. By relating this story in an intensely dramatic manner, the teacher will impress it deeply upon the children. Procure a picture of St. Michael, a large one, if possible, and exhibit it throughout the day; call attention to it frequently. Have a smaller picture pasted on the calendar.

Practice:
1. To stay away from children who use bad words.
2. When I hear bad words I will whisper, "Praised be Jesus Christ."

OCTOBER

The Feast of the Holy Guardian Angels— October 2

Who remembers the story about St. Michael? Very well, James, what can you tell us about him? That is good, James. Now, Grace, can you tell us anything about the angels that remained in heaven? What do you think they do? Can you see the angels? Why not? I am going to show you a pretty picture this morning. See! (Show picture of Guardian Angel. See picture on page 164.) Who do you think that is? (Point to angel.) Yes, it is an angel. How do you know it is an angel? (Because he has wings.) Why does the angel have wings? Do you remember what I told you about the angels a few weeks ago? The angels are God's messengers. A messenger must go very quickly and that is why in pictures, angels usually have wings. The angels do not really have wings, because they have no bodies, but we cannot imagine how any one looks without a body, and so when we make pictures of God or of the angels we must make them look like people here on the earth.

God sends His angels to this world so that they may guard and protect us. *Each one of us* has an angel to watch him day and night. We call this angel our Guardian Angel. You have a Guardian Angel and so have I. He is here right now in this room with us. Your angel is right beside you now; sometimes he whispers to you not to be lazy or disobedient. When he sees a little boy or girl disobey mother or father or the teacher, he is sad. Be very careful, therefore, not to displease this dear angel.

On the picture you see also a little child playing carelessly where there is danger. Now just as you see the child's Guardian Angel caring for him and watching over him so your own Guardian Angel cares for you and watches over you. How often you are in danger when crossing streets! How many little boys and girls are killed every year by automobiles! Some children are drowned, others are burned, others are crippled for life. Remember the many times when you were almost hurt. What saved you? It was your Guardian Angel. You ought to be very thankful to him for helping and guarding you, and you should try never to displease him. By doing all the things I have been telling you to do to please Jesus, your Angel Guardian will also be happy and pleased. Say this little prayer now with me to your Guardian Angel. Try to learn it as soon as possible and then you can say it very often during the day, especially when you are in danger.

> Angel of God, my guardian dear,
> To whom His love commits me here;
> Ever this day be at my side,
> To watch, to guard, to rule and guide.

Look very carefully at the picture. Do not forget that your angel is by your side day and night. And when you do wrong, your angel is sad. You do not wish to make your angel sad, do you? Now while you look at the picture, I will read to you a very pretty poem about the Guardian Angel.

> Dear Angel, ever at my side,
> How loving must thou be,
> To leave thy home in heaven to guide
> A little child like me.
> *Father Faber.*

Practice:
1. When I cross the street, I will ask my Guardian Angel to protect me.
2. When I go to bed, I will ask my Guardian Angel to watch over me.

St. Thérèse the Little Flower of Jesus— October 4

On January 2, 1873, the hills and valleys of Normandy were covered with snow. In the home of Mr. Martin in the city of Alençon, four little girls were fast asleep. Suddenly the father came to waken the two older girls and tell them that they had a new baby sister.

Mary Louise, who was thirteen, sat up in bed. Pauline, eleven years old, jumped up at once to go to see the baby. But their father told them to be quiet, lest they wake the other children. He said they must wait till morning to see their little sister. So they settled down to sleep again.

Mr. Martin went back to the room where the new baby was asleep in her mother's arms. Then he and Mrs. Martin prayed earnestly that God would choose this child for Himself, and never let her soul be soiled by mortal sin.

Early in the morning the four little girls crowded around the baby's cradle. They loved her at once, because she was very beautiful. Her eyes were blue and bright as stars, and her hair was golden. She smiled, and they clapped their hands and jumped for joy.

Two days later, the children went to the Church of Our Lady to see the baby baptized. Her oldest sister, Mary Louise, was her godmother. She was named Mary Frances Thérèse.

Some months afterwards, Mrs. Martin went to Mass one morning, leaving the baby asleep in her cot. When she returned she found little Thérèse on a chair beside the bed, sound asleep. The cot was overturned on the floor. She knew that the baby's Guardian Angel had saved her from being hurt.

Happy months passed. When the baby began

to walk, she followed her mother everywhere. Whenever little Thérèse climbed the stairs she stopped on every step to call, "Mama!" If her mother forgot to answer, the little one stood and called again and again till she heard her mother say, "Yes, darling!" Little Thérèse was sweet and loving towards her dear mother. Thus she made her very happy. Though she was so lovable, this small girl was very stubborn until she was three years old. Then she understood that God does not want His children to be stubborn. So she never again disobeyed anyone who had the right to command her.

To obey perfectly was hard for Thérèse, because she liked to have her own way. But when she disobeyed, even before she was three, she always was sorry right afterwards, and begged forgiveness.

Once when she was swinging, her father called to her, "Come and kiss me, little Queen." Usually she obeyed her father, but this time she just sat still, and answered pertly, "You must come for it, Papa." Her father refused and went away.

Mary Louise was present, and she scolded Thérèse, saying, "How naughty to answer Papa like that!" Then Thérèse was sorry and began to cry. She hurried into the house and ran up the stairs, not even waiting to call her mother, as she usually did. She wanted to find her father and tell him how sorry she was. Her father was glad to have his little daughter be so humble as to come to ask his pardon, and he forgave her immediately.

Little Thérèse was unkind once to her dear mother, too. One morning Mrs. Martin wanted to kiss her baby before going downstairs. Thérèse seemed to be asleep. But Mary Louise said, "Mama, I am sure she is only pretending." So her mother bent down to kiss her forehead. Then Thérèse hid herself under the bedclothes, and said in a whining tone, "I don't want any one to look at me."

Her mother was displeased with her and told her so. Then she went downstairs. Soon she heard Thérèse at her side crying. The baby had got out of her cot and had run downstairs, stumbling over her long nightdress as she hurried.

Thérèse clasped her mother's knees and lifted her tear-wet face. "Mama," she cried, "I am sorry for being naughty. Forgive me." Then her mother picked her up in her arms and kissed her many, many times.

Fathers and mothers understand that sometimes their little ones are cross because they do not feel well. So they forgive them quickly. But when children are just naughty, the parents may have to punish them so that they will remember not to be bad again. But they forgive the children as soon as they say they are sorry. And so, too, does the Good God forgive His children.

You see, it was no easier for Thérèse to obey her parents than for other children. Before the age of three she was proud. If she had not been well trained she might have grown up to be a different person from the dear, sweet saint whom everyone loves so much.

Once her mother said to her, "Thérèse darling, if you will kiss the ground I will give you a penny." A penny meant a fortune to a small girl in those days.

But Thérèse drew herself up and said, "No, thank you, Mama; I would rather go without the penny." As little Thérèse grew older she became very humble, and not at all like the proud baby.

Thérèse obeyed through love and not through fear of punishment. This is the right way to obey. She was even more careful to obey her parents when they were away than when they could see her.

Whenever she did anything wrong she always told them, even though they could not find it out from any one else. Once she ran to her mother and confessed, "Mama, I have pushed Celine. I slapped her once, but I'll not do it again."

Celine would never have told on her little sister, because she loved her. So Thérèse told on herself. She loved her parents too much to conceal anything from them.

> O Little Flower, teach us to obey
> Our parents, in your ready, loving way,
> That we may bring them many pretty flowers
> Of kindly deeds, to cheer their weary hours.

The Little Flower's Love for Her Parents, Sister M. Eleanore, C.S.C.

Girlhood of the Little Flower

When little Thérèse was only four years old, her dear mother died. God sent His lovely angel of death, whose wings are gray outside but lined inside with gold, to take her to heaven. Mrs. Martin was sorry to leave her husband and children. But she was glad to go to heaven to live with God. Besides, she knew her four babies who had died were there waiting for her.

The Little Flower was very sad, though she did not tell anyone how she felt. She took her sister Pauline for her "little mother." But soon Pauline went to be a nun. She wanted to belong entirely to Jesus and pray always for those people who will not pray and who hurt Jesus by their sins.

Then Thérèse understood that Jesus wanted all her love for Himself. So while she was growing up and going to school, she gave up everything that might have taken her love from Jesus. She obeyed the Priests and the Sisters who taught her. She knew they wanted to help her become worthy to belong to Jesus.

When Thérèse was ten years old, she became very sick, so sick that the doctors said she could not live. Her father had a Novena of Masses said in the Church of Our Lady of Victory in Paris.

On Sunday during the Novena, her sisters were praying at her bedside. Mary Louise knelt before the statue of Our Lady which was in the room. Suddenly the statue seemed to come to life and gave the sick little girl the most beautiful smile ever seen. All the pain left Thérèse and she was well again. Our Blessed Lady loved the Little Flower because she had given herself entirely to Jesus. So she made her well.

Thérèse had made up her mind to enter the convent at the age of fifteen. But she had many troubles before she could do so. The superiors of the convent thought she was too young. So did the Bishop, though she did her hair up when she went to see him so that he would think she was grown up. These refusals nearly broke her heart. But she was patient and did not complain, because she knew Jesus was just trying her courage.

At last her father took her to Rome to see our Holy Father, the Pope. When she was in his presence her heart beat very fast. She knelt down at his knee before all the people and asked him to let her enter the convent. But even he told her she must wait till the superiors of the convent would consent.

It seemed that all hope was gone. But when Thérèse got home again she prayed and prayed and prayed. Then a letter came saying that she could enter the convent. This was on December 28, the Feast of the Holy Innocents. The superiors said that she could enter at Easter time.

The Little Flower in the Convent

Thérèse spent the next three months in getting ready to belong to Jesus. She did many hard things. She never excused herself or answered back when blamed for anything. She gave in to others. She was very generous and did not keep things for herself. At last the happy day came when she could enter the convent.

Thérèse had to leave her dear father and her home and all the gay things of life that might have been hers if she had not entered the convent. The parting was hard. But she was willing to do anything for Jesus. She would have Him, and that would be enough for her. She said:

"Dear Jesus, all I have to Thee I give;
I am content if I for Thee may live."

Something very sweet happened for Thérèse when she first put on her nun's dress. Because she was born when the world was white with snow and because she was so pure, she wished for snow on this happy day. But the morning was mild and clear. So she offered her disappointment to Jesus, saying she asked nothing for herself.

After the ceremony was ended she looked out the window. Lo, the earth was covered with sparkling snow. She was so pleased. Jesus had granted her wish. Nobody else could ever do such a wonderful thing to please her.

Thérèse received the name Sister Thérèse of the Child Jesus when she became a nun. She lived in the convent for nine years. During all that time she obeyed her superiors even in her smallest action. She wanted to be the servant of every one. She liked to do the hardest tasks.

She never lost patience, no matter what happened.

This was not easy. Most people feel like scolding when others cause them trouble. The Little Flower felt so, too, but she conquered her feelings.

Little Thérèse was an artist. She spent many hours in making pictures. She used every moment of her time well, because she knew people should not waste time. So it sometimes happened that she had to leave her work just as it was when the prayer bell rang. When she returned she sometimes found things out of place or gone. Did she become cross or scold? No, indeed.

She said that it was hard not to get angry. But she knew that Jesus would not like to have her get angry. So she never did. You see, Jesus likes to have us smile away little troubles that others cause us.

This dear little saint was very sick for a long time before she died. She did not complain, but offered her pain to save sinners. She helped Jesus in this way. He gave His life to save sinners, you know, and anybody who is good and bears pain happily can help Him make sinners be sorry for their sins.

People who suffer much for God are called martyrs. So little Thérèse was a martyr. After she had endured this pain so gladly for God, she died. When she awoke from the lovely sleep of death, lo, she was in heaven.

> Dear Jesus, grant us so to live
> That when Death comes to close our eyes,
> We, like Thy chosen Little Flower,
> May open them in Paradise.

The Reward of the Little Flower's Obedience

The Fourth Commandment promises a reward to the obedient child. It says, "Honor thy father and thy mother, that thou mayst live long upon the land which the Lord thy God will give thee."

The Little Flower has proved to us that God keeps His promises. She was always loving and obedient. And she will live on earth till the end of the world.

It is true that when she was only twenty-four years old she died and went to heaven. But the saints and angels can go everywhere. She knew before she died that she would spend her time in heaven in doing good upon earth. Her work is to make people love God.

Little Thérèse is very famous and very powerful. She has been dead only a few years. Yet more books have been written about her than even about our great George Washington, who gave our country freedom and was our first president.

From an actual photograph of the Saint.
ST. THÉRÈSE, THE LITTLE FLOWER OF JESUS

All the Catholics in the world and many Protestants pray to this little saint and ask her for favors. Is not that a lovely way of living on the earth, even if one has died? She lives in her own land of Normandy, in France. She lives also in every country in the world. So her reward for obedience is very great.

Because she always did what God wanted her to while she lived on earth, God does what she wishes Him to do in heaven. He lets her spend her time in heaven in doing good on earth. This is what she wishes to do.

She wishes to help everybody to know God and

love Him. She asks God to work miracles for those who pray to her for help. God does what she asks, even though miracles are great things. No person could work miracles without God's help; but God helps saints to work miracles.

We should pray to the Little Flower with great faith and hope. If the favor we ask is pleasing to God, she will obtain it for us. Will it not be wonderful if, when we come to heaven, we can say, like little Thérèse, that we always did what God wished? If we obey our parents and the priests and the Sisters, and keep the commandments of God and of the Church, then we, like the Little Flower, shall please God. And He will reward us. If it is hard for us to be good, let us ask little Thérèse to help us.

> O Little Flower of Jesus,
> Help us God's will to know,
> And help us to obey Him,
> As through our lives we go.

The Little Flower's Love for Her Parents, Sister M. Eleanore, C.S.C.

Saint Francis—October 4

Many, many years ago, there was born in a beautiful city of Italy a little boy who grew up to be a very holy man. He was always kind, gentle, loving and cheerful. This man was called St. Francis. His parents were very rich, but Francis gave everything he had to the poor, because he wished to be like Jesus Who was so poor when He lived in this world. Francis went about day after day preaching to the people of the love of the good God. He often told them how Jesus loved them, and how He loved also the birds and the animals and the flowers. He told them, too, how our good God is so kind that He watches over us all, even over the little birds. St. Francis dearly loved birds and flowers. When he walked along the roads or in the fields, the birds would fly to his shoulders. One day while he was walking along the way, he saw many birds in the trees and on the ground. They were singing and chirping merrily as if they wanted to show how glad they were that St. Francis was there. The birds flew down about the saint. St. Francis spoke to the birds and they listened quietly all the while: "My little brothers and sisters, listen to me. God loves you dearly; He is very good to you. He gives you the beautiful fields and the lovely trees; He gives you wings to fly, and water from these brooks to drink. He gives you feathers to keep you warm. So you have much to be thankful for. Sing His praises, my little brothers and sisters, and thank Him for all His goodness to you."

St. Francis of Assisi Embracing Our Lord

When St. Francis had finished speaking, he made the Sign of the Cross over them and they flew away singing their sweetest songs. St. Francis watched them and smiled. He was pleased that the birds were so attentive to what he said.

St. Francis was always kind and gentle. People loved this dear saint, because he was so cheerful and spoke to them of the love of God.

We, also, like St. Francis, can try to be kind

and gentle and loving. This month we are trying to learn to have pleasant and cheerful thoughts, and to do many kind and loving deeds to please Jesus and His blessed Mother. We are going to ask St. Francis to help us to be kind

ST. DOMINIC RECEIVING THE ROSARY FROM THE BLESSED VIRGIN

and cheerful and so make others love God more and more. As we grow older we shall learn many more lovely things about this beautiful Saint.

Feast of the Most Holy Rosary—October 7

Do you know what this is? (Show the children a rosary.) It is a rosary. What do we do with a rosary? Do you know how to pray the rosary? That is something you shall learn to do. Do you know why we call it the rosary? The word "rosary" means a crown or wreath of roses. Do you think the rose is a pretty flower? Do you like roses? Would you be pleased if some one were to give you some roses? In some countries it is the custom to put a wreath of roses on the head of a person we wish to honor.

Now of all persons we wish to honor, the Blessed Virgin comes first; kings and queens wear crowns, golden crowns, on their heads. This is a mark of great honor. The Blessed Virgin is our queen. She is often called the Queen of Heaven. As our queen we wish to crown her. The best way for us to do this is by saying the rosary.

Each Hail Mary we say is a rose and the whole rosary is a wreath of roses. The Blessed Virgin is pleased when we offer her this gift.

Try then, dear children, to learn to say this beautiful prayer. (Father Finn's *Boys' and Girls' Prayer Book*, pages 131-148, contains a practical and attractive plan for children to learn the rosary, a practical illustration of which is herewith given.)

How to Say the Rosary

This is the way to say the rosary. Take the cross, or sometimes it is a medal at the end of the rosary, in your right hand and make the Sign of the Cross with it on yourself, and while you look at it say the Creed, "I believe in God," etc.

On the first large bead say the Our Father. Now there come three small beads close together. On each of these beads say a Hail Mary. After the third say a Glory be to the Father.

Say an Our Father on the next large bead. Then come ten small beads close together. Say ten Hail Marys on these beads, and at the end a Glory be to the Father. Say an Our Father on the next large bead and again ten Hail Marys. Do this till you reach the end of the rosary. We say one Our Father and ten Hail Marys five times.

We can say the rosary much better if we think of things in the life of Our Lord and His blessed Mother. These things are called Mysteries. If you look well at the pictures and read what follows, it will help you to understand better what the saying of the rosary and the Mysteries mean. (The teacher may then show the pictures of the Mysteries, telling the story of each Mystery as outlined in the text accompanying these following or similar pictures.)

The Five Joyful Mysteries

1. THE ANNUNCIATION

The Angel tells the Blessed Virgin that she will be the Mother of God.

The Blessed Virgin Mary was in her room at prayer one day. An angel appeared to her and said, "Hail, full of grace, the Lord is with thee." He said that through the Holy Ghost she would become the Mother of God.

This showed that God loved Mary very much. He knew that she was the best and most holy woman in the whole world.

2. THE VISITATION

Our Lady visits her Cousin Saint Elizabeth.

The angel had also told our blessed Lady that God would soon send a baby to her cousin Elizabeth. So she went at once to visit her and told her what had happened. She remained with her cousin, who was quite old, to wait on her. The Blessed Virgin loved to visit the sick, to help the poor, and was always kind to old people.

3. THE NATIVITY

The Infant Jesus is born to the Blessed Virgin on Christmas Day.

A little while later, on Christmas Day, the child was born to our blessed Lady and she called Him Jesus. It was night. The stars shone brightly. Some men were tending their sheep in the fields. Suddenly an angel appeared to them. The angel told them of the birth at Bethlehem of Jesus, the Saviour of the world. Then a great many more angels appeared and sang "Glory to God in the highest and peace on earth to men of good will." After that the shepherds hurried to Bethlehem and, finding the Holy Family in a stable, knelt alongside the Blessed Virgin and St. Joseph and adored the Infant Jesus in the crib.

4. THE PRESENTATION

The Blessed Virgin takes the baby Jesus to the Temple to be blessed.

The Blessed Virgin took the Infant Jesus to the temple. There she offered Him to God, His Father. It was then that Simeon, the priest who took the divine Baby in his arms, saw that Jesus was the Redeemer promised by God.

Simeon had waited many years to see the Redeemer, and he was very happy to hold the baby Jesus in his arms.

The Blessed Mother was happy too, because she was offering her little Son to God. It was the law in those days that boy babies were to be taken to the temple and given to God. The Blessed Mother always did what God wanted her to do. This was because she loved God.

5. THE FINDING IN THE TEMPLE

Mary and Joseph find Jesus in the Temple among the learned men.

When Jesus was twelve years old, the Blessed Virgin and St. Joseph took Him to the city to attend the ceremonies of a great feast day called the Pasch. Big crowds of people had come too. When it was over, all started for home. Then our blessed Lady and St. Joseph found out that Jesus was not with them. They did not worry about it at first, because they felt He had most likely gone back with some of their friends. But when they did not find Him, they feared He was lost. They looked for Him for three days. At last they found Him. He was in the temple, talking to the priests and doctors, who wondered how He knew so much about God and religion.

The Five Sorrowful Mysteries

1. The Agony in the Garden

Our Lord suffers cruel pain in the Garden of Olives the night before He died.

After the Last Supper, Jesus went into the Garden of Olives. Leaving His friends, He went away to think of what would happen the next day. It was a terrible thing to think about. Jesus knew how He was going to suffer and He did not have to do it. Yet He would do it, to save us from our sins.

2. The Scourging at the Pillar

Jesus is tied to a post and lashed with whips.

Then Judas, the traitor, led soldiers to this garden to arrest Jesus. Judas kissed Jesus, to show the soldiers who He was. They took hold of Our Lord and brought Him before Pilate. He told the soldiers to tie Jesus to a post. Then they took heavy whips and beat Him until His back was covered with blood.

3. The Crowning with Thorns

A crown made of sharp thorns is pressed on the head of Jesus causing great pain.

Pilate gave Our Lord to the Jews, so they could put Him to death. The soldiers made a crown of thorns and pressed it deep into His head. Then they mocked Him, saying, "Hail, King of the Jews."

4. Jesus Carries His Cross

Though weak from pain, Our Lord is forced to take up His heavy cross.

Though He was weak from pain and loss of blood, Jesus was forced to take up the cross and carry it on His shoulders. It was so heavy He fell three times on the way to Calvary.

5. The Crucifixion

Jesus, after nails had been driven through His hands and feet, is nailed to the cross.

For three hours Our Saviour hung on the cross. His body was racked with pain. His heart was heavy with the sins of the world. Then He died.

The Five Glorious Mysteries

1. The Resurrection

Our Lord rises from the dead on the third day after His burial.

The third day after His death, Jesus rose from the dead just as He said He would. He did this to prove He is God. His friends coming to His tomb found the stone removed and the body of Our Lord no longer there. Only God could raise Himself from the dead.

2. The Ascension

Our Lord ascends into heaven in the presence of the Apostles.

Jesus came to His friends many times after He rose from the dead. He told them to go everywhere and teach everybody what they must do to be saved. He wanted them to make the whole world Catholic. After forty days, before their eyes, He ascended into heaven.

3. The Descent of the Holy Ghost

The Holy Ghost comes down upon the Apostles.

A little while later, the friends of Jesus were together. The Holy Ghost came down upon them in the form of little flames. After that they did many wonderful things through the power of God the Holy Ghost.

4. The Assumption

Our blessed Lady is taken into heaven by Our Lord, her divine Son.

Jesus could not let His Mother die and be buried and remain dead like other people. So after her death and burial, she was taken by angels and carried into heaven.

5. The Crowning of the Blessed Virgin

Our blessed Lady is crowned Queen of Heaven by her divine Son, Our Lord.

What joy there was in heaven among the saints and angels. Her divine Son crowned her Queen of heaven. Our Lady is the greatest of all the creatures God made.

If you know how to pray the rosary learn to say it with greater devotion. Offer your dear Mother Mary these beautiful flowers as often as you can. Say at least a part of the rosary each day. The Blessed Virgin will obtain many graces for you if you are faithful in saying the rosary.

Saint Theresa of Jesus—October 15

The saint whose feast we are celebrating today was born many years ago in Spain. St. Theresa had good parents. They were rich, and they trained their children to love and serve God faithfully. While Theresa was yet small her greatest delight was to hear her mother tell stories of the saints. Her mother told her many beautiful things about the great love the saints had for God and how much they did for the honor and glory of God. As soon as Theresa was old enough to read, she read all she could about the lives of the saints. Above all she took pleasure in reading about the martyrs. She longed to give her life for God. She used to sit for hours thinking about how wonderful it would be for her to be martyred for the sake of Jesus.

Theresa had a little brother with whom she usually played. This little boy was also very much interested in the lives of the saints and he and Theresa talked many times about the glory of being martyrs. One day the two of them made up their minds to run away from home to go to Africa to be killed for their faith in Christ. They had no idea where Africa was. They had

The Infant Jesus Appearing to St. Theresa

heard that many Christians were being put to death there for their faith, so they thought they would go there and become martyrs. Do you think that was a wise thing for them to do? Of course, Theresa and her brother were very young at that time. They were not any older than some of you. They loved Jesus dearly and wanted to do something to show Him how much they loved Him. So they started off for Africa. You can imagine the two children trudging along the road that morning, carrying with them a little bread for their dinner. They walked on bravely for a long time. They did not think about the worry they were causing their dear mother. They thought only of going to be killed for Jesus' sake. While they were crossing a bridge, they met their uncle who promptly scolded them for running away and took them home to their parents. Theresa and her brother were very much disappointed that they were not allowed to go to Africa.

When Theresa was old enough she went to a convent, where she lived many years, doing much good to all. Theresa became a great saint. She did many wonderful things for God. She had to suffer much, which was just as hard as to be a martyr. By her good example she helped many souls to know and love God and to serve Him faithfully.

St. Theresa as a child loved to hear about the saints. This made her wish to be one also. When she heard how the saints loved and worked for Jesus, she was filled with a great desire to do something to show her love for Him. She would often say, "If these can do so much and suffer so many hardships for God, why can't I also do something?" So she made up her mind to become a saint, and you know how well she succeeded. You can imitate Saint Theresa in many things. She loved God so much that she wished to suffer all sorts of pain for love of Him. She worked hard for many years to bring souls to know and love Him also. God did not want her to go to Africa. He had other work planned for her.

God wishes you also to do something for Him. He has planned how you can help to win souls for heaven. But he wants you to learn to obey your parents and teachers, to study your lessons, to imitate the saints in their love for Him and to be faithful to your duties as children. Then later on He will tell you what He desires you to do to serve Him. Ask St. Theresa to help you to do your duty as a good Christian child so that some day you may be able to love and serve Jesus as she did. Say a special prayer to this great saint to-day that she may obtain for you many graces and blessings.

St. Raphael, the Archangel—October 24

A long time ago, in a country far from here, there lived a pious man and his wife and son. This man's name was Tobias. His son was also called Tobias. There were many wicked people in that country, but Tobias and his family served God faithfully. The father was a very kind man and helped the poor and the sick in every way he could. Once, while resting after a day of hard work, some dirt from the nest of a swallow fell upon his eyes and made him blind. This was very hard for Tobias for now he could no longer help his neighbors. He was very patient, however, and did not get cross and complain because this happened to him. He continued to serve God and prayed every day for patience in his sufferings.

When the father became old and thought he would soon die, he called his son and told him always to be kind to his mother, to care for her in her old age, and to keep the commandments of God. Afterwards he sent his son to a city far away to collect some money which he had lent to a man there. But before going, the father told the son to get some one to go with him since the journey was long and dangerous. The young man went out and, lo, standing before him was a beautiful young man, dressed as if ready for a journey. Tobias did not know the young man, but he asked him if he knew the way to the city to which he was to go. The young man said that he did, and when Tobias asked him to show him the way, the stranger was glad to go with him. They started out together and by night came to a river. When Tobias bathed his feet in the river a big fish came up and seemed about to eat him. Tobias was frightened but the young man told him to take hold and pull it out of the water. When Tobias had done this, he told him to cut out the heart, and the gall and the liver and to save them for later use.

After this they went on and in a few days reached the city. Here they stopped for a while at the house of relatives. The young man went to the person who owed Tobias the money and when he had received it he came back to young

Tobias. After a while, Tobias made ready to return home. How glad his father and mother were to see him again! Then Tobias took the gall of the fish he caught and rubbed it over the eyes of his father and at once he could see again. They praised God and thanked Him for this great blessing. When they wanted to thank the young man for all he had done for Tobias they saw him suddenly become more beautiful. A bright light shone about him. He now told them that he was the Angel Raphael who had been sent by God to protect Tobias. Then the angel disappeared and returned to heaven.

The story of this angel is very interesting, my dear children. It shows you how God sends His Angels to guard and guide you. True, you cannot see your Guardian Angel as Tobias saw the Archangel Raphael. But your Angel is at your side nevertheless. He guards, guides and protects you and tells you what to do, just as the angel Raphael did to Tobias. If you follow him, you also will be rewarded for your obedience. Never forget to ask your Guardian Angel to help you. Never go away, especially if you have to pass through dangerous places, without asking your Angel to go with you and to protect you. Often think of your Angel walking by your side as you imagine the Angel Raphael must have walked beside Tobias on his journey.

NOVEMBER

Feast of All Saints—November 1

There is one feast, my dear children, which should be a feast of great joy to all of us. On this day we celebrate the feast of all the saints in heaven. You notice that now and then I say to you, "To-day is the feast of St. Theresa, or to-day is the feast of St. Francis." But there are so many saints that we do not have days enough in the year for all of them. So we have one day on which to honor all the saints.

The saints are the special friends of God. They loved and served Him faithfully while they lived in this world. Now they are in heaven with God. Some of these saints we know better than others. What saint can you name? Yes, first of all the Blessed Virgin, then you know St. Joseph. Can you name some other saints? St. Francis, St. Theresa, St. Anthony. There are many saints of whom we do not know anything, not even their names.

Some of the saints died for Jesus. We call these martyrs. Even little children gave their lives for Jesus. Some day I shall tell you about St. Agnes, a young girl, who died for Jesus, and of St. Dorothy, another young girl who gave her life for the love of Jesus. So you see, dear children, that this great feast ought to remind you that you also can become a saint, if you try. To become a saint you must be pure. Your heart must be free from sin. You must love God and keep His commandments.

When you think of the saints so happy now with God in heaven, think also that you too will one day be as happy as they, if you live the life of a good Catholic child now and later on continue to lead a holy life. Ask your patron saint to pray for you that you may please Jesus by your love and devotion. Do not forget to pray often to all the saints. They can help you, for they are God's friends.

Feast of All Souls—November 2

Yesterday, dear children, we had the feast of All Saints. This day is so called because there are so many saints in heaven that we cannot know all their names and also because the year has not enough days to give each saint a special feast day. But to-day we have a feast that does not make us feel so happy and cheerful as yesterday's. To-day we are reminded of the souls in Purgatory. Now what do I mean by the souls in Purgatory? What is Purgatory? What kind of a place is it?

You know, dear children, that when a person dies with a mortal sin on his soul, he cannot get to heaven. His soul must go to hell. He will never again be able to get out of it. Which souls go to heaven? The souls of those persons who die in the state of grace and are free from the stain of sin.

But many persons die with the stain of small sins on their souls. These cannot enter heaven at once. They must remain in Purgatory until their souls are entirely free from all stains. These are the souls for whom we pray in a special manner to-day. These holy souls suffer many terrible pains in Purgatory. Our prayers and our good works help them to leave this place sooner.

My dear children, perhaps among the souls in Purgatory you have a father or a mother, or a sister or brother or some other dear relative. Will you let them suffer without trying to help them to be released from their pains? What can you do for them? How can you help the suffering souls? You can do much for these poor suffering souls. First of all, you can frequently assist at Holy Mass for them. This is one of the best ways to help them. Then, if you have already received your First Holy Communion, you can often receive Our Lord in your heart and ask Him to help the souls in Purgatory. You can offer your prayers and good works for them. In your visits to Jesus in church, ask Him to have mercy on the souls suffering in Purgatory. Do all your actions for the relief of the holy souls. Obey more promptly, treat your playmates more kindly, be pleasant and agreeable for the love of the holy souls.

Often say this prayer: "Eternal rest grant unto them, O Lord, and let perpetual light shine upon them; may they rest in peace." Say, "My Jesus, mercy," frequently during the day to gain the indulgence for the souls in Purgatory.

Do not forget that some day you may be in Purgatory. How glad you will then be if by the prayers and good works of a little child you are released from your sufferings. Make a special resolution now to do all you can during this month to help the sufferings souls in Purgatory.

St. Elizabeth of Hungary—November 19

St. Elizabeth was the daughter of a king. She was therefore a princess. Her father and mother, the King and Queen of the country, were fervent Catholics. Little Elizabeth was a lovable child, gentle and sweet-tempered towards all. When she was but four years old she had to leave her parents to go to live in a strange country. You can imagine how deeply her dear mother grieved when she saw her little girl go far away, perhaps never to come back again. When she arrived in the country to which she was sent, she had to live in a big castle. This castle was the home of a great prince, whose son, Louis, Elizabeth was to marry when she was old enough. You see, in those days, dear children, people used to promise their children in marriage when they were very young.

Elizabeth had been well trained by her good mother. Young as she was she loved to pray and to think of God. She knew how to deny herself for the love of God. Her pious mother taught her to be especially kind towards the poor. Whenever she could, Elizabeth gave money or food to them. She saved all her pocket-money for them. She was not fond of rich dresses or fine jewelry. Once on a great feast she was dressed in rich finery and wore a gold crown on her head. When she knelt before the crucifix in church and saw the crown of thorns on the head of Jesus, she wept bitterly and taking off her crown said: "How can I, a poor sinner, wear a crown of gold, when Jesus wears a crown of thorns?" She was ashamed to be dressed so richly when Jesus was so poor for love of us.

When the father of Louis died, his mother and sister treated little Elizabeth very unkindly. They made fun of her piety and laughed at her when she prayed. And because she liked the poor and waited on them whenever she could, they called her a servant and not a princess. They even tried to turn Louis against her, but he saw what a beautiful soul she had and would listen to nothing they said against her. However, Louis was often away from the castle and poor Elizabeth had to suffer much. Yet she was always patient and gentle. You see, dear children, how even a rich princess had to bear many hardships. Whether you are rich or poor, you will have much to bear for the sake of Jesus. When you try to do what you know is pleasing to God, some wicked people will laugh at you and mock you and persecute you. The saints give you an example of what you should do when you are treated in this way.

St. Elizabeth was far away from her home and her country. In those days it was not easy for her to write to her parents. Her father and mother did not know that she was treated so cruelly. They would have sent soldiers to guard her and bring her home. Elizabeth did not wish her parents to know what she suffered. She bore everything patiently and thus she became a great saint. How often you complain when things do not go as you wish. At times you may have to live with somebody who does not treat you well. You may have to be with children who tease you or hurt you by unkind words. Think of the good St. Elizabeth then and ask her to help you to bear your cross.

When Elizabeth was old enough she was married to Louis. He was very kind to her and loved her dearly. He allowed her to visit the sick, to help the needy, to go to church and to do all that her heart desired. Elizabeth was like an angel among her people. The people loved her and treated her with great respect.

But Elizabeth's happiness did not last long. Her husband went to the Holy Land to fight for the Holy Sepulchre and while there he died. Now began another time of great suffering for Elizabeth. She was driven out of her palace one cold winter's night. She was not allowed to take anything with her. Her poor little children were shivering in the cold. They went from house to house to find shelter, but the ungrateful people, afraid of the cruel man who had put out Elizabeth, refused to help her. At last she found shelter in a stable. Now you might think Elizabeth would complain and perhaps say that God did not care for her, else He would not send her so many troubles. But no; instead she went to a church where the priests were singing the praises of God and made them sing a hymn of thanksgiving for all the sufferings He sent her.

After some time she was taken back to her palace, but she no longer cared to stay in the world. She sent her children to a good school, and she herself lived alone in a little hut. She spent her days praying and serving the poor and the sick. She gave all her money to build and keep up hospitals and she herself washed and cared for the sick and the poor.

The life of St. Elizabeth is full of suffering and trials. St. Elizabeth bore everything patiently. In spite of all she had to endure, she was always kind to the poor. She loved the poor as her children. What can you do to imitate this saint? Perhaps you may say that you are not rich like St. Elizabeth. That is quite true. But still you can be good to the poor. I shall tell you how. You can share your bread and butter, your apple or orange, your candy and ice cream, and give it to the poor. In every church there is a poor box into which people drop the money they wish to give to the poor. Do you ever put anything into that box? You can also help the poor by giving a glass of water to some one who is thirsty or tired. You help the sick by running errands for mother, when one of the family is sick. You can also do little errands for a sick neighbor. Whatever we do for others for the love of Jesus, He will receive as being done to Himself. Always love the poor. With the permission of your parents, give them something of what you have. Speak kindly to any poor or crippled person you know. Never make fun of these poor beings.

Often ask the good St. Elizabeth to help you to love the poor for God's sake. Ask her to obtain for you a share of her great love for Jesus.

DECEMBER

St. Nicholas—December 6

This saint is one whom children ought to love very much. St. Nicholas is the saint whom many people now call Santa Claus. You see, dear children, father and mother often tell you that if you are not good children Santa Claus will not bring you anything for Christmas. That makes some children behave; but good boys and girls do not need to be afraid of Santa Claus. He loves good boys and girls.

Now I shall tell you what Saint Nicholas has to do with Santa Claus. St. Nicholas lived many years ago. He was a good boy. When he was old enough he became a priest and afterward a bishop. At that time there were many poor people living in the place where St. Nicholas was. He was very sorry for these people and tried to help them all he could. But he never wanted any one to know that he helped them. So he always quietly went to the houses of the poor at night and left baskets of food and clothing. In the morning when the people awoke they found the good things St. Nicholas had left for them.

St. Nicholas was especially kind to little children. He loved them dearly and always had some good things, such as nuts and fruit for them. Of course, St. Nicholas is dead many years. But there are many good people now who try to imitate this kind saint and so, every year at Christmas time, they bring many things to people. The little children are especially remembered and they receive toys and candy and fruit and many other things from Santa Claus. You see, dear children, this is the way people try to imitate the good St. Nicholas. In some countries the people called St. Nicholas Santa Claus and now every one who brings good things to others at Christmas time is called a Santa Claus, because he is doing what St. Nicholas did.

The Immaculate Conception of the Blessed Virgin Mary—December 8

This great feast, my dear children, reminds us of the purity and holiness of the Blessed Virgin. Do you remember what we call the sin which every one has received from Adam and Eve? Yes, original sin. Every person that comes into this world has the stain of original sin on his soul. The Blessed Virgin alone was without this sin. God wanted her to be the Mother of His Son. He did not wish the devil to have any power over her, and so the Blessed Virgin was free from all stain of sin. Therefore you must be pure to please your dear Mother Mary. Try to keep your soul free from all sin in order to imitate the purity of the Blessed Virgin. God gave Mary to you as your Mother, and He wished you to be pure and holy; for if you wish to be her child you ought to have a pure heart.

Ask your dear Mother Mary every day to help you to keep your soul free from all sin. Say three Hail Marys every day that she may obtain for you the grace to keep your heart pure. Often say this prayer also: "O Mary, by thy Immaculate Conception, purify my body and sanctify my soul."

This day is kept as a holyday. On this day people must go to church to hear Mass as on Sundays. When you go to church on this feast, pray earnestly that the Blessed Virgin may help you and your parents and your brothers and sisters and all your friends and relatives to live holy and pure lives. Ask the Blessed Virgin also to make a good child of you so that she may count you as one of her own children.

JANUARY

St. Sebastian—January 20

Boys always like stories of soldiers, do you not, boys? Well, to-day I shall tell you the story of a brave soldier who lived a long time ago. This soldier was called Sebastian. He was tall and strong and very brave. He had to be near the King to guard him. He fought hard for the King and was not afraid of anything. At the time Sebastian lived, the King whom he served made a law that all people that believed in Jesus Christ should be arrested and killed. This King was a proud King and he thought he himself was a god. Many good people were arrested and thrown before wild animals to be eaten by them. Some were tortured by being thrown into kettles filled with burning oil. Even children and women were tortured and killed. Tomorrow I shall tell you about the dear girl saint, St. Agnes, who was also killed by the orders of this wicked King.

Sebastian during all this time, helped the Christians as much as he could. He told them to be brave and to suffer patiently, for soon it would all be over and they would be in heaven with Jesus. At last some one told the King that Sebastian was a Christian. The King became very angry when he heard this. He did not believe it and sent for Sebastian. When Sebastian came, the King asked him if he were a Christian. At this, the brave Sebastian proudly said, "I am." He knew that the King would have him put to death, but he was not afraid; he was glad to die for Jesus. The King now became furious and ordered Sebastian to be shot to death, with arrows. Do you know what an arrow is? This was a very cruel way to kill a person, but Sebastian was brave. He was glad to suffer for Jesus. The men who were to kill Sebastian shot arrows at him till at last they thought he was dead. But Sebastian was not dead. A pious lady had him carried into her house. She took such good care of him that he became well again. One day the King was standing on the marble steps in front of his palace, when all at once

Sebastian appeared before him. Now the King thought Sebastian was dead. He therefore thought he saw a ghost. But when Sebastian spoke to him, he knew he was alive and he was so angry that he had him clubbed to death right there on the marble steps. This is how St. Sebastian died. Do you not think he was a brave soldier?

St. Agnes—January 21

Dear children: To-day we celebrated the feast of a beautiful saint. It is the feast of the dear St. Agnes. The name Agnes means "pure." Her parents gave her that name because they wished their little girl to be pure as snow. Her parents were rich, but they were also very pious people. Little Agnes grew to be a lovely child. Everybody loved her; she was so sweet-tempered that she never gave way to angry words or looks. She did not, like many little girls to-day, spend all her time thinking about how pretty she was, or what fine clothes she had. Instead she prayed and learned to work so that she could help the poor. She loved to take care of the poor people who came to her house every day. She was especially kind to those that had no one else to look after them. Her greatest pleasure was to speak to Jesus, and while still very young she promised Jesus that she would always keep her heart spotlessly pure. Jesus helped her to keep this promise. Agnes was never heard to say anything that was even in the slightest way wrong. She took great care to please Jesus in everything she did. Day and night she thought of Jesus and how she could love Him more.

When Agnes lived, cruel and wicked men who hated Jesus tried to kill everyone that loved Him and believed in Him. So they hunted the Christians, and when they found one, tortured him to make him give up his faith. When Agnes was about thirteen years old she was arrested and taken to the Judge. He tried everything to make her deny Jesus. But Agnes would not listen to him. He promised to make her richer than she was, to give her everything great and good in this world, but Agnes paid no attention to him. At last he tried to scare her by threatening her with all kinds of terrible things but Agnes remained firm. She prayed to Jesus to help her. When the Judge saw that he could do nothing with her, he ordered that she be put to death by having her head cut off. Agnes heard this and cheerfully went with the men that were to kill her. But she was so young, so gentle and pure, that she seemed more like an angel than a human being. With a quick sharp blow of the sword, the executioner cut off her head.

Her good parents thanked God for the holy child God had given them. They were sorry, very sorry, of course, to see her suffer, but they knew that she would soon be in heaven with Jesus. Agnes was pure and holy. If you, dear children, wish to be pure you must imitate St. Agnes. You must lead a pure life; you must pray to Jesus that He may help you always to keep your heart for Him alone. Pray to St. Agnes; ask her to help you to live good, pure lives, that you, too, may one day be happy with Jesus in heaven.

St. Francis de Sales—January 29

St. Francis de Sales, the saint whose feast we celebrate to-day, is loved and honored throughout the whole world. He was noted for his gentleness and kindness. Even as a little child, Francis was known to be always cheerful and pleasant. People loved this little boy and his parents took special care to train him well. Little Francis also showed a great love for the poor and needy. He could not bear to see poor people and when it was possible he gave them food or clothing.

St. Francis de Sales was born in France. He was the son of rich parents. His father was very strict with him and trained him to be truthful and honest. His mother was a pious woman who spent her time teaching her children to lead holy lives. With such good parents it is little wonder that Francis became so great a saint. Little Francis was trained by his mother to overcome himself in small things; that is, she trained him to do cheerfully and gladly all those little things which most children find very tiresome and disagreeable. She rarely allowed him to have sweet things, such as candy and cake. She taught him to do without these for the love of Jesus Who suffered so much for us. Though his parents were rich, as I said before, little Francis was always dressed in plain clothes. In those days it was the style to dress the children of rich people, even the boys, in fine and expensive clothes. Francis' mother showed her little son that it was better to spend the money thus saved to help the poor. His clothes were clean and neat and Francis was happy to do something for God's poor.

As soon as the child was old enough to understand her, she spoke to him of the love of God and of the fatherly care He has for all of His children. One of the first things little Francis learned to say was, "God and my mother love me very much."

His father also trained his son to be good. He spent much time teaching him the things that would one day make him great. He loved his little Francis dearly, but he would not excuse his faults. He punished him when he found Francis doing something he ought not to do. He was particularly strict with him in regard to honesty and truthfulness.

One day little Francis found a bright-colored girdle which one of the men working about the place had laid down. When Francis saw it he was delighted with its beautiful colors and took it with him. Shortly afterwards the man came for his jacket and girdle but the girdle was missing. No one knew what had become of it. When the father of Francis heard about it, he thought he would ask the little boy if he knew anything about the belt or girdle. At once Francis acknowledged that he had taken it and falling down on his knees asked his father to forgive him. Some of the men present asked the father not to punish the little boy. But the good man knew that such little acts of dishonesty often lead to greater faults. So he gave Francis a spanking and told him that since it was the first time he had done such a thing he would let him off easy. But should it ever happen again he would punish more severely. Little Francis was ever after careful about taking things and would never so much as take an apple without permission.

Thus Francis grew to be quiet, mild and gentle. His mother made it her chief business to train his heart and mind; she taught him the "Our Father" and "Hail Mary" and other prayers. The little Francis gave her great delight by the pleasure he took in learning these prayers. Francis was a bright lad; he had a good memory and could easily remember all his mother told him about the good God, the Blessed Virgin, the angels and the saints. He listened with the greatest attention to the lives of the saints and often while his mother told him about what the saints did to please God, little Francis would say, "I want to be a saint, too."

This little boy was so pleased to hear about God and His Blessed Mother and the saints that he could not keep it to himself. He called together his playmates and told them what his mother had taught him. He would take a little bell and ring it to call the children together. At this time Francis was only five years old. You see, dear children, this boy was a little apostle; he was doing what he could to make others love Jesus. He tried to bring many souls to our dear Lord.

As you might imagine, Francis was very devout at his prayers. He did not turn around to see who was coming into church when he prayed there. He was also very gentle and cheerful with every one, especially with his brothers and sisters and playmates. He was very careful about always telling the truth. He was ready to acknowledge any fault he had committed and would never excuse himself. He hated a lie so much that he was willing to suffer anything rather than tell the smallest untruth.

Francis also showed a great love towards the poor. Although not yet two years old, his greatest delight was to receive something which he could hand to a poor person. As he grew older he showed his love for the poor in many ways. Often he would share with them the food he had. His pious mother many times took the boy with her on her visits to the poor and the sick. She would allow him to give the articles of food and clothing she had brought with her to the sick and needy. This was a great pleasure to Francis. It was his greatest joy to make others happy.

With all this Francis was a real boy. He loved to play with his little friends and often took walks with them into the woods. He would tell them stories of the Lives of the Saints and they listened to them with great attention. No one ever said a bad word in his presence. Every one respected him and the boys were ready to do anything he might suggest.

As Francis grew older his father sent him away to school. He studied so hard that he was soon at the head of his class. Later on he wished to become a priest, but his father objected to this plan. However, Francis begged his father so hard that at last he gave his consent. After some time, Francis became a bishop and for many years worked greatly for the honor and glory of God. He converted many to the true faith.

There are many things this dear saint did that you, dear children, can imitate. Francis was kind, cheerful and gentle. Although he became angry easily, he tried so much to overcome that fault that he was called the "meek saint." You know what it means to be meek and humble. If so pious a boy as this saint had to work so hard to become meek, surely you will not stop after trying for only a short time to learn to control your temper. Make up your mind to become a saint as did St. Francis de Sales. Say to yourself every morning, "I will become a saint." Then ask St. Francis de Sales to help you to become one. Ask him to obtain for you the grace to live as God wills you to live.

To-day think often of this dear saint and try to imitate his example. Try to think what he would do if he were in your place. Thank God for having given for our example so great a saint.

FEBRUARY

The Purification of the Blessed Virgin Mary —February 2

The feast we celebrate to-day is very interesting. It has two names. Sometimes it is called the feast of the Purification and at other times it is called Candlemas Day. On this day candles are blessed. You saw some people take candles to church to be blessed by the priest.

When Jesus was forty days old the Blessed Virgin Mary and Joseph carried Him to the temple. There they offered Him to God. They also offered two doves as a sacrifice for Jesus. There was at that time in the temple a holy priest who was very old. When this priest, whose name was Simeon, saw the Infant Jesus, he took Him in his arms and thanked God for having let him live to see the Savior of the world. This holy old priest called Jesus a "light to the revelation of the Gentiles." The candles which are burned on our altars are to remind us that Jesus is the light of the world.

On this day also, our dear Mother Mary was told by the holy man Simeon that a sword should pierce her heart. He meant to tell her that she would have to suffer much for Jesus' sake. This was one of the great sorrows of our Blessed Mother. How it must have hurt her heart when she saw her little Jesus playing so happily, and she thought that one day cruel men would nail Him to a cross!

To-day's feast is one that gives us much to think about. Thank God every day that He has given you the grace to know Jesus, the Light of the World. Ask God to let the Priests and Brothers and Sisters who work in heathen lands, bring souls to know Him. Ask the Blessed Mother to help you to be patient when you have anything to suffer. Ask her to help you to keep pure and holy so that you may one day see Jesus and be with Him forever in heaven.

Saint Blase—February 3

This morning, dear children, the priest blessed your throats. Why did he do this? To keep you from getting sore throat? Yes, but do you know why your throats were blessed to-day and not yesterday or the day before? It is because to-day is the feast of St. Blase. Who was St. Blase? Why do the priests bless the throats of the people on his feast? I shall tell you the story of St. Blase and then you will be able to answer all these questions.

St. Blase was a holy bishop who lived many years ago. He was kind to every one, especially to the sick and the poor. So he did all he could to help the people when they came to ask his help. One day a woman brought to him her little boy who had swallowed a fishbone. The bone stuck in his throat and he was choking to death. St. Blase made the sign of the cross over the boy and at once the fishbone fell out of his mouth and the boy was saved.

People pray to St. Blase to ask him to protect them against all diseases of the throat. Of course, dear children, you know that God is pleased when we ask the saints to help us. But it will be useless to ask Saint Blase to cure a sore throat, or to keep you from having tonsilitis or diphtheria if you do not take the proper care of yourself. God wants you to do all you can to keep yourself well. But even with the best of care it sometimes happens that you will become ill. You may therefore ask this good saint to help you, that you may not get any of those diseases which many children get every year.

Have a great devotion to this saint and do something special in his honor. Say a prayer to him so that God may not let you suffer from disease of the throat, or, if you have such disease that you become better again. Pray often then that through the help of St. Blase, God may protect you and your dear brothers and sisters and all your little playmates and friends from all diseases of the throat and all other ills of body and soul.

St. Valentine's Day—February 14

To the Teacher:—The feast of St. Valentine will give the Catholic teacher a splendid opportunity to encourage children to send messages and greetings of Catholic import and meaning to their friends instead of such that are not only foolish but often pagan in character and which take the form of valentines, as they are called. What purpose does it serve to let the children cut out hearts, darts, cupids, and the like, to send to their friends? How much better to suggest to the children to make religious pictures and booklets to send to their friends! A message of cheerfulness and encouragement to the sick, to those in affliction, in imitation of the thoughtfulness of St. Valentine is much better. The sending of valentines has assumed great proportions. Catholic teachers can start a crusade against this custom by introducing a counter movement which will serve to perpetuate the real motive that actuated St. Valentine. It will not do merely to frown on the custom or to voice disapproval; to combat it effectively something better must be substituted. This plan has been tried in some schools with great success. It appealed, not only to the children, but to the adult members of the family as well. If the children cannot make booklets, introduce the custom of sending holy pictures. It will be a good investment, even if the teacher must supply the pictures. Children do not usually make much use of holy pictures unless they are taught to mount them on construction paper or paste them in booklets. This is an interesting occupation for them and at the same time much good can be accomplished if they study the picture and write a sentence or two under each.

The Courage of St. Valentine

The story of St. Valentine is very interesting and it shows that even when the saints were suffering every kind of pain and torture, they had the courage to go on and do all they could to help others. St. Valentine was a priest who did much good among his people. At the time he lived, wicked men were trying to kill every one that believed in Christ. They were especially anxious to kill those that were teaching the people to know Christ. St. Valentine was not afraid, but he went about doing his work, helping his people. When he was put into prison he did not forget his friends. He spent his time praying for them and in writing little letters to them. He tied these messages around the necks of pigeons and sent them to his friends. You can imagine how glad they were to get a letter from the good Father Valentine as they called him. These letters cheered the people and helped to make them strong in their faith. Now you know why people send valentines. However, instead of sending such silly messages as some people are sending to-day, we shall send kind letters to the sick, the poor, the helpless to cheer them in their sufferings. That is what St. Valentine did.

I have a little plan for you. I know you will wish to be like St. Valentine and make others happy. Now you say, "How can we do that?" I shall tell you. It is very easy. Suppose you make a booklet containing some beautiful pictures of the Infant Jesus or the Blessed Virgin or some other saint. I know you can make somebody happy by sending them such a booklet. What do you think of my plan? Do you wish to do this? To whom can we send the booklets? That can be easily settled. There are many children in hospitals or in orphan asylums. Don't you think they would like your little books? Would it make them feel better? Would

St. Valentine want you to do that? Make up your minds to-day which pictures you wish to use for your booklet. You can paste the pictures into it during your spare time. To-morrow we shall get them ready to send away. While you are making booklets, think of St. Valentine and the messages he sent to his friends. Ask him to help you to make others happy, especially those that are sick or in trouble.

A ST. VALENTINE'S BOOKLET

Practice:

1. I will make the best booklet I know how to make.
2. I will not spend any money on silly valentines, but I will make pictures or booklets to send to my friends.

> Hearts good and true
> Have wishes few
> In narrow circles bounded,
> And hope that lives
> On what God gives
> Is Christian hope well **founded**.
>
> Small things are best;
> Grief and unrest
> To rank and wealth are **given**;
> But little things
> On little wings
> Bear little souls to Heaven.
>
> *Father Faber.*

MARCH

St. Patrick—March 17

To-day you see people wear bits of green ribbon or shamrocks. If you would ask them why they do this, they would tell you because it is St. Patrick's Day. Of course you will wonder who St. Patrick is, and why people wear green ribbons or shamrocks on his feast. So I shall tell you the story of St. Patrick and then you will see why people wear green ribbons or shamrocks to honor this saint.

St. Patrick lived many years ago. His parents were good people and they did all they could to teach their little boy to love and serve God. Patrick was a pious little fellow. He tried to obey his parents and kept his soul pure and spotless. One day Patrick and his little sister were playing in a field when the girl slipped and fell. As she fell she struck her forehead against a sharp stone. The stone cut her head and the girl seemed to be dead. As soon as little Patrick saw his sister lying so quietly and bleeding so much from the deep cut, he knelt down beside her and prayed. Then he rose and made the sign of the cross over her and at once the wound healed and his sister was cured. Only a slight mark remained as a reminder of what had happened.

Patrick was a bright boy and took great pleasure in his studies. When he was old enough his parents sent him away to a school. But one day a terrible thing happened. Some wicked men came to the place and captured many men and boys and carried them away to a strange country. Patrick was among them. This was

ST. PATRICK

very hard, indeed. Do you not think that he prayed to God to bring him home safely to his parents? The bad men sold Patrick to a man that made him take care of his sheep and swine. Even in this great trouble, Patrick did not forget to pray. After a long time, Patrick succeeded in getting back home once more.

Later he made up his mind to go back to the country where he had been captive and to preach to the people about Jesus Christ. So Patrick came to Ireland to teach the people there to know God and to serve him. This was not an easy task. It was hard for these people to understand some of the things Patrick told them. One day he was telling them about the three divine Persons in God, the Father, the Son and the Holy Ghost. To make it easier for them to understand this, he showed them a shamrock. In our country you often see clover leaves. These are shaped like the shamrock and from this they learned to remember the three divine Persons in God. There were many shamrocks growing in Ireland. This made the land look green for the whole place was covered with these little plants. Do you know what clover is? Have you ever seen any? Because the land was so green people called it "Emerald Island" which means green island. Now you see why people wear bits of green ribbon or shamrocks on Saint Patrick's Day. They want to show that they honor St. Patrick for what he did for Ireland. St. Patrick taught them to know Jesus Christ and showed them how they could serve God best. He lived many years in Ireland and did much good.

When you see people wear green ribbons or shamrocks, think of all that St. Patrick did to teach the people of Ireland the true Faith. Thank God for having given St. Patrick the grace to save so many souls. Try to imitate the example of St. Patrick by leading a holy life, so that people may learn from you to love God and to serve Him faithfully.

The Archangel Gabriel—March 18

Do you remember the story I told you about the Archangel Michael? What did he do? Do you also remember what I told you about the Archangel Raphael? Now I shall tell you about another archangel, the Archangel Gabriel. This angel was sent by God from heaven to earth to tell the Blessed Virgin that she was to be the Mother of God. Do you remember the story of this angel coming to our Blessed Lady while she was praying in her little room. All at once the room was filled with a heavenly light and there stood before the Blessed Virgin a most beautiful Angel. This was the Archangel Gabriel.

Dear children, God also sends his angel to you. He has given each of you a Guardian Angel. You cannot see him, but yet he is always at your side. When you say that beautiful prayer, "Angel of God, my Guardian dear," imagine

THE ANNUNCIATION

you see your angel standing beside you, just as the Blessed Virgin saw the Archangel Gabriel.

When the Archangel Gabriel came to Mary he said, "Hail, full of grace, the Lord is with thee; blessed art thou among women." When do you say these words? Yes, in the Hail Mary. When you say the Hail Mary think also of the Angel Gabriel.

St. Joseph—March 19

Next to the Blessed Virgin we honor St. Joseph as the person who was most dear to Our Lord. St. Joseph was the foster father of Jesus. Jesus did not have an earthly father; His Father was in heaven. St. Joseph took care of the Holy Child and His Mother. He worked for them in his carpenter shop. He was poor; he did not live in a fine house. God chose a poor man for the foster father of His Son. God wanted to show us that He loved the poor; His only Son was poor; Jesus lived and died poor.

We do not know anything about St. Joseph when he was young. Probably he lived just as other boys of those days, but he was purer and holier than any of them. He was meek and humble. He loved God with all his heart and served Him every day of his life. Can you imagine, dear children, what a great saint he must have been to be chosen by God to care for Jesus. To be with Jesus all day; to live for Jesus, to work for Him, to care for Him and His Blessed Mother, what a wonderful life that was! St. Joseph was pure and holy. That is why he was chosen to live with the two holiest persons who were ever on earth. How happy he must have felt, when after a day of hard work, Jesus ran to meet him. Joseph took good care of Jesus and Mary. You remember how kind and gentle he was when he and the Blessed Virgin had to leave their little home in Nazareth to go to Bethlehem. How sad he was, when they could find no place to stay when Jesus was to be born. How happy he must have been when he held the dear Babe in his arms on the first Christmas night! How carefully he watched over Jesus and Mary on the Flight into Egypt. Surely he was greatly troubled that Herod wanted to kill the Child. He never complained or grumbled that he had to work so hard. He might have thought that God ought to make him rich so that he could care better for Jesus and Mary. His days were spent in work and prayer. All day long he thought of Jesus and His Blessed Mother

All he did was for them. What a wonderful example St. Joseph gives you, dear children. See how he worked from morning till night for Jesus. Everything he did was for Him. His thoughts were all on Jesus. And when he came to die, he died in the arms of Jesus and Mary. What a happy death. That is why we pray to St. Joseph for a happy death. We ask him to obtain for us the grace to die in the arms of Jesus and Mary as he did. But if you wish to

St. Joseph and the Infant Jesus

die as he did, you must also live as he did. St. Joseph never did anything great or grand. He was only a poor carpenter. He never built big houses, or made fine furniture for rich people or kings. He worked for the poor. He lived and died poor.

Pray often that St. Joseph may help you to be satisfied with what you have. Do not grumble and complain when you do not have the fine clothes and expensive toys you like. By working and praying as St. Joseph did, you will also be able to keep yourself free from sin. If you are always busy the devil cannot tempt you for you will have no time to listen to him.

Try to have a great devotion to this dear saint, for Jesus will hear his prayers for you. He cannot refuse his dear foster father who never refused Him anything when He was on earth. Ask St. Joseph to help you in your prayers, especially for a happy death for all in your family. Say often, "Jesus, Mary and Joseph, I give you my heart and my soul. Jesus, Mary and Joseph assist me in my last agony. Jesus, Mary and Joseph, may I die in your holy company. Amen."

The Annunciation—March 25

We learned just a few days ago about St. Michael, who cast out the bad angels from heaven. We are now going to hear something about another archangel whom we call Gabriel. Angels are messengers; that is what the word angel means. God sends the angels to earth to speak to the people to whom He wants to send a message. We can not see these angels. Once in a while, however, God allows some one to see an angel. This is what happened one day, a long time ago, in a little town of Galilee. There lived in this place a lovely young girl, the most beautiful that ever lived. This beautiful girl was Mary, whom we call the Blessed Virgin.

One day when Mary was devoutly kneeling at prayer, a soft light filled the place and a beautiful angel suddenly stood before her, who said to her: "Hail, full of grace, the Lord is with thee; blessed art thou among women." Mary looked in wonder at the angel when he told her that he was sent to tell her that she was to be the Mother of Jesus. Mary bowed her head and answered the angel: "Behold the handmaid of the Lord; be it done unto me according to thy word."

The picture you saw on page 215 shows the Blessed Virgin kneeling down and saying her prayers, and the angel appearing to her. There you see the Archangel Gabriel telling her the great news.

APRIL

St. Isidore—April 4

This saint was a great bishop who was one of the most learned men of his time. As a boy Isidore found it very hard to learn his lessons at school. This discouraged him very much so that he ran away from school. On his way he rested at a roadside spring. Do you know what a spring is? Here he noticed a stone which had been hollowed out by the water dripping on it. This caused him to think. He thought to himself that if it was possible for the water to wear away the hard stone by steadily dripping upon it day after day, week after week, month after month, and year after year, it ought also be possible to get something into his mind if he kept at it long enough. So he went back to school. He studied hard every day and kept at it until he became very learned. He thanked God for helping him and showed his gratitude by using his learning to convert many people.

My dear children, you can learn a lesson from this saint. Many times you may find it very hard to learn. Think of St. Isidore. Have patience, work hard every day; keep at it all the time and you will succeed. Ask God to help you as St. Isidore did. Then perhaps you also may be able some day to do much for the honor and glory of God.

Blessed Herman Joseph—April 7

In a large city of Germany there lived many years ago a poor family, who had a son named Herman. Herman's mother had a great devotion to the Blessed Virgin and she trained the little boy to love and honor the Mother of God. They had a little altar on which a statue of the Blessed Virgin was placed. Every day Herman and his parents prayed before this altar, asking the help of the dear Mother of God. While yet a very small child, little Herman found the greatest happiness in praying before this altar. He would look at the statue and speak to the Blessed Virgin just as he spoke to his own mother.

When Herman grew older, his mother told him about Jesus in the Blessed Sacrament of the Altar and Herman wanted to be taken to church to visit Jesus. She told him also about the beautiful large statue of the Blessed Virgin there. When she took him to church, Herman's joy was great. He spent many hours praying before the altar of the Blessed Virgin. He told her all his little troubles. He spoke to her as a child speaks to his mother. When Herman was old enough to go to school, he learned diligently. At recess, while the other boys were playing, Herman stole away to church to pray before the altar of the Blessed Virgin. Herman's parents were very poor. Often there was not enough to eat in the house. Then Herman would tell the Blessed Virgin about his troubles and, like a good mother, she helped him.

One day, he told her that he had no shoes; his parents were too poor to buy him any. The Blessed Virgin told him to lift up a stone near the altar and there he would find money for shoes. Herman did as he was told and found the money. The Blessed Virgin told him to come to her every time he needed something. A kind person once gave him a beautiful apple. Herman ran to church, went up to the altar and offered it to the Blessed Virgin. He was much pleased that he had something to give her. "See, Mother," he said, "what a beautiful apple I have brought for Jesus!" And the Blessed Virgin stooped to take the apple from the hand of little Herman and gave it to Jesus. This was a miracle, for God wanted to show that He was pleased with Herman's good heart. When you share an apple or something else with a poor child, it is as pleasing to Jesus as if you gave it to Him.

Later on Herman went to a monastery to become a Brother. He was then given the name Joseph, and that is why he was afterwards known as Herman Joseph. He loved this name, for he honored St. Joseph very much as being near to the Blessed Virgin. After a life of great holiness Herman died.

Like this humble saint, you can have a great love and devotion to our Blessed Mother. No one who loves and honors Mary will be lost, for if you truly love and honor her, you will follow her example and lead a holy life. Often ask the Blessed Herman Joseph to obtain for you a great love for the Blessed Virgin. Like him, go to Mary in all your troubles. Tell her what you need and she will help you as she helped the Blessed Herman Joseph.

MAY

Blessed Imelda—May 14

Blessed Imelda is the little patroness of First Communicants. I wonder do you know why? Well, because her First Holy Communion, which was also her last, was so heavenly in every way.

This dear little girl was born in Bologna, Italy, about the year 1322. When she was still a mere child she was taken to a convent and brought up among the Dominican Sisters. In those days, you know, even tiny tots were taken to convents, where they grew up like so many fragrant lilies. This fair Italian maid was also given a little Dominican habit to wear. How lovely she must have looked—only imagine! And she was just as sweet as her name; Imelda, means, "Go, give honey!"

Now, there was one thing above all other things that Imelda longed for, and that was Holy Communion. But though at the time of this story she was already ten years old, she was not allowed to receive her Lord; for it was then the custom not to let young people receive Holy Communion so early as they do now. Oh, how little Imelda used to yearn for the Bread of Life! With what eager eyes she would watch the Sisters receive the Blessed Sacrament!

One day, when the Sisters had gone back to their places after receiving, it happened. What? The miracle! For suddenly a little Host was seen floating in the air just above the kneeling Imelda. And there it stayed suspended. Jesus wanted to give Himself to the loving girl, you see. Quickly a priest was called. He came with a golden paten. The Host gently came down upon it. And the priest gave Holy Communion to the enraptured maiden. O the love that burned in her heart then! Her one great desire had been granted. For a long time she knelt motionless in an ecstasy of joy with a love-light from heaven on her fair young face—for so long a time, in fact, that some of the Sisters came up gently to speak to her.

Then they found that her first Communion had also been her last; for Jesus had taken her up to heaven to enjoy Him forever.

Imelda had fallen into the sleep of death.

Tell Us Another, Winfrid Herbst, S.D.S.

St. Paschal Baylon—May 17

My dear children: In the lives of the saints of God we find many things which we can imitate. These saints were the friends of God to whom He gave special graces. But the saints were human beings the same as we are. I told you several times that even as little children many of them showed their love for God. Even in their early childhood they tried to live holy lives. St. Paschal Baylon was one of the saints who even as a small child lived a life of great holiness. This saint was born of poor parents. Little Paschal showed a great love towards the Blessed Sacrament. One day, when he was only two years old, he disappeared from his home. There had been some gypsies in the town at that time and the parents feared that they might have stolen their little boy. So they searched everywhere, but could find no trace of Paschal. At last the father and mother went to church to ask God to help them find their child, when to their great surprise and pleasure they found the little boy sitting on the altar steps looking at the tabernacle. Little Paschal knew that Jesus lived there and he wished to be with Him. Many times later he ran away from home to go to church to visit Jesus, but as his parents were afraid something would happen to him on the streets, he was forbidden to go alone. This hurt the little fellow very much but he cheerfully obeyed his parents.

He had also a great devotion to the Blessed Virgin. When he was out in the fields with his sheep, he would kneel down before a figure of the Blessed Virgin which he had carved out of a piece of wood. Paschal's parents were so poor that they could not send him to school. He wished to learn to read, but he had no one to teach him. See how happy you should be to have a chance to learn to read and write. Little Paschal would have been so happy had he been able to go to school, because he wanted to learn all he could about God and the angels and saints. But what did Paschal do in order to learn to read? Whenever he went out with his sheep he took with him a book. Then he asked the people who passed to tell him the letters. The people were pleased with Paschal's eagerness to learn and helped him to learn to read and write. This is how he was able to study his catechism. As soon as he was able to read he would go to a lonely place with his sheep and when they were quietly eating the grass, he took out his catechism or other pious reading and studied and read as long as he could. No wonder God blessed him with so many graces.

St. Paschal was eager to learn to read because he wanted to be able to learn more about God and the saints. Try to be like St. Paschal, dear children, and love to read about God and the wonderful things He did for us. Love also to read about what the saints did for the love of God. It was hard for this saint to learn to read and write; how easy it is for you. You have your teachers to help you and to show you how to learn. Your good parents give you a chance to go to school; they willingly buy books and other things that you need for school. Make good use of your time, therefore, and learn all you can so that you may know, love and serve God better every day.

St. Paschal became a great Saint. He loved to spend hours before the Blessed Sacrament. He also had a great devotion to the Mother of God. Later in his life he became a Franciscan brother. He served God cheerfully for many years.

JUNE

St. Anthony of Padua—June 13

Dear children: You hear so much said about praying to St. Anthony, that I think you will want to know something about him. St. Anthony lived many years ago. He was the son of rich parents. They were devout and God-fearing. They trained their little son, whose name was Fernandez, or Ferdinand, in great piety and love for God. His mother taught him a great love for the Blessed Virgin. All his life, the saint showed this love and devotion towards his heavenly Mother.

When he was old enough to go to school, he learned his lessons so well that his parents and teachers were greatly pleased with him. He was diligent and attentive and never shirked his duty in school. The little boy was as beautiful as a young flower just about to open. He was pure and innocent and showed a kind and loving heart for all.

When he was fifteen years old he went to a monastery to become a friar. That is, he wanted to leave the world and live for God alone by praying and working for souls. One day while he was at a certain monastery the bodies of five Franciscans who had been martyred in Africa, were brought to the place. Ferdinand was so fired with a love for martyrdom that he asked if he could join the Franciscans so that he also might be sent to Africa and become a martyr for Christ. He was allowed to join the Franciscans and then his name was changed to Anthony. He was on his way to Africa when he became very ill. On his way home a great storm arose and the ship on which he was, landed in another country. Here he met the great St. Francis of Assisi. After this St. Anthony was sent to preach and teach. He worked many miracles. One day, when the people of a certain city would not listen to his preaching, St. Anthony went to the sea and spoke to the fishes. They came to the top of the water and quietly listened to his words. After the sermon he made the sign of the cross over them and they went back into the water. When the people saw this, they were ashamed that they had not listened to the saint. Afterwards many were converted. During his life he worked so many miracles that he is called "the great wonder worker." That is why so many people have such great devotion to St. Anthony. Every Tuesday there are devotions in his honor in some churches. People pray to St. Anthony especially to recover lost things, because he has helped so many to find them.

One time while the saint was praying in his room, the Infant Jesus came down and put His little arm around his neck. You can imagine how happy St. Anthony was to hold the Infant Jesus in his arms. St. Anthony is usually pictured with the Child Jesus in his arms. St. Anthony must have loved Jesus very much for it was certainly a great favor to hold the Infant Jesus in his arms. What a happiness it will be for you if you also love the Infant Jesus so that He will gladly come into your heart when you receive Holy Communion. Prepare yourself for Jesus so that He may joyfully come to you and rest in your heart. Pray to St. Anthony, not only for lost things, but also that He may help you to love Jesus more every day. When you see a picture of this saint, think about the great happiness you also may have if you receive Jesus into a pure heart.

THE INFANT JESUS APPEARS TO ST. ANTHONY

St. Germaine Cousin—June 17

This saint was born in France many years ago. Her parents were poor people, but they were pious and trained their daughter to love God tenderly. Germaine was an only child. When a baby she was so sickly that her parents thought she would not live long. But her mother took such good care of her that she grew stronger, though she was never very well. Germaine's mother taught her to love prayer. She taught her how she could pray all day by offering up to God all her work and play. She told her about Jesus and His love for us, about the Blessed Virgin and the saints and angels. Little Germaine listened attentively to her good mother. She never grew tired of hearing about these things. She tried to please her mother by obeying her promptly and cheerfully. She was always gentle and patient. Her greatest pleasure was to go to church to visit Jesus in the Blessed Sacrament.

Germaine's parents were poor, yet the pious girl loved to share the little she had with others poorer than herself. Before she was six years old, Germaine had a painful ailment. Her body was covered with ugly sores. But she did not cry or get cross or fretful. Some children are disagreeable when they are ill. They expect every one to wait on them. The mothers of such children have little rest day or night. Such children are selfish and do not think of others. Little Germaine was not at all like such children. She was very patient and never complained. She was satisfied with everything her mother did for her and tried hard not to give any trouble. After a while she became well again and as she grew older she became more beautiful every day. She reminded all who saw her of a lovely flower blooming in the early spring. She was so pure and humble that all were sure that she was one of God's special friends.

When Germaine was seven years old, the priest who knew the purity of her innocent heart, wished her to receive her First Holy Communion. You can imagine, dear children, what joy that was for the little girl. But just as she was about to begin her preparation for this great event, her mother became very ill and after a short time died.

Now began a hard time for the poor child. Her father hired a woman to keep house for him, but this woman did not like Germaine and treated her with the greatest cruelty. Germaine was patient and never complained of this to her father. After awhile her father became ill and Germaine had to take care of him. They became very poor now, for there was no one to earn money.

The woman left them, for they had no money to pay her and Germaine had to care for her father and do the housework too. They were now so poor that they had nothing to eat. Germaine had to go out begging. Many times she was roughly sent away from the houses where she asked for food, but many also were kind to the poor little girl. All this time Germaine continued to pray and visit Jesus in church as often as she was able.

Her father at last became well again. Then he married a second time, but this woman also was very unkind to Germaine. The girl had to do the hardest and meanest kind of work. She was treated as a slave. As the years went by the stepmother became more and more cruel and at last she made Germaine leave the house and sleep in the stable. During the day she had to take care of the sheep. This she liked to do, for then she could pray as much as she wished. She went to Mass every morning. Before she left for Mass she took the sheep out into the pasture, and sticking her crook, that is, the shepherd's staff, into the ground, the sheep grazed about it and never strayed from the place during the time she was gone. This is how God showed how much He was pleased with Germaine. She spent the greater part of the night in prayer. People passing by the stable at night often heard a sweet voice singing most wonderfully. Often, too, a wondrous light was seen coming from the stable.

For many years, Germaine had to bear the bad treatment of her stepmother. Her father was too busy to bother about her and Germaine never complained to him about her stepmother. Finally God changed the cruel woman's heart and she saw how wicked she had been. She tried to be kind to Germaine and wished her to live again with them. But she begged to be allowed to remain in the stable. One night while she was praying, an angel appeared to her and told her that she would soon die. This pleased her very much and she at once began to prepare herself. She became ill suddenly, and after having received the last sacraments asked her father to let her stay one more night in the stable. The next morning she was found peacefully sleeping the sleep of death. The sheep were gathered around her as if they knew that they had lost their best friend. Germaine was dead. She had gone to Jesus.

What a beautiful life this dear saint led here on earth! Germaine did not have any earthly joys and pleasures, but she found great happiness in bearing everything patiently for the love of Jesus Who suffered so much for all of us. Germaine was always patient. She never scolded or grumbled because she was neglected and ill-treated. She prayed much and loved to be alone with Jesus. What can you do to imitate this saint?

St. Aloysius Gonzaga—June 21

Of all the saints whose feasts we celebrate in the year, St. Aloysius is the one chosen to be the special patron of boys throughout the whole world. This saint lived such an innocent life that he is the model for all Catholic boys. St. Aloysius was born of noble, pious parents. His father was a powerful lord and lived in a grand castle. His good mother had a great devotion to the Blessed Virgin. She trained little Aloysius to love Mary as his heavenly Mother. His first prayer was the "Ave Maria," the Hail Mary. The little child liked it so well that he repeated it over and over. Instead of learning silly rhymes or songs, ask your parents to teach you the sweet prayers to our Blessed Mother. If you have a baby brother or sister at home, you can teach the little one to say the holy names of Jesus and Mary, or if they are able to learn more, the Hail Mary. Teach them the little prayers and songs you learn at school. Tell them about the Blessed Virgin and the saints and they will grow to love them also.

Little Aloysius loved to hear about the saints and what they did for Jesus. Being the son of rich parents he had everything he wanted. He had rich clothes, beautiful toys and the best of food. But he cared little for any of these things. He loved to pray before a picture or a statue of the Blessed Virgin. When he was only five years old he was often found in a corner praying.

The father of Aloysius was a great soldier and he wished his little son to grow up to be a soldier too. So he took him along in the camp where the soldiers were drilling. Aloysius liked to see the soldiers in their fine uniforms. He liked to watch them march. He was then about seven years old. While he was in camp with the soldiers Aloysius heard bad words. He repeated these words without knowing what they meant. As soon as he was told that these words were wicked, he wept to think that he had offended God. Aloysius never forgot this fault and all his life time he did penance for it. From that time he tried to live for Jesus alone and he made a rule for himself according to which he lived. He

ST. ALOYSIUS

was very strict with himself, but kind and gentle to others. He loved to play with his companions and he took part in the games and sports of those days.

He received his First Holy Communion when he was twelve years old. For the rest of his life he always had a great devotion to the Blessed Sacrament and prepared himself with great care for Holy Communion. He was most remarkable for his purity. No one ever knew him to say anything or do anything in the least against the holy virtue. He was careful about his companions and would not allow any that used bad words in his presence. That is one reason why St. Aloysius is the patron for boys and young men.

Because Aloysius was to become a great soldier his father sent him away to a school where he should learn to be a soldier. But Aloysius did not like this kind of life. He did not enjoy the feasts and pleasures of the king's palace where he had to spend many days. In the midst of all the grand and brilliant festivities he was ever thinking of God. Aloysius wanted to become a priest and join an Order. His father was very angry when he heard this, but the young boy begged so hard that at last he was allowed to go. He lived only a few years, but he served God so well that when he died he was honored by all as a holy youth.

St. Aloysius is the model for all Catholic boys. He loved the Blessed Virgin so much that he never forgot to put himself under her care each day. His life was pure and holy. He is also the patron saint for young men preparing for the priesthood.

Pray often to St. Aloysius for the grace to keep your hearts pure. Ask him to obtain for you the grace never to yield to any temptations against holy purity. Ask him to pray for you to keep you from bad companions who would lead you into sin. Pray that he may obtain for you a great love for Jesus in the Blessed Sacrament and for the Virgin Mother Mary. Like St. Aloysius try to lead a holy life that you may one day die a holy death and live with Jesus forever in heaven.

St. John the Baptist—June 24

Do you remember the story of the Visitation of Our Blessed Mother? This story tells us that one day the Blessed Virgin left her home in Nazareth and went over the hills to visit her cousin St. Elizabeth. The Blessed Virgin remained with St. Elizabeth for some months. St. Elizabeth had a little boy who was six months older than Jesus. This boy was named John. When John grew older, his mother often took him with her when she visited the Blessed Virgin. Then he and Jesus played together.

Would you not like to have been with Jesus

The Blessed Virgin's Rose Garden

and little John? How pleasantly they must have played together. Do you think they quarreled or fought? No indeed. They played quietly and peacefully. How happy their mothers must have been when they watched them play!

When St. John grew to be a man he went into the desert to live. He wished to get the people ready for the coming of the Redeemer. For this reason he stayed in the desert and preached to the people who came out to see and hear him. He talked to them about the Savior and told them to make ready for Him. John baptized the people. St. John baptized Jesus and a voice from heaven was heard to say, "This is My beloved Son, in Whom I am well pleased."

St. John is called the Baptist, because he baptized so many. Later on St. John was killed by order of a wicked King. His head was cut off and put in a basin and brought to the King. This was a horrible death, but St. John was glad to suffer for Jesus.

7. CHARTS, POSTERS AND BLACKBOARD DRAWINGS

Charts, posters, blackboard drawings, mottoes and slogans are helpful in emphasizing character talks. These aids are especially useful if they refer in their general aim and outline to some outstanding event or feast of the month, or to the religious dedication of the month. These visual aids are effective means to arouse ambition, to spur the class to greater efforts, and to stimulate interest in some particular phase of school work.

The suggestions given may be carried out by drawings either on the blackboard or on large sheets of paper, by cut-out pictures arranged as posters, or by means of charts. The drawings may be made from a smaller picture and enlarged with the aid of a pantograph and then colored.

The Blessed Virgin's Rose Garden

For the month of OCTOBER several devices may be used. One of these is the "Blessed Virgin's Rose Garden." Draw a picture of a garden showing a number of rosebushes. If the class is not large, let each child have his own rosebush. When a pupil has been regular at Mass or at the recitation of the rosary, let him draw a rose on the bush; or let him cut out a picture of a rose and paste it on the bush. If the class is too large, have a rosebush for a certain number of children, five being the proper number for one rosebush. The group that has the most roses at the end of a specified time receives a special award.

The Rosary

Another seasonable device for OCTOBER is the rosary. Large beads are cut out of colored paper. These are arranged to form a rosary on the blackboard or on a large sheet of paper. As a child distinguishes himself by good conduct or satisfactory lessons his name is printed on a bead. Any child who has his name on ten small beads will be permitted to write his name on a large bead. This device may also be carried out by letting each child make a small rosary for his own use. Each of these smaller rosaries is mounted on a separate card. The cards are then arranged about the room, making an attractive decoration. When a child has succeeded in attaining the specified standard set by the teacher, he is permitted to color a bead of his rosary. When all the beads on one card have been colored, the pupil is allowed to make a second rosary.

Little Friends of the Holy Souls

For the month of NOVEMBER make a poster representing Purgatory. Above it write the words, "Little Friends of the Holy Souls." Below this space the teacher may list a number of little sacrifices and prayers that small children can offer for the Souls in Purgatory. This list may take the form of a Spiritual Bouquet. Make the practices simple and practical; for example, acts of obedience, kindness, patience and the like. It is not advisable to use the term "mortification." Teach the children to form the habit of self-control by subduing their desires and inclinations for the love of God and to please Jesus and Mary.

Friends of Jesus

The dominant idea for DECEMBER is preparation for the Birth of Jesus. A poster of the Birth of Jesus will be appropriate for this month. Under the picture the words "Friends of Jesus" may be printed or cut out and pasted.

Sheep Around the Crib

Another attractive scheme is to sketch on a large sheet of paper the hills and plains of Bethlehem, showing in the background the stable in which Jesus was born and representing the sheep and the shepherds by picture cut-outs. Pin the

THE HOLY SOULS HELPED BY HOLY MASS

The names of the children in the class should be listed and marks given for good behavior, regular attendance at Mass, or satisfactory lessons. A scene similar to the one shown in the upper part of the Calendar for December, page 167, will suggest the idea for the poster.

sheep to the paper. Move them forward toward the stable each day as a reward for good conduct or special efforts to make little sacrifices to please Jesus. If the teacher wishes, each child may have a sheep. The child's name is then written or printed on the sheep. This plan is also very effective if one sheep is used to represent each day of the month. The children will be interested in seeing how many sheep they can get near the stable before Christmas.

The Crown of Thorns

The following is also a helpful design to interest the children in promptly obeying the rules of the class for the love of Jesus:

Flowers for May

For the month of MAY, the following device has been found valuable. Mount a picture of the Blessed Virgin on a sheet of paper. Around this picture draw a vine forming an arch over it. If two arches are drawn, one may serve for the boys and the other for the girls. If the class is small one arch will be sufficient, one-half being allotted to the boys and the other half to

THE INFANT JESUS WITH SHEEP REPRESENTING THE CHILDREN

Mount a large picture of the Sacred Head of Christ and around it draw a crown of thorns. Divide this crown into two parts, one part being for the boys, the other for the girls. When one division has succeeded in making a good record for the day, a thorn is removed and a flower substituted for it. This device stimulates great interest in the practice of little acts of self-denial so necessary to prompt obedience to the small and apparently insignificant rules of the school.

the girls. To excite greater interest in any activity, let the side that distinguishes itself during the day, paste a flower on the vine. As the number of the flowers increases the interest of the class will likewise increase.

Similar projects might be designed for the other months. For March, charts or posters on which lilies have been drawn or pasted might be used with good results. Let each child have a lily; the petals are filled in when he secures a point. Contrariwise, a petal may be erased or taken off if he fails to keep up his standing.

Flowers for Our Blessed Lady

A variety of other flowers may be used for the same purpose.

8. NAME DAYS AND BIRTHDAYS

Make a special note of the patron saints of the children in the class. On the patronal feast of any of the children, give the child a picture of his patron saint, if you can procure one. Congratulate the child in the morning and tell the class something about the saint whose feast is celebrated. The children will be delighted with this little attention and will more readily remember their patron saint.

To make children feel that you take an interest in them and their affairs, make a special effort to remember the birthdays of the little ones. At the beginning of the year make a list of the birthdays of the children as they occur. A good plan is to make a large school calendar and write the names of those whose birthday occurs on a certain day in the block for that date. In this way no date will be forgotten.

When a birthday of a child occurs place a little silk flag on his desk. At the beginning of the morning exercises tell the children that to-day is John Smith's birthday. Then let them rise and say, "John, we wish you a happy birthday." If they know a suitable song let them sing it.

Another plan that pleases the children is to draw a star or some other pretty design on the blackboard and write therein the name of the child whose birthday occurs. These little attentions delight the children and teach them to be thoughtful and considerate of others.

SECTION II

SAND TABLE PROJECTS

1. SAND TABLE WORK

The use of the sand table in teaching religion is by no means a new idea. For many centuries the Church has used kindred forms of teaching, under one name or another, to impress upon the people the sacred mysteries, by picturing them as objective realities that would affect the intellect through the senses. Thus we have St. Francis of Assisi giving expression to his conception of the birth of Christ in a scenic representation. At Greccio in Italy, in the year 1223, he constructed a crib and grouped about it figures of the Blessed Virgin and St. Joseph, the ox, the ass, and the shepherds who came to adore the new-born Savior. The widespread use of the crib throughout the Christian world to-day, the religious fervor which it arouses in the hearts of the people, are striking proofs of the value of the sand-table idea in teaching religion. In like manner, the Stations of the Cross, particularly those in which the figures stand out in relief, embody the idea that underlies all sand-table work. The various groups of statuary found in churches, convents and monasteries also employ the same idea. The reproduction of Calvary, the Pietà and other grottoes and shrines dedicated to the Blessed Virgin—all are sand tables on a large scale.

Early in life, the constructive instinct of the child manifests itself. Who of us will ever forget the thrill we got out of the mud pies we made, or the houses and forts we built in the sand? The same delight that children take in digging sand by the seashore, or in making mud pies, or building houses and forts in the sand, may be made a means of mental growth in the schoolroom. A prominent educator speaking to parents said: "Give the child a clean sand-pile, let him be free to play as he wishes, and you may be sure he will develop a greater ability to self-expression and independent thinking than he would by any other form of play or work." Teachers in Catholic schools would neglect a valuable factor in the education of the child, were they to disregard the use of the sand table in the teaching of religion. The stories in the Bible History, incidents in the life of Christ and the saints will furnish suitable subject matter for sand table reproduction. Children love this kind of work and if it is so planned that each child will have on the finished table something he has made, the sand table will prove one of the most valuable as well as one of the most interesting helps in the class room.

The proper arrangement of geographical features, such as hills, valleys, plains, rivers and lakes affords the children an opportunity for close observation. The use of tiny dolls, statuettes, home-made figures and cut-out pictures will represent the people in the story. To the child the little forms in the sand are pictures in nature just as truly as the bundle of rags is a beautiful doll. The imagination readily supplies what is lacking in size and color. The real source of delight to the child is this power of imagination, for a toy, so perfect that nothing is left to the imagination, is soon cast aside.

The acts of association between the forms in nature and their signs in the sand should be, as far as possible, unconscious; that is to say: let the child himself select the figures or representations for his work. This will lead him to associate these signs with his ideas, and in this way he will be prepared to give a natural expression to his concepts.

The sand table need not be an expensive article. Frequently a father or older brother of one of the children will volunteer to make the table. The boards on the bottom should be strong; those on the sides should be finished and about four or five inches high. The size of the table will depend upon the size of the room and the amount of space available for the table. Large ones are more easily worked and give a better opportunity for developing the story. Sometimes two or three tables may be used with good effect. A piece of galvanized tin or, if the table is small, a piece of glass may be used to cover the bottom to prevent the sand from falling through the cracks. Ready-made tables of galvanized iron or steel are very expensive; the home-made sand table will serve the purpose just as well. There is no standard size. For ordinary purposes, a table seventy-two inches long, from twenty-seven to thirty inches wide, and about four or five inches deep, will prove satisfactory. Both small and large tables may be used with good success.

Equipment

Probably the greatest difficulty in this work will be gathering the necessary materials. The children will experience less difficulty in this than the teacher might expect. They are accustomed to all kinds of make-shifts in their play, and for this reason they will have little trouble in collecting the necessary supplies. The principal equipment will consist of the following: sand, dolls, statuettes, paper cut-outs to represent bridges and houses. A few suggestions are given here to enable the teacher to plan the work more easily. The regular lessons in construction work, paper cutting and drawing will aid the children in preparing many articles for their sand table projects.

Sand

The best kind of sand is the ordinary sand used for building purposes. This kind holds together more firmly when moistened. The sand should always be slightly moistened before working it. White sand is not so good because it does not pack so well as common sand.

Trees

Trees may be represented in many ways. Small twigs on which artificial leaves and blossoms have been fastened are often used. Palm trees may be made by rolling stiff brown paper for the trunk and pasting green leaves on the top. Round pieces of wood stained brown may serve as trunks. Crumpled pieces of green tissue paper or crêpe paper fastened to a match stem or a toothpick will also serve as trees. Empty spools make good stands for trees. These should be covered with sand so that they cannot be seen. Pictures of trees cut from magazines and pasted on stiff paper may also be used.

Grass

Natural or artificial moss, sawdust dyed green, or green paper, plain or crêpe, will serve to represent grass.

Water

A mirror, a piece of blue or silver paper, or a piece of plain white paper will give a realistic appearance. Small stones or shells along the shore add a touch of naturalness to the scene. A strip of paper cut irregularly will represent a river winding through a valley or between hills.

Roads, Streets, Hills and Mountains

Roads and streets can easily be pictured by using white sand, salt, flour, black dirt or gravel. Hills, valleys, mountains and plains are easily made in the slightly moistened sand. Sometimes a small piece of rock placed here and there and covered with moss and sand will make the hills and mountains very realistic.

Snow

Artificial snow can easily be obtained, especially during the Christmas season. Flour or cotton is a good substitute.

Houses, Bridges, Fences

Houses can be made from cardboard or heavy drawing paper and suitably colored. Cardboard boxes, cartons, or heavy wrapping paper may also be used. Houses made from cigar boxes, with cornstalks or branches of trees for logs, give the scene a more natural appearance. Care should be taken to make the houses on the same scale with the rest of the articles used, so that there may be no lack of proportion.

Directions for constructing houses, boats, log huts, churches, trees and other articles for use with sand-table work will be found in the section on construction work (pp. 268 ff.).

Clay for Modeling

A very simple and satisfactory molding clay may be made from flour, salt and powdered alum in the following proportions: One cup of flour, one cup of salt and one teaspoonful of alum. Mix with enough water to mold easily. By wrapping it in a damp cloth after it has served its purpose the clay can be used again and again.

People, Animals

Small dolls, dressed clothes-pins, paper cutouts, statuettes or toy figures can easily be procured by the children. Toy animals, especially dogs, sheep and horses, can be used.

Some teachers arrange a background for each sand-table project. Attractive settings can be made by simply tacking up a large sheet of wrapping paper. On this draw the background with white or colored chalk or with crayola. If the sand table is in front of a blackboard, draw the background on the blackboard. This will add greatly to the general appearance and completeness of the work. The sky, mountains, hills, and even trees may be drawn, and the objects on the table so arranged as to present a continuation in the general scheme of the pictures.

How to Work Out a Project on the Sand Table

Relate the story in an interesting manner, carefully describing the persons, places and events. When the story is quite familiar to every one, begin to plan the illustration. Give a more extensive study of each part, placing on the sand table the objects as the story progresses. If the class is not too large, permit the children to stand around the table so that all can see it. Let the children put the objects in their proper places.

2. SAND TABLE PROJECTS IN RELIGION

Adam and Eve in Paradise

Make the table as beautiful as possible. Place different types of trees in the garden. Flowers, shrubs and plants of various kinds should be shown. Cut small pieces of colored paper to represent the fruit on some of the trees. Surround the garden with shrubbery. A lake in the foreground will add charm to the picture. Show Adam and Eve walking together on the shore of the lake. Place a few birds and animals in different parts of the garden. The Tree of Knowledge should stand out prominently with a serpent coiled beneath it.

Adam and Eve Driven Out of Paradise

By moving the shrubbery and placing it back about one-third from the edge of the right of the table, the outer section may be used to represent the bleak world into which Adam and Eve were driven from the garden of Eden. An opening in the shrubbery will represent the gate through which they were driven. Represent Adam and Eve near the gate. An angel with a sword in his hand should be shown driving Adam and Eve out of the garden of Eden.

Cain and Abel

Let the sand table represent a large field. In the one section show Abel and his flock of sheep, while in the other section represent Cain. A rude fence constructed of splints or small pieces of wood should enclose the field of Cain. In each section represent an altar. These altars can be made of cardboard and painted to represent stone. On each altar place the representative offering of each. Place a sheep on a few pieces of red tissue paper to show Abel's offering. A picture of fruit cut out, or artificial fruits may represent the offering of Cain. By cutting the red tissue paper into strips the appearance of fire will be effected.

Cain Kills Abel

Show Abel lying on the ground with Cain standing over him, a club in his hands. Turn the sheep in Abel's pasture, so that they appear to be running away.

Noe and the Ark

Arrange a group of mountains in the background. To the right in the distance show a portion of water. About the center of the table place an ark. This ark may be made of wood or cardboard. Arrange the animals in pairs entering the ark. Noe and his family should be standing together watching the animals enter the ark. Place a few trees here and there.

Noe and His Family Leaving the Ark

By removing the trees or plants shown in the preceding setting, the effect of a bleak landscape can be obtained. Show the animals leaving the ark. To the left, show an altar around which Noe and his family are grouped. A piece of paper properly colored may represent the rainbow just behind this altar.

The Story of Moses

One portion of the sand table may be used to represent the palace of Pharao. On the grounds surrounding the palace, soldiers are seen on guard. Trees, shrubbery and walks may be skillfully arranged in this section. The other section may represent the camp of the Israelites. Tents made of paper may be placed near the River Nile which may be shown in the center of the table. An oblong piece of mirror or silver paper laid across the center will do to represent the river passing through the country. On the banks, bulrushes are represented by pieces of paper cut or torn. Place a small basket with a tiny infant representing Moses near the shore of the river. Show Miriam standing behind the bulrushes watching her baby brother.

The Story of Joseph

The story of Joseph is well-adapted to sand table reproduction.

Represent Jacob sending Joseph to see how his brothers are getting along with their flocks. One end of the table might represent the brothers of Joseph and their sheep. A few stones arranged around a small pit dug in the sand may represent the cistern. The other end of the table might be used to show the merchants with their camels.

The teacher might also show Joseph as governor of Egypt. The brothers, their bags filled with grain, may be pictured in this scene.

Joseph meeting his father will also prove interesting.

The Birth of Christ

To get the most out of this project, begin as early as the first week in December. Arrange the sand table to represent the hill country around Bethlehem. Show a few hills with low valleys here and there on the right; near the center of the table group a number of houses to represent Bethlehem, and to the left in the rear make a cave in the hillside and build a stable in front of it. Show shepherds and their flocks in various places on the hills and in the valleys near Bethlehem. During the first week in December, show the Blessed Virgin and St. Joseph coming over the hills from the right on their way to Bethlehem. Move them forward a little each day.

In the second week, show them leaving the town of Bethlehem in the center and going towards the cave on the hillside. Change the position of the shepherds and the sheep.

In the third week, show the Infant Jesus with Mary and Joseph in the stable. Group the shepherds and the sheep near the stable.

In the fourth week, show the arrival of the Magi. Let them first be seen coming over the hills; then gradually place them nearer and nearer to the stable. Finally show them kneeling in adoration before the Infant Jesus.

Material for the story of the Birth of Jesus and the various incidents in His early life may be found in "Morning Talks," pp. 3 ff., and "Catholic Teaching for Children," by Winifred Wray; "New Testament Stories," by C. C. Martindale, S. J.; "A Simple Life of Jesus for His Little Ones," by a Sister of Notre Dame.

Tell the story several times until the persons, places and events become quite familiar to the children. Then make a more intensive study of each part.

Begin, for example, with the life of the Blessed Virgin at Nazareth and relate again the story of the Annunciation. The next day tell about the visit of the Blessed Virgin to her cousin Elizabeth. Then relate the story of the journey of Joseph and Mary from Nazareth to Bethlehem. Ask the children: "Where did Mary and Joseph live before they went to Bethlehem?" "In Nazareth." "Why did they leave Nazareth?" "Because the Emperor ordered that every man should go to the town to which his father belonged, so that his name should be written down there."

"Have you ever seen a picture of Our Lady and St. Joseph on their way from Nazareth to Bethlehem? The Blessed Virgin is riding on a donkey with St. Joseph walking beside her taking care of her. Let us now show Mary and Joseph on their journey. They had to travel over hills and through valleys."

On one side of the sand table, heap up the moist sand to represent several hills. In the plains and valleys show some sheep grazing. If you have no statues to represent Mary and Joseph cut out the figures and place them in the sand on one of the hills in the distance, to make it appear that they are just beginning their journey over the hills.

"Where are Mary and Joseph going?" "To Bethlehem."

"Let us now make Bethlehem. We shall place it right here." Arrange a section of the table near the center to represent the town of Bethlehem. A fence encloses a space in which a number of houses are ranged along a narrow street. Place a number of people here and there; also one or two donkeys. On one side of the fence there should be an opening for a gate.

"Where did Mary and Joseph go when they found no place in Bethlehem?"

"They left the town and found shelter in a poor miserable stable."

"Let us make this stable." Build the stable of strong cardboard and cover it with sand and moss. Hollow out a cave in one of the hills at the other end of the table and place the stable in front of this cave. Later in the month, place figures of the Infant Jesus and Mary and Joseph partly in the cave and partly in the outer space covered by the stable.

Now the whole scene is complete. Move the figures of the Blessed Virgin and St. Joseph a little nearer to Bethlehem each day. In the third week arrange the interior of the stable for the birth of Jesus. Place a star above the stable.

The Flight Into Egypt

This will require a re-arrangement of the setting. Let the sand table show a desert scene. A few palm trees around a well, represented by a small mirror, will picture an oasis. Show the Holy Family on the way to Egypt. A lion or some other wild beast should be shown in the distance.

The Holy Family at Nazareth

Arrange the table to represent the hill country about Nazareth. Show a few houses in the town. The home of the Holy Family should be larger than the rest. The Holy Family might be represented outdoors, Mary seated near the door working, Joseph doing some carpenter work and Jesus assisting him. There are many ways in which this project may be carried out. The teacher will allow the children free play of their imagination in arranging this scene.

The Stations of the Cross

This will be found an interesting project. Let the children cut out pictures of the stations from calendars, old magazines or discarded Bible Histories. Paste these on stiff cardboard and arrange them properly on the sand table. The table should be laid out to represent the way from Jerusalem to the top of Mount Calvary. Make the road from the city to the top of the hill rough and stony. A little gravel strewed about the street will help to give it this appearance. The houses in Jerusalem should be built in the style found there.

Calvary

Give prominence to the hill of Calvary. Construct three crosses of wood or heavy cardboard and place them in the ground of the top of the hill. A crucifix fixed in the ground might be used to represent the cross of Our Lord.

A Grotto of Lourdes

During the month of May it might be interesting to have the children make a miniature grotto of Lourdes on the sand table. The mountains and hills surrounding Lourdes can easily be made. From a picture of the grotto or one of the many imitation grottoes that can be seen in many Catholic magazines and periodicals, the children will be able to get an idea of the form of a grotto. A number of persons might be shown in procession to the grotto.

Through the Year with the Sand Table

September: The story of the Creation; Adam and Eve.

October: The Guardian Angel.

November: The story of Thanksgiving.

December: The Story of the Birth of Jesus.

January: The Three Wise Men.

February: The Flight into Egypt.

March: St. Joseph and the Boy Jesus in the Workshop.

April: Calvary.

May: Lourdes.

June: Corpus Christi—Altars and Procession.

3. MISSIONARY PROJECTS ON THE SAND TABLE

The sand table may be used for a study of missionary activities in various countries. These projects will arouse the interest of the children and will serve to stimulate missionary activities and the missionary spirit. The various monthly publications devoted to missionary purposes will provide ample material for the portrayal of life in missionary countries.

The story of the country, illustrating the dress, the customs, the characteristics and the religious worship of the inhabitants, will prove

SAND TABLE PROJECTS

a fascinating method of impressing upon the little ones the great needs of the missions and the missionaries engaged in the work of bringing the Faith to these lands.

The following outlines will serve to show only a few of the many projects that might be arranged.

China

Arrange the table to represent a scene in a Chinese city. Build Chinese houses and pagodas and show some of the inhabitants grouped about a missionary priest. A few dolls dressed as Sisters will make the scene more interesting. Out of cardboard construct buildings to represent the church, convent, school and orphan asylum.

American Indians

Arrange the table to represent an Indian settlement; wigwams constructed of paper might be set up around a log church. Erect a large cross made of two sticks of wood in front of the church. Use cut-out figures of Indians and animals. Place a log cabin near the church to represent the priest's house. Show the missionary near the cross. Some Sisters instructing the Indians might be shown on another section of the sand table.

Eskimo

The study of the Eskimo is one of the most fascinating projects for the children of the first and second grades. For the sand-table work, an Eskimo village will prove instructive. At one end of the table show the sea, which may be of blue paper covered with glass, over which paraffin was poured. Place a rock near the shore of the sea and cover it and the remainder of the table with cotton batting and artificial snow. The igloos or Eskimo huts may be built of pulp made by tearing newspapers into small pieces and soaking in water for a few days. Stir this

A Sand Table Project on the Missions

mixture thoroughly and mold the pulp into igloos. Arrange these igloos to form a village. The sledges may be made from pieces of wood or from spool boxes. Small pieces of fur may represent the polar bear. Dogs formed from clay, or toy dogs, may be harnessed to the sledge. Clothes-pin dolls can easily be dressed in Eskimo style. Seals and reindeer can also be modeled or cut out of paper. A large igloo may represent the church. A group of Eskimo children near the church will give the children special delight.

Africa

A village in Africa can be simply arranged. A few huts made of clay and straw, and several palm trees will portray the scene. The priests and Sisters should be clothed in white. The natives wear little clothing.

Since the children of the lower grades study these countries only in a general way, the teacher will use the missionary project merely as a means to inculcate a love for the missionary work of the Church and to create a desire to assist in promoting missionary enterprises. By means of the illustrations cut from missionary magazines, the teacher will be able to give the children a pretty fair idea of the dress and customs, religion and peculiarities of the people. By skillful suggestions the teacher will be able to lead the children to picture correctly the geographic features of the country to be studied.

A mite box or a mission bank placed near the sand table will remind the children of the duty of making occasional sacrifices for the missions.

SECTION III

DRAMATIZATION

1. DRAMATIZATION IN THE CLASSROOM

There is in the heart of every child a desire to "act things." Children in the kindergarten and the primary grades are in the dramatic stage of their development and spontaneously put all their ideas into action. When they hear about a wolf prowling about and stealing upon his prey, they immediately imagine themselves to be that wolf and begin to imitate his actions. In like manner, they imagine themselves to be lions, tigers, elephants, birds, horses, and even flowers. The small boy can be a horse or a man with equal ease and enjoyment, and to be an Indian is his special delight. When children study any process, whether they be riding horseback, paying out money or sweeping the house— they wish at least to go through the motions. Things mean little to the child without these motions and for this reason impersonation and dramatic expression hold a valuable place in the work of the kindergarten and primary grades.

Dramatization is more formal than dramatic expression. In it we take something that is not in the form of play and definitely change it into such form. The principal objective in dramatization is to develop the imagination and to stimulate thought and oral expression. Dramatization is the child's interpretation of life; therefore, to be of any value in the schoolroom, the dramatic play should come from the child's own imagination. It is the means of making the child live in himself that which he is attempting to express.

Dramatization is of unquestionable value so long as the children naturally act out their own conceptions of the story. So long as the children are young enough to see in imagination the real story which they are acting, they will derive much benefit from this form of expression.

The teacher must exercise great care in the use of dramatization. Almost every diversion in school has its dangers. An attempt to develop pupils in one way may impede the development of some other equally important quality.

Some teachers fail in teaching dramatization. This may be due to several causes. The teachers may have no definite method of procedure; they may look upon dramatization as a recreation, and have no definite objective in view; they may select only the naturally active children, neglecting the timid and less active; they may aim at a finished production, and therefore practice, rehearse and polish until the children lose all interest and the result is stilted and lifeless.

Lack of Definite Method

Before attempting any dramatization the teacher should have well-defined ideas on the subject. Many children have never seen a play and consequently do not know how to proceed. The teacher should lead her pupils by skillful questions and suggestions to see the actions in the story and to interpret and express them correctly.

Dramatization Not a Form of Recreation

Dramatization is considered by some teachers as a form of recreation and consequently there is a tendency to conduct it without having a definite objective in view. This leads to haphazard work on the part of the pupils, who derive little or no benefit from such a procedure. The teacher should regard this form of expression as an aid to impress deeply on the minds and hearts of the children the lesson the story is intended to convey.

Dramatization Should Benefit All Pupils

Some teachers choose the characters from among those pupils who are naturally active and who possess marked abilities in dramatic expression, while the timid and less active children are neglected. Thus the dramatization benefits chiefly those who are less in need of such means to stimulate their imagination and to develop the expression of their ideas, while the more retiring and less talented are given little opportunity to develop their latent powers along these lines.

A Finished Production Is Not the Aim

The teacher should not aim to secure a finished production. Such an aim would defeat the purpose for which dramatization has been introduced into the school. A simple presentation of

A Dramatization

the story is all that is expected. Dramatization should be a spontaneous expression of the individuality of those taking part. The play should not be rehearsed until it becomes mechanical and thus loses all educational value.

The Kind of Stories to be Used for Dramatization

Not all stories are suitable for dramatization. There must be action in the story and it must have dramatic value. It is a mistake to attempt to dramatize each and every story found in the

Reader, the Bible History or the Lives of the Saints.

Excellent material may be found in the Readers, the Bible History, the Lives of the Saints and the numerous stories illustrating incidents in the lives of children—incidents that teach some great lesson, such as honesty, uprightness, self-sacrifice, kindness to animals, gratitude, etc.

Children like stories of animals because they understand them and like to be with them. They like stories portraying family life, for they are familiar with it and thus readily grasp the meaning of the incidents following each other in natural sequence. In fine, they like stories that call their imagination into action.

Besides the Bible History, which furnishes many stories suitable for dramatization, Catholic teachers can find abundant material in the Lives of the Saints. There are numerous incidents in the Lives of the Saints that illustrate the wonderful, at times supernatural, power which the saints exercised over animals. Boys and girls find endless delight in the story of St. Francis and the wolf of Gubbio. With what a thrill they listen to the account of the wolf "shaking hands" with Brother Francis.

St. Francis and the birds, St. Anthony preaching to the fish, St. Anthony and the mule, the hermits St. Paul and St. Anthony and the lion in the desert, these are only a few of the stories that delight the hearts of the little ones.

Method of Procedure

In the beginning only the simplest stories should be used, that is, only those stories should be dramatized which are most easily grasped by the children. Having decided what story is to be used, read or tell it in as dramatic and interesting a manner as you can. Tell it and retell it as many times as necessary to make the children so thoroughly familiar with it that they can tell it themselves.

The next step is to determine the characters, their actions and words. Before the reproduction of the story by dramatization, it is well for the teacher to have a few of the pupils tell what some of the characters said, and how they said it. The descriptive parts should be told by the teacher first, until the children are able to tell them. When the children have gained sufficient power in dramatization, the descriptive parts may be omitted.

The selection of the children for the various characters should now be made. The pupils should be encouraged to do all they can in deciding upon the parts, the actors, scenery, costumes, etc., and in arranging the details of the dramatization.

Recall the characters and places in the story and describe them vividly and clearly. Review the events in the order of their occurrence, so that the pupils see them clearly and distinctly. To assist the children to recall these events in their proper order and to aid them to select the important details in the story, skillfully question the class. These questions should be systematic, progressive and to the point.

Having decided upon the characters, their actions and their places in the play, proceed to discuss the conversation occurring in the story. Again lead the children by a series of questions to develop the dialogue as it occurred in the story. A set form of words should not be insisted upon. The children should get the sense, not the exact words. Allow them to use the form natural to them, provided they bring out the idea so that the next speaker may get his cue.

Attention must be paid to the language of the children and the manner in which they express their conception of the story. The children should be instructed to speak clearly, distinctly, and loud enough to be heard by all in the room. Mistakes in grammar should be corrected after the play is finished. Correcting a child in the midst of a performance tends to make him self-conscious and probably will spoil the rest of his act.

Planning for the stage setting, stage properties, costumes and other paraphernalia brings into play the imagination. Children delight in "make-believe" and readily supply in imagination what is wanting in reality. Nearly all stage properties can be imaginary, for successful work of this kind should be a training of the imagination.

DRAMATIZATION

Summary and Illustration

The method of procedure, then, may be summed up as follows:

1. Read or tell the story.
2. Select the characters, their words, actions and the part they play in the story.
3. Arrange the setting of the play.
4. Select the dialogue.
5. Study the language expression.
6. Decide upon the stage properties, costumes, make-up and other details.

The dramatization should be free and carried out by the pupils according to their own plans. The teacher should remember that dramatization is not to be a finished production, smoothly performed by a selected few, while the rest of the class passively look on.

Every class has some children who possess considerable dramatic ability. However, the teacher must not allow these children to take all parts. If the play is to benefit the whole class, it will be necessary that each child take part in its production. The more talented ones can be used at the beginning. Great care must be taken not to allow these children to know that they are the "star" actors. A play in which a large number of less talented pupils take part will be of greater value than a brilliant performance by a limited number of talented children.

No child should be forced to take part. The prospect of speaking before his classmates will frighten a timid child. A better plan would be to allow the timid ones to be mere spectators for a time.

Their interest will soon be aroused, and, encouraged by the success of others, they will eventually join their classmates in the play. The watchful teacher will help these timid pupils by giving them easy parts—parts that will require no speaking and very little action. In this way they will soon gain sufficient courage to take active parts.

Summary and Illustration

Briefly stated, the procedure in dramatization is as follows: First, tell the story in the most entertaining manner. Tell it and retell it several times in exactly the same manner. Children do not tire of a good story well told and for the story to be of value the children must know it so well that it becomes a part of themselves. Secondly, the teacher must make sure of the details, the sequence of events, the part that particular persons or animals play in the story, for she cannot leave out one step without destroying the unity of the story.

The next step is to decide upon the characters by recalling the people in the story; then discuss the location of the events, that is, the places in the story. Then recall the conversation, or the talking done in the story.

The staging and costuming used in dramatizing stories should be extremely simple. Children are experts in the art of "make-believe" and are quite ready to accept makeshifts in staging, costumes and other paraphernalia.

Pupils should not be required to memorize the dramatized form. Bible quotations, however, should be given as accurately as possible.

Encourage the children to interpret the story and carry out the dramatization of it in a manner thoroughly consistent with its spirit and content.

Never force a child to take part. If left to himself, he will soon ask to take part and his actions will then be free from all constraint and fear of being ridiculed.

Sometimes children should be permitted to select the players. Children are the frankest critics in the world and will make good judges in this matter.

Remember that dramatization is only a means to an end, not an end in itself, and, if rightly used, will become an invaluable aid in classroom work.

As an illustration of the method of procedure let us take the story "Christ Blessing Little Children." After the story has been read or told, the teacher might proceed to ask questions such as,

About whom is this story?

What is Jesus doing?

What are the children doing?

What are the Apostles doing?

Why are the Apostles trying to keep the mothers and the children away from Jesus?

Why was Jesus tired?

Did Jesus want the little children to come to Him?

How do you know?

What did Jesus say?

How did the Apostles act when they tried to keep the children away from Jesus?

How did the mothers act?

Show me how you think the children crowded around Jesus.

Do you think the children were happy?

What did Jesus do when the children crowded around Him?

What did the mothers do when Jesus blessed their children?

How do you think the Apostles acted when Jesus said He wished the little ones to come to Him?

Now, children, let us try to play this story. How many persons were there? First, there was our dear Lord; then there were the Apostles, the mothers, and the children.

Who will be Our Lord? (*The impersonation of the Lord, the Blessed Virgin and other holy personages should be carefully considered and great care should be exercised in selecting the children who are to represent these characters.*)

Whom shall we choose for the Apostles?

How many do we need?

Now, we need a few girls who will take the part of the mothers.

Whom shall we select?

The others can be the children.

Select a few to be those children who approach closer to Our Lord. The other children may stand around. If the class is very large, divide it into two or three sections, allowing one group to give the play first, another group the next time, and so on till all have had a turn.

Now comes the question of the staging of the play. The teacher should have this carefully planned out beforehand. This will enable her to guide and direct the class in presenting the story in a systematic manner.

Where shall we play the story? Where did Jesus rest after His hard work? Let us suppose that the front of the room is the place where Jesus and the Apostles rested. (*The children will readily suggest the proper positions of Jesus, the Apostles, the mothers and the children.*)

Next review the dialogue or conversation.

What did the Apostles say?

Did all speak at once?

No; did each Apostle have something to say?

Who answered them?

What do you think did any one of the mothers say?

Now another Apostle answered this mother. What did he say?

And what did another mother probably say?

Continue in this manner, calling on one child here and there to answer until the conversation in the story has been fairly well fixed in the memory.

Correct faulty expressions. As far as possible, let the children use the words in the book if they have been reading the story from the Bible History or their Readers.

After the children have a fair idea of the characters and the conversation, complete the arrangements by deciding upon the stage properties, costumes and other details.

Our Lord probably rested under a tree. How shall we represent the trees? the field? the flowers?

What kind of a day do you think it was? Why?

The time spent in discussing these points is well spent, for it will help to give a better dramatic interpretation of the story.

The selection of the children who should take part may sometimes be left to the class, for children are frank critics and often make a better choice than the teacher. However, this is not always practical and the teacher should use her judgment in this respect and choose the method best suited for each individual dramatization. It might be well to vary the method of selecting the characters and keep the attention of the class centered on the important points in the lesson or story.

2. STORIES DRAMATIZED

CAIN AND ABEL

SCENE: *Let two stands represent the altars on which the sacrifice of each is placed. A few fruits such as apples, oranges and the like represent the sacrifice of Cain. A sheep cut out of cardboard or a toy sheep represents the offering of Abel.*

CHARACTERS: *Cain, Abel, Voice of God.*

VOICE OF GOD: Why art thou angry? And why is thy countenance fallen? If thou do well, thou shalt be rewarded; but if thou do ill, punishment shall forthwith be present at thy door: Keep away from sin.

CAIN (*Walks towards Abel*): Come, let us go forth into the fields.

(*They walk away together. Cain turns, suddenly strikes Abel. Abel falls and Cain runs away.*)

VOICE OF GOD: Where is thy brother Abel?

CAIN: I know not; am I my brother's keeper?

VOICE OF GOD: What hast thou done? The voice of thy brother's blood crieth to Me from earth. Therefore, cursed shalt thou be upon the earth.

(*Cain covers his face and runs away.*)

THE BUILDING OF THE ARK

SCENE: *Several boys are engaged with tools building an ark. A few boards, one or two hammers, a saw will answer. A toy tool chest can be easily secured.*

CHARACTERS: *Noe, three sons, and a number of men.*

FIRST MAN: What are you doing?

NOE: We are building an ark.

SECOND MAN: Why are you building an ark? Are you and your family going to sail on the sea?

NOE: Oh no! God commanded me to build this ark for He intends to destroy the whole world and all creatures in it.

THIRD MAN: Oh ho! just listen to what Noe is saying. God is going to destroy us all because we are so wicked! ha! ha!

NOE: Yes, unless you repent and do penance, you shall all perish, you and your wives and your children.

FOURTH MAN: Don't worry about us, Noe! We are going to enjoy ourselves and have a good time. You can't scare us with such talk.

ALL: Come on, let's go and enjoy life. (*All leave.*)

SEM: Father, do you think God really means to destroy everything?

NOE: Yes, my son. He has told me that unless the people repent and turn away from their wicked ways, He will destroy all.

CHAM: How glad I am, that we are to be saved.

JAPHET: Yes, let us thank the Lord and praise His great mercy.

NOE: The time is soon at hand. We have now worked a hundred years and soon the ark will be completed.

SCENE II. *Entering the Ark.*

CHARACTERS: *Same as preceding. Wives of the sons of Noe. Three girls.*

SEM: Now all is completed. What shall we do now?

NOE: Gather now the beasts, a pair of every kind as the Lord has commanded and take them into the ark.

CHAM: We have stored a sufficient supply of food for all.

JAPHET: Behold, we are now ready, let us enter.

(*A number of boys and girls may be chosen to represent the animals. The animals form in line to enter the imaginary ark. Noe, his sons and their wives follow.*)

NOE'S OFFERING—THE RAINBOW

SCENE: *Animals leave the ark.*

Noe, his sons and their wives are seen surrounding an altar. Teacher's desk may represent the altar. A rainbow drawn on the blackboard behind the desk, or a large sheet of paper properly colored may serve as the rainbow.

CHARACTERS: *Same as in preceding scene.*

NOE: Praise the Lord for His goodness towards us.

VOICE OF GOD: Never again will I destroy mankind by a flood. The rainbow in the clouds shall be the sign of My covenant with the earth.

THE STORY OF JOSEPH

This story may be divided into several parts. Each part may be dramatized separately; or, the entire story may be presented at one time.

SCENE I: *Joseph at home.*

Joseph is seen with Jacob. Jacob is giving Joseph a new coat made of many colors.

CHARACTERS: *Jacob, Joseph.*

JACOB: Come here, my son. See what a beautiful gift I have for you!

JOSEPH: What is it, dear father?

JACOB: See, a beautiful new coat!

JOSEPH: Oh, dear father, what a beautiful coat! What lovely colors!

JACOB: Are you pleased with it?

JOSEPH: Yes, dear father, many, many thanks! I do not know how to thank you.

JOSEPH: My dear son, your ready obedience to me in all things gives me great pleasure. Would that your brothers also pleased me so much!

JOSEPH: Dearest father, I am sorry that my brothers cause you so much worry. I am sure they do not know that they grieve you so much.

JACOB: My heart is heavy when I think of them. I

wonder what they are doing now. Go now, Joseph, to thy brothers and see if all be well with them and the flocks.

JOSEPH: I go at once. Farewell, dear father.

JACOB: Farewell, my son, the Lord be with you.

(*Exit Joseph.*)

SCENE II: *Joseph and his brothers.*

The brothers of Joseph are guarding their flocks in a field. Joseph appears in the distance. Joseph wears the coat of many colors.

CHARACTERS: *Joseph, ten brothers, a few merchants.*

RUBEN: See, who is coming there!

SIMEON: It is Joseph. And what do I see? He is wearing the new coat which our father gave him.

DAN: It seems to me that father loves Joseph more than any of us. He gives him anything he wishes.

LEVI: I suppose he is coming to spy on us again. The last time he was with us he told father what we were doing and you remember quite well how displeased with us father was.

ASER: I think we ought to get rid of him.

ALL: Get rid of him! What do you mean?

ASER: Why kill him, of course!

SEVERAL TOGETHER: Kill him! Kill him! But how?

ASER: That can be done very easily. We can strike him over the head as he comes along, and throw his body into this cistern. Then we can say that a wild beast ate him.

JUDA: No, no! do not kill him, I beg you. Why should we spill innocent blood? He is our brother. Throw him into this pit. That will scare him. We can decide later what to do with him.

SEVERAL TOGETHER: Yes, I suppose, that will be the best at present. But we shall have to get rid of him soon. He is becoming too overbearing.

(*Enter Joseph.*)

JOSEPH: Good morning, dear brothers. I have brought your dinner. Our father sends you his greetings.

SEVERAL TOGETHER: Good morning, dear brother. So our father has sent his darling out to spy on us again.

DAN: We'll show you how we treat tale-bearers. Here! catch hold of him. Strip off his fine coat and cast him into the cistern. He can remain there as long as he likes.

(*They seize Joseph, strip off his coat and throw him into the pit.*)

(*Brothers sit down to eat. While they are eating a number of merchants pass by.*)

JUDA: What does it profit us to kill our brother? It is better he be sold to these merchants, and our hands be not defiled; for he is our brother.

GAD: You are right, Juda. Let us sell him to these merchants. They will take him to a strange country where he will be treated as a slave.

JUDA (*to merchants*): Do you wish to buy a slave? We have a young boy here we should like to sell? What will you give us?

MERCHANT: Let us see the slave.

(*Brothers pull Joseph out of the pit. The space behind the teacher's desk might serve as a pit.*)

JUDA: Here he is.

MERCHANT: A fine looking lad. We will give you twenty pieces of silver.

JUDA: Agreed. Take him with you.

JOSEPH (*weeping*): Oh brothers, you do not mean to sell me! Have pity on me! Oh, have pity on me!

ZABULON: No, you shall go with these men. You will soon find out now what your fine dreams mean.

ISSACHAR: Now, we'll see who will bow before you.

JOSEPH: Oh, my brothers, for the sake of our dear old father, have compassion on me! Do not sell me to these men!

MERCHANT: Enough of this. Come, we paid for you; you are ours. We have no time to lose.

JOSEPH: Oh my father, my poor father! Oh, would that I were dead!

(*Exeunt Joseph and the Merchants.*)

SCENE III: *Joseph as a prisoner.*

Joseph in prison. Two other men in prison.

CHARACTERS: *Joseph, the Chief Butler and the Chief Baker of King Pharao.*

JOSEPH: Why are you so sad?

BUTLER AND BAKER: We have dreamed a dream last night and we have no one to explain it to us.

JOSEPH: Does not the interpretation come from God? Tell me your dream.

CHIEF BUTLER: I dreamed I saw a vine on which were three branches: these blossomed and brought forth ripe grapes. I took the cup of Pharao and pressed the grapes into the cup and gave it to the king.

JOSEPH: After three days the king will set you free. Remember me then, and ask the king to take me out of this prison, for I am innocent.

CHIEF BUTLER: Thank you, my friend. I shall remember you before the king.

CHIEF BAKER: I dreamed I had three baskets of meal upon my head; and the birds came and ate the meal in the uppermost basket.

JOSEPH: After three days the king will have you hanged.

(*Chief Baker is sad.*)

SCENE IV: *Joseph as a Prince.*
PART I: *Joseph in prison alone. Appears sad and sorrowful.*
CHARACTERS: *Joseph, messenger.*

JOSEPH: Here I am, after more than two years still in prison. The Chief Butler has forgotten me entirely.

(*Enter Messenger.*)

MESSENGER: Arise. The king wishes to see you.
Joseph rises and goes with the messenger.

PART II. SCENE: *King Pharao on his throne, surrounded by courtiers.*
CHARACTERS: *Joseph, messenger, Pharao, courtiers.*

MESSENGER: Your Majesty, here is Joseph.

KING: Ah, my friend. I am glad you are come. Our Chief Butler tells me you interpreted his dream correctly. I want to ask you the meaning of two dreams I had which trouble me very much.

JOSEPH: Your Majesty, God alone gives the interpretation of dreams. May it please Him to grant your petition. But what were your dreams?

KING: I dreamed I stood by the River Nile. And there came out of the water seven kine, very beautiful and fat, and they fed in marshy places. After them came also seven other kine, lean and ugly, and they devoured the fat ones. Then I awoke. After that I slept again and had another dream.

JOSEPH: Go on. Relate also your second dream.

KING: This time I saw seven ears of corn grow up on the stalk, and the ears were full and fair. After these sprang up seven other ears, thin and blighted, which devoured all the beauty of the former. After this I awoke once more. Tell me now, what my dreams mean.

JOSEPH: Your dreams mean that for seven years there will be plenty of crops. Then will follow seven years of famine throughout all the land.

KING: Yes, I believe that is what my dreams mean. But what shall I do?

JOSEPH: Choose a wise man, O King, and make him ruler over Egypt. In the years of plenty, let him store up the crops so that there may be plenty of food when the time of famine comes.

KING: Can I find such another man that is full of the Spirit of God? Thou shalt be over my house, and thy command all the people shall obey.

JOSEPH: Thank you, my lord, I shall do as you bid me.

KING: As a token of the power I give you, I place this ring upon your finger.

(*King puts ring upon Joseph's finger; he also places a chain of gold around his neck. Joseph is then seated in a triumphal chariot.*)

HERALD: Bend your knees to Joseph; for he is the Governor of the whole land of Egypt.

(*Exeunt all in procession.*)

THE STORY OF MOSES

SCENE I: *Miriam and her mother discussing what disposition to make of Baby Moses. The mother holds the baby in her arms.*

MIRIAM: Oh, mother! what if that terrible man had found our dear little baby? I was so afraid baby would cry.

MOTHER: God be praised. The Lord our God watched over us and guarded our little treasure. But we cannot keep baby any longer. What shall we do? I cannot bear to part with him.

MIRIAM: Mother, I know where we can hide baby. You know where the rushes grow so tall in long rows near the river. I often hide there to see the princess go by. Hide baby brother there and I can play with him every day.

MOTHER: If the princess walks there, I am afraid it will not be a good place for baby.

MIRIAM: Oh, mother, the princess will not hurt baby. She is good and kind. She saw me one day hiding in the rushes and she said, "Do not be afraid, little girl. Come out and let me see you."

MOTHER: If the princess is so kind, then that may be the best place to hide him after all.

MIRIAM: Let us put him in a strong basket and carry it down to the bank. I will hide in the bulrushes and watch over him.

MOTHER: While you get the basket, I will get baby ready. Poor little darling, how I wish I could keep you. But I know the Lord our God will watch over you and protect you.

SCENE II: *A large space in front of the room represents the river. Plants placed on either side represent the bulrushes. Miriam is seen hiding. Baby Moses is in a basket in the river near the bank.*
CHARACTERS: *Baby Moses, Mother, Miriam, the princess, attendants.*

MIRIAM (*sees princess coming towards the river*): How beautiful she is! Oh! (*she sees the basket*).

PRINCESS: Oh, you dear little baby! Did we wake you? Don't cry, dear. No one will hurt you. This must be one of the Hebrew babies. But I will save him. Call one of the Hebrew women to come to me.

MIRIAM (*comes running up*): Dear princess, may I bring a woman to you?

PRINCESS: Are you the little girl I saw hiding in the rushes?

MIRIAM: Yes, dear princess.

PRINCESS: If you know a woman who will be kind and good to the baby you may bring her.

MIRIAM: Thank you, dear princess. I will go at once.

(*Exit Miriam. Returns with mother.*)

MIRIAM: Noble lady, here is a woman who will take care of the baby.

PRINCESS: Take this baby to your house and care for him. Do not be afraid. When the baby is older he shall live with me in the palace. I will pay richly for all you do for him. Only take good care of him.

THE ADORATION OF THE SHEPHERDS

SCENE: *A large field. Some shepherds are seen with their flocks. The sheep, represented by small children, are huddled together in a corner as if sleeping.*

CHARACTERS: *Five or six shepherds; a number of Angels; sheep.*

FIRST SHEPHERD: It is getting late. Let us go to sleep. Whose turn is it to watch tonight?

SECOND SHEPHERD: It is my turn. I think you had all better turn in now. All is quiet in Bethlehem.

(*Shepherds lie down on ground to sleep.*)

(*Second shepherd sits quietly, gazing over the city. Becomes drowsy and gradually falls asleep also. Singing is heard, first very soft, then gradually louder. Second shepherd awakes. Rubs his eyes.*)

SECOND SHEPHERD: Hark! What is that? I thought I heard some wonderful music. (*Singing grows louder.*)

THIRD SHEPHERD (*suddenly awakened*): What heavenly music I hear! (*Other shepherds awake.*)

ANGEL: Fear not, for behold I bring you good tidings of great joy. For this day is born to you a Savior, Who is Christ the Lord, in the city of David. And this shall be a sign to you. You shall find the Infant wrapped in swaddling clothes, and laid in a manger.

(*A number of other Angels appear. All sing "Glory to God in the highest." Shepherds look wonderingly at the Angels. Angels gradually disappear singing the hymn.*)

SHEPHERD: What is it that he says? Let us go over to Bethlehem.

SHEPHERD: Yes, let us see this word that is come to pass, which the Lord hath showed to us.

(*Arrange a crib in some other part of the room. The shepherds approach it and kneel down before it. Form a tableau while the class sings a Christmas hymn such as "Holy Night, Silent Night." Exeunt shepherds.*)

THE ADORATION OF THE MAGI

SCENE I: *The Magi gazing at the wonderful star.*
CHARACTERS: *Casper, Melchior, Balthasar.*

CASPER: Do you see that bright star in the sky?

MELCHIOR: Yes; I wonder what it is.

BALTHASAR: It must be a new star. I have never seen it before.

CASPER: See! how brilliant it is!

MELCHIOR: What can it mean? Let us look in the writings of the learned men and see if anything has been foretold about it.

BALTHASAR: I remember now reading about the coming of a Messias. A wonderful star is to appear at His birth.

CASPER AND MELCHIOR: This must be His star.

MELCHIOR: Where is the Messias to be born?

BALTHASAR: In Judea, for He is to be the King of the Jews.

CASPAR: Let us go to Judea to see this new-born King, this heavenly Messias.

MELCHIOR AND BALTHASAR: Yes, let us go at once to adore Him and offer Him our gifts.

SCENE II: *The Magi near Jerusalem.*
CHARACTERS: *Magi, servants.*

CASPER: The Lord be praised. We are near Jerusalem.

MELCHIOR: Our long journey is at an end and we shall soon behold the glory of the Lord.

BALTHASAR: What joy, what happiness to see the promised Messias!

MELCHIOR: Let us give thanks to God for calling us to adore the Redeemer of the World.

CASPER: See, the wondrous star has disappeared!

BALTHASAR: Let us enter the city and go to the palace of the king. We shall surely find the child there.

SCENE III: *Palace of Herod.*
CHARACTERS: *King Herod; courtiers; the Magi, servants, doctors of the law.*

CASPER: We greet thee, O king. We are strangers in this land. Where is He, that is born King of the Jews?

KING HEROD: The new-born King of the Jews? What do you mean?

MELCHIOR: We have seen His star in the East and are come to adore Him.

KING HEROD (*to himself*): What do they say? The new-born King of the Jews? If there is to be a new King of the Jews, I shall no longer be King!

(*To his courtiers*) Go call the doctors of the law.

(*Exit one or two courtiers.*)

(*Enter two or three doctors of the law.*)

Where is the new King of the Jews to be born?

FIRST SCRIBE: It is written here that Christ, the King of the Jews is to be born in Bethlehem of Juda.

KING HEROD: Go and diligently enquire after the child and when you have found Him, bring me word again that I also may come and adore him.

MAGI: We thank thee, O king.

(*Exeunt Magi and servants.*)

SCENE IV: *Magi on way to Bethlehem.*
CHARACTERS: *Magi; servants; a crib.*

MELCHIOR: Behold! the star! the star!

BALTHASAR: It is leading us to the birthplace of the Messias. Let us follow.

CASPER: See! it stops over a house yonder.

MELCHIOR: Let us enter.

(*The Magi now kneel before the Crib. The servants bring the gifts. Arrange as a sort of tableau.*)

JESUS BLESSING LITTLE CHILDREN

SCENE: *A few of the Apostles enter and mothers with their children enter from the opposite side.*

APOSTLE: Where are you going?

MOTHER: We are going to see Jesus.

APOSTLE: Go home and don't bother Jesus.

MOTHER: No, we love Jesus and we want to tell Him so.

APOSTLE: Jesus has been teaching all day and is very tired.

MOTHER: Jesus is never too tired to talk to little children.

(*Jesus and the other Apostles enter.*)

APOSTLE: Don't you see how pale and worn He looks?

JESUS: "Suffer the little children to come unto Me and forbid them not for of such is the Kingdom of Heaven."

A CHILD FACING THE REST: Did you hear what Jesus said?: "Suffer the little children to come unto Me and forbid them not for of such is the Kingdom of Heaven?"

APOSTLE: There's no use talking, let them go.

APOSTLE: Let them go, Peter.

A CHILD: Jesus, You are not too tired to talk to us, are You? The Apostles wanted to send us away and we would not listen to them.

A little child then goes up to Jesus and says the following prayer:

> Take, Lord, this heart of mine,
> And make it thine.
>   J. F. X. O'Connor, S.J.

ALL: *Hymn: "Suffer That the Little Children"— Hymnal and Prayer Book.*

ST. FRANCIS AND THE WOLF

CHARACTERS: *Several boys and girls to represent the people of Gubbio; three or four boys to represent St. Francis and his companions; one boy to take the part of the wolf.*

SCENE: *Several persons are talking excitedly, pointing towards the woods. Francis and his companions come walking along. The people run up to him.*

FRANCIS: My good people, what is the matter? You seem very much frightened.

BOY OR GIRL: We are frightened. Did you not hear about the terrible wolf that is killing our sheep? Last night he came into town and carried off a man.

ANOTHER BOY OR GIRL: Yes, and this morning we found the bones strewn all over this place. What shall we do? This dreadful wolf will soon kill us all.

BOY: No one dares go near him. He is so fierce and powerful.

FRANCIS: Dear friends, in the name of God, I will go out to meet the wolf.

SEVERAL: No, no, good Brother Francis, do not go. The wolf will eat you.

FRANCIS: Let me go, good people. God will protect me.

(*Francis goes forward; wolf comes from woods, walks toward the people; Francis blessing himself approaches the wolf. The wolf runs towards Francis. Francis makes the Sign of the Cross over the wolf. The wolf stops at once, looks at St. Francis.*)

FRANCIS: Come here, Brother Wolf. I command you, in the name of God, that you do not harm me or any other person.

(*Wolf approaches Francis and lies down at his feet.*)

FRANCIS: Brother Wolf, you have done much harm. You have even killed men. You ought to be hanged. You are a bad wolf. Every one is afraid of you and hates you.

(*Wolf appears ashamed.*)

I want to make peace between you and the people, so that you do no more harm, and so that they will forgive you.

(*Wolf appears pleased; reaches out his paw.*)

FRANCIS: If the people of this town promise to feed you, will you promise not to kill any one? Will you promise not to do that again?

(*Wolf "shakes hands" with Francis. Francis walks away, the wolf follows him meekly.*)

ST. FRANCIS PREACHING TO THE BIRDS

SCENE: *The classroom represents a large field; the desks are the bushes and trees.*

CHARACTERS: *St. Francis, two or three friars, any number of boys and girls to represent the birds. St. Francis is seen walking along with his brothers. He notices the birds.*

FRANCIS: See our little brothers and sisters, the birds! Wait for me here on the road, and I will go to preach to them.

(*Francis walks towards the birds. The children leave their desks and come to the front of the room. Some may be seated on the floor. All listen attentively.*)

FRANCIS: My little sisters, you ought always to thank God for being so good to you. You have pretty feathers, which are warmer in winter than in summer. God gives you food and drink. He gives you shelter. He cares for you every day. So thank Him always.

(*Francis makes the sign of the cross over them. Birds begin to sing. An appropriate hymn might be sung by the children. Children then return to their places.*)

BLESSED HERMAN JOSEPH AND THE INFANT JESUS

Tell the story of Blessed Herman Joseph and have the children dramatize it. The story might be divided as follows:

1. Little Herman at home. Imagine his mother speaking to him of their poverty, having nothing to eat in the house. Little Herman goes to church, tells the Blessed Virgin and the child Jesus his troubles. The Blessed Virgin tells him to lift the stone; there he finds money for shoes and food.

2. Herman Joseph plays with his little friends. Steals away to visit his blessed Mother in church. He speaks to her.

3. Herman Joseph brings the apple to the Infant Jesus.

SCENE I: *A Playground. A number of boys are playing a game. Little Herman approaches.*

CHARACTERS: *Blessed Herman. Seven boys.*

FIRST BOY: Ah! Who comes here? It is Herman. Let us ask him to join our game.

SECOND BOY: No. Do not ask him. He never plays with us very long.

THIRD BOY: Well, let us ask him to play a game with us.

FIRST BOY: Here, Herman, come and play with us. We want you to join us in our game.

HERMAN: All right, boys. But I can't stay very long. For I have an errand to do.

FOURTH BOY: Oh, that can wait. Let's have a game now.

(*Boys play marbles, or other game.*)

HERMAN: I must go now, or I shall be late.

SEVERAL BOYS: Why, we only started to play! We're just getting interested.

HERMAN: I am sorry, boys. But I cannot break my word. I must go now.

FIFTH BOY: Oh, let him go. I suppose he wants to run to church to pray. I see him go there every day.

SIXTH BOY: Well, that is all right. I for my part think it time for all of us to stop playing. It is getting late.

HERMAN: Goodbye, boys. I shall play with you tomorrow.

SEVENTH BOY (*taking a beautiful apple from his pocket*): Here, Herman, take this apple. I have another one for myself.

HERMAN: Oh, thank you, George, you are very kind.

SEVENTH BOY: That's all right. Goodbye. (*Exit.*)

(*Boys gradually leave. Herman is alone.*)

HERMAN: What a lovely apple! Ah, I know what I shall do with it. I will give it to my Blessed Mother. I will ask her to take it for the Infant Jesus.

(*Exit Herman.*)

SCENE II: *The Altar of our Blessed Lady. Herman kneeling before it.* (*Place a statue of the Blessed Virgin on the teacher's desk, if there is no shrine or altar in the classroom.*)

HERMAN: See, dear Mother, this beautiful apple! Please take it. It is all I have and I want to give you something to show you how much I love you and the sweet Jesus.

BLESSED VIRGIN: (*Let a girl standing near the statue speak*): Thank you, dear Herman. I shall give it to Jesus as you wish.

HERMAN: Dearest Mother, I wish I could give you more, but you know that I am only a poor little boy.

BLESSED VIRGIN: Do not worry, dear child. You please me much when you keep your heart pure. Jesus loves little boys and girls who obey their parents. Be obedient, be pure and holy and by this you will show better than in any other way that you love us.

HERMAN: O my Mother, help me! You know I love you, dear Mother, and I am sure you will be with me. Keep me safe, Mother dear, and let me come to heaven with you when I die.

PANTOMIME
BLESSED HERMAN JOSEPH

CHARACTERS: *Blessed Virgin—represented by a little girl, or a statue may be used.*
Herman Joseph—a little boy.

SCENE: *A little girl, wearing a white veil stands on a chair to represent the statue of the Blessed Virgin. The little girl holds a doll in her arms to represent the Infant Jesus.*
Let the class sing or recite the poem, while the boy impersonating little Herman Joseph dramatizes or rather pantomimes the action.

> Little Herman every morning
> Went to church to Mary's shrine,
> There to see the Infant Jesus
> In His mother's arms recline.

Little Herman Joseph walks slowly up to the Virgin and Child, holding his beads, or folding his hands devoutly.

> And he came one morning early
> With an apple in his hands,
> Golden-colored cheeks of rose,
> On his toes he stretching stands.

Taking a rosy apple from his pocket, Herman Joseph offers it to the Infant Jesus. He stands on tiptoe while offering the apple.

> Reaching up towards Mary's statue—
> "What an apple, Mother! Look!"
> "Take," he says, "give it to Jesus."
> And the Blessed Virgin took.

Herman Joseph holds up the apple, he looks pleadingly at the Blessed Virgin. The Blessed Virgin takes the apple from him.

> Smiling sweetly, she to Jesus
> Gave the gift of innocence,
> And the heart of little Herman
> Throbbed with joy when going thence.

The Blessed Virgin gives the apple to Jesus. Herman folds his hands, throws a kiss to the little Infant, and skips happily away.

THE BOY AND THE WOLF

There was once a boy who had the care of a great many sheep.

For sport, the boy would cry from time to time, "The wolf! The wolf!" when there was no wolf near him.

Many times in this way, he had drawn the men in the fields from their work.

At last, the men made up their minds that they would not go again, though the boy cried, "Wolf! Wolf!"

Soon the wolf did come.

Then the boy cried, "The wolf! The wolf! The wolf!" as loud as he could; but no one went to help him.

So the wolf killed the boy and many of the sheep.

SCENE: *A field.*
CHARACTERS: *Several boys (representing men at work in the field)*

A cry is heard:
"Help! help! the wolf! the wolf!"
FIRST BOY: What's that?
SECOND BOY: Some one calling for help.
THIRD BOY: It's a wolf! Let us run and help to drive him away.
(*Boys run out. They return in a short time.*)
FOURTH BOY: Well, now, what do you think of that? Not a wolf in sight.
FIFTH BOY: Yes, I felt like going after that rascally boy. What did he mean?
SIXTH BOY: Oh, well; perhaps the boy thought he saw a wolf and wanted to warn us.
SEVENTH BOY: Let's get back to work. We'll never finish at this rate.
(*Cries of "Wolf! Wolf! Help!" heard again. Boys stop and listen.*)
EIGHTH BOY: There it is again! Perhaps the boy is only teasing us. Let's wait a while.
(*All continue to work. Cries heard again. "Wolf! Wolf!"*)
NINTH BOY: It sounds as if some one is in danger. I'm going to see if I can help.
BOYS: Let's all go and try to kill the wolf.
(*All leave. After a short space of time all return.*)
BOYS: Well, well, some one is surely playing a trick on us. I couldn't see sign of a wolf.

BOY: Neither could I. I don't believe there is a wolf here after all. Some one is trying to tease us.

BOY: I saw a boy run away through that wood just now. I wonder if he is not the one who called for help.

BOY: Well, I'm not going to stop my work again. If it is such fun for that boy to see us run, it is not such fun for us to lose our time.

ALL: No, we will not stop our work again.

(*All work again. After a brief silence, the cry* "Wolf! Wolf!" *sounds louder than before. Boys look up, listen, shake their heads and continue work. Cries come nearer and nearer.*)

BOY: Let him call this time. We're not going to run again.

BOY: The rascal thinks we are going to keep it up all day.

(*A boy comes running breathlessly crying:* "The wolf! the wolf! Help! help!" *He falls to the ground holding his hands to his throat as if bitten.*)

BOYS (*gathering round him*): Oh, look, the wolf killed him. See, there he is, the terrible beast. He is eating a sheep.

BOY: What a terrible thing this is; but that is what happens when boys do not tell the truth.

BOY: Yes, had he not deceived us so many times we would have helped him. But when a person once tells a lie it is hard to believe him again.

LEGEND OF CORPUS CHRISTI

Material for Dramatization

One fine morning in the month of June old Mother Birchtree told her children not to be a bit frightened should some one come in the course of a few hours and cut them down. "Yours may be a glorious lot," she said, "but only the fine, tall, straight trees will be taken. Listen, my children, it may be your happiness to stand honorary guard when the Lord Jesus moves in triumph through the streets on the feast of Corpus Christi to-morrow. It is indeed true that afterwards you will have to die, but you will see that which is the most beautiful on the face of God's earth, and you will be giving your lives for Him. I could not see Him when I was young, because I have grown crooked." And Mother Birch sobbed.

Nearly all the young Birches were delighted with the prospect; only a few tried to hide themselves, faint-heartedly, behind their mother. The others were proud of the honor that might be accorded them and looked forward with joy to the hour of their glorious sacrifice. "After having seen that which is fairest under the sun," they said to each other, "we can afford to die; for then a nameless longing would consume us, and we should die slow deaths anyhow. As it is we shall die like so many martyrs."

Now, one tiny little Birch heard all this, too; but it was too frail, too small, too gentle—a mere baby Birch. And when it hesitatingly asked whether it would probably be taken also, the others only looked sympathetic and shook their leaves most doubtfully. Then the little Birch became very sad indeed; not even its mother, nor the sunshine, nor the birds that sang so jubilantly in its branches every morning, could console it in its sorrow. To see the Lord Jesus! Oh, the twinkling stars up above its head so high had told it so much about the dear, good God; when the others were asleep it used to listen to their wonderful talk for a long, long time. To adorn the way along which He would walk; to see Him; to die for Him—what an enviable lot!

Suddenly the tread of heavy feet was heard, and rough voices sounded. Ah, surely, many of the youthful Birches, so brave but a moment before, must have trembled then, even in spite of themselves. But they were quickly cut down, one after the other. With pain, and yet joy, did Mother Birchtree look upon her children as they fell before her very eyes. Theirs was to be a happy lot indeed!

"Oh, if they would only come to me," the weak little Birch sobbed in a whisper.

"Enough," called out one of the voices. So it was not to be taken along after all! Oh, how it had hoped against hope that it would be needed anyhow! A dewdrop ran down its fair white trunk like a tear.

"One is still wanting," a voice said again, "but there is not a single fair tree left. Ah, here, this one will do. . . ." A blow, a fall, and the little Birch, happy in its very pain and all aglow, was piled on the wagon with the rest.

It is the great feast of Corpus Christi. All in a row the Birches stand proudly side by side along the flower-covered road, young and fresh and smiling in their bliss, each beauteous leaf trembling in adoration, the favored guard of honor of the Lord God, Jesus in the Blessed Sacrament, to be adored forever! But where is our little Birch the blessed one? Oh, the good fortune that fell to its lot! In addition to other larger and leafier trees two smaller ones were wanted in order to have two evenly matched trees to adorn the high altar in the open. They were placed just next to the tabernacle. And one of them was our thrice happy little Birch!

Tell Us Another, Winfrid Herbst, S.D.S.

3. GYMNASTIC STORIES

Play is one of the child's natural activities and one of the most potent factors in his physical and mental development. Through the medium of play the senses are made acute, the powers of observation and attention are developed, the imagination is stimulated, and the body is given the needful exercise.

In the primary grades there should be frequent opportunities for the children to exercise their muscles, to satisfy their desire to do something, and to work off their abundance of animal spirits.

The gymnastic story affords a fine opportunity for exercise. Activities done in rhythm should be used to cultivate a sense of rhythm. The cultivation of rhythm will give ease, dignity and grace to carriage and foster greater freedom in all bodily movements. The first exercises for the cultivation of rhythm in children must of necessity be simple. Suitable phonograph records will aid the teacher to secure the proper rhythm. While a musical instrument is a great help to the teacher in this work, she will be able to get along quite well, if the children are familiar with simple songs written in the desired meter. At first the teacher may merely say "Clap," "Swing," while the children carry out these movements.

Primary teachers generally are familiar with the various rhythmic plays, mimetics, and gymnastic stories. We would here suggest the use of these also in connection with the Bible and other stories selected from the Reader or the Lives of the Saints. All of these stories contain action. The class might be asked to imitate the various activities of the characters in the story; for example, in the story of Blessed Herman Joseph, the class might imitate the boys on the playground, in walking, stooping, throwing stones, bending and jumping. Then when Herman leaves his companions to go to church, they might carry out the actions of little Herman in leaving his playmates to visit the statue of the Blessed Virgin, there, in his childlike simplicity, to offer his beautiful apple. Let the class mark time, left, right,—left, right, as if marching together to church. Let them in imagination walk up the church steps, enter the church, genuflect, approach the altar, kneel, step forward to offer the apple to the Blessed Virgin, bow before her statue, genuflect before the Blessed Sacrament, and leave the church.

Incidents in the life of the Little Flower will furnish a variety of activities. When the Little Flower of Jesus was a child, she knew very well that Jesus likes to have children come to visit Him. She often asked to be taken to church. Her nurse used to take her to church when they went for their afternoon walk. The class might imitate the Little Flower's visits to church in the following manner:

The Little Flower of Jesus and Her Nurse Go to Church

After having told the story the teacher will ask:

How many little boys and girls would like to take a walk to the church to visit Jesus this morning? Let us play going to church as the "Little Flower" did. Let us pretend it is very early in the morning and we want to turn over for another sleep before we start out. Put your heads down on the desk and go to sleep. When I clap my hands, all wake up and sit tall and straight.

(*Clap.*) Good morning, little boys and girls, did you all have a good sleep? Now let us start out on our walk. But first we shall take a trip to the country and pick some flowers for Jesus. (*Pupils stand up in proper position. Mark time: left, right—left, right; keep step to music if desired. Class halt.*)

Oh, here is a puddle of water; let's jump over it. (*Children jump.*)

Here we are at the park. Oh! look at the pretty flowers (*turn head first to the right, then to the left*). How sweet they smell! (*First to the right, then to the left.*) Let us sit down and pick some flowers to take along to church. See how many we can pick without moving from our places. Oh! there is a pretty pink flower! See if we can reach it. (*Stretch toward right.*) See, there is another. (*Stretch toward left.*) There I see a lovely white flower. (*Continue picking flowers for a little while.*) Now, let's lay our flowers aside, and see if we can gather the beautiful flowers on that bush. See if we can reach the beautiful flower at the top. (*Pupils reach and stretch upward, standing on toes, imitating the picking of flowers, reaching with both hands, one hand holding the branch, while they pick the flowers with the other. Bend forward to lay the other flowers on the ground.*)

Now let us arrange our bouquet for Jesus. (*Children bend and pick up flowers.*)

We will sit down for a little while and listen to the birds sing. Do you hear that sweet song? (*Pupils hold hands behind ears, first right, then left.*)

Now let us take a look around, so that we shall be able to tell father and mother all we have seen. Look at the dear little chickens! See! there is one little chickie all alone! (*Pupils look to the front.*)

Now, let us visit Jesus and give Him our pretty flowers. Before we go, we will breathe some of the good fresh air very deeply. (*Breathing exercise.*)

Are we ready to go now? (*Mark time: left, right,—left, right.*)

Here we are now at church. Boys, remove your hats! (*Boys make motion of removing hats.*)

Let us enter softly, for Jesus is here. (*Walk slowly and reverently.*)

(*The children now genuflect reverently, then kneel, fold their hands, say a short prayer together, step to the altar, lay down their flowers, genuflect and turn to leave the church.*)

Now, we are back at school once more, and we must get busy with our books. Some other time I shall tell you another story which you can act out.

SECTION IV

MUSIC

1. MUSIC IN THE CLASSROOM

Some one has said, "Music is the best gift of God; it is the only art of heaven given to earth; it is the only art of earth we take to heaven." Music is now recognized as an essential factor in the training of children. In the standard course of music for the schools certain aims, materials, methods and attainments are definitely outlined for each grade. Catholic schools are fortunate in having at their command various systems by Catholic authors for the teaching of church music.

In accordance with the wish of the late Holy Father Pope Pius X the members of our Catholic congregations are to take part in the singing of the liturgical services, and hence the children in our schools must be taught to love and appreciate the beauty of music and to sing as naturally as they read or speak. The beauty of the Gregorian Chant will never be truly appreciated by our people unless the children in our schools are trained in the proper manner of singing and in the appreciation of the beauty and spiritual significance of good music.

One of the main purposes of music in the schools should be the development of music appreciation in the child. This development naturally depends largely upon the type of musical experience provided for the child. Therefore, school music should first of all cultivate the child's natural response to music heard and his interest in hearing and expressing it. A child should be trained to enjoy good music. He should be educated to discriminate between what is good and what is commonplace. In the early grades the teaching of music should consist mainly in having the children sing many good songs, properly graded and selected. Emphasis should be placed upon obtaining response and stimulating desire for expression. At this stage in the child's musical education, musical appreciation means simply the enjoyment of singing, with musical and emotional response. Hearing a beautiful selection many times is necessary for the full appreciation of its aesthetic and spiritual significance.

Whatever the method in use in the music courses of our schools, we must take into consideration the fact that the child's impressionable mind will be greatly influenced by the quality of music he hears at home and in school. The phonograph, the player piano and the radio are to-day important factors in the musical life of the nation. By means of these wonderful inventions, we may now not only *hear* the world's great music, but we may *study* it, its form, its content, and thus get the whole message of the composer. Again and again we may hear the selection, analyze its phrases, motives, periods and movements, until we obtain a real understanding of the science of music as well as of its emotional and cultural values.

Before the invention of the phonograph, school music was limited to what pupils themselves could produce, the teacher of music could give, or some gifted artists would furnish on rare occasions. Now it is possible to hear the world's best artists in the classroom at any time and as often as desired. It is obvious that the use of the phonograph in the classroom affords a rich opportunity for studying music, furnishing the foundation for the development of rhythm, singing, music appreciation, ear-training, instrument study and all the other phases of this beautiful art. It would consequently be a serious mistake on the part of the Catholic teacher to neglect this valuable factor in the musical training of the child.

In the first grade the child is given a foundation in musical experience upon which the formal instruction of the succeeding years is based. This musical experience consists of some form of rhythmic response, such as marching, clapping, and the like, to good rhythmic music. It likewise includes listening to phonograph records, piano pieces, and songs. In the first school years the principal work of the child is to sing well-chosen songs and to listen to good music.

2. CREATING MUSIC

School children to-day are given many opportunities for self-expression. Drawing, construction work, clay modeling, projects of various kinds provide so many means of expressing the ideas in the child mind. Children are encouraged to express themselves in many ways and these activities gain for them a wider outlook on life and life's problem.

One of the most thrilling acts of self-expression is the composing and singing of original melodies. The musical conversation is an invaluable aid in this regard. Often it will be interesting to let the class compose words suitable for the musical phrasing. Many times it is advisable to arrange the words first and then to compose the melody.

The idea of composing a song to be sung by the class is very fascinating to the children. Just as an intensive interest in the work in religion is aroused by letting the children express themselves freely through drawing, paper cutting, poster and sand table work, so the study of music is intensified by encouraging the children to compose original melodies and songs. It is quite obvious that only simple songs consisting of three or four phrases should be attempted.

To get the best results from work of this type, the teacher might try the following plan:

First draw a staff on the board. Then call for a melody for the first phrase. From the number of answers given choose the one that is deemed best. The notes are then written on the staff. Next call for a melody for the second phrase. If two or more seem good, write them on the board and let the class decide which is more suitable. Proceed in the same manner for the remaining phrases. After the entire melody has been accepted by the class let the children sing it in concert and individually.

One or more stanzas of poems by Father Tabb, Father Faber, Father Ryan, Alice and Phoebe Cary and others furnish good words to be set to music in this manner, thus giving the children in the lower grades an opportunity for developing their creative ability.

Once the children have learned to express themselves by means of original musical melodies the teacher may feel assured that she has given them a real love for music and has created a wider interest in its study.

The following melodies have been developed in the manner suggested above and are fair examples of what children can do if properly directed.

THE CHILD ON CALVARY

Words by Father Tabb

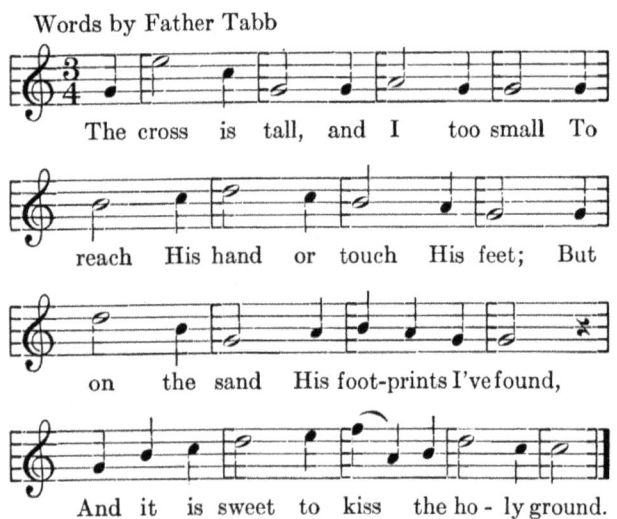

LITTLE BOY, LITTLE GIRL

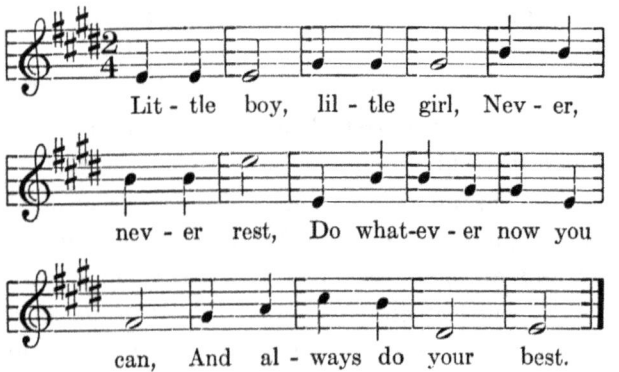

3. MUSICAL CONVERSATION

An interesting device that will help to develop good musical phrasing is the "Musical Conversation." Let the teacher or a child sing a musical phrase and have the class answer with another musical phrase. Sometimes the procedure is varied; the teacher may call on one child to answer; that child in turn may ask a musical question of another. Or a child may ask the first question and several may be called on to answer. After two or three answers have been given, the teacher may write them on the board, and the entire class may be called upon to read the selection.

The "Musical Conversation" may be conducted in this manner:

Teacher. What did we learn in music yesterday, Alice?

Alice. We learned to ask questions in music and to answer them.

Teacher. Yes. Will some one now ask the class a musical question? Very well, James, you may try.

James. (sings) || 1 3 | 5 4 | 3 2 | 3. ||

Teacher. Good. Now I wonder who will answer this question? Mary, will you try?

Mary. (sings) || 5 4 | 3 3 | 3 2 | 1. ||

Teacher. That is fine. But sometimes we may be able to get more than one answer. Will some one else try to answer James' question? Dorothy.

Dorothy. (sings) || 5 1 | 7 6 | 5 3 | 1. ||

Teacher. Good. Now, I am going to write the question on the board and under it I shall place the first answer. Then I shall repeat the question and write the second answer under it.

(*The teacher writes the four phrases on the board.*)

Teacher. Now, let us all together sing the question and answers. But before you begin what must you remember?

Class. We must remember to drop our jaws and pronounce distinctly.

(*Class sings the four phrases from the board.*)

Teacher. What do we have on the board, Joseph?

Joseph. We have two musical questions and two musical answers on the board.

Teacher. Good. But can you tell me that in a shorter way?

(*No answer.*)

Teacher. I shall tell you one word that expresses the four phrases on the board. The word is "melody." Class repeat the word.

Teacher. How many measures have we in this melody, John?

John. We have sixteen measures.

Teacher. Correct. But instead of saying sixteen measures, we shall say that we have four phrases. Therefore how many measures to a phrase, Anna?

Anna. There must be four measures to a phrase.

Teacher. And if we have sixteen measures and four measures to a phrase, how many phrases do we have, Thomas?

Thomas. We shall have four phrases.

(*The teacher sings one measure.*)

Teacher. What part of the melody did I sing, David?

David. You sang a bar.

(*The teacher goes to the board and makes a bar.*)

Teacher. What is this, children? Class answers, "A bar."

Teacher. You see, David, I can make a bar, but I cannot sing one. Now do you remember what you call the part I sang?

David. Yes, Sister, it is a measure.

Teacher. Very well, David. That is correct.

Teacher. Now let the first row sing the first phrase; the second row, the second phrase; the next row, the third phrase; and the others, the last phrase.

(*The class sings the melody as directed. Many other variations may be introduced by the teacher. This work is interesting and stimulates the children to activity.*)

4. THE SINGING OF SONGS IN THE CLASSROOM

Regardless of what system or course in music we follow we should recognize that the fundamental purpose is to develop musical thought, musical hearing, and musical expression. Children ought to fill the world with the beauty of their song. But to attain this end we must give attention to their voices. A child's voice can become a wonderful instrument for producing beautiful music. To secure natural voice production select songs within the proper compass of the child's voice. Give some attention to correct breathing since breathing influences the quality of the tone. Careful phrasing is an aid to proper breathing.

Song singing is one of the most important activities carried on in schools. When songs have been carefully chosen and properly taught, they ought to be sung over and over again for the enjoyment and beauty found in them. Let the children sing the songs merely for the satisfaction they get from their beauty.

The child learns to sing, not by memorizing many rules and detailed processes, but by hearing others sing and imitating them. In this way he gets some idea of melody and rhythm and soon notices the different tones. He learns the scale by hearing others sing it. This enables him to lay the foundation for learning to read at sight any simple song or hymns placed before him.

The musical education of the child is best begun with class singing in the do-re-mi system. Simple rote songs at the beginning will train the ear for musical tones and will serve to keep up the interest in the singing lesson. Vocal music should be a constant factor in the schoolroom, especially in the primary grades. Twenty minutes given to singing during the day will be time well spent. A good rousing song at the opening of school will inspire the pupils to take up their work with enthusiasm. A song at the close of the day is calculated to remove all unpleasant thoughts from the mind, and the child will go home contented and happy. Singing has also a very wholesome effect upon discipline. Nature songs, patriotic and religious hymns, with a few simple exercises, should constitute the work of the first and second grades. Music if properly correlated with all other subjects, especially with religion, will promote not only aesthetic development, but will stimulate also mental and moral growth.

5. MUSIC IN ITS RELATION TO PLAYS AND GAMES

Rhythmic play, gymnastic stories, and mimetic exercises are fast supplanting in the lower grades the more formal gymnastics or calisthenics. Children should be allowed great freedom of expression in rhythmic play in response to the suggestion of rhythm and form in a musical selection. At times, the music is intended to suggest or represent. Children spontaneously respond to these suggestions. For example, when the children hear a lullaby, they at once begin to sway in the rhythmic motion of the lullaby; likewise, a march played on the graphophone will elicit the desire to step.

Whether the little folks will be interested in music depends largely upon the teacher. The teacher should love music and know it well before she attempts to present it to the children. From the very beginning, only good music should be presented. A large number of musical records properly graded and suitable for classroom use are obtainable.[1] To use records indiscriminately, that is, to use marches, songs, and other musical selections that have not been carefully graded and adapted for children, will do harm, for the records to be used in school are specially made for educational purposes.

When the child comes to school his voice and ear have rarely been trained, but such training comes naturally with activity. Hence the primary aim should be to develop rhythm activity. The best way to do this is by means of records produced by miniature orchestras. Let the children play the simple rhythm in two's, three's, and four's, that is, let two, three or four children act the rhythm first. The following selections are suitable for this purpose:

"Rataplan" ....Donizetti
"Shadows" ....Schytte
"Gypsy Rondo" ....Haydn
"Serenata" ....Moszkowski

[1] The Columbia Graphophone Company, New York, and the Victor Talking Machine Company, Camden, N. J., produce a series of such records. They will gladly supply catalogues and graded lists offering valuable suggestions as to the various uses of these records in connection with school work.

When the step is fairly well known, then you may gradually and systematically give the child good, pleasing music, and let him live in it. Put on a record, and let the child express himself. A few pupils at a time may take turns at acting in the way suggested by the music. Play, for instance, "The Wild Rider." Ask the children what it makes them feel like doing. Run? Hop? Skip? Let them try it out. When the right action is given, let the pupil who hit upon it first, be the leader in directing groups to gallop with the music. When the children are interested, let them learn the names of the piece and the composer. Show them his picture and tell them something about his life. After the selection has been taught the child should recognize the piece and know the composer as soon as he hears the piece played. The child will soon be so trained that when he hears a new selection he will ask at once what the name of the piece is, and who wrote it.

A Recommended List

"Knight of the Hobby Horse" and
  "The Wild Rider"   Schumann
"The Huntsmen"   Gurlitt
"March"   Hollaender
"Soldier's March"   Tschaikowski
"Gounod Toy March"   Tschaikowski
"March of the Little Lead
  Soldiers"   Pierne
"Doll's Cradle Song" and "The
  Top"   Bizet
"Trumpeter and Drummer"
"Rock-a-bye"
"Sleep, Baby, Sleep."
"Lullaby"   Mozart

After this rhythm has been mastered, at least in part, the swing-sway or lullaby rhythm is begun, that is, the children sway with the music.

It will be noticed that all the pieces named suggest action.

"Wild Rider"   Free gallop
"Hobby Horse"   Backward and forward pull
"Toy March"   Stiff, stilted walk
"Hollaender's March"   Free walk and a bow
"Huntsmen"   Pantomime story
"Doll's Cradle Song"   A small sway

"Rock-a-bye"	A long sway
"Sleep, Baby, Sleep"	A medium sway

It takes longer to develop these pieces when the children themselves work them out, under the teacher's supervision, than if the teacher simply tells them and shows them what to do, but the fact that the children are encouraged to take the initiative makes them feel that it is their own production, and the music becomes a part of themselves.

In the second grade, review these first grade selections and gradually add some with less of the rhythmic element and more of the beautiful in melody. "Morning," by Grieg, an excerpt of his suite, is one of this type. The following list offers suggestions for the Second Grade:

"Morning"	Grieg
"Sweet and Low"	Barnby
"Lullaby"	Taubert
"Sandman"	Brahms
"Lullaby"	Brahms
"Soldier's March"	Schumann
"Rider's Story"	Schumann
"Toy Symphony"	Haydn
"Cradle Song"	Schubert

The teacher must be prudent in giving these selections. One at a time, presented in an attractive way, will serve to rouse the children's interest and lead them to form a correct taste in music. Review until they know the old selections well, before presenting a new one.

A few minutes of the opening exercise will be well spent in this work of review. Let the children take turns in suggesting what should be played. The indifferent child will soon learn the compositions, in order not to miss his chance to make out a "music program." When the room is stuffy, open the windows and let the children "play" one of their pieces. They will enjoy "swinging the birdies on the tree-top" or galloping around the room to Schumann's music more than a formal health exercise dictated by the teacher. At the same time they will feel refreshed and go back to their work with lighter hearts and greater love for the beautiful. When a love for good music has been cultivated in the lower grades, the interest will not flag in the upper grades.

A list of suitable records for the first and second grades may be found in "Music Appreciation Taught by Means of the Phonograph," by Kathryn E. Stone,[1] Chicago. The teacher who wishes to make use of the phonograph for the purpose of creating a love and intelligent enjoyment of music in her pupils will do well to secure a copy of this book. A partial list of the records suggested for the first and second grades is given here.

1.
"Of a Tailor and a Bear"	MacDowell
"The Wild Horseman"	Schumann
"Spinning Song"	Kullak
"The Little Hunters"	Kullak

2.
"Minute Waltz"	Chopin
"The Bee"	Schubert

3.
"Rock-a-Bye Baby"
"Sweet and Low"
"Cradle Song"
"Adeste Fideles"
"The First Noel"
"Nazareth"

4.
"The Postilion"
"Lullaby"
"Spanish Gypsy"
"The Linden Tree"
"Pull a Cherry"
"Nightingale"
"The Fire"
"See-Saw, Margery Daw"

5.
"Marche Miniature"	Tschaikowski

6.
"Anvil Chorus," from "Il Trovatore"	Verdi

7.
"Minuet"	Beethoven

8.
"The Swan"	Saint-Saens
"Melody in F"	Rubinstein

6. DEVICES TO AID THE SINGING TEACHER

The Singing Voices of the Children

A young child has but a tiny singing voice. The objective of the singing teacher in the beginning should be to attain sweetness and correctness of tone rather than power of voice.

[1] See bibliography, "Books for the Teacher."

Every normal child can be taught to sing. A child's voice should be characterized by its lightness, sweetness, and flexibility. Harsh tones force the delicate mechanism of the child's voice and will cause strain and perhaps even permanent injury to the voice. Children should be cautioned against unnecessary yelling, screeching and shouting. A good tone may be secured by having the children sing softly at all times. The voice should be thrown forward. Merely telling the children to throw their voices forward will help but little, the teacher ought to show how this is done.

A simple device to remind the children to throw their voice forward is to draw a chimney on the board. From this chimney smoke issues in curls. Make the smoke light and dark. The syllable "Noo" is written upwards in the smoke. The following verses may help to stimulate the interest of the children:

> See from out the chimney bright,
> Smoke is rolling, soft and light.
> "Noo" is what the ringlets say,
> See they swell, then die away.

Another device is to tell the children that to bring out their voices correctly the tip of the tongue should touch the roof of the mouth.

How to Help Monotones

Some children cannot sing a tune correctly. Some may be able to follow the melody, but cannot sing in perfect tune; others have no idea whatever of singing in tune. These children are usually classed as "monotones." Monotones should have special attention. No matter how poorly a child may sing at first, encourage him to believe that he can learn to sing if he will try his best.

A useful device that will often help monotones is the "calls." These provide excellent material for beginning rote singing and teaching the correct use of the voice. The calls used are generally the "name calls" and the "street calls." The calls may be made in various ways: The teacher may call the children, and have all reply; she may call individuals to reply; the children may call one another; or one child may give the call and be answered by a row or a group. The best type is probably the "name call." One child calls another by name and the one thus called answers.

The "street calls" may also be given in a variety of ways. If these calls are used early in the year, the children will greatly enjoy the exercise. Encourage the children to make their own calls. Teachers should not allow the class to sing these calls exclusively till all can sing them correctly. Other songs ought to be learned during this time, but the teacher returns to the calls after each lesson for the benefit of those who do not get them correctly. The calls are only an aid for drill in singing and ear-training.

Playing engine, having the monotones sing tu-tu-tu, in imitation of an engine, also helps. When they have acquired the ability to hold this tune, let them try other similar tunes in different keys.

Another device for eliminating monotones is to classify the voices, that is, to arrange the best voices in one row, the next best in the next row, and so on, leaving the last row for the monotones. Name the first row, the canaries, the next the bluebirds, and so on till the row of the monotones who receive no name. Tell them that as soon as they are able to carry a tune you will put them in a row with the others.

Giving the children music seats is another helpful device. Let the children having the best voices occupy the last row across the room, the next best, the row in front of these, and so on, placing the poorest singers in the front row. This will let the good voices be heard by the poorer ones. Sometimes let the last row, the best singers, sing a phrase, the next row repeat it and so on down to the first row. This will often help the monotones to get the right tune.

NAME CALL

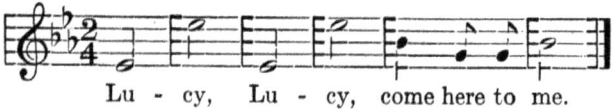

Lu - cy, Lu - cy, come here to me.

STREET CALL

B'na - nas, b'na - nas, nice ripe b'na-nas to-day.

Mottoes and Slogans for the Music Class

Good music is the sunshine of the heart.
Lift up your voices.
By singing for God we imitate the angels.
Sing and be happy.
Good music is the language of heaven.
Drive away gloom and sadness with music.
What is home without music?
Children's voices reach heaven.

7. FOLK SONGS

It is generally admitted by authorities in music that the development of modern musical literature has been greatly influenced by a revival of folk music. Folk songs and rhymes, folk dancing and singing games—all played an important part in the lives of people in the early times. Songs were learned by ear and thus were passed on from one generation to another. Any one who would understand and appreciate the higher forms of musical art should become familiar with the folk songs of the different nations. Folk music makes the strongest appeal to children in their early years. In the following list of songs taken from "Catholic Education Music Course," by Justine Ward, this fundamental principle is recognized and an opportunity is given to the child to become familiar with the sweet melodies of bygone centuries.

FIRST GRADE

"It is Love" music adapted from a theme by Mozart
"Christmas Carol—A Welcome to Jesus" — Noel Bourguignon
"Jesus' Love" — Folk Song
"The Father's Love" — Beethoven
"Dearest Lord, We Thank You" — Adapted from German Folk Song
"Little Robin, Never Fear" — Folk Song
"A Story" — Samuel Cole
"The Mother's Prayer" — Folk Song
"Christmas Carol" — German Carol, 15th Century
"Lullaby" — Haydn
"Hymn for First Communion" — Spanish Noel

SECOND GRADE

"Marching Song" — French Folk Song
"Lullaby of the Infant Jesus" — Old German Song
"The Annunciation" — German Folk Song
"High on the Hillside" — French Folk Song
"Why?" — Old English Carol
"The Spring" — French Folk Song
"Emmanuel" — Old German Melody
"The First Noel" — Old English Carol
"Garden and Cradle" — Adapted from Old French Melody
"The Cat and the Pigeon" — French Folk Song
"Joseph and Jesus" — German Folk Song
"The Fairy Ship" — French Folk Song
"The Son of Man" — Adapted from Mozart
"The Visible Creation" — Beethoven
"Adam and Eve" — Schubert
"Jesus, Tender Shepherd" — Mozart

In like manner the following titles from "The Progressive Music Series" (Catholic Edition) edited by Rt. Rev. Joseph Schrembs, D.D., Bishop of Cleveland and Very Rev. Gregory Huegle, O. S. B., will appeal to the teacher.

FIRST GRADE

"God's Greatness" — Dielman
"Faith of Our Fathers" — Rt. Rev. Joseph Schrembs, D.D.
"Song of Praise" — Joseph Haydn
"Children of the Heavenly King" — Ignaz Joseph Pleyel
"On Christmas Day in the Morning" — Edward B. Birge
"Angele Dei" — Missa de Angelis

SECOND GRADE

"See Amid the Winter's Snow" — Rt. Rev. Joseph Schrembs, D.D.
"Hark, Hark, My Soul" — Rt. Rev. Joseph Schrembs, D.D.
"Bread and Butter" — French Folk Song
"Morning Song" — German Folk Song
"At Sunrise" — Franz Schubert
"Bed in Summer" — English Folk Song

"Approach of Winter"   From the Dutch
"Dear Harp of My
   Country"   Welsh Folk Song
"The Sturdy Blacksmith"   W. A. Mozart
"Pop Corn Song"   W. Otto Miessner

8. SONGS FOR THE LITTLE ONES

Teachers in Catholic schools are guided in their choice for suitable material for exercises, songs and hymns by the outlines in their respective courses of study. However, teachers sometimes wish to vary their programs somewhat and use other songs and hymns for special occasions. The list given here presents a wide range of material for use in the primary grades. It contains many favorite selections.

CHRISTMAS—The Infant Jesus

"What Lovely Infant," Father Finn's Carol Book, C. C. Birchard & Co., Boston, Mass.
"Jesus, Teach Me How to Pray" ibid.
"The Christmas Tree" ibid.
"We Three Kings of the Orient" ibid.
"Silent Night," Twice Fifty-Five, C. C. Birchard & Co., Boston, Mass.
"Holiest Night," New Hymn Book for Church and School, Benziger Brothers, New York, N. Y.
"O Cruel Herod! Why Thus Fear," Manual of Catholic Hymns, Benziger Brothers, New York, N. Y.

THE NEW YEAR

"Father, Let Me Dedicate," Manual of Catholic Hymns, Benziger Brothers, New York, N. Y.

THE BLESSED SACRAMENT

"We Thee Adore," Diocesan Hymnal, J. Fischer and Bro., New York, N. Y.
"Jesus, Lord, Be Thou My Own" ibid.

THE BLESSED VIRGIN

"Mother, O Forget Me Not" ibid.
"Maiden Mother," Roman Hymnal, Fr. Pustet & Co., New York, N. Y.
"Hail Queen of Lovely Blooming May," Manual of Catholic Hymns, Benziger Brothers, New York, N. Y.

ST. JOSEPH

"Bring to Me, Dearest Father," Diocesan Hymnal, J. Fischer & Bro., New York, N. Y.
"Holy Patron Thee Saluting," Manual of Catholic Hymns, Benziger Brothers, New York, N. Y.

ST. ALOYSIUS

"Hail! Aloysius, Hail!" Manual of Catholic Hymns, Benziger Brothers, New York, N. Y.

RENEWAL OF BAPTISMAL VOWS

"True to My Vows," New Hymn Book for Church and School, Benziger Brothers, New York, N. Y.

FIRST HOLY COMMUNION

"Jesus, Thou Art Coming," Manual of Catholic Hymns, Benziger Brothers, New York, N. Y.

MISSIONS

"Oh, Priceless Love," Manual of Catholic Hymns, Benziger Brothers, New York, N. Y.

MORNING HYMN

"Honor Be to God in Heaven," New Hymn Book for Church and School, Benziger Brothers, New York, N. Y.

EVENING HYMN

"In This Dark Night," New Hymn Book for Church and School, Benziger Brothers, New York, N. Y.

GUARDIAN ANGEL

"Dear Angel Ever at My Side" ibid.

HYMN OF PRAISE

"Holy God, We Praise Thy Name," Roman Hymnal, Fr. Pustet & Co., New York, N. Y.

PATRIOTIC SELECTIONS

"America," The Gray Book of Favorite Songs, Hall & McCreary Company, Chicago, Ill.

"America the Beautiful," Twice Fifty-Five, C. C. Birchard & Co., Boston, Mass.

"Salute to the Flag," Jessie L. Gaynor in Songs of the Child World, John Church Company, Cincinnati, O.

"Our Flag Is There," Johnstone, A. E., and Loomis, H. W., Lyric Music Series Primer, Scott, Foresman and Company, Chicago, Ill.

HOME—CHILDREN

"Father's and Mother's Care," Song Stories for Kindergarten, Clayton F. Summy Company, Chicago, Ill.

"This Is the Mother," Songs for Little Children, Milton Bradley Co., Philadelphia, Pa.

"Slumber Boat," Songs of the Child World, John Church Co., Cincinnati, O.

"Lullaby," Brahms, Twice Fifty-Five, C. C. Birchard & Co., Boston, Mass.

"The Carpenter," Songs for Little Children, Milton Bradley Co., Philadelphia, Pa.

"Carpenters," Johnstone, A. E., and Loomis, H. W., Lyric Music Series Primer, Scott, Foresman & Co., Chicago, Ill.

MISCELLANEOUS SELECTIONS

"Sweet and Low," Twice Fifty-Five, C. C. Birchard & Co., Boston, Mass.

"Blacksmith," Dann (Hollis) Music Course, First Year, American Book Co., New York.

"Dapple Gray," Ibid.

"Tick Tock," Ibid.

"Happy Thought," Ibid.

"A True Story," Johnstone, A. E., and Loomis, H. W., Lyric Series Primer, Scott, Foresman and Co., Chicago, Ill.

"Japanese Parasol," Ibid.

"The Lost Balloon," Ibid.

"The Leaves' Party," Songs of the Child World, John Church Co., Cincinnati, O.

"Thanksgiving Song," Ibid.

"The Bird's Nest," Ibid.

"Baby Chickens," Johnstone, A. E., and Loomis, H. W., Lyric Music Series Primer, Scott, Foresman and Co., Chicago, Ill.

"We Thee Adore"—Teaches reverence and love for the Blessed Sacrament.

"Maiden Mother"—gives a lesson to the little ones and is an incentive to good conduct.

"Blacksmith"—teaches a lesson in etiquette and kindness to animals.

"Dapple Gray"—shows kindness to animals.

"Japanese Parasol"—"The Lost Balloon"—teach lessons in economy; taking the proper care of toys.

"Slumber Boat"—is used to arouse love for little brothers and sisters.

"Thanksgiving Song"—teaches love and respect for grandparents.

"Jesus, Lord Be Thou My Own"—is a preparation for Holy Communion.

"The Leaves' Party"—teaches behavior at play and kindness to others.

Brahms' "Lullaby"—teaches love for the little ones.

"We Three Kings of the Orient"—may be used in connection with the dramatization of the Adoration of the Magi.

"Silent Night"—may be sung in connection with the Christmas celebration.

"Salute to the Flag"—shows love for the flag and inculcates reverence for our country's flag.

Valuable material for songs for the little ones may be secured from the following publications:

The Catholic Education Music Course, The Catholic Education Press, Washington, D. C.

Music Education Series, T. P. Giddings and Others. Ginn and Company, Boston, Mass.

Dann (Hollis) Music Course, American Book Company, New York.

The Progressive Music Series, Catholic Edition edited by Rt. Rev. Joseph Schrembs, D.D., and Rev. Gregory Huegle, O. S. B. Silver, Burdett and Company, New York, N. Y.

The Universal School Music Series, Damrosch, Gartlan & Gehrkens. Hinds, Hayden and Eldridge, Inc., New York, N. Y.

The Lyric Music Series, Scott, Foresman and Company, Chicago, Ill.

Book of Songs, R. Foresman. American Book Company, New York, N. Y.

Primary Melodies, E. W. Newton. Ginn and Company, Boston, Mass.

Folk Songs and Other Songs, Oliver Ditson & Co., New York, N. Y.

Congdon Music Readers, C. H. Congdon, New York, N. Y.

Lilts and Lyrics, Clayton F. Summy Co., Chicago, Ill.

Songs of the Child World, John Church Co., Cincinnati, O.

Twice Fifty-Five, C. C. Birchard & Co., Boston.

The Rose Book, Ibid.

The Community Book, Ibid.

The Gray Book of Favorite Songs, Hall and McCreary, Chicago, Ill.

The Golden Book of Favorite Songs, Ibid.

The Child's Song Treasury—Mary B. Ehrman, Auburn Ave., Cincinnati, O. This contains the following favorite poems set to music:

"Song of the Creation"..Cecil F. Alexander
"Night and Day".......Mary Mapes Dodge
"Beautiful Things".......Ellen P. Allerton
"Little Things".........Francis S. Osgood
"A Birthday Gift".....Christina G. Rosetti

REFERENCE BOOKS

Music Appreciation Taught by Means of the Phonograph—Kathryn E. Stone, Scott, Foresman and Company, Chicago, Ill.

Music Appreciation for Little Children, Educational Department, Victor Talking Machine Company, Camden, N. J.

Listening Lessons in Music, Agnes Moore Fryberger, Silver, Burdett and Company, Chicago, Ill.

The Victrola Book of Opera, Educational Department, Victor Talking Machine Company, Camden, N. J.

Music Appreciation in the Schoolroom, Music Education Series. Ginn and Company, New York, N. Y.

Music Appreciation for Every Child, Glenn DeForest, Silver, Burdett and Company, Chicago, Ill.

Music Appreciation Records, Ginn and Company, New York, N. Y.

SECTION V

CLASSROOM AIDS AND DEVICES

1. SCHOOLROOM DECORATIONS

The more homelike the atmosphere of the primary room the easier it is to accustom the children to their new life. The first grade should not resemble a curio shop, nor a junk shop either, with all kinds of useless ornaments and objects standing around. Useless material should have no place in the primary room. The schoolroom is a workshop and the sooner the children get to work the sooner they forget that they are in a strange place.

In the course of the year, the classroom decorations should be such as will be in conformity with the proper observance of the special festivals and holidays of the season. The decorations should be simple throughout. When posters, pictures, charts and other objects have been used, they should be removed. If it is desired to use them later for an exhibit or review, they should be put away carefully so that they may be produced with little trouble when needed.

Some teachers object to blackboard decorations. In primary rooms there is usually much space at the top of the board which the little ones cannot reach. This space might well be utilized for appropriate decorations. Borders, drawn with chalk or "cut out" pictures of birds, fruits, flowers, paper cut-outs illustrating incidents in the Bible History and the Lives of the Saints, all these will serve as suitable decorations for the blackboard. Care should be taken to have variety. Try never to have the same border or pictures a second time.

Where it can be done, use plants and flowers in pots and vases, branches or sprigs of blossoms; even paper flowers add to the charm and beauty of a classroom. But do not let these stand in the same place too long. Change their position from time to time. A new cover on a flower pot, a new piece of decoration on the stand or table will make a pleasing change.

Pictures in the Schoolroom

Children are always greatly interested in pictures. Sometimes a picture will make an impression on a child that will last for years. No matter how cheery and beautiful the classroom may be, fine pictures can be added to advantage. It is far better to have one picture and that a good one well-framed, than to have a number of cheap prints. Besides some very good religious pictures of Our Lord Blessing Little Children, the Head of the Boy Christ, Our Blessed Mother, or The Holy Family, there might be some good nature study animal pictures. The latter pictures develop ideas, supply imagery, and aid sense training. Attention is called to the illustrations given in the various parts of the book of religious pictures.

Besides patriotic pictures and reproductions of works of art the auditorium in a Catholic school should have a portrait or picture of the Pope, the Bishop of the Diocese and the Pastor of the Parish.

Children in the primary grades ought to know the name of the Pope, their Bishop, and their Pastor and his Assistant.

Pictures, posters, charts, and other similar materials should be changed in the course of the time they are in use. It might be well to remove one or the other for a day or two, then return it as the need may arise. When they have served their purpose and are not used for merely decorative purposes, they should be removed. The poster "God Sees Me" ought not to be removed, but its position should be changed from time to time.

Let simplicity and utility be the keynote of the decorations in the primary room.

A Poster Design

2. PRACTICAL AIDS AND DEVICES

A Bee-Hive

Draw a bee-hive and show bees swarming around it. The words "Our Busy Bees" printed above the hive, bring out the purpose of the device. On the space below the design, write or print the names of those children that merit distinction on account of their diligence and application to study.

An Airship Race

Let the children cut out airships to be used for this device. Draw a landscape scene on a sheet of paper large enough to accommodate all the airships. At the beginning of the month allow each child to write his name on an airship and when he attains to a certain standing in his class in any study, let him move his airship upwards. A scale at the right or left side of the drawing will give the standard grade for each advance to be made. The child whose airship reaches the highest point first, receives a suitable reward.

A Race Across the Country

This familiar device consists of a map representing the country and a road connecting two given points. A number of signs along this road indicate the degrees of advancement. Each child has an automobile cut out of pasteboard and suitably colored. As he makes progress in any particular study his automobile is moved forward toward the goal.

Instead of a map, the teacher may draw a scene to represent a race course. Any other design will also answer. The point is that the children are to work towards a certain goal. The automobiles are moved forward or turned backward according to the success or failure to attain the given standard.

The Flight of the Birds

In autumn when the birds are leaving for their winter homes, and in spring, when they return, a device showing the flight of the birds and their return will prove both fascinating and helpful. Let the children cut birds from heavy paper and color them according to the kinds of birds they wish to represent. Each child writes his name on a bird. Draw a scene with a number of trees and on the right or left of the picture mark the scale according to which the departure or return of the birds is to be regulated. The scale may begin with 5% increasing 5% at each succeeding mark. As the child gains good marks his bird is moved higher and higher until it reaches the desired height.

"The Return of the Birds" will show the birds coming from the distance advancing according to the degree of proficiency. In this latter case the scale is marked at the top of the picture.

In this as well as in the Aeroplane Race and the Race Across the Country, when a child loses his standing, his bird, aeroplane or automobile is set back accordingly.

Across the Sea or Across the Lake

This may be used in the same manner as the other races suggested. In "Across the Sea" use steamships; in "Across the Lake" small boats may be used.

A variety of similar devices will suggest themselves to the teacher. If the children are permitted to help in making the picture or poster greater interest will be aroused. For instance, in drawing a landscape scene, the children might be permitted to draw the trees and houses; or they might cut out trees and paste them in their proper places. Let the children make the aeroplanes, birds, automobiles, ships, boats, and other objects used in any of these plans.

Birds on Wires

Birds sitting on telephone or fence wires are a familiar sight to most children. The sight may suggest a device that will prove interesting to children. Draw lines on the blackboard to represent the wires. Let the children cut out, using white or colored paper, a number of birds in various positions. Paste the best cuttings on the board. This makes a very attractive border.

This design may also be used to arouse the enthusiasm of the class. By moving the birds along the wires the progress in any given line of work may be recorded. If the birds are used for this purpose, the wires should be drawn on a sheet of dark paper so that the birds may be pinned on. They can then be more easily removed and advanced to a higher position.

Birds on Trees

On the blackboard or on a large sheet of paper, draw several trees, or if you wish, one large tree. Write or print each child's name on a bird cut out of heavy paper. As progress is made move the birds up on the tree. If a child fails, place his bird on a lower branch. The branches of the tree should be so arranged as to represent a certain degree of progress. The topmost branch is 100%. Children like this device and the amount of interest created in a lesson will more than reward the teacher for the extra work.

Another interesting device is to fasten a strip of adhesive kraft paper along the edge of the blackboard with the adhesive side out. On this strip paste a row of birds. The adhesive strip makes it possible to arrange the birds in many different positions.

The same device may also be used to make a border of flowers, fruits or leaves.

Banners and Pennants

Banners and pennants are valuable in securing good results in classroom discipline. They may be made from cardboard cut out in the desired shape and trimmed with crepe paper. Many different kinds of banners and pennants can be made. The most convenient sizes are 6 x 18, 12 x 24, 14 x 20, or 18 x 36. Other sizes may be found equally satisfactory. Letters may be cut out and neatly pasted on the banner or pennant. Always place a cross or some other religious emblem on the banner or pennant.

Cardboard cut in different shapes, such as hearts, shields, circles, triangles, stars always prove helpful in the classroom. When colored cardboard is used and the lettering is neatly done, these devices are both artistic and effective.

Pictures of saints and other religious subjects add to the design and serve to keep the children in touch with the religious sentiments inculcated in the morning talks and other religious instructions given throughout the day.

On these banners, pennants, shields and other similar devices any of these inscriptions will be appropriate: "Banner Class, Mission Helpers, Little Missionaries, Star Class, Infant Jesus Class, Friends of Jesus, Blessed Virgin Class, Our Little Workers." Many other suitable titles will suggest themselves to the teacher.

Badges—Armbands

Little folks are delighted when they may wear some mark of distinction, such as a badge or an armband. It is surprising how much a bit of bright-colored ribbon or crepe paper will help to excite the interest and sustain the enthusiasm of the little ones. Make badges and armbands of ribbon or crepe paper. Cut out letters and paste neatly on the badge or band. Fasten a blessed medal to the badge; the children will always be more pleased to wear a medal when it is fastened to a piece of colored ribbon. For the armband cut out a small cross and paste it above the letters used. Crepe paper is inexpensive and may easily be replaced when soiled.

Home-Made Stencils

Sometimes teachers have pictures they wish to reproduce on the blackboard. The plan suggested here might prove helpful to them. First trace the outline of the picture on thin paper. Now remove the thread from the needle and bobbin of the sewing machine and stitch carefully through this outline. The stencil is now complete and ready for use. The details can readily be filled in on the blackboard.

A Scrap Album

A scrap album is the child's delight. So are the scrap envelopes, which by the way, are very convenient for the classroom. Let the children make the envelopes from poster or construction paper, or from wall paper. These envelopes should be about 4 x 6 inches in dimension. Place in them pictures cut out from old magazines, story books, calendars, etc. The pictures should be such as the children can use in their work.

These pictures may be used in various ways. One method is to place five pictures in each envelope, together with slips of paper on which are written the names of the objects in the pictures. For busy work, the children match the names with the pictures. When they can do this readily, let them write short sentences about each picture. One picture may be selected and a short story written about it.

These pictures may also be used for oral language work. Let the child select a picture from his envelope and tell the class about it. This oral work may consist in giving a short description of the picture or telling a story about it.

Allow the children who have done good work in the written and oral exercises to paste their pictures in a scrap book. This scrap book may be made from several sheets of plain paper, securely bound and fastened with a piece of ribbon. The prettiest picture might be pasted on the outside cover. The sentences or stories are written beneath the picture.

The above suggestions will prove valuable in preserving any pictures the children may bring the teacher for their Bible lessons or stories from the Lives of the Saints. Usually all the pictures brought by the children cannot be used, but the best might be selected and preserved in the envelopes until later.

Friday Afternoon Programs

Friday afternoon is usually a trying period for both the teacher and the children. At the end of the week little energy is left and often all the pent-up mischief of the week crops out in the last hour of the last day of the school week. Therefore the wise teacher will set aside this time for some special exercises. These exercises may take the form of a specially arranged program consisting of songs, recitations, poems, memory gems, dramatization, and stories learned during the week or month. Let the children take an active part in the arrangement of the various numbers. On Friday morning a few minutes may be spent at the end of the morning session in talking over the afternoon's program. As much as possible let every child take part. Make the children feel that they are responsible for the success of the affair. The teacher may make suggestions here and there, but on the whole, let the children feel that they are arranging the program. The time given to these exercises will be well spent. Instead of ending the week in a tired and perfunctory manner, the teacher and the class will close the week with a feeling that something has been accomplished and that some progress has been made.

Each Friday the order of the program should be changed so that there will be no danger of the exercises becoming tiresome. When a song has been well learned or a story well told or a poem or a lesson well read, ask the children if they do not think that it would be a good thing to use for Friday afternoon. They will soon make the suggestions of their own accord and the interest thus aroused will amply repay the teacher for the trouble she takes to arrange for the exercises of Friday afternoon.

Bulletin Board

A bulletin board is useful in the classroom and even in the lower grades the teacher will find it helpful. It can be used for a number of purposes: posting notices, reports, averages, making announcements and displaying work.

The bulletin board is more frequently used for displaying work. In the lower grades the teacher may wish to show the children how a piece of work ought to look when completed. Or, she may desire to encourage a child by displaying his work.

The bulletin board may be called into service when the teacher has some specially interesting picture to show to the class. The picture may be fastened by means of thumb tacks, or by pasting strips of adhesive paper to the edges. The picture may be left on the bulletin board for a number of days so that all the children may have an opportunity to examine it. The bulletin board may also be used to display the work of the class at the end of the term or any other given period. The teacher may find it practicable to have two or more bulletin boards in use at the same time.

If the bulletin board is made of beaver board or plaster board it may be used instead of a blackboard. Simple landscapes may be drawn and appropriate picture cut-outs pasted on these, making complete posters. The board may be washed and cleaned and be ready for use at any time.

A good bulletin board may be made from beaver or plaster board. This can be purchased in suitable sizes. A piece about 4 x 6 feet is a desirable size for lower grade rooms. The board may be painted black, green or yellow. A frame consisting of strips of wood about three inches wide may be nailed along the edge. This frame can be varnished. Instead of the strip of wood for the frame the edges may be covered with heavy paper, plain or colored. Ready-made bulletin boards may be purchased from dealers in school supplies.

Exhibiting Work

Teachers should from the beginning preserve all good examples of the children's work in art and construction. At the end of the year a quantity of interesting material will then be available for exhibition. Time is lost by making things just for the purpose of exhibition. With this end in mind the teacher should file examples of the children's work at various times. Allow the children to arrange their work on a large sheet of cardboard, before filing it.

The best work accomplished in the class may be mounted on a dark paper and hung in the space assigned for exhibiting the work. Such work will stimulate other pupils to greater endeavor and at the same time will keep before the eyes of all the kind of work the teacher wishes the pupils to do.

The best drawing and construction work of each week may be displayed in a special place and then later all such exhibits may be assembled and exhibited in a space set aside for this purpose. This special space should be called the "Honor Corner." It may be well occasionally to call in the Superior, the Principal or other teachers to commend the work the children are doing. The pupils should also be encouraged to invite their parents to see the work. At the end of the term the teacher will not need to spend additional time selecting suitable material for the exhibit for she will have a sufficient supply of material on hand.

Suggestions for Busy Work

1. Pictures from discarded books, catalogs, magazines and other sources can be mounted by the children upon gray bogus paper or mounting board of uniform size, classified and arranged in sets, as class needs may indicate. They can be filed in portfolios and catalogued in the same manner as books.

2. Cut small pictures from magazines. Paste one in the left hand corner of each child's paper. Tell him he is to make up a story about his picture; he may look in his book for words he is unable to spell, but the story must be entirely his own. Children are enthusiastic about writing their own stories. It is a splendid means of promoting self-activity and makes the bright child work to his fullest capacity. The results are most gratifying.

3. From the "Messenger of the Sacred Heart" which contains many beautiful pictures, valuable material may be secured for helps in teaching religion. In each issue a series of pictures is presented with a full descriptive text. These pictures may be cut out and mounted and arranged in sets. Their meaning may be explained to the children. In this way events in the life of Our Lord or the Blessed Virgin will become better known to the little ones. The pictures may be hung around the room, or may be placed around the blackboard ledge. On certain days the class may be asked to give short talks on the pictures.

4. To familiarize the children with the mysteries of the Passion of Our Lord, and particularly to teach them the meaning of the Stations of the Cross, the following method will be found useful: Secure pictures of the Stations of the Cross from discarded catalogs and mount them on heavy paper. Explain the meaning of the pictures, carefully describing the event portrayed. After the entire set has been explained allow the children to relate the story of the Stations. Vary this procedure occasionally by asking them questions. Ask, for instance, what happened at the First Station, the Second, and so on. At which Station did Jesus fall the first time? If the children will familiarize themselves with the Story of the Passion as contained in the form of the Way of the Cross in Father Finn's Boys' and Girls' Prayerbook, it will help them to carry out this idea.

Correct Copying

The children in the lower grades often make mistakes through carelessness when doing work at their desks. To prevent the children from forming careless habits and to assist them in learning the use of the margin, paragraph and punctuation marks, give them a short but interesting lesson to copy correctly. Those who have no mistakes may be permitted either to find a picture on the lesson and trace it, or to color a duplicated copy. Then let them copy the lesson again on good paper leaving room for the picture. If this work is neatly and correctly done, they may paste the picture in its place, and the paper is hung up or kept until enough papers have been gathered for a book of model work. When the children have a certain number of lessons completed in a satisfactory manner, a cover to fit the papers is made in the drawing class and the papers put in the form of a reading book. Those pupils whose work is not correct and neat may not put their work on good paper until they can copy correctly. In this way it takes but a short time for children to learn to copy correctly and they form correct habits in using the margin and the paragraph.

Charts to Teach the Use and Meaning of Religious Articles

To teach the children the use and meaning of the various articles used in the service of the Church such as candles, candlesticks, tabernacle, chalice, vestments, the teacher can make charts by cutting out from discarded catalogs of church goods, illustrations of the different articles and pasting them neatly on a piece of heavy cardboard.

These home-made charts are perhaps more useful than those that may be purchased because the children can help in making them and also because the teacher may explain one article at a time while she is pasting the picture on the chart, thus teaching the children its meaning and use.

To Teach the Story of the Passion of Christ

In teaching the different scenes of Our Lord's Passion and Death, particularly the Way of the Cross, the sand table is an effective aid. The stations may be cut from a catalog and mounted on heavy paper or cardboard. A mound of sand with a cross will represent Calvary. The Stations are arranged in their proper order along the road leading to the top of the mound. Gather the little ones around the sand table and tell them the story of each Station. The teacher may begin with the explanation of the Fourth Station—Jesus Meets His Afflicted Mother—because the children will understand this scene most easily, and then follow up in order with the explanation of the Meeting with the Holy Women, or Veronica Wiping the Face of Jesus, the Crucifixion and Death, and then fill in the other Stations as the children are ready for them. Let the children repeat the stories. In a comparatively short time they will learn the meaning of each station and correctly repeat each incident pictured.

To stimulate the interest of the children assign one Station to a child for study. Then let the children in order tell their story to the class. In connection with this work, teach simple little prayers, ejaculations, or suggest the practice of slight acts of self-denial. For instance when speaking of the Fifth Station, suggest to the children that as Simon assisted Jesus, so they can help their mothers. Let them form some resolution, such as, "I will help mother with the work out of love for Jesus."

Another device to help the children to learn the important events in the life of Christ is to express these in a certain number of key sentences. For instance, "Jesus turned water into wine" may serve as a key sentence for the Miracle at Cana. Pictures, charts and posters may be used to illustrate these sentences. Each event is enlarged upon and explained to the children and then the sentence is repeated until most of them know it by heart. After all the sentences have thus been treated, assign a sentence to each child in the class. Then as a special exercise for visitors, let each one recite the sentence assigned and show the picture that is to accompany it. Or, let one child recite and another show the picture.

3. SCHOOL MANAGEMENT

Little children like to enact the parts of other beings. Let them play at being butterflies, sunbeams, angels, birds, kittens, mice, etc. To teach reverence in prayer, let the children play at being angels. When they move about the classroom, when they put aside their work, when they rise, remind them of the rôle they are enacting; for instance, if they are playing "butterfly" for that day, tell them to use their "butterfly feet" and move about as lightly as a butterfly. The little ones enjoy this game and will try to move about quietly and quickly. On a rainy day they may play at being "sunbeams."

These little games create a new atmosphere in the room and help to maintain classroom discipline.

Passing to and from Seats

Young and inexperienced teachers often encounter great difficulty in getting the children to enter and leave the room quietly and orderly and to pass to and from their seats for class exercises in a regular manner.

Get the children accustomed to wait for your

command before they rise to leave their seats for any exercise. When you have the attention of the class say, "Class rise on two counts—1—2." Or "left—right." When you give the command, "Class rise on two counts" the children prepare to rise, that is they place their left foot in the aisle ready to rise. On the count of "one" they rise, on "two" they assume an upright position, ready for the next command. The teacher may then say "Turn"—one—two—one—two and so on until the children have reached the appointed place. Instead of counting the teacher may let the children march to music. A good phonograph with suitable records for little children will prove helpful inasmuch as it saves the teacher's voice and energy. When passing to the blackboard, let the children march as suggested before. Do not allow them to take chalk and erasers until you give the command. Let the children stand at their places facing the front of the room, then say, "turn, one—two." The children turn towards the board, take the chalk and eraser and are now ready for work. When the work at the board is completed, the teacher says, "Place erasers; one—two." The children then return to their seats. Sometimes the teacher will have to let the children change the direction of marching when returning to their seats and another group is to go to the board. This will depend largely upon the amount of space there is in the aisles between the rows of desks and in front of the blackboard.

When the children have learned to take their places in a quiet and orderly manner, let them hop, skip, fly or run to their places, acting out the suggestion of playing sunbeams, butterflies, birds, or kittens.

Dismissing the children to the accompaniment of music is good as it may correct a slouching or swaggering gait, and leave a pleasant impression of the day.

To Secure Regular Attendance

1. Place a flag outside the classroom if the entire class is present.
2. In the front of the room have two large signs, one marked "Boys" and the other marked "Girls." If all the boys are present, place a flag on their sign; if all the girls are present, the flag is put on their sign. If all the boys and girls are present, the teacher may, as a reward, tell them a short story. If only one section has perfect attendance, give that section some little privilege; for example, special time to make a poster or drawing, or, permission to use the class library. Any little privilege that will serve to stimulate friendly rivalry between the boys and girls will prove valuable.
3. Instead of using a flag as suggested in the foregoing, mark 100% for the side having perfect attendance.
4. Cut out a large cross and paste it on a piece of heavy mounting board. On this cross, paste a small star for each day the class has a perfect attendance record.
5. On rainy or stormy days, arouse the interest of the children by giving them supplementary readers, calling them story books.[1] Of course, the use of supplementary readers should not be confined to rainy days. A love of reading cannot be created too early. Every primary grade teacher should be supplied with a number of supplementary readers. Permit the children to read silently, and help them over difficult words; later on let them read the stories aloud to the class.
6. Tell the children "weather stories" on rainy or disagreeable days. Let them expect a story about a snowstorm or a flood on such days. Suit the story to the weather.
7. Allow the children to paste a gold star on a small piece of cardboard for each week of perfect attendance. If the cardboard is cut in the shape of a star, for example, and the stars arranged in some sort of design, the children will take a special delight in having a gold star to record their perfect attendance.
8. Display a banner each day the class has perfect attendance. When there are several grades in the same room, use a banner for each grade. Suppose there are three grades in one classroom, then the teacher might use three banners, one white, one blue and the other red. The grade having all its members present may put up its banner for the day.

[1] For a list of some supplementary material see bibliography at end of book.

This will keep up a friendly rivalry and help to secure better attendance.

To Cure Tardiness
1. Have an honor list to record the names of those who are on time.
2. Give gold stars as a reward.
3. Have interesting opening exercises.
4. Give the children special help before school; that is, help them with any lessons in which they have difficulties.
5. Have an attendance contest between the boys and girls, or between the different grades in the room.

To Secure Punctuality
1. Start the day with an interesting program.
2. Allow the children who are in school before time to look at picture books, story books, or children's magazines.
3. Let the children help you to get ready for the day's work, for instance, to open the windows, clean the blackboard, decorate the blackboard with cut-out pictures, and the like.
4. When the plan is feasible, dismiss the class one-half hour earlier on Fridays if the class had 100% attendance and punctuality during the week. This is a very effective plan, and by dismissing one-half hour earlier no time is is lost, because on account of the perfect attendance and punctuality of each child more work was accomplished through the week. Dismissing the children even fifteen minutes earlier is a privilege for which the most negligent and indifferent pupils will strive. However, in some schools such a plan might conflict with the school regulation requiring a common dismissal.

To Teach the Making of a Good Intention
To accustom the children to acquire the habit of making a good intention before each action of the day, some teachers train their pupils to make a small cross at the head of each paper they begin, directing them at the same time to say, "All for the honor and glory of God," or some similar ejaculation. This is a praiseworthy custom and one that will insure much spiritual profit for the children.

To Teach Thoughtfulness
Teach the children to be thoughtful of others. A good way to do this with little ones is to let them send the booklets they have made to their sick classmates or to a sick person in the neighborhood. Teach them the joy of giving happiness to others. Train them to work for others and to be especially thoughtful of the poor, the sick and the helpless. Tell them that what they do for others out of love for Jesus will be looked upon by Him as having been done to Himself.

When they have a number of pictures mounted, or posters completed or booklets made, suggest that they select the best to give away.

When a child is absent for any length of time on account of illness, let the children send little gifts made by themselves. When they are able to write let them compose a letter and send it to their little classmate. A "Golden Rule Club" might be formed, the object of which is to be kind and thoughtful towards others in every way, at all times and in all places. Make a large banner on which a foot rule is drawn. Paint this in gold and under it paste the letters GOLDEN RULE CLUB. Cut these letters from gilt paper or paint them with gold paint. On the banner write or print the names of those who are trying to be kind and thoughtful.

Let the teacher train the little ones to be especially thoughtful of their parents. Let the children therefore remember their parents in some way on their birthdays and namedays, on Christmas, and on Thanksgiving Day. It might also be well to suggest a May Day Basket for mother, and a poem for Father's and Mother's Days.

Teaching Pupils to Be Tidy
1. Give each aisle in the room the name of a street. Let the children choose the name of their aisle. The children in that row are the residents on that street and are responsible not only for the floor which represents the street and the yard, but also for their desks which are their houses. The children will vie with each other to see who can keep the cleanest street. The

winners may have a treat of an additional cutting or tearing lesson for the week.

2. To arouse greater interest in keeping the desks and floor clean give each aisle the name of a building. If all the children in a row keep the floor clean and have their desks in order a small flag may be placed on the first desk in that row. Besides, some special privilege might be given to the children in that row.

other emblem on the desks of those who keep them neat. Or, you may allow the children in the winning row to wear a pretty ribbon or a flower or some other mark of distinction.

Lessons in Peace

Since the close of the World War there has been more or less agitation for universal peace. But peace must be purchased at the price of

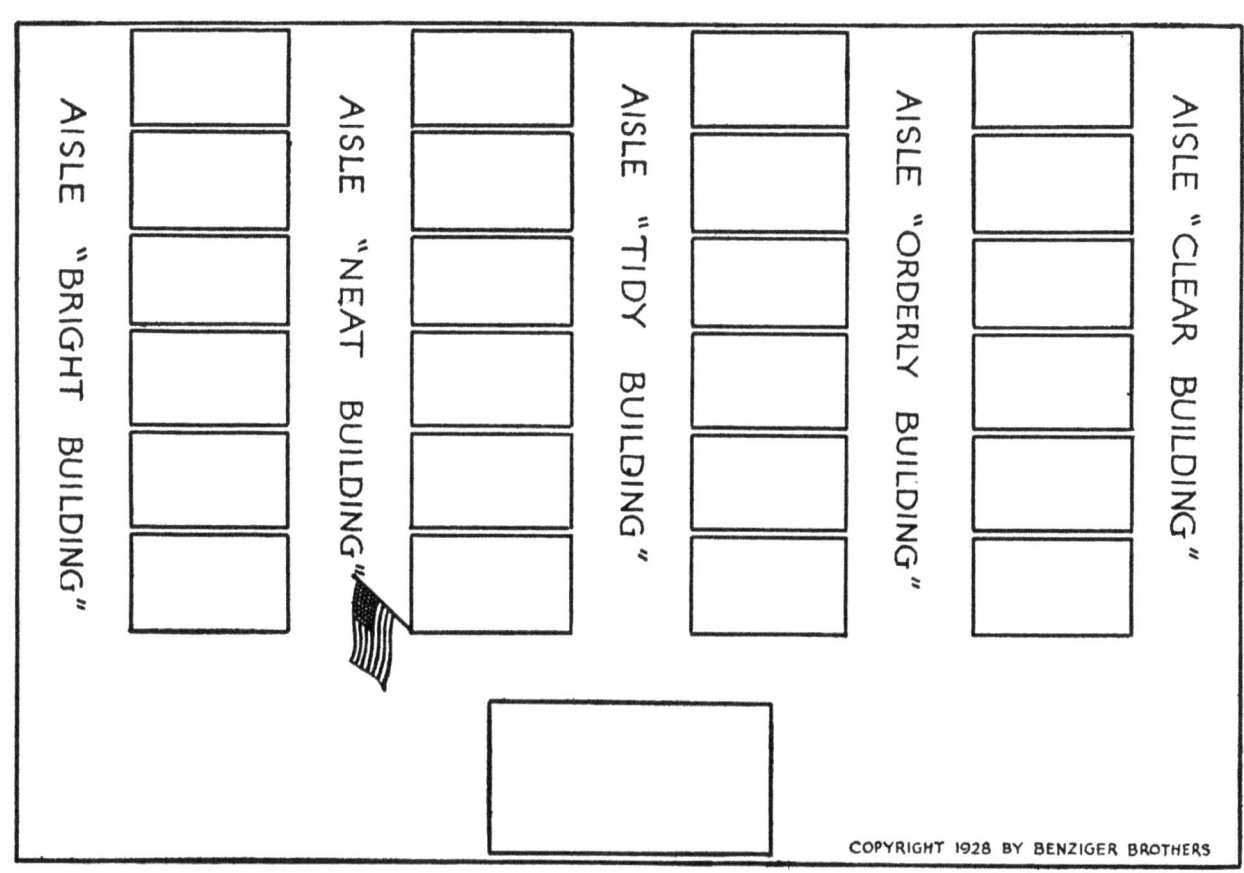

A NEAT CLASSROOM

3. Divide the class into sections, each row bearing the name of a street or town. Appoint a health officer for each row. The duty of this officer shall be to report all children whose desks and floor are not clean.

4. Call the class a park. Each row represents one of the driveways or walks in this park. Ask the children to try to keep their driveways clean and free from all paper so that people will use their driveway to visit the park. The row that has a perfect record for neatness should be rewarded in some manner.

5. When the class is small place a flag or some

sacrificing pride, jealousy, greed of power and wealth, and hatred. A nation is made up of individuals. A nation is the embodiment of the thoughts, habits and ideals of its people. The peace and general prosperity of a nation depend to a great extent upon the mutual co-operation of its individuals. It would seem, then, that if nations are to be taught to live peaceably with one another, the individuals composing a nation must first learn to observe self-control, kindness, fair play, justice and mutual co-operation.

The early years of school life are the important period for the development of those traits and virtues which will enable the little ones to grow into a nation of peace loving people. Children ought to be taught to respect the rights of others, to play fair and to co-operate with others. Teachers in primary grades ought to make use of every opportunity to instil into the hearts of the little ones the fundamental principles of peace and charity. "Little children, love one another," ought to be inscribed in letters of gold on the walls of every classroom and particularly of the lower grade classroom. Children must be taught to nourish love and good will towards all. This is as essential as the teaching of religion, good manners of citizenship. In fact it cannot be separated from religion. Religion is the corner stone, the keynote to world peace. The angels sang on that first Christmas morning: "Peace on earth to men of good will."

Teach the children, therefore, to live peaceably with their playmates and friends. Train them to show by their daily actions that they wish to live in peace with others. For this purpose give little lessons from time to time in which the following subjects may be discussed: 1. The careful handling of toys: often children strike or destroy their playthings for the mere pleasure they derive from doing so; this conduct may easily develop into a habit of striking their playmates and destroying things that belong to others. This is a harmful habit. 2. The treatment of animals; children ought to treat animals kindly and should never be allowed to torment them. Cruel children usually develop into cruel men and women. 3. Treating brothers and sisters kindly. 4. Acting kindly towards their playmates and companions. Let the teacher be careful to seize every opportunity for the developing of peaceful habits. Let her bear in mind the greeting Our Lord so frequently used while here on earth, "Peace be to you." She will have opportunity for noting the tendency to quarrel if she observes her charges on the playground or at the blackboard. Children who may seem to be very peaceable otherwise, may be in many a fight on the playground, and at the blackboard they may display their selfishness by taking the best piece of chalk or the new eraser.

As a representative of God, let the Catholic teacher spread the gospel of peace, remembering that the boys and girls under her care are the future men and women of the nation.

SECTION VI

DRAWING AND CONSTRUCTION WORK

1. CORRELATING THE COURSE IN ART WORK WITH THE COURSE IN RELIGION

Since a course in art work is presumably prescribed for most of the Catholic schools, the suggestions herewith presented are to be viewed in the light of supplementary work. There has been, doubtless, in the hearts of many Catholic teachers a desire to extend the prescribed course to include practical problems in connection with the teaching of religion. A lack of definite plans and suggestions has handicapped many teachers in their efforts to adapt the principles of drawing and construction work to the lessons in Catechism and Bible History.

The desire to do is inherent in the child and the wise teacher will use this creative instinct with good results in the teaching of religion. Sand table work, dramatization, and posters will increase the interest and effectiveness of the lessons in religion. Many of the problems arising from the use of these visual aids will require the pupils to make the various objects used in illustrating the dominant idea or ideas. For example, in the study of the Sacrifice of the Mass, the lesson will be intensified and made much more effective if the children learn to construct the altar, the candles and candlesticks, the tabernacle, the missal (see Figure 3, page 270) and the other appurtenances for the celebration of holy Mass. Likewise, in presenting the feasts of special interest to the children, a better conception of the significance of the day can be obtained by letting the children construct

DRAWING AND CONSTRUCTION WORK

the various objects used to illustrate the meaning of the respective feast.

The plan herewith presented is to serve the teacher as a guide in preparing for the work to be assigned to her pupils.

2. LITTLE THINGS FOR LITTLE HANDS TO DO

September

Draw a fish; (see figure 1, page 270) a cross. Make a booklet.

Cut out a fish and a cross freehand.

Paste the cross on the cover of the booklet and the fish inside the booklet.

October

Draw the ships of Columbus; a wolf; trees; Indians.

Illustrate Columbus at the gate of the Convent of La Rabida.

Make a banner.

Cut out the ships of Columbus; boats; Indians; trees; a banner; St. Francis; a wolf; birds, (see figure 2, page 270) beads for the rosary; the first group of letters.

Make these posters:
  The Landing of Columbus,
  The Guardian Angel,
  St. Francis and the Wolf,
  St. Francis Preaching to the Birds.

Sand Table Projects:
  Columbus, his Voyage and Landing,
  The Guardian Angel,
  Missionaries among the Indians.

November

Draw a church; some children going to church; a cross, and a crown to illustrate the victory of the saints.

Cut out the church; the second group of letters; the words "PRAY FOR THE DEAD."

Construct a church; an altar; candles and candlesticks; altar cloth; trees.

Make these posters:
  Thanksgiving Day, people going to church to hear Mass.
  A family at table giving thanks to God for the food.

Sand Table Projects:
  Thanksgiving Day; carry out the idea suggested for the poster.
  Erect an altar complete with crucifix, candles and candlesticks and altar cloth.

December

Draw and color sheep; shepherds; dogs; camels; the houses of Bethlehem, low and flat.

Cut out sheep; shepherds; dogs; camels (see figure 8, page 270); trees.

Construct the stable of Bethlehem; make the houses of Bethlehem.

Make a Christmas calendar.

Make the poster, "The Birth of Jesus."

Sand table project: "The Birth of Jesus."

Model sheep, camels, dogs, shepherds for the crib.

January

Draw the Wise Men; the Flight into Egypt.

Cut out stars; figures to illustrate the Flight into Egypt; lambs; camels; donkey (see figure 5, page 270); Eskimos; icebergs; dogs; sleds; the third group of letters; the word "JESUS"; the word "OBEDIENCE."

Make an Alphabet Booklet.

Make these posters:
  The Three Kings,
  The Flight into Egypt,
  Agnus Dei,
  Missionaries among the Eskimos.

Sand Table Projects:
  The Flight into Egypt,
  The Holy Family at Nazareth,
  Missionaries among the Eskimos.

February

Draw doves; (see figure 6, page 270) candles and candlesticks; the prison of St. Valentine. (see figure 7, page 270).

Cut out candles and candlesticks; the prison of St. Valentine and paste it on a sheet of paper.

Make these posters:
  The Boy Jesus at Home in Nazareth,
  The Holy Family,
  Candlemas Procession.

Sand Table Projects:
  The Boy Jesus in the workshop of St. Joseph,

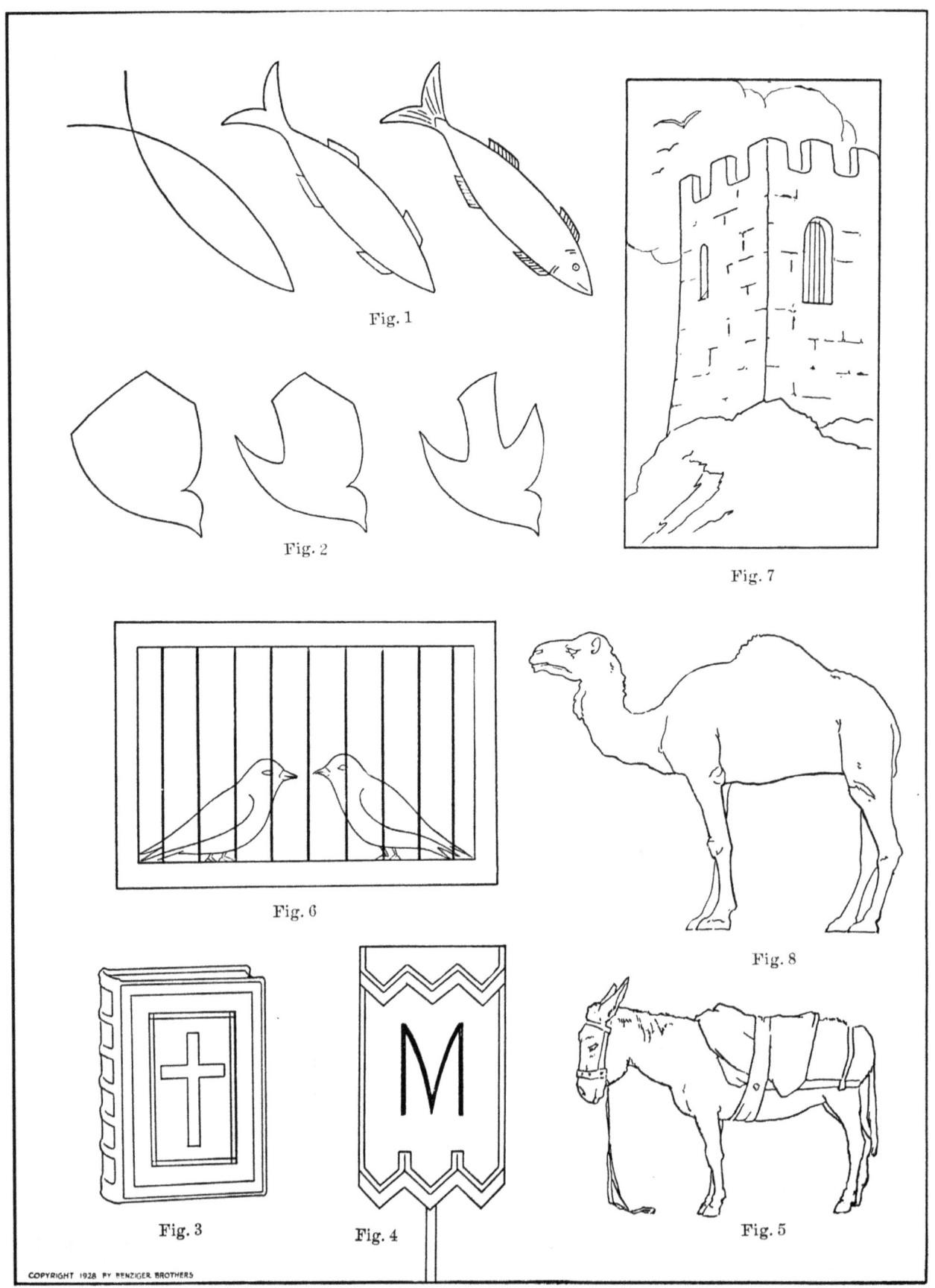

Things to Make

St. Valentine in prison.
Make a St. Valentine Booklet.

March
Draw a lily; a shamrock.
Cut out a lily; a shamrock.
Make these posters:
  St. Joseph and the Child Jesus
  The Annunciation,
  The Way of the Cross; Calvary.
Sand Table Projects:
  The Way of the Cross,
  Calvary.
Make these Booklets:
  St. Patrick—shamrock on the cover page and a picture of St. Patrick inside.
  St. Joseph—a lily on the cover page and a picture of St. Joseph inside.
  Easter—a cross on the cover page and a picture of the Resurrection inside.

April
Draw a rainbow and color it.
Cut out pictures of the Resurrection; the fourth group of letters.
Make a Mass Booklet.
Make the Poster "The Way of the Cross."
Sand Table Project:
  The Resurrection.

May
Draw a dove as the symbol of the Holy Ghost.
Make a banner of the Blessed Virgin (see figure 4, page 270), a badge for a Child of Mary.
Cut out the fifth group of letters.
Poster: Cut out the words AVE MARIA and mount them on a large sheet of paper.
Construct an altar of the Blessed Virgin.
Sand Table Projects:
  The Grotto of Lourdes,
  An altar of the Blessed Virgin,
  Missionaries in China.

June
Draw or cut out a monstrance.
Cut out the letters "SACRED HEART OF JESUS."
Make a poster of the Sacred Heart using the above letters.
Sand Table Projects:
  Corpus Christi procession, showing altars, monstrance, banners.
  A Sacred Heart Shrine.

3. SUPPLEMENTARY WORK IN DRAWING AND CONSTRUCTION

If there is no regular course prescribed for Art Work and Industrial Training, the following hints and helps may be useful in giving the children some training along these lines so that they may be able to carry out the various projects in connection with the study of religion. A few preliminary exercises are given to introduce the work.

Teaching Direction
Teach the children direction. Drill them to recognize right, left, upper, lower. To illustrate this it is best to use a book or a piece of paper. Let the children show the directions as you call them out. Reverse the exercise by letting the children name the direction as you point to them. Be careful not to confuse their sense of direction by your position.

Single Curves
Through continuous movements in the air and on their desks, let the children form circles. Let them repeat this until they can form a fairly good circle or part of a circle. Count while they are doing this. Get them accustomed to rhythm. Now let them make circles on the blackboard. Show them how they can make cats and rabbits from these. If practicable, let the children use crayola for their work at their desks.

Show the children how to make a fish by drawing two simple curves. The fish is chosen as a symbol of Christ. Tell the children that the fish was used formerly to represent Christ, particularly in the days of the persecutions. Teach them to draw a cross, the line from top to bottom to be made first, the other to be drawn from left to right.

Color Perception
Let the children draw lines or strokes using, red, yellow and blue chalk or crayola. Let them tell you the names of the colors as they use them. Place several apples before the children and draw them out as to their knowledge of

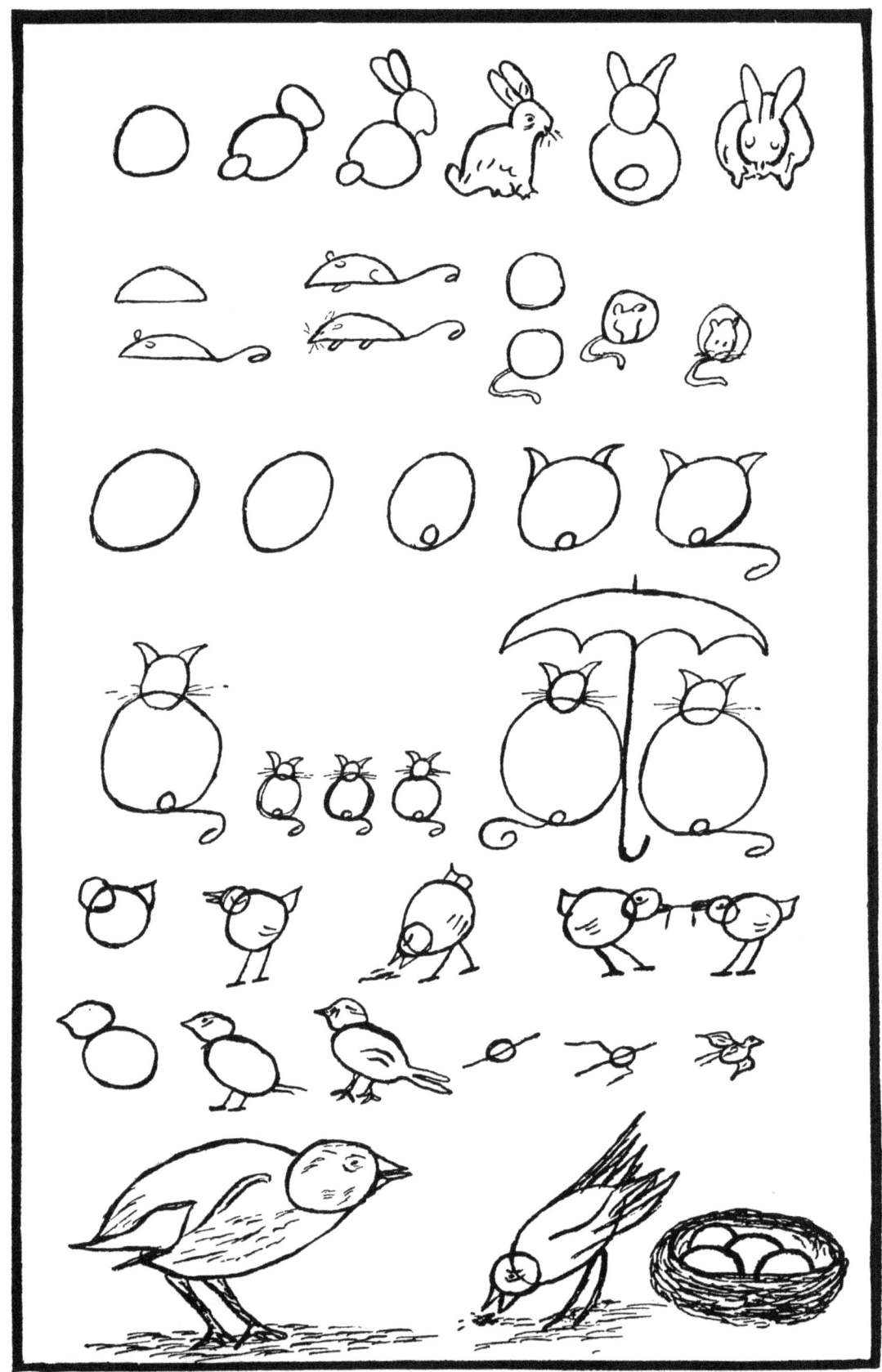

FORMING OF CIRCLES

DRAWING AND CONSTRUCTION WORK

color, shape, and size. Let the children draw a circle to represent an apple and then color it. Other round fruits may also be drawn and colored. Use familiar fruits and vegetables to illustrate circles and curves, such as, peach, orange, plum, pear, tomato, onion, and potato.

Tearing Trees

The ability to tear trees from paper is one that will serve to add much interest in the construction of posters. With a little practice the children will be able to tear trees of different forms and sizes. Emphasize the importance of clean tearing, without ragged edges. The trees may be colored and used in constructing the background for the posters.

A simple preliminary exercise for landscape work is to tear several trees of different shapes and sizes. Draw two lines on a piece of construction paper to represent hills and arrange the trees to illustrate a forest. The perspective must be carefully watched.

Making and Decorating Envelopes

An envelope or some other receptacle for holding the cuttings will be found necessary. At an early stage in the construction work an envelope is more conveniently handled than a box.

Use a piece of paper 9 x 12 inches. Fold over about two inches from the top. Now fold the opposite edge of the paper to this crease. When the edge has been folded to the first crease, we have an envelope with the sides open.

To close the edges, cut strips of paper 5 inches long and 2 inches wide and fold them lengthwise into halves. The folded strips are then pasted along the right and left edges of the envelope.

Simple designs may be used to decorate this envelope. Place the ruler on the envelope so that one edge fits along one long edge of the envelope, and draw a line along this. Draw a straight line along the other side. Cut squares or circles of colored paper and paste in the squares formed at each corner.

Let the children suggest other suitable designs. Try out the designs suggested by the pupils on the blackboard and allow the children to copy those they like best.

4. PAPER CUTTING

Much interesting and instructive work may be done by means of paper cuttings. Children should be carefully shown the proper manner of holding the scissors, opening and closing them. They should practice cutting strips of newspaper till they acquire the ability to cut evenly. Show them the proper way to hold the paper. A little practice will enable the children to cut the paper without leaving ragged edges.

Play games with the scissors. Let the children cut along certain marked lines. Let them imagine the scissors to be a car and the lines the track on which it is to run. The children do not want to get their car off the track. When cutting circles it will be necessary to show them that the proper thing to do is to turn the paper and not the scissors. If the teacher tells the children to imagine the scissors to be a fish with its mouth open, she will have little trouble in getting them to feed the paper to the fish. As soon as the children are able to cut a clean edge along marked lines and to cut circles, give them plenty of practice by cutting dolls, toys, furniture, houses, flowers and other interesting articles from newspapers, magazines and catalogs. This will prepare them for free-hand cutting later.

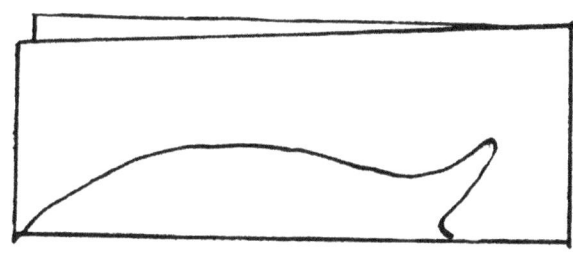

How to Cut a Fish

Paper cutting is one of the most valuable and interesting forms of busy work for children in the primary grades. It trains both the fingers and the eye and delights the child. It is at the same time one of the simplest helps for the little ones and can be used from the very beginning of the child's school work.

To cut a fish, fold a small piece of paper, any desired size, and cut along the open edge in the shape of a fish. This is easily done as the chil-

BORDER DESIGNS FOR BOOKLETS AND POSTERS

dren will know the approximate length and width from drawing it. To make a cross, cut two strips of paper, one shorter than the other, and paste them in position. A fish or a cross cut from tinfoil or colored paper makes a very attractive ornament for a booklet.

Border Designs

Often a border design on the cover page of a booklet, envelope or sheet of drawing is desired. Very simple and attractive borders can be made with dots and dashes systematically arranged. Circles, lines, squares, triangles, either drawn, stenciled or cut out make neat designs for this purpose. On page 274 is a variety of designs which may be made by the little ones with very little effort, but which will give the work a finished appearance. This type of work will present an unusual opportunity to develop taste in orderly arrangement and in selecting colors that harmonize. The designs given are merely suggestive. Many other ideas will present themselves to the teacher and the pupils.

An easy way for children to make circles is to let them take a button and draw around it. Cut out these circles and paste them on the cover to be decorated. Several designs may be produced by arranging the circles in groups. By cutting the edges of the circles other forms may be produced. Half circles can also be used for pretty decorations.

Cut small squares of colored paper and arrange them alternately with circles for border designs. A pleasing variety may be secured by orderly arrangement of the circles and squares. Half squares make good borders also.

Cut triangles of various sizes. Arrange in groups. Paste smaller ones and draw a straight line beneath each

Tree Stencils

Tree stencils can be made by folding a piece of paper and tracing on it half of the outline of the tree desired. By cutting out this outline and opening the paper, we have a stencil. If this is placed on another paper and firmly held in

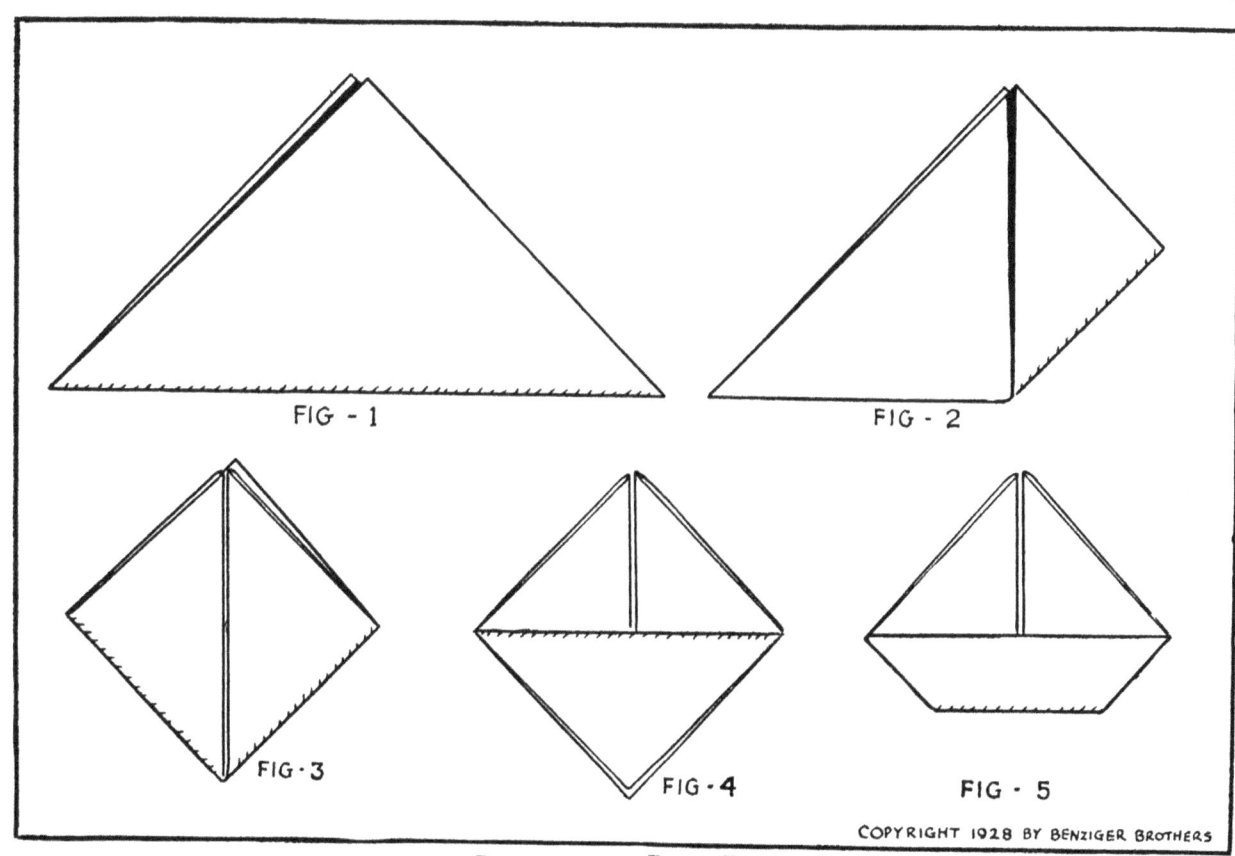

DIAGRAM FOR A PAPER BOAT

place and a crayon rubbed over the stencil the result will be a tree design which may be repeated as often as desired. Simple flower designs may be produced in like manner.

Very interesting border designs may be made from Biblical subjects. A cut-out figure of sheep, the Wise Men, doves, candles, candlesticks repeated as a border design always please the children. These also may be cut as stencils.

How to Make a Boat

A number of boats are used to illustrate the landing of Columbus. In the first and second grades, the boats should be very simple. Use a piece of construction paper six inches square. Fold this square into a triangle (Fig. 1). Then bring the right corner to meet the top corner (Fig. 2). In like manner bring the left corner to the top corner (Fig. 3). Now reverse the paper and fold the two square pieces down into a triangle (Fig. 4). Then bend the lower part of this up halfway (Fig. 5). Now color the lower part of the boat.

How to Make a Rosary

To make the beads for the rosary use paper of any color. White paper may also be used and colored afterwards. Strips of paper about one-half inch wide are best for this purpose. Double the paper and redouble it until you have a small square about the size of a rosary bead, then round the corners. For the large beads, fold the paper into larger squares and cut round in the same manner as for the smaller beads. Now paste the large and the small beads in their regular order on a piece of construction paper. Arrange the beads in any desired position. The cross is made by cutting two thin strips, one smaller than the other. First paste the cross at the lower right or left end of the mounting paper, then the beads. A little piece of paper cut in the shape of a triangle is put at the beginning of the five decades. The children may draw chains between the beads.

How to Make a Small Banner

To make a small banner, use a strip of paper, any color, 2½ by 3½ inches. Fold in half lengthwise and cut flaps. For the pole use a narrow strip of paper. Fasten this at the back of the banner and keep the lower part even with the longest flap. If the flaps of the banner are cut even make the pole longer in proportion. Cut and paste a cross in the center. For the month of May a double banner may be made by cutting another flap, to be pasted on the first line leaving a little border along the edge. The letter "M" is cut out and pasted in the center. Different kinds of banners may be made.

Trees

The following method serves to show how many varieties of trees may be made for use with sand table work. Take a piece of green construction paper. The size of the paper depends upon the height and width of the trees desired. The width however should be about three times the height. Fold this into three equal parts. The best way to do this is to fold A over B and then both over C (Fig. 6). Fold this again (Fig. 7) and from the open side cut the trunk and branches as shown. It will be well to draw the outline first before cutting (Fig. 8). After a little experience, the children will be able to cut the trees without drawing them first. After the cutting there are three trees. The three trees pasted together form a tree that will easily

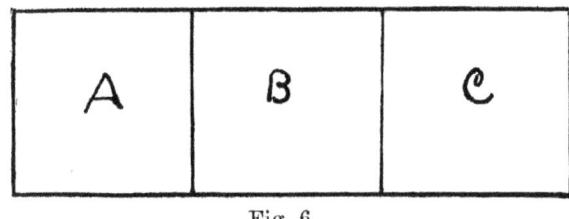
Fig. 6
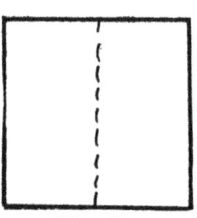
Fig. 7

Fig. 8

Diagrams for Paper Trees

DRAWING AND CONSTRUCTION WORK

FIRST GROUP

SECOND GROUP

THIRD GROUP

LETTER CUTTING

FOURTH GROUP

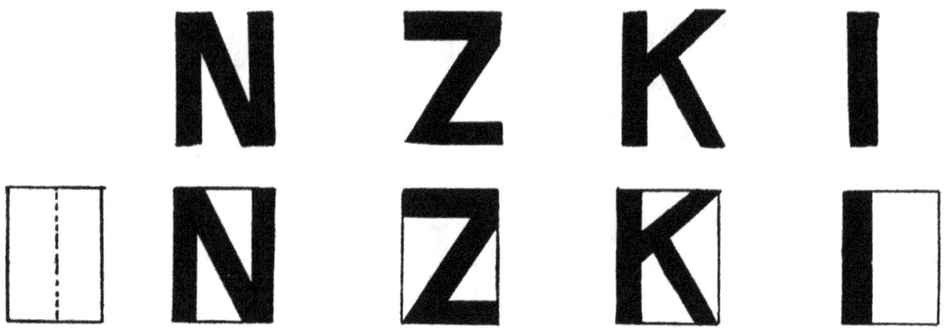

FIFTH GROUP

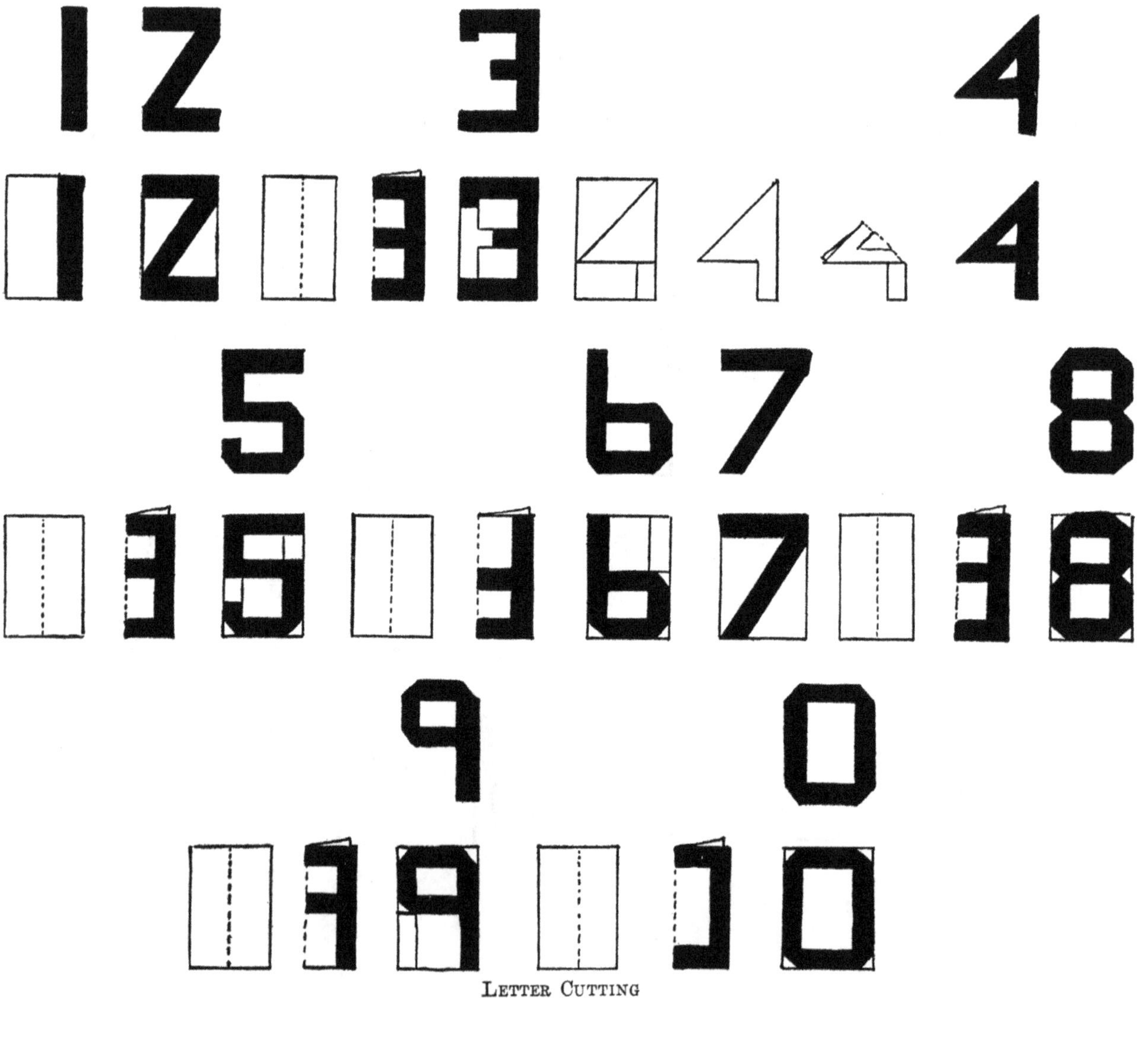

LETTER CUTTING

stand. This is very useful for sand table work. Any size or shape of tree may be cut and pasted in this manner.

5. LETTER CUTTING

Letter cutting is a very interesting and useful occupation. Children may be required to cut out words and this will give them practice in spelling, and will prove an interesting way to teach them spelling.

As a preliminary exercise for letter cutting let the children take a sheet of paper, colored or white, about 6 x 9 inches. Let them fold this paper in the following manner: turn the lower edge so that it meets the upper; crease and open. Now fold the lower half to meet the center crease; turn the paper and fold and crease the upper half. Now cut the paper at the creases; this will give four strips. Take one of these strips, fold in half, crease, fold again, then crease and fold a third time. Now open and cut at the creases. This will give you eight blocks. Fold and cut each of the other strips as needed. Each of the blocks so cut is to serve for a letter. A uniform size is thus secured.

To get the best results from the instruction in cutting letters, the teacher ought to demonstrate the method of cutting to the class. Stand before the class, hold the paper up high enough so that all can see what you are doing. Before cutting a letter draw a sketch of the block of paper you are going to cut and make a mark on this showing where they are to hold their thumb. Then mark the vertical and horizontal lines of the letter they are to cut. (See illustration.)

For convenience the letters are divided into four groups. The figures form the fifth group. In the beginning proceed slowly so that the children may become acquainted with the proper method of cutting. The cutting of each letter may be done as follows: after drawing the outline on the board take one of the little blocks cut as directed before. Hold the paper before the class and say: "Level cut at top, level cut at bottom, and vertical cut. Now we have the letter C." The paper should not be turned while cutting. The cutting of the other letters should be directed in the same way.

6. CONSTRUCTION WORK FOR THE SAND TABLE

In doing construction work for sand table projects great care should be taken so as not to let a few children do all the work. Every child should have a chance to take part in this activity. When there is occasion to use a number of trees, houses or other objects, the less talented children should have a hand in making some of them. There will always be some object made by these pupils that can be used.

A House

There are many occasions to use houses for sand table projects. These may be made from cardboard boxes, from cartons and from heavy wrapping paper. Construction paper or other heavy paper may be used in the following way. Take a piece of paper 9 inches square and fold as follows: turn the lower half up until it meets the upper edge; crease, and fold a second time in a similar way. Now open and turn the paper, folding and creasing it as directed before. You now have 16 squares. Mark off the upper row of blocks as 1-2-3-4 and the lower row as 5-6-7-8. Make a cut along each of these squares cutting along the heavy line (Fig. 9). Then lay square 2 over square 3 and paste; also square 6 over square 7 and paste. Now fold squares 1 and 4 so that the edges overlap. Fold over and paste squares 8 and 9 in a similar manner.

The house is now complete (Fig. 10). Windows and doors may be cut out or they may be drawn or pasted on. This method may also be used for making log houses and churches.

Log House

To make a log house proceed as in the manner described for making a house. To make logs take a strip of soft paper, any desired length, and 2 inches wide. Roll this lengthwise around a pencil. Paste along the edge of the strip before removing from the pencil. The paper may be colored before rolling; this will make the logs look more natural. Now paste the rolls to the side and ends of the house. If doors are cut out the size of the rolls must be regulated accordingly. The roof may be finished by covering it with strips of paper, one inch wide, cut into fringes and pasted on, one over the other, allowing the fringed part to show.

window in the steeple may be made with crayon. The church may be finished by drawing fine lines to suggest stones or bricks. Stained glass window effect may be produced by brushing various colors of water paint on a sheet of paper.

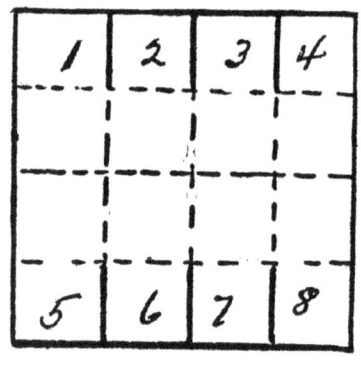

Fig. 9

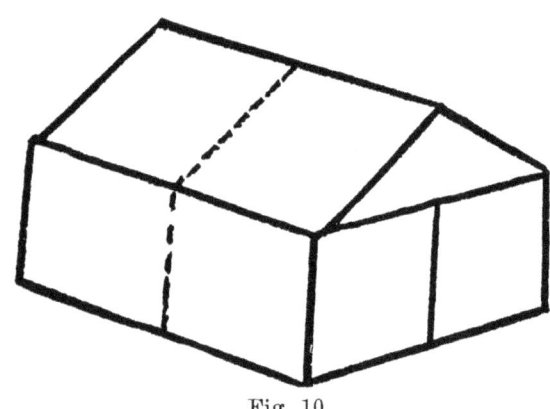

Fig. 10

DIAGRAM FOR A HOUSE

Church

To make a church for the Thanksgiving Day project follow the plan suggested for constructing a house. To make the steeple fold a piece of

The blend gives the appearance of stained glass. Cut out the windows and paste them to the walls of the church. By drawing heavy frames around these windows the effect is heightened.

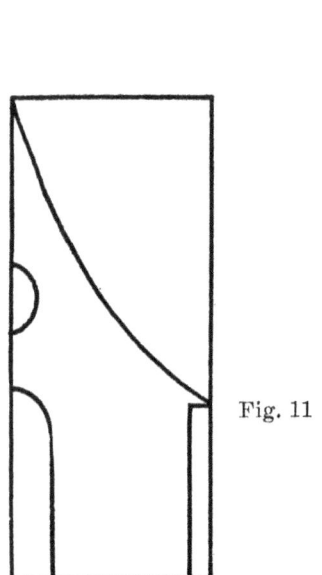

Fig. 11

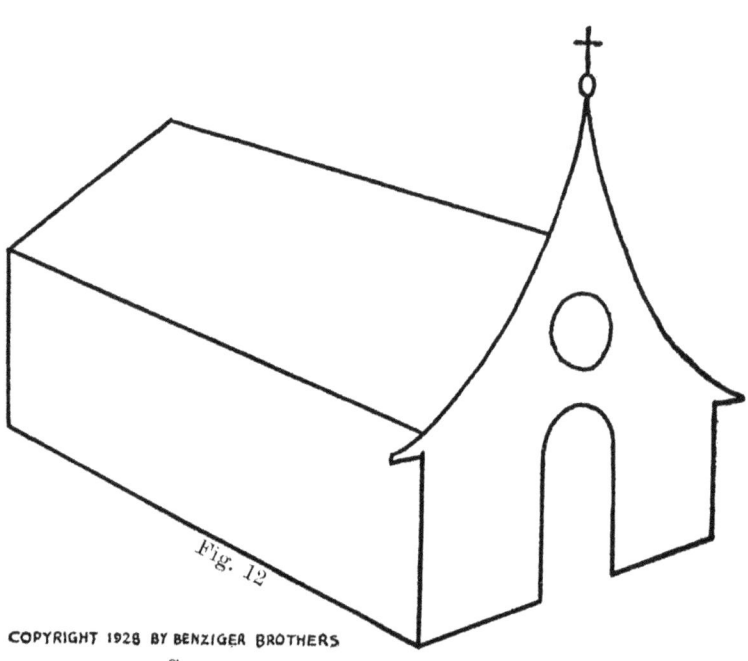

COPYRIGHT 1928 BY BENZIGER BROTHERS

DIAGRAMS FOR A CHURCH

paper of the width of the front of the house and high enough to harmonize with the rest of the building (Fig. 11). Cut this the shape of a steeple and paste to the front of the house (Fig. 12). The doors are then cut out and a rose

Cornstalk Houses and Furniture

Cornstalk houses and furniture are particularly valuable for picturing colonial scenes on the sand table. Houses, tables, chairs and other articles are easily made from cornstalks. For purposes of this kind use only that part of the stalk from the tassel to the first or second joint. If the stalk is too dry soak in water for a few hours. Then wipe dry and use.

For a church or a log cabin, notch the logs at the corners. Split the stalks for the roof. The logs may be held in place with pins.

Cigar Box Furniture

Cigar box furniture is easily made. The wood is soft and can readily be cut. Empty spools may serve as stands for beds, chairs and tables. Furniture made from cigar boxes may be painted or enameled and is then very attractive.

Houses of Bethlehem

A number of houses will be necessary for the sand table project on the Birth of Christ. The houses of Bethlehem are low and have flat roofs. These are easily made of construction paper. Use some heavy paper, any color desired, preferably grey or brown, and fold as illustrated (Fig. 13). For ordinary sand table work use a sheet of paper about 6 x 12 inches. One or two larger houses and several smaller ones may be used with effect. Before pasting the ends, cut out the openings for windows and doors.

An Altar

Altars are used for a number of projects. Children delight to make altars, candles, candlesticks, vestments and other articles used in church. This work furnishes an opportunity for explaining the meaning and purpose of these objects.

To make an altar use heavy paper about 9 x 12 inches. Other sizes may also be used. Fold the paper into 16 blocks and cut along the heavy lines as illustrated. Now fold and cut the upper part of the altar as shown in Fig. 14. Many pleasing designs may be made by cutting this part in imitation of the different styles of altars. Next cut out a tabernacle. For this use a piece

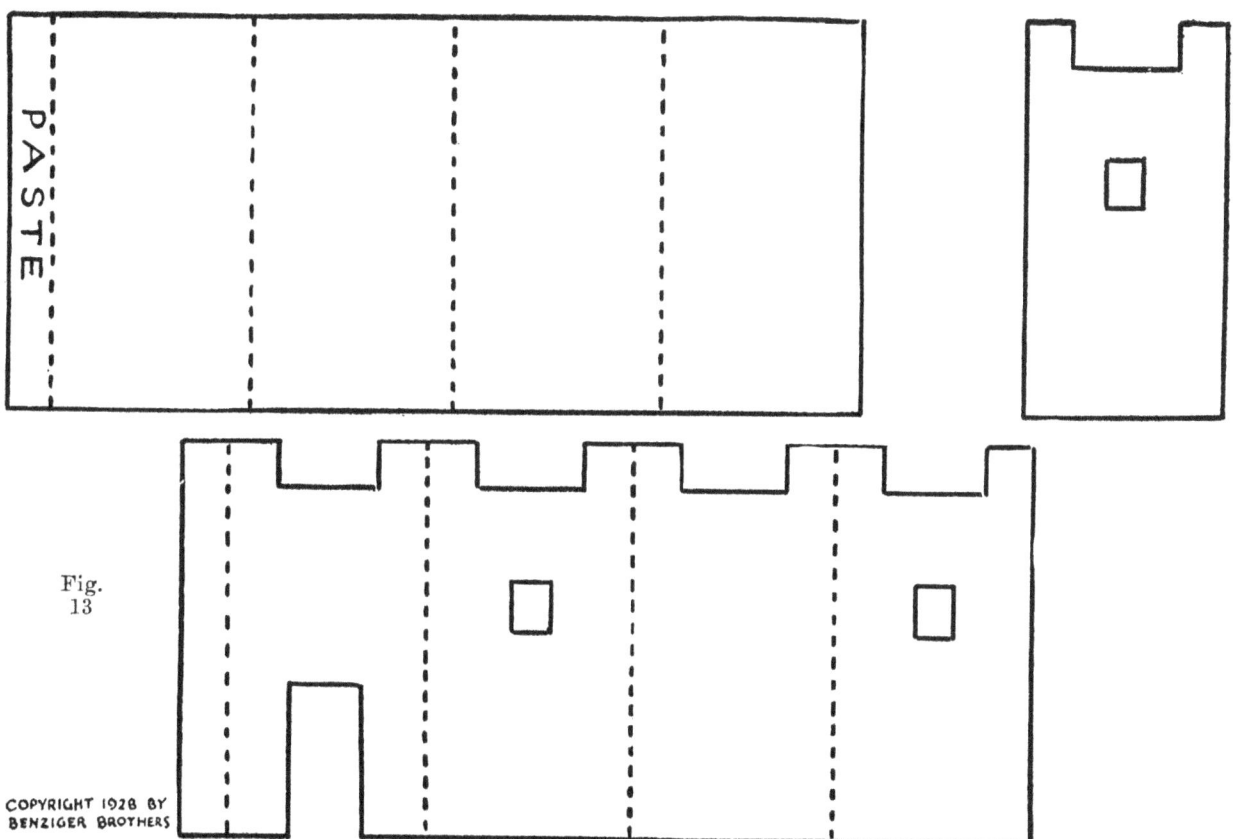

DIAGRAMS FOR THE HOUSES OF BETHLEHEM

of gold paper, folded and cut out and pasted on the center. If gold paper is not easily obtained use yellow paper or color a piece of white paper.

If the teacher desires, the children may cut out candles, candlesticks and altar cloth and paste them on the altar.

The sides are then folded in box shape and pasted.

Candlesticks

Candles and candlesticks are used in the Candlemas Day poster and also in the Corpus Christi sand table project. The children should confine themselves to the use of simple designs that may easily be cut out. Let them observe the various shapes of candlesticks. For the Candlemas Procession plain candles without candlesticks are used. These are easily cut out (Fig. 15 and Fig. 16).

In the Corpus Christi project candlesticks will be required for the altar or altars erected on the sand table. The size will depend upon the size of the altars. Use construction paper; fold this and trace the outline. Cut along the pen edge; both sides will then be alike. Paste the part cut on heavy cardboard, cut out and finish by adding a stand made of a strip of stiff cardboard. Paste the candles made of white paper to the candlesticks.

7. TELLING STORIES WITH PICTURE CUT-OUTS

At the end of the story period or reading lesson, the children may be permitted to illustrate the story or some part of it by cutting or tearing paper. This activity furnishes one of the most delightful and useful occupations. Children are always interested in making posters.

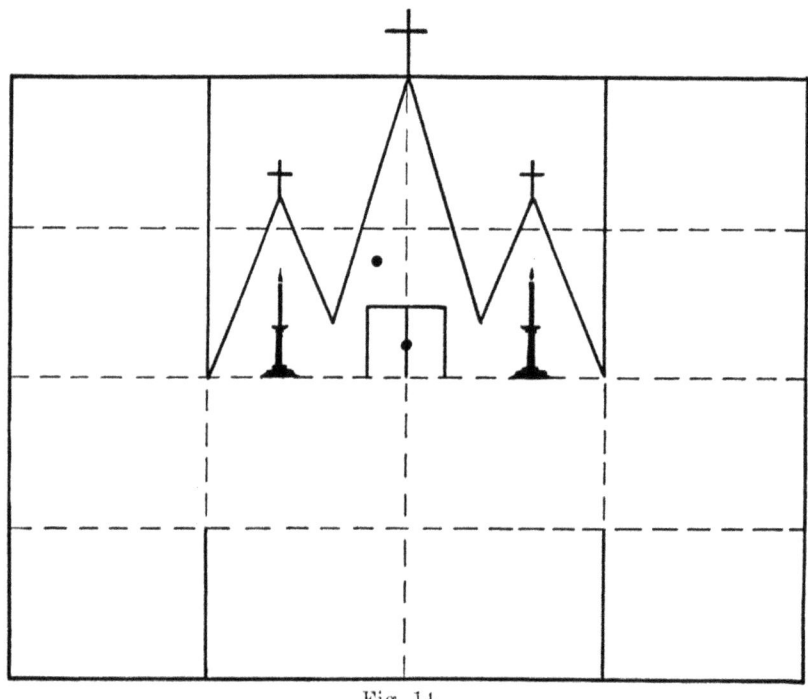

Fig. 14
DIAGRAM FOR AN ALTAR

If they are permitted to plan the picture and to cut out free-hand the pictures used, the project will be far more valuable than if they used ready made cut-outs.

For illustrating stories, large or small posters may be used. It is better to use the large size for smaller children. A piece of kraft paper about 40 x 60 inches is about the correct size. For the smaller posters, manila or tag board about 12 x 20 inches, or any other convenient size, will be suitable.

The children may begin by cutting one object in the story, as, for example, the wolf in the story of St. Francis and the Wolf. The entire class may cut trees, for a variety of trees will be needed when a forest or landscape scene is to be shown. The teacher may also assign different parts of the story to different children. After the cut-outs have been prepared, let the class arrange their work in the proper sequence of events on the large sheet of paper.

The picture is then built up. The background or setting is decided upon first, and then the

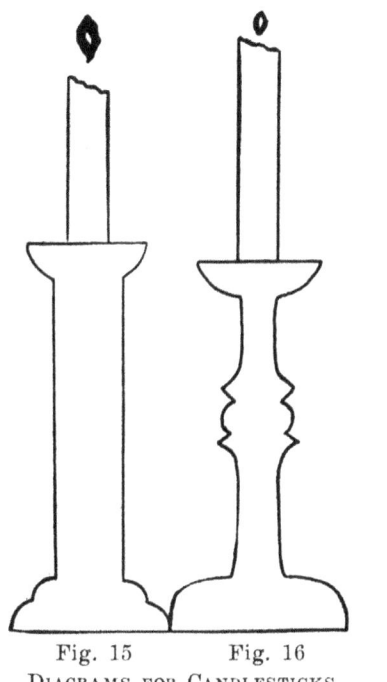

Fig. 15   Fig. 16
DIAGRAMS FOR CANDLESTICKS

sky, mountains and hills are drawn. Next the cut-outs are pasted in their proper places. The teacher will, of course, direct the class and incidentally tell them many things about picture composition. The children will soon learn the principles of perspective. The coloring of the picture should also be directed. After a few lessons the children should be able to create their own pictures.

The story of St. Francis and The Wolf, or of St. Francis and the Birds, will furnish a good opportunity for this kind of work. The class may cut out trees, people, birds, St. Francis and the wolf. The arrangement of these pictures is simple and will give the children an occasion to learn the principles of picture composition. In connection with the study of Bible History and of incidents in the Life of Christ and the Saints, the children will find much interesting material for telling stories in pictures.

8. THE USE OF POSTERS IN TEACHING RELIGION

Most teachers are more or less familiar with the use of posters in connection with a number of school activities, but not many Catholic teachers have adapted this method to the teaching of religion. Some suggestions are presented here, in the hope that our teachers may find them helpful in making the study of religion more practical and vital. A careful study of the rich material at the command of Catholic teachers will convince them that to neglect this force in the teaching of the Catechism, Bible History and the Lives of the Saints, is to neglect one of the most valuable aids at their disposal.

Poster work is making a picture in mass by means of paper cut freely in various shapes and forms and mounted according to the laws governing good composition in art. In posters the general points and characters of the picture are represented in mass. Fine lines and details are omitted. The laws of perspective and proportion together with good spacing must be observed. Many beautiful posters are made of black and white paper. When colors are used, they should be in harmony with nature, using light and shade as much as possible.

Each picture has two parts, the sky and the ground. The sky is small, the hills smaller; the foreground is the largest. This is not so in reality, but it appears so to the eye. In planning a poster some general points must be observed. The season, the locality, and the colors to be used are to be considered. They must be kept as true to nature as possible. After these matters have been decided upon, sketch the design so that a more definite idea of what is to be done may be had. Begin with the sky and work downwards, drawing the hills next, if any are to be represented, then the foreground, and lastly add figures and other details that are necessary.

Poster work prepares the child for the study of the fine arts. It teaches observation of nature, the seasons, the weather, the physical laws. It makes one think logically and develops the power of reasoning and expression.

9. POSTER PROJECTS

Guardian Angel Poster

This poster will prove agreeable work for the children, for they love to deal with angels, especially their Guardian Angels. Let the children bring pictures of angels cut out from calendars or magazines. An attractive picture

St. Francis and the Wolf

This is another pleasing subject. Let the children cut out the trees, the wolf and the figure of St. Francis. If the latter is too difficult, let them cut out a picture of the saint from a calendar or magazine. If the teacher wishes the children to show the people of the town of Gubbio, let the children cut these out freehand or from picture magazines. This poster will afford a good opportunity for teaching perspective.

DESIGN FOR A GUARDIAN ANGEL POSTER

DESIGN FOR POSTER—ST. FRANCIS AND THE WOLF

can be made by proper arrangement of the setting. The poster will prove more gratifying if the picture has a modern setting, for example, children crossing a street in a dangerous section of the city where there is much traffic; children playing games, surrounded by dangers; and others of similar nature.[1] Let the poster represent a scene that might occur any day in the life of children. Show primarily the guiding hand of the Guardian Angel.

[1] Cf. picture of Calendar for October, page 164.

St. Francis and the Birds

The birds and the trees will give the children an opportunity for many cuttings. This poster is easily made and will present a pleasing scene when properly arranged.

The Landing of Columbus

This subject gives an opportunity for a variety of cuttings. Let the children cut out boats, ships, birds, trees and Indians. Columbus and his men are also to be cut out. For these the children in the first and second grades will find it more convenient to use pictures. Indian huts or wigwams may also be cut out.

After the children have learned to make the various objects required for the poster begin planning the arrangement. Give the pupils free scope in this respect. Discuss freely the story and let them suggest the proper placing of the

DESIGN FOR POSTER—ST. FRANCIS AND THE BIRDS

objects. Use a sheet of kraft paper about 28 x 72 inches; tack it to the wall. Let the children first build up an Indian camp. Let one part of the poster represent the land on which the Indians lived and the other section, the ocean on which the ships of Columbus were seen. Arrange the Indian camp by pasting the wigwams in place, showing some Indians, birds, trees and canoes near the shore. On the water paste the ships of Columbus. Columbus and his men may be shown standing on the shore in the act of erecting a cross and thanking God.

Thanksgiving Day Poster

To carry out the Catholic idea in this poster, arrange the scene to represent people going to a Catholic Church.[1] A simple landscape torn out of paper with a church cut out and inserted may be used for this purpose. The landscape may be constructed in the following manner:

Material required: 1 sheet of dark blue paper about 6 x 9 inches. 1 piece of white paper to represent snow, 4½ x 6 inches. 1 piece of dark brown or black paper 6 x 3 inches.

Tear the white paper to obtain a snow effect. Begin tearing at about one-third from the bottom. Do not tear the paper straight. Tear up and down to make it look like a hill. The lower line should be kept even. Paste the white paper thus torn on the dark blue, making the lower part even. Paste only at the corner. If the teacher wishes, she may use white paper for the background instead of the dark blue, and let the children color it with crayola.

To cut the church and spire fold the piece of brown paper along the edge lengthwise and crease. Measure off about two inches and cut slant at the top, being careful to hold the paper on the closed side. Now cut in about ¾ inch slantingly and then cut again at the top. After this a window may be cut out. The window should be circular to represent a rose window. A piece of yellow paper pasted under this window and decorated with some design will add to the effect. Next the doors are cut out. The church is now ready to be pasted on the dark blue paper. In pasting the church slide it under the snow. Now cut two pieces of paper for the cross of the steeple.

The windows, doors and cross may also be drawn with crayolas instead of cutting them out.

Get the children interested in observing the shape of the churches in their neighborhood. Draw attention to the spires. The month of

[1] Cf. the calendar picture for Thanksgiving Day, page 165.

November furnishes an excellent opportunity for teaching a few of the important symbols employed by the Church. We may take as an objective this month the meaning of the spires and steeples on the church and the mystical signification of the primary colors, red, yellow and blue.

The first of November set aside by holy Mother Church for the veneration of the glorious army of saints in heaven, calls us to raise our hearts and minds to the celestial home and to God, the Author and Giver of all good. The towering spires and lofty steeples of our churches beckon to us to raise our hearts and thoughts heavenward. Tell the children to observe the spires on the churches they see.

The primary colors, red, yellow and blue also have a deep significance. The mystery of the Blessed Trinity may be explained to the children by comparing it with the light coming through a prism. Show the class a prism and let them observe the different colors as the light falls on it. The following will serve as an illustration and comparison in explaining the Blessed Trinity: red signifies love—Christ; yellow, light—Holy Ghost; blue, eternal Truth—Father.

The Birth of Jesus

The construction of this poster and others relating to the Infant Jesus contains many possibilities for interesting occupation. Let the children cut out the various objects required for the presentation of the events connected with the Birth of Jesus, for example, the shepherds, sheep, the stable of Bethlehem, the crib, the Blessed Virgin, St. Joseph and the Infant Jesus. For the latter it will be better to use a picture

DESIGN FOR THANKSGIVING DAY POSTER—A CHURCH

cut from catalogs or magazines than to attempt freehand work. Let the children plan the arrangement of the poster.

The Three Kings

The children will be able to cut out nearly all the objects needed for this poster. The wise men, the camels, servants and gifts can be cut from paper. A simple presentation of the subject is all that is required from children in lower grades.

The Flight Into Egypt

This is a simple picture showing the Blessed Virgin and St. Joseph taking the Holy Child to Egypt. The children will be able to cut the figures required. It might be well to let the children cut out each figure separately and then

Design for Poster—The Birth of Jesus

Design for Poster—The Adoration of the Magi

DRAWING AND CONSTRUCTION WORK

arrange them in proper groups. The children ought to be able to suggest a good background for this poster.

The Boy Jesus at Nazareth

This will give an opportunity for many interpretations. Let the children select the part of the life of Jesus in Nazareth that appeals to

tools used by a carpenter, such as the hammer, saw, plane and workbench.

The Annunciation

Arrange this poster according to any one of the pictures of the Annunciation. Let the children cut out pictures of the Blessed Virgin and the angel.

POSTER DESIGN—THE FLIGHT INTO EGYPT

them most. For example, Jesus helping St. Joseph; Jesus and the Blessed Virgin; Jesus playing with St. John; Jesus praying.

The Holy Family

A suitable illustration of this would be to show the three holy persons engaged in some sort of work. St. Joseph might be shown using his tools, while Jesus is helping him, and the Blessed Virgin may be engaged in some household duty. Let the children plan the general arrangement of the poster.

St. Joseph and the Child Jesus

Jesus helping His foster-father in the carpenter shop will be an interesting subject. The children will take a delight in cutting out the

A Candlemas Procession

Since children take such delight in showing the various objects and articles used for the services of the Church, let them make a poster illustrating the procession which takes place on Candlemas Day or the feast of the Purification.[1] The altar boys are easily cut out. Cut out and paste, or draw, a window along the wall. The children may cut as many altar boys and candles as they wish for the procession.

The Way of the Cross

Probably the most satisfactory way for presenting this subject will be to make a series of posters each representing one of the scenes along

[1] Cf. picture of Calendar for February, Candlemas Day Procession, page 173.

POSTER DESIGN—CANDLEMAS PROCESSION

the road to Calvary. These smaller posters may be arranged on a large sheet of paper to present the Way of the Cross as a unit. Again, the project may be completed as one poster. Represent the city of Jerusalem on the extreme left, leaving the main part to show the road to Calvary, which can be shown on the right.

Calvary

This may be a part of the foregoing poster or it may be a separate project. Three crosses made of white paper against a black or gray background, pasted on the top of the hill drawn or cut out will be sufficient for the pupils of the first and second grades. If the teacher so wishes figures of soldiers and other people may be added. (Silhouette)

The Resurrection

This subject can be illustrated by using a picture cut from magazines or catalogs. Freehand cut-outs may be a little too difficult for the children in the first and second grades.

An Altar of the Blessed Virgin

A simple illustration of an altar with a picture of the Blessed Virgin will help to bring out the idea of veneration of the Blessed Virgin and the honor and respect due her. Let the children suggest a suitable background.

Various Subjects

A number of simple posters consisting of letters cut out and suitably mounted are also

POSTER DESIGN—"CALVARY"

SACRED HEART OF JESUS

AVE MARIA

AGNUS DEI

JESUS

OBEDIENCE

PRAY FOR THE DEAD

Designs for Posters of Various Subjects

suggested. Among these may be mentioned the following: Ave Maria, Sacred Heart of Jesus, Pray for the Dead, Jesus, Obedience, Agnus Dei. The last subject may be represented by cutting out the figure of a lamb bearing a cross. The words "Agnus Dei" are cut out and pasted beneath the figure of the lamb.

Illustrations of incidents in the lives of the Saints and Bible stories will furnish additional and abundant material for posters. Many of these can also be used for blackboard borders. The story of the Wise Men makes a good blackboard border. Cut out the camels and the Wise Men and paste them on the board and repeat the design along the border.

children will be led to discuss the subject of enlisting in the service of God. Show the priest administering the sacraments, helping the sick and needy, consoling the afflicted. Show Sisters teaching in the schools, waiting on the sick, caring for orphans, working among the poor and the aged.

Alphabet Posters Illustrating the Lives of the Saints

Making alphabet posters to illustrate the Lives of the Saints is an interesting occupation for the little ones.

Cut one letter of the alphabet each day or each week. Mount it on manilla paper about 9 x 12

Missionary Poster Design

Missionary Posters

Missionary posters can be made from pictures cut out of mission magazines. Let the children show the missions in China and Africa by using the illustrations found in mission magazines. Missions among the Indians and Eskimos may be shown by cutting out the figures of Indians, Eskimos, huts, dogs, trees, and other subjects. Add pictures of priests and Sisters at work among the people. Use these posters to arouse a missionary spirit in the children.

Posters may also be used to awaken interest in religious vocations. Let the children bring pictures of priests and Sisters engaged in mission work or other activities, and by arranging these in a variety of ways to suggest the works of mercy performed by priests and Religious, the

inches. Instruct the children to find pictures of the saints whose names begin with that letter. The work of finding the pictures should be done at home, while the cutting and mounting may be done in class. On each poster write a sentence or a rhyme to describe the picture. In the first and second grades the sentences should be very brief.

This method may also be used to show a number of related events in Bible History. Thus to picture the successive parts in the story of the creation of the world, a poster showing each of these events may be made. In like manner the story of Moses may be treated. After the posters have been completed, assemble them in their proper order and let the children tell the stories as illustrated.

10. MAKING BOOKLETS

Much enthusiasm is created by permitting the children to make booklets in which to paste pictures, drawings and cut-outs. Children find pleasure in making something to keep. Nothing delights them more than work which may be preserved and shown to those at home. For this reason making booklets proves an interesting occupation.

Many kinds of booklets may be made. The simplest form is made by folding a piece of paper 9 x 12 inches. To show the children how to fold the paper, hold it on the board, short edge to the bottom. Fold the short edge up until it meets exactly the upper corner; then crease the fold with the nail of the thumb, pressing back and forth several times.

have the children make a book large enough for all the letters in the alphabet. A cover and eight leaves is the most that can be conveniently handled by smaller children. If it is desired to complete the alphabet, several books may be made, using different colors for the covers. Place the eight leaves and the two pieces of tinted paper in a pile. Punch this at the center of the back along one short edge about three-quarters of an inch from the edge. About three and one-half inches above and below this hole punch others. The books may be fastened by paper fasteners or with macramé cord. The letters of the alphabet may be cut out and pasted one on each leaf. A cut out picture of the object it represents may be mounted at the right of the letter and the word written or printed below this. Later the child may write a sentence about the object.

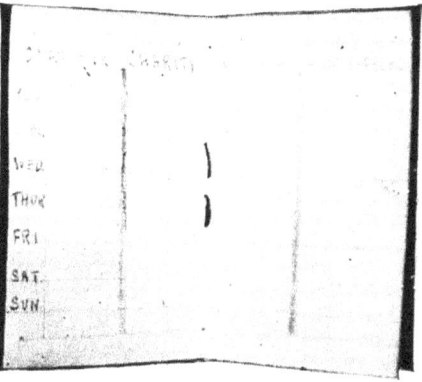

MODELS FOR BOOKLETS

One of the first lessons in September is to make a booklet consisting of a cover and two leaves. On the cover a cutting of the cross is pasted and on one of the inside leaves a fish is shown.

Many varieties of booklets may be made during the year. The following are some suggestions: Alphabet, Flowers, Bird, Health, Pictures, Safety, the Creation, Thanksgiving, Christmas, Easter, the Saints, Mother's Day, St. Valentine's Day, Holy Mass.

One of the most common forms of booklets used is the Alphabet Booklet. To make this use drawing paper for the leaves and tinted construction paper for the covers. The paper may be of any size, but 9 x 12 seems to be most convenient for the little ones. It is not advisable to

"Catholic Nursery Rhymes: The Life of Our Lord in Verse for Children," by Sister M. Gertrude, M. A., Sisters of Charity, offers fine material. For example:

"A" is for ANGEL St. Gabriel fair,
   Who appeared as our Lady was kneeling in prayer.

"B" is BETHLEHEM, dear little town!
   As the birthplace of Jesus it has great renown.

Creation Booklet

In the early part of the year the children may be interested in making a Creation Booklet. For this cut sheets of drawing paper into large circles about 6 or 9 inches in diameter. On the cover page let them paste the letters "Creation Booklet" cut from colored paper. Then on each of the pages illustrate the days of Creation.

Picture Booklet

During the month many pictures are studied by the children. To preserve these it will be well to let the children paste them in booklets. They may then be taken home, or may be sent to a sick classmate, to the little orphans, or to crippled children.

Bird Booklet

Pictures of birds are often brought to school by children. They make a pleasing booklet when pasted neatly on the page with a sentence or two describing the bird or its song written beneath it. Children like to gather pictures of birds.

Flower Booklet

Flowers may be cut out and pasted in booklets. These make beautiful gifts for sick children or for others. Short sentences written beneath the picture will make the booklet more valuable.

Fruit Booklet

Children find much pleasure in making booklets in which to paste pictures of various fruits. Magazines and seed catalogs furnish many pleasing varieties of pictures that can be cut out and used for this purpose.

Booklets cut in the shape of various designs are always interesting to the children. They may be cut in the shape of a bell, heart, star, circle, or shield. A pleasing variety may be obtained by adapting the shape to the particular kind of booklet made; for example, the Valentine Booklet may be heart-shaped, St. Patrick Booklet in the shape of a shamrock, the Easter Booklet may be lily-shaped or in the form of a cross.

Saint Booklet

Mount the pictures of saints in a special booklet and under each let the children write short sentences about the life of the saint.

Thankful Booklet

Around Thanksgiving Day let the children prepare a Thankful Booklet. This booklet is to consist of several pictures with suitable inscriptions. The thought of thankfulness to God for father, mother, baby brother or sister, pets, the home, food and clothing may be used to illustrate this booklet. On the cover paste the words "My Thankful Book" cut out of colored paper. On the first inside page paste a picture of a man to represent father; under it let the child write or print the words "My Father." Next a picture of mother with the words "My Mother" written or printed. Then a picture of a baby, with "My Baby Brother," or "My Baby Sister" written beneath it. Add pictures of a house, of several articles of food for the Thanksgiving Day dinner. Lastly a picture of the child, a photograph if possible, is pasted on the last page, with the words "Myself" written or printed under it. Other objects may also be included in this booklet. Pictures of grandfather, grandmother, uncle, aunt, a church, school, playground, and books may be used to show for what a child ought to be thankful.

Christmas Booklet

For the Christmas Booklet a pleasing variety may be suggested by cutting or drawing the different objects shown around the crib; for instance, the Crib with the Infant Jesus, angels, sheep, shepherds, dogs. Paste a picture of the Birth of Jesus on the cover. For the Infant Jesus use a picture. There are a number of pictures which will be suitable for this purpose. Sheep, shepherds and dogs are easily cut out. Let each child select the objects for his booklet.

St. Patrick Booklet

A border design of shamrocks can be easily cut and pasted on the cover. The words "St. Patrick" cut out of paper and pasted below this border will make a neat center for the cover. On the inside page paste a large shamrock. A picture of St. Patrick would also be appropriate.

St. Joseph Booklet

The St. Joseph Booklet might consist of a lily as a cover design and some of the carpenter tools cut out and pasted on the inside pages. A hammer, a saw, a plane are easily cut out. Use black paper for the tools. The booklet might be of grey paper while the inside paper may be of another color.

A Penance Booklet

At the beginning of Lent let the children make a Penance Booklet. This is made of grey paper as symbolic of penance. The letters and decorations are to be black. The cover bears the word "Penance." A large black cross is pasted on the first page. The other inside leaves are used for marking the prayers and work of penance performed by the little ones. Only a few practices should be marked. At the end of Lent the children may be permitted to take their booklets home.

Easter Booklet

Teach the children to draw or cut out a lily or some other appropriate flower for the cover. On the inside pages paste a cut-out picture of the Resurrection with the words "Christ Is Risen" cut out and pasted beneath it. A cross and a lily are also very appropriate for the cover.

The booklet may be tastefully decorated with one of the border designs.

Mass Booklet

Making this booklet proves very interesting to the little ones. About the month of May the children are ready to make an altar. Before this, they can be taught to cut out candles and candlesticks. A tabernacle is cut from gold paper or from yellow paper to represent a golden tabernacle. Then a chalice or ciborium is cut out of the same kind of paper. When the children are able to make fairly good cut-outs, let them paste them in a booklet to be called their Mass Booklet. Cut out and paste the word "Holy Mass" on the cover. On the inside pages paste the chalice, the tabernacle and lastly the candles and candlesticks, etc. The children may draw or cut out a missal and paste it on the back cover.

The letters "Holy Mass" should be cut out and pasted above the cross on the cover.

Mother Booklet

As suggested in the section on Mother's Day a booklet made especially for mother will be a very suitable gift for this day. Cut out the letters M Y M O T H E R and arrange them neatly on the cover. On the inside pages a carnation drawn or cut out will suggest the thought of the day. The words "God Bless My Mother" pasted on another page will be indicative of the prayers offered for mother. In the second grade the children may add a list of prayers in the form of a spiritual bouquet. Another suggestion is to draw a carnation on one of the inside pages and on the petals of this print the prayers offered for mother.

Mission Booklet

Making a mission booklet is a good way to inculcate a missionary spirit among the children. Let the pupils bring from home any pictures they may wish to use for this purpose. In nearly every home there should be found a missionary magazine of some kind. The teacher may also be able to collect from her friends a number of old mission magazines and she should let the children select and cut out the pictures they wish to use. This will be excellent busy work for them. Naturally many of the pictures will have to be explained and in this way it will be possible for the teacher to tell her class many interesting facts about the missions. Besides, the practice will also stimulate a spirit of helpfulness. The children can be led to offer their prayers and good works for the missions. Give the children free scope in planning their booklets. Later have a display in the class room giving a prize for the one that is the best arranged and that contains the most appropriate pictures.

Vocation Booklet

The children in the primary grades are not too young to have something said to them on the subject of vocations. Many of them are quite able to form definite ideas on the subject. To bring out these ideas and to arouse in them a desire for a religious or priestly vocation let the class make Vocation Booklets. Let the boys, for example, find pictures of priests and brothers, either of individuals or groups. Mission magazines will furnish many interesting illustrations of activities in which priests and brothers function. Pictures in the daily and weekly papers and other magazines are also serviceable. The girls in like manner may be kept busy looking for pictures of Sisters engaged in their various labors for the salvation of souls. This will interest the children and by occasional explanations and the telling of stories in which the work of priests and Religious is discussed, the teacher may be able to nurse the seeds of many vocations.

Literature on Art and Construction Work

Applied Art, drawing, painting, design, and handicraft, arranged for self-instruction of teachers, parents and students. Pacific Press Publishing Association, Mountain View, California, 1920.

Abbott Art Texts: Simple Graphic Art Ideas; Graphic Aids in Figure Drawing; Graphic Aids in Decorative Design, Abbott Educational Company, Chicago, Ill.

Blackboard Story Telling, H. Keel-Smith, Rand McNally and Company, Chicago, Ill.

Construction Work for the Primary Grades, Edward F. Worst, Bruce Publishing Co., Milwaukee, Wis., 1921.

The School Arts Magazine, Davis Press, 44 Portland St., Worcester, Mass.

BIBLIOGRAPHY

BOOKS FOR THE TEACHER

ANTONIA, SISTER M., (SISTER OF CHARITY, B.V.M. DUBUQUE) The Religious Teacher *(New York, N. Y., Benziger Brothers)*

BAGLEY, W. C., Classroom Management *(New York, N. Y., The Macmillan Co., 1907)*

BAIERL, J. REV., A Course in Christian Doctrine *(Rochester, N. Y., Rev. J. Baierl)*

BARRETT, S. M., Practical Pedagogy *(New York N. Y., D. C. Heath & Co., 1908)*

BARRY, W. F., The Hygiene of the Schoolroom *(New York, N. Y., Silver, Burdett & Co., 1909)*

BENEDICTINE SISTERS, Teaching for God *(St. Louis, Mo., The Queen's Work)*

BETTS, G. H., Classroom Management *(Indianapolis, Indiana, Bobbs—Merrill Co., 1917)*

BRIDGHAM, A. M., Day by Day in the Primary School *(Chicago, Ill., Beckley, Cardy & Co., 1924)*

BROOKS, S. S., Improving Schools by Standardized Tests *(Boston, Mass., Houghton Mifflin & Co., 1924)*

BROTHERS OF MARY, Manual of Christian Pedagogy *(Dayton, Ohio, Brothers of Mary, 1911)*

The Polite Pupil *(Dayton, Ohio, Brothers of Mary, 1911)*

BROTHERS OF THE CHRISTIAN SCHOOLS, Catechist's Manual *(Philadelphia, Pa., John Joseph McVey, 1912)*

BROTHERS OF THE CHRISTIAN SCHOOLS, Elements of Practical Pedagogy *(New York, N. Y., Christian Brothers)*

BROWNLEE, J., Character Building in School *(Boston, Mass., Houghton Mifflin & Co., 1917)*

BROWNSON, J., To the Heart of the Child *(New York, N. Y., Encyclopedia Press, 1918)*

BRYCE, C. T., and SPAULDING, F. E., Aldine First Language Book *(New York, N. Y., Newson & Co., 1913)*

Aldine Language Method *(New York, N. Y., Newson & Co., 1917)*

BURKE, C. E., Child Study and Education *(New York, N. Y., Benziger Bros., 1908)*

BURNS, VERY REV. J. A., C.S.C., Catholic Education *(New York, N. Y., Longmans, Green & Co., 1921)*

Principles, Origin and Establishment of the Catholic Schools in the United States *(New York, N. Y., Benziger Bros., 1907)*

Growth and Development of the Catholic School System in the United States *(New York, N. Y., Benziger Bros., 1912)*

BURRAGE, S., and BAILEY, H., School Sanitation and Decoration *(Boston, Mass., D. C. Heath & Co., 1911)*

CABOT, E. L., Ethics for Children *(Boston, Mass., Houghton Mifflin & Co., 1910)*

CALL, A. P., Power Through Repose *(Boston, Mass., Little Brown and Co., 1911)*

CATHER, K. D., Educating by Story Telling *(Yonkers, N. Y., World Book Co.)*

CECILIA, MADAME, Home Truths for Mary's Children *(New York, N. Y., Benziger Bros., 1911)*

The Training of Children and Girls in their Teens *(New York, N. Y., Benziger Bros., 1914)*

CHRYSOSTOM, BROTHER, The Development of Personality *(Philadelphia, Pa., John Joseph McVey, 1917)*

COLGROVE, C. P., The Teacher and the School *(New York, N. Y., Charles Scribner Sons, 1911)*

COLLINS, A., Library for Catholic Elementary Schools *(Washington, D. C., National Catholic Welfare Council, Bureau of Education, 1927)*

CONCANNON, H., A Garden of Girls *(New York, N. Y., Benziger Bros., 1928)*

CONSTANTIUS, BROTHER, The Young Christian Teacher Encouraged (St. Louis, Mo., B. Herder Book Co., 1911)

COOPER, REV. J. M., Fair Play (Washington, D. C., Catholic Education Press, 1923)

DOOLEY, W. H., The Education of the Ne'er-Do-Well (Boston, Mass., Houghton Mifflin & Co., 1916)

DRANE, A. T., Christian Schools and Scholars (New York, N. Y., Benziger Brothers, 1922)

DRINKWATER, REV. F., The Way into the Kingdom (New York, N. Y., Benziger Brothers)

DUNNEY, REV. J. A., The Parish School, Its Aims, Procedure, and Problems (New York, N. Y., The Macmillan Co., 1921)

EADES, J., Modern Ideas and Methods for School Teachers and Students in Training (New York, N. Y., The Macmillan Co., 1924)

EATON, MOTHER MARY, Consider the Child (New York, N. Y., Longmans, Green & Co.)

FITCH, J. G., Lectures on Teaching (New York, N. Y., The Macmillan Co.)

FLURY, E., Practical Hints on Education to Parents and Teachers (New York, N. Y., Benziger Bros., 1910)

FREEMAN, E. N., Mental Tests (Boston, Mass., Houghton Mifflin & Co.)

Psychology of Common Branches (Boston, Mass., Houghton Mifflin & Co.)

GEORGE, M. M., Character Building (Chicago, Ill., A. Flanagan Co., 1909)

The Primary Plan Book (Chicago, Ill., A. Flanagan Co., 1912)

GILBERT, C., What Children Study and Why (New York, N. Y., Silver, Burdett & Co.)

GILLET, M. S., The Education of Character (New York, N. Y., P. J. Kenedy & Sons, 1914)

GILMAN, N., and JACKSON, E., Conduct as a Fine Art (Boston, Mass., Houghton Mifflin & Co.)

GREENWOOD, J. M., Successful Teaching (New York, N. Y., Funk and Wagnalls Co., 1906)

GREGORY, B. C., Better Schools (New York, N. Y., The Macmillan Co.)

HART, J., In the Schoolroom (New York, N. Y., Hinds, Hayden and Eldridge)

HIGGINS, J., Fundamentals of Pedagogy (Boston, Mass., D. C. Heath & Co.)

HODGE, C. F., Nature Study and Life (New York, N. Y., Ginn and Co.)

HUBBARD, E., Little American History Plays for Little Americans (Boston, Mass., H. Sanborn & Co.)

HULL, E. R., Collapses in Adult Life (New York, N. Y., P. J. Kenedy & Sons)

The Formation of Character (St. Louis, Mo., B. Herder Book Co.)

JOYCE, P. W., Handbook of School Management (New York, N. Y., Longmans, Green & Co.)

KANE, W. T., For Greater Things (St. Louis, Mo., B. Herder Book Co., 1915)

KELLEY, Zeal in the Class Room (New York, N. Y., P. J. Kenedy & Sons)

KENDALL, C. N., and MIRICK, G. A., How to Teach the Fundamental Subjects (Boston, Mass., Houghton Mifflin & Co.)

KIRKPATRICK, E. A., Fundamentals of Child Study (New York, N. Y., The Macmillan Co., 1917)

KIRSCH, F. M., The Catholic Teacher's Companion (New York, N. Y., Benziger Bros., 1924)

KREBS, H. C., Being a Good Teacher (New York, N. Y., Hinds, Hayden & Eldridge, 1918)

LEO, BROTHER, The Story of St. John Baptist de la Salle (New York, N. Y., P. J. Kenedy & Sons, 1921)

LORD, REV. D. A., S.J., Our Nuns (New York, N. Y., Benziger Bros., 1924)

MAC EACHEN, REV. R., The Teaching of Religion (New York, N. Y., The Macmillan Co., 1921)

MCCALL, W. A., How to Measure in Education (New York, N. Y., The Macmillan Co., 1922)

MCCORMICK, REV. P. J., History of Education (Washington, D. C., Catholic Education Press, 1915)

MAHER, REV. M., S.J., Psychology (New York, N. Y., Longmans, Green & Co., 1911)

MARIQUE, P., History of Christian Education (New York, N. Y., Fordham University Press)

MEUMAN, E., Psychology of Learning (New York, N. Y., D. Appleton & Co., 1913)

MILDRED, SISTER M. (Sisters of St. Francis, Glen Riddle, Pa.) Supervision in the Catholic Elementary School (Glen Riddle, Pa., Sisters of St. Francis, 1925)

Assignments and Directions in the Study of Religion (New York, N. Y., Benziger Brothers, 1920)

MOORE, REV. T. V., Dynamic Psychology (Philadelphia, Pa., J. B. Lippincott Co., 1924)

NEWMAN, CARDINAL, Idea of a University (New York, N. Y., Longmans, Green & Co.)

NIST, REV. J., Private First Communion Instructions (St. Louis, Mo., B. Herder Book Co., 1914)

O'SHEA, M. V., Everyday Problems in Teaching (Indianapolis, Ind., Bobbs—Merrill Co., 1912)

PAGE, D. P., Theory and Practice of Teaching (New York, N. Y., The American Book Co.)

PARKER, S. C., General Methods of Teaching in Elementary Schools, Including the Kindergarten (New York, N. Y., Ginn & Co., 1922)

Types of Elementary Teaching and Learning Including Practical Technique and Scientific Evidence (New York, N. Y., Ginn & Co., 1923)

PAULA, SISTER MARIE (Sisters of Charity Mt. St. Vincent, N. Y.), Talks to Teachers (New York, N. Y., Benziger Bros., 1925)

Shibboleths (New York, N. Y., Benziger Bros., 1928)

PEAR, T. H., Skill in Work and Play (New York, N. Y., E. P. Dutton & Co.)

PHILIP, BROTHER, Considerations for Christian Teachers (Baltimore, Md., John Murphy Co., 1922)

RICKABY, REV. J., S.J., Four Square (New York, N. Y., J. F. Wagner, 1908)

RUEDIGER, W., Vitalized Teaching (Boston, Mass., Houghton Mifflin & Co.)

RYAN, J. H., Catechism of Catholic Education (Washington, D. C., National Catholic Welfare Council)

SCHREMBS, RT. REV. J. and REV. J. HUEGLE, O.S.B. Progressive Music Series, Catholic Edition (New York, N. Y., Silver, Burdett & Co.)

SCHWICKERATH, REV. J. H., S.J., Jesuit Education (St. Louis, Mo., B. Herder Book Co.)

SHIELDS, REV. T. E., Philosophy of Education (Washington, D. C., Catholic Education Press, 1917)

Teachers' Manual of Primary Methods (Catholic Education Press, 1912)

The Making and Unmaking of a Dullard (Washington, D. C., Catholic Education Press, 1909)

SIGNOR, A., Material, Aids and Devices for Teachers (Dansville, N. Y., F. A. Owen Co., 1925)

SISTERS OF LORETTO (Loretto, Ky.), Loretto Series, Language Busy Work (St. Louis, Mo., A. B. Dewes Printing and Stationery Co., 1924)

SISTERS OF ST. JOSEPH, Politeness (St. Louis, Mo., B. Herder Book Co., 1923)

SLOANE, REV. P., The Sunday School Teacher's Guide to Success (New York, N. Y., Benziger Bros., 1908)

SLOMAN, L., Some Primary Methods (New York, N. Y., The Macmillan Co., 1927)

SMITH, J., Faith and Duty (New York, N. Y., Benziger Bros., 1920)

SPALDING, MOST REV. J. L., Aphorisms and Reflections (Chicago, Ill., A. C. McClurg & Co.)

Education and the Higher Life (Chicago, Ill., A. C. McClurg & Co.)

Means and Ends of Education (Chicago, Ill., A. C. McClurg & Co.)

Things of the Mind (Chicago, Ill., A. C. McClurg & Co.)

Thoughts and Theories on Life and Education (Chicago, Ill., A. C. McClurg & Co.)

SPENCER, MARY E., Foods and Nutrition (Washington, D. C., National Catholic Welfare Council, Bureau of Education)

Health Education Bibliography (Washington, D. C., National Catholic Welfare Council, Bureau of Education)

Health Through the School Day (Washington, D. C., National Catholic Welfare Council, Bureau of Education, 1924)

Medical Supervision in Catholic Schools (Washington, D. C., National Catholic Welfare Council, Bureau of Education)

STEVENS, J., The Question as a Measure of Efficiency in Instruction (New York, N. Y., Teachers College, Columbia University)

STUART, J., Education of Catholic Girls (New York, N. Y., Longmans, Green & Co.)

SULLIVAN, REV. J., The Visible Church (New York, N. Y., P. J. Kenedy & Sons)

SUZZALO, H., Teaching of Primary Arithmetic (Boston, Mass., Houghton Mifflin & Co., 1912)

Teaching of Spelling (New York, N. Y., Teachers College, Columbia University, 1911)

THOMPSON, FRANCIS, Complete Poems (New York, N. Y., Modern Library)

TIERNEY, REV. R., S.J., The Teacher and Teaching (New York, N. Y., Longmans, Green & Co., 1917)

TOMPKINS, Philosophy of School Management (New York, N. Y., Ginn & Co.)

URBAN, REV. A., Easy Catechetics for the First School Year (New York, N. Y., J. F. Wagner, 1910)

WAITS, H., Practical Problems of the School (Boston, Mass., Benjamin H. Sanborn & Co.)

WALSH, J., M.D., Health Through Will Power (Boston, Mass., Little, Brown & Co.)

WARD, JUSTINE, Catholic Education Music Course (Washington, D. C., Catholic Education Press)

WARNER, E., Character Building Readers (New York, N. Y., Hinds, Hayden & Eldridge)

WEIGAND, REV. J., A Simple Course in Religion for the Little Ones Preparing for Their First Holy Communion (New York, N. Y., Benziger Brothers, 1924)

WEIGAND, REV. J., The Catechist and Catechumen (New York, N. Y., Benziger Brothers, 1924)

WILLMANN, J. and REV. FELIX KIRSCH, O.M. Cap, The Science of Education (Beatty, Pa., St. Vincent's Archabbey)

WILSON, H., Modern Methods of Teaching (New York, N. Y., Silver, Burdett & Co.)

ZULUETA, REV. F. DE, S.J., The Child Prepared for First Holy Communion (New York, N. Y., Benziger Brothers, 1911)

BOOKS FOR CHILDREN

ALPHABET OF SAINTS, AN. RHYMED, by Father Benson, Reginald Balfour and S. C. Ritchie; drawn by L. D. Symington (Benziger Brothers, New York, N. Y.)

BOYS' AND GIRLS' PRAYER BOOK. By Father Francis J. Finn, S.J. (Benziger Brothers, New York, N. Y.)

CATHOLIC NURSERY RHYMES. The Life of Our Lord Jesus Christ in Verse for Young Children. By Sister Mary Gertrude, M.A., Sisters of Charity, Convent Station, N. J. Profusely illustrated in colors. (Benziger Brothers, New York, N. Y.)

CATHOLIC TEACHING FOR YOUNG AND OLD. A brief Course in Catholic Doctrine, Explaining the Important Events in the Old and New Testaments, with Instructions on the Creed, the Commandments, the Sacraments, the Ceremonies, etc., of the Catholic

Church. By W. Wray. Illustrated. *(Benziger Brothers, New York, N. Y.)*

CHILD'S RULE OF LIFE, A., by Father Robert Hugh Benson, with Pictures by Gabriel Pippet. A Book of Rhymes and Pictures. *(Longmans, Green & Co., New York, N. Y.)*

CREDO, THE CREED IN PICTURES FOR CHILDREN. *(B. Herder Book Co., St. Louis, Mo.)*

ILLUSTRATED LIVES OF PATRON SAINTS FOR BOYS by Mary E. Mannix. Illustrated. *(Benziger Brothers, New York, N. Y.)*

ILLUSTRATED LIVES OF PATRON SAINTS FOR GIRLS by Mary E. Mannix. Illustrated. *(Benziger Brothers, New York, N. Y.)*

LIFE OF CHRIST IN PICTURES, THE, by Rev. George A. Keith, S.J. *(Extension Press, Chicago, Ill.)*

LITTLE CHILDREN'S THOUGHTS AND PRAYERS FOR HOLY COMMUNION by Sisters of Notre Dame. Illustrated. *(Benziger Brothers, New York, N. Y.)*

LITTLE LIVES OF THE SAINTS FOR CHILDREN, by Th. Berthold. Illustrated. *(Benziger Brothers, New York, N. Y.)*

LORD JESUS, THE,—HIS BIRTHDAY STORY. *(Extension Press, Chicago, Ill.)*

MASS FOR CHILDREN, THE. Instructions in Story Form for Use in the Primary Grades with Colored Drawings Accompanying Text According to Modern Educational Methods. By Rev. William R. Kelly. 36 pictures. 18 in colors, 18 in black and white. *(Benziger Brothers, New York, N. Y.)*

OLD TESTAMENT RHYMES by Father Robert Hugh Benson. *(Longmans, Green & Co., New York, N. Y.)*

OUR FIRST COMMUNION. Instructions in Story Form with Colored Drawings Accompanying Text According to Modern Educational Methods. Based on Essential Requirements, Canon 854 of the New Code of Canon Law. By Rev. William R. Kelly. 36 pictures. 18 in colors, 18 in black and white. *(Benziger Brothers, New York, N. Y.)*

OUR SACRAMENTS. Instructions in Story Form for Use in the Primary Grades with Colored Drawings Accompanying the Text According to Modern Educational Methods. By Rev. William R. Kelly. 49 pictures. 17 in colors, of which 7 are full page. 32 in black and white in the text. *(Benziger Brothers, New York, N. Y.)*

RELIGION HOUR. Story Lessons in Conduct and Religion Based on "Teacher Tells a Story." By Rev. Jerome D. Hannan, D.D. Heavy paper covers, colored picture on cover, frontispiece and 30 text illustrations in colors. Books I and II. *(Benziger Brothers, New York, N. Y.)*

ROSARY FOR CHILDREN, THE. The Story of the Holy Rosary told to Children in Word and Picture. By Sister M. Ambrose, O.P., Sister of St. Dominic, Adrian, Mich. *(Benziger Brothers, N. Y.)*

TALES OF FOREIGN LANDS. A Series of Stories for the Young. Collected by Rev. Joseph Spillmann, S. J. 12 vol. *(B. Herder Book Co., St. Louis, Mo.)*

TALES OF THE ANGELS. By Father Faber. *(Benziger Brothers, New York, N. Y.)*

THOUGHTS AND PRAYERS ABOUT THE ROSARY FOR LITTLE CHILDREN by Sisters of Notre Dame. *(Benziger Brothers, New York, N. Y.)*

WONDER DAYS, THE. The Story of the Divine Boy of Nazareth in Word and Picture for Children. By Marion Ames Taggart. *(Benziger Brothers, New York, N. Y.)*

WONDER GIFTS, THE. A Simple Explanation of Confession, Holy Communion and Confirmation in Word and Picture for Children. By Marion Ames Taggart. *(Benziger Brothers, New York, N. Y.)*

WONDER OFFERING, THE. The Holy Mass in Word and Picture simply explained for Children. By Marion Ames Taggart. *(Benziger Brothers, New York, N. Y.)*

WONDER STORY, THE. The Birth and Childhood of the Infant Jesus in Word and Picture, Simply Told for Children. By Marion Ames Taggart. (Also in French or Polish.) *(Benziger Brothers, New York, N. Y.)*

MATERIAL FOR STORIES

(Material for stories may be found in the following books).

ALONG THE MISSION TRAIL, by Rev. Bruno Hagspiel, S.V.D. 5 vols. *(Society of the Divine Word, Techny, Ill.)*

AMERICAN INDIAN FAIRY TALES, by Margaret Compton. *(Dodd, Mead & Co., New York, N. Y.)*

AMERICAN MYTHS AND LEGENDS, by Charles M. Skinner. 2 vol. *(J. B. Lippincott Co., Philadelphia, Pa.)*

ANECDOTES AND EXAMPLES ILLUSTRATING THE CATHOLIC CATECHISM, by Rev. Francis Spirago. Edited by Rev. James J. Baxter, D.D. *(Benziger Brothers, New York, N. Y.)*

BIBLE STORIES FOR LITTLE CHILDREN. Illustrated. *(Benziger Brothers, New York, N. Y.)*

BLACKFEET TALES OF GLACIER NATIONAL PARK, by J. W. Schultz. *(Houghton Mifflin & Co., Boston, Mass.)*

BLUEGOWNS. TALES OF THE CHINA MISSIONS, by Alice Dease. *(Foreign Mission Society, Maryknoll, N. Y.)*

BOOK OF SAINTS AND FRIENDLY BEASTS, by Abbie Farwell Brown. *(Houghton Mifflin & Co., Boston.)*

BOOK OF THE EPIC, THE, by Helene A. Guerber. *(J. B. Lippincott Co., Philadelphia, Pa.)*

BOYHOOD AND MANHOOD OF JESUS, by Vy. Rev. R. A. O'Gorman, O.P., *(Benziger Brothers, New York, N. Y.)*

BOY'S KING ARTHUR, THE, by Sidney Lanier. *(Charles Scribner's Sons, New York, N. Y.)*

CATECHIST, THE—or, Headings and Suggestions for the Explanation of the Catechism of Christian Doctrine. With numerous quotations and examples from Scripture, and an appendix of anecdotes and illustrations. 2 vols. By Rev. G. E. Howe. *(Benziger Brothers, New York, N. Y.)*

CATHOLIC YOUNG PEOPLE'S FRIEND. A Monthly. *(Angel Guardian Press, Chicago.)*

CHILDREN'S CHARTER, THE. Talks to Parents and Teachers in Preparing Little Children For Their First Communion, by Mother Mary Loyola. *(Benziger Brothers, New York, N. Y.)*

FAIRY TALES FROM "ARABIAN NIGHTS," Edited by E. Dixon. *(G. P. Putnam's Sons, New York, N. Y.)*

FATHER PAUL'S STORY BOX TALES OF A CHINESE MISSIONARY, by Elsa Schmidt. *(Society of the Divine Word, Techny, Ill.)*

FATHER TIME'S TALKS WITH PEOPLE HE MET, by Rev. C. D. McEnniry, C. SS. R. 5 vols. *(B. Herder Book Co., St. Louis, Mo.)*

FIELD AFAR STORIES. 3 vols. *(Foreign Mission Society, Maryknoll, N. Y.)*

FOLK TALES EVERY CHILD SHOULD KNOW, edited by H. W. Mabie. *(Grosset and Dunlap, New York, N. Y.)*

HEROES OF ICELAND, by Allen French. Adapted from Dasent's translation of "The Story of Burnt Njal." *(Little, Brown & Co., Boston, Mass.)*

HEROES OF THE MISSION FIELD, by Herman Wegener, S.V.D. *(Society of the Divine Word, Techny, Ill.)*

IRISH FAIRY TALES, by James Stephens. *(The Macmillan Co., New York, N. Y.)*

JESUS OF NAZARETH. The Story of His Life Written For Children by Mother M. Loyola and edited by Father Thurston, S.J. Illustrated. *(Benziger Brothers, New York, N. Y.)*

KING OF THE GOLDEN CITY, THE, by Mother Mary Loyola. *(P. J. Kennedy & Sons, New York, N. Y.)*

KNIGHTLY LEGENDS OF WALES OR THE BOY'S MABINOGION, by Sidney Lanier. *(Charles Scribner's Sons, New York, N. Y.)*

LEGENDS (EVERY CHILD SHOULD KNOW), edited by H. W. Mabie. *(Grosset and Dunlap, New York, N. Y.)*

LEGENDS OF THE MIDDLE AGES, by Helene A. Guerber. *(The American Book Co., New York, N. Y.)*

LITTLE FLOWER'S LOVE FOR HER PARENTS, THE, by Sister M. Eleanore, C.S.C., Ph.D. Profusely illustrated in colors. *(Benziger Brothers, New York, N. Y.)*

LITTLE FLOWER'S LOVE FOR THE HOLY EUCHARIST, THE, by Sister M. Eleanore, C.S.C., Ph.D. Eleven illustrations in colors after original drawings. *(Benziger Brothers, New York, N. Y.)*

MANA. A Monthly for Children. *(Salvatorian Press, St. Nazianz, Wis.)*

MERRY ADVENTURES OF ROBIN HOOD, by Howard Pyle. *(Charles Scribner's Sons, New York, N. Y.)*

OUR YOUNG PEOPLE. A Monthly for Children. *(Catholic Deaf Mute Institute, St. Francis, Wis.)*

ROSARY FOR CHILDREN, THE. The Story of the Holy Rosary Told for Children in Word and Picture, by Sister M. Ambrose, O.P., Sister of St. Dominic, Adrian, Mich. *(Benziger Brothers, New York, N. Y.)*

SAINT OF THE EUCHARIST, ST. PASCHAL BAYLON, by Rev. Oswald Staniforth, O.S.F.C. *(Benziger Brothers, New York, N. Y.)*

SCHOOL MATE. A weekly paper. *(Buechler Printing Co., Belleville, Ill.)*

STORIES OF THE MIRACLES OF OUR LORD, Told to Children. By a Religious. *(Benziger Brothers, New York, N. Y.)*

STORY OF KING ARTHUR AND HIS KNIGHTS, by Howard Pyle. *(Charles Scribner's Sons, New York, N. Y.)*

STORY OF ROLAND, by James Baldwin. *(Charles Scribner's Sons, New York, N. Y.)*

STORY OF ST. FRANCIS OF ASSISI FOR CHILDREN, by Sister M. Eleanore, C.S.C., Ph.D. With colored illustration. *(Benziger Brothers, New York, N. Y.)*

STORY OF THE LITTLE FLOWER OF JESUS, by Rev. Daniel A. Lord, S.J. *(Benziger Brothers, New York, N. Y.)*

SUNDAY SCHOOL INSTRUCTIONS FOR EVERY SUNDAY OF THE YEAR, by Rev. M. Phillips. *(Catholic Union Store, Buffalo, N. Y.)*

TEACHER'S STORY TELLER BOOK, by Alice O'Grady and Frances Throop. *(Rand, McNally & Co., Chicago, Ill.)*

TEACHER TELLS A STORY. Books One and Two. Story Lessons in Conduct and Religion for Every Day in the School Year; Containing also Teachers' Helps for Use with "Religion Hours." Books 1 and 2. By Rev. Jerome D. Hannan, D.D. *(Benziger Brothers, New York, N. Y.)*

TELL US ANOTHER, by Rev. Winfrid Herbst, S.D.S. *(Salvatorian Press, St. Nazianz, Wis.)*

THE CROSS IN JAPAN, by Cecilia Caddell. *(Burns, Oates and Washbourne, London)*

UNCLE REMUS, HIS SONGS AND HIS SAYINGS, by Joel Chandler Harris. *(D. Appleton & Co., New York, N. Y.)*

WITH THE HERALDS OF THE CROSS, by Rev. Norbert Weber, O.S.B. *(Society of the Divine Word, Techny, Ill.)*

WORKERS ARE FEW. REFLECTIONS UPON VOCATIONS TO FOREIGN MISSIONS, THE, by Rt. Rev. J. F. McGlinchey. *(The Press of the Society for the Propagation of the Faith, Boston, Mass.)*

YOUNG CATHOLIC MESSENGER, THE. Weekly publication. *(George A. Pflaum, Dayton, Ohio.)*

ALPHABETICAL INDEX

Adam and Eve, story of, 85; sand table project of, 230
Agnes, St., feast of, 209
Album, scrap, 261
Alcott, Louisa, quoted, 6
All Saints, feast of, 142, 205
All Souls, feast of, 205-206
Aloysius, Gonzaga, St., feast of, 221-222
Alphabet of Saints, poster of, 292
Angel, Guardian, *see* Guardian Angel
Anger, method of controlling, 75
Animals, kindness to, 27; Little Flower and, 28
Anne, St., 135, 136
Annunciation, feast of, 216
Anthony of Padua, St., apparition of Infant Jesus to, 93; feast of, 219-220
Apostles, the, 146
Apostolate, the Child, 146-154
Ark, *see* Noe and Ark
Armbands, 261
Art, correlation of, with religion, 268; literature on, 296
Articles, religious, charts to teach meaning and use of, 264
Attendance, devices to secure regular, 265
Bacon, Francis, quoted, 67
Badges, 261
Bank, design for, 37
Banners, 261
Baptism, grace of, 148
Baseball player, example of, 63, 64
Bee-hive, device, 259
Benson, Rt. Rev. Msgr. Robert Hugh, quoted, 79
Betham-Edwards, Matilda, quoted, 38
Bethlehem, 89, 90, 95
Birds, kindness towards, 31; flight of (device), 260; on trees, on wires (devices), 260; booklet of, 294
Bishops, prayers for, 153
Blase, St., feast of, 211-212
Blessed Mother, example of, 11; 134-142 *passim;* feast of Nativity of, 191-192; feast of Immaculate Conception of, 208; feast of Purification of, 211; feast of Annunciation of, 216; rose garden of (device), 224
Blessed Sacrament, St. Teresa on Jesus in, 88; institution of, 115; 126-133, *passim*
Blessed Virgin, *see* Blessed Mother.

Blunt, Hugh Francis, quoted, 112
Boniface, St., apparition of Infant Jesus to, 93
Booklets, how to make, 293; Suggestions for, 293-296
Borrowing, 60
Boy and Wolf, story of, dramatization of, 245-246
Browning, Elizabeth Barrett, quoted, 72
Bulletin board, how to make, 262; use of, 262
Cain and Abel, sand table project on, 230; dramatization of story of, 238-239
Calendars, how to make, 157; subjects for, 157; pictures of, 161-187
Callista, Sister Mary, quoted, v-vii
Calls, name, 254; street, 254
Calvary, Jesus dies on, 121; poster of, 290
Candlemas Day, procession on, poster of, 289
Carlyle, Thomas, quoted, 51
Cary, Alice, quoted, 26, 49, 61, 76
Cary, Phoebe, quoted, 41-42, 43, 49
Catholic Educational Review, quoted, v, vii
Charts, suggestions for, 224; to to teach use and meaning of religious articles, 264; to teach Passion of Our Lord, 264
Cheating, 58
Cheerfulness, 6
Child, Christian, duties of, 79, 80, 81, 82
Child, Lydia Maria, quoted, 29
Child's Rule of Life, A, quoted, 79
Christ, obedience of, 41; sand table project of birth of, 231
Christmas, story of, dramatized, 99; program for, 190; poster and device for, 225; booklet for, 294
Church, visits to, 132
Ciborium, 126
Cigar box furniture, 281
Cleanliness, 49
Colesworthy, quoted, 33
Columbus, Christopher, courage of, 64
Columbus Day, program for, 189
Communion, Holy, and Last Supper, 115
Communion, spiritual, how to make, 145
Confession, help of, 77, 78; sorrow in, 92

Conscience, compared to a watch, 76, 77, 78.
Construction work, 271-279; for sand table, 279-282
Copying, 263
Cornstalk houses and furniture, 280-281
Cousin, St. Germaine, feast of, 220-221
Coward, 64; Pilate a, 120
Creation, booklet on, 293
Crib, Christmas, 85; model for, 91; origin of, 227
Cross, Exaltation of Holy, feast of, 193
Cutting, paper, 273-274; letters, 279
Decorations, blackboard, 258-259
Dessert, denial of, 81
Devices: Blessed Virgin's rose garden, 224; rosary, 224; Christmas crib, 225; crown of thorns, 226; flowers for May, 226; flowers for March, 226; birthdays and name days, 227; to aid teacher of singing, 253-255; bee-hive, 259; airship race, 259; cross-country race, 259-260; flight of birds, 260; birds on wires, 260; birds on trees, 260; banners, pennants, badges, ornaments, 261; to secure regular attendance, 265; to cure tardiness, 266; to secure punctuality, 266; to teach making of good intention, 266; to teach thoughtfulness, 266; to teach tidiness, 266-267
Dodge, Mary Mapes, quoted, 40
Dramatization, method of, 234-238; of story of Christmas, 99; of story of Cain and Abel, 238-239; of building of the ark, 239; of story of Joseph, 239-241; of story of Moses, 241-242; of adoration of shepherds, 242; of adoration of Magi, 242-243; of Jesus blessing little children, 243; of St. Francis and wolf, 243; of St. Francis and birds, 244; of Blessed Herman Joseph, 244; of boy and wolf, 245-246; material for, 246-247
Drawing, 271-279
Drawings, blackboard, suggestions for: Blessed Virgin's rose garden, 224; rosary, 224
Easter, booklet for, 295
Egypt, flight into, story of, 103-104; sand table, project of, 232

INDEX

Eleanore, Sister M., C.S.C., quoted, 119, 120, 196, 199
Elizabeth, St., mother of St. John the Baptist, 107
Elizabeth of Hungary, St., feast of, 206-207
Emery, Susan L., quoted, 137
Envelopes, making of, 273; decoration of, 273
Exaltation of the Holy Cross, feast of, 193
Faber, Father, quoted, 93, 96, 108, 127, 133, 135, 142, 146, 148, 149, 150, 195, 212
Family, Holy, sand table project of, 232
Feasts of the Church: Nativity of Blessed Virgin Mary, 191-192; Most Holy Name of Mary, 192-193; Exaltation of Holy Cross, 193; Seven Sorrows of Blessed Virgin Mary, 193-194; St. Michael, Archangel, 194; Holy Guardian Angels, 194-195; Little Flower of Jesus, 195-199; St. Francis of Assisi, 199-200; Most Holy Rosary, 200; St. Theresa of Jesus, 203-204; St. Raphael, Archangel, 204-205; All Saints, 205; All Souls, 205-206; St. Elizabeth of Hungary, 206-207; St. Nicholas, 207-208; Immaculate Conception, 208; St. Sebastian, 208-209; St. Agnes, 209; St. Francis de Sales, 209-211; Purification of Blessed Virgin, 211; St. Blase, 211-212; St. Valentine, 212-213; St. Patrick, 213-214; St. Gabriel, Archangel, 214-215; St. Joseph, 215-216: Annunciation, 216; St. Isidore, 217; Blessed Herman Joseph, 217-218; Blessed Imelda, 218; St. Paschal Baylon, 218-219; St. Anthony of Padua, 219-220; St. Germaine Cousin, 220-221; St. Aloysius Gonzaga, 221-222; St. John the Baptist, 222, 224.
Fighting, 74
Fish, how to cut, 273
Flowers, booklet of, 294
Francis de Sales, St., feast of, 209-211
Francis of Assisi, St., cheerfulness of, 5; imitation of, 5; quoted, 6; and birds, 8; and wolf, 11; and animals, 28; example of, 146-147, 152; feast of, 199-200; and Christmas crib, 227; dramatizations on life of, 243-244; posters of, 284
Franklin, Benjamin, quoted, 61
Fruit, booklet of, 294
Gabriel, St., Archangel, feast of, 214-215

Garden of Olives, 114-117
Generosity, antidote of selfishness, 87
God, presence of, 40; obedience to, 39; *passim*
Golden Rule, 87, 93
Greccio, crib at, 227
Greediness, 86
Guardian Angel, 13, 14, 76, 79, 80, 82, 98, 145, 146, 151, 153; feast of, 194-195; poster of, 284
Hallowen, 142
Harrison, Virginia, quoted, 70-71
Heathen, prayer for, 37
Heaven, 39
Herbst, Winfrid, quoted, 40, 42, 87, 94, 127, 128, 131, 218, 246-247
Herman Joseph, Blessed, 141, 144; feast of, 217-218; dramatization of story of, 244; pantomime of, 245
Herod, 101; and slaughter of Holy Innocents, 103
Holy Innocents, 103
Holy Souls, see Purgatory, Souls in
Holy Week, program for, 190
Home, cheerful words in, 8; politeness in, 19; happiest place on earth, 23
Honesty, in school, 58; in play, 59; rules of, 59
Imelda, Blessed, and the Blessed Sacrament, 131; story of, 144; feast of, 218
Immaculate Conception, 83; feast of, 208
Innocents, Holy, see Holy Innocents
Intention, good, devices to teach making of, 266
Isidore, St., feast of, 217
James, St., on the tongue, 73
Jesus, example of, 11; love of, for children, 16; in the tabernacle, 16; birth of, 83,84; unselfishness of, 85; in Blessed Sacrament, 88; death of, 121; visits to, 132, 133; dramatization of blessing of children by, 243
Joachim, St., 135
John the Baptist, St., 107; feast of, 222, 224
Joseph, sand table project of story of, 230; dramatization of story of, 239-241
Joseph, St., prayer to, for a happy death, 82; feast of, 215-216; booklet of, 294
Judas, 113-120
Keys, Golden, 24
Kimball, Harriet McEwen, quoted, 44
Kindness, charm of, 9; to poor and sick, 9
Labor Day, exercises for, 188-189
Last Supper, 114

Law, obedience of Joseph and Mary to, 95; obedience of children to, 95
Lincoln, Abraham, 83
Little Flower of Jesus, kindness of, to animals, 28; and Blessed Sacrament, 132; and Blessed Virgin, 141; feast of, 195-199
Little Flower's Love for Her Parents, quoted, 119, 196, 199
Little Flower's Love for the Holy Eucharist, quoted, 120
Lost articles, what to do with, 60
Lourdes, Grotto of, sand table projects of, 232
Lying, 54, 55, 56, 57
Machabees, courage of, 65
Magi, see Wise Men
Manners, good, in school, 20
Mary, St., see Blessed Mother
Mass, booklet of, 295
Meals, prayers at, 80
Memory Gems, use of, 4
Michael the Archangel, St., feast of, 194
Miller, Emily H., quoted, 6
Missionaries, saving money for, 37; work of, 37, 150
Missionaries, Little, 150-154
Missions, sand table projects on, 232-234; posters on, 292; booklet of, 295
Monotones, how to help, 254
Morning exercises, how to conduct, 3
Moses, story of, sand table project of, 230; dramatization of, 241-242
Most Holy Name of Mary, feast of, 192-193
Mother's Day, program for, 190-191; booklet for, 295
Mottoes, for music class, 255
Music, creating, 249-251; lists of selections of, 252, 253, 255-258; devices to aid teacher of, 253-255; reference books on teaching of, 258
Mysteries of the Rosary, 201-203
Nazareth, 95
Neatness, 49; in school, 52
Nicholas, St., feast of, 207-208
Noe, and Ark, sand table project of, 230; dramatization of story of, 239
Obedience, necessity of, 38; to parents, 41; to teachers, 42; of Christ, 41
O'Connell, William, Cardinal, quoted, 114
Osgood, Frances S., quoted, 54
Ostensorium, 126
Pantomime, of Blessed Herman Joseph, 245
Parents, appreciation of, 33; obedience to, 35-41

INDEX

Paschal Baylon, St., and the Blessed Sacrament, 131, 132; story of, 144-145; feast of, 218-219
Passion, lessons of Our Lord's, 118; charts to teach, 264
Patrick, St., feast of, 213-214; booklet of, 294
Peace, and happiness, 10; lessons in, 267-268
Penance, booklet of, 295
Pennants, 261
Petals of a Little Flower, quoted, 137
Pets, care of, 32
Pictures, suggestions for, 259; use of, in story telling, 282-283; booklet of, 294
Pilate, Pontius, Jesus taken before, 118; has Jesus scourged, 119; condemns Jesus to death, 120; cowardice of, 120
Pius X, Pope, and music, 248
Poe, Edgar Allen, quoted, 139
Politeness, golden keys and, 24
Ponies, runaway, example of, 69
Poor Richard, quoted, 61
Poor Souls, *see* Purgatory, Souls in
Pope, prayer for the, 153
Posters, suggestions for: Purgatory, 224; birth of Jesus, 225; crown of thorns, 226; flowers for May, 226; flowers for March, 226; Guardian Angel, 284; St. Francis and wolf, 284; St. Francis and birds, 284; landing of Columbus, 284-285; Thanksgiving Day, 285-286; birth of Jesus, 286; Three Kings, 286; flight into Egypt, 286-287; Jesus at Nazareth, 289; Holy Family, 289; St. Joseph, 289; Annunciation, 289; Candlemas procession, 289; Way of the Cross, 289-290; Calvary, 290; Resurrection, 290; Altar, 290; missionary, 292; alphabet illustrating lives of saints, 292
Prayers, at Meals, 80
Priests, prayers for, 153
Proctor, Adelaide A., quoted, 138-140
Programs, suggestive, for Labor Day, 188-189; Columbus Day, 189; Halloween, 189; Thanksgiving Day, 189-190; Christmas, 190; Holy Week, 190; Mother's Day, 190-191; for Friday afternoons, 262

Projects, sand table; how to work out, 229-230; Adam and Eve, 230; Cain and Abel, 230; Noe and Ark, 230; story of Moses, 230; story of Joseph, 230; birth of Christ, 231; flight into Egypt, 232; Holy Family, 232; Stations of the Cross, 232; grotto of Lourdes, 232; missionary projects, 232-234
Promises, keeping, 61
Punctuality, devices to secure, 266
Purgatory, Souls in, prayers for, 153; poster of, 224
Purification of Blessed Virgin Mary, feast of, 211
Quinn, John Francis, S. J., quoted, 85
Race, airship (device), 259; cross-country (device), 259-260
Raphael, Archangel, St., feast of, 204-205
Resurrection, poster of, 290
Rosary, the, feast of, 200; how to say, 200-203; blackboard drawing of (device), 224
Rossetti, Christina, quoted, 84, 87, 88, 92
Rule, Golden, 87
Ryan, Father Abram, quoted, 87, 98, 116
Sacrament, Blessed, *see* Blessed Sacrament
Sacred Heart of Jesus, 118, 121, 128, 129
Saints, 142-146; alphabet poster of lives of, 292; booklet of, 294
Sanctuary Lamp, meaning of, 124
Sand table, value of, 227-228; how to make, 228; equipment of, 228; sand for, 229; representation of people, scenery, etc., on, 229; construction work for, 279-282; *See* Projects, sand table.
Santa Claus, *see* St. Nicholas
School, neatness in, 52; honesty in, 58
Sebastian, St., feast of, 208-209
Selfishness, 86, 147
Seven Sorrows of Blessed Virgin Mary, feast of, 193
Shepherds, visit of, to Jesus, 97; dramatization of story of, 242
Shields, Thomas Edward, Memorial School, v
Singing, devices to aid teacher of, 253-255
Songs for Sinners, quoted, 112

Spencer, Mary E., quoted, 66, 68, 69
Starr, Eliza Allen, quoted, 92
Stations of the Cross, how to make, 124, 125; sand table project of, 232; poster of, 289-290
Stencils, making of, 261; use of, 261
Stevenson, Robert Louis, quoted, 17, 19, 34
Stoddard, Mrs. E. R., quoted, 73
Stories, gymnastic, method of acting, 247-248; use of pictures in telling, 282-283
Sunshine Club, 17
Sympathy, 22
Tabernacle, 126
Tardiness, devices to cure, 266
Teachers, obedience to, 42
Teeth, manner of brushing, 68
Temple, Jesus and His parents visit, 110; the finding of Jesus in, 111; Blessed Virgin in, 137
Thackeray, W. M., quoted, 14
Thanksgiving Day, story of, 35; meaning of, 35; program for, 189-190; booklet for, 294
Theresa of Jesus, St., 87; love of, for Blessed Virgin, 134; feast of, 203-204
Thompson, Francis, quoted, 102
Thoughtfulness, devices to teach, 266
Thoughts, cheerful, 6; reason for controlling, 71; concentration of, 72
Tidiness, devices to teach, 266-267
Tongue, St. James on, 73; control of, 73; three gates for control of, 74
Valentine, St., feast of, 212-213
Visitors, how to treat, 21
Vocations, booklet of, 295
Wallace, L. M., quoted, 113
Ward, Lydia Avery Coonley, quoted, 38
Washington, George, 83
Watch, comparison of, with conscience, 76, 77, 78
Watts, Isaac, quoted, 34, 47
Wise Men, 99, 100, 101, 102, 126; dramatization of story of, 242-243
Words, cheerful, in the home, 8; kind, and peace, 9
Work, time for, 46; exhibition of, 262; busy, suggestions for, 263
Work booklet, 50.

www.ingramcontent.com/pod-product-compliance
Lightning Source LLC
Chambersburg PA
CBHW080531170426
43195CB00016B/2531